Art and Identity in Scotland

This lively and erudite cultural history of Scotland, from the Jacobite defeat of 1745 to the death of an icon, Sir Walter Scott, in 1832, examines how Scottish identity was experienced and represented in novel ways. Weaving together previously unpublished archival materials, visual and material culture, dress and textile history, Viccy Coltman re-evaluates the standard clichés and essentialist interpretations which still inhibit Scottish cultural history during this period of British and imperial expansion. The book incorporates familiar landmarks in Scottish history, such as the visit of George IV to Edinburgh in August 1822, with microhistories of individuals, including George Steuart, a London-based architect, and the East India Company servant, Claud Alexander. It thus highlights recurrent themes within a range of historical disciplines, and by confronting the broader questions of Scotland's relations with the rest of the British state it makes a necessary contribution to contemporary concerns.

VICCY COLTMAN is a professor of history of art at the University of Edinburgh, where she is an authority on eighteenth-century visual and material culture in Britain. The author of four books including two monographs, an edited and a co-edited volume, Coltman has been awarded fellowships by the Whitney Humanities Center at Yale, the Huntington Library, the National Gallery of Washington DC and the British School at Rome, amongst others. In 2006 she was awarded a Philip Leverhulme Prize in recognition of her outstanding contribution to History of Art. Coltman is currently the academic lead on a MOOC, a Massive Open Online Course on 'Bonnie Prince Charlie and the Jacobites', in collaboration with the National Museums Scotland.

Art and Identity in Scotland

A Cultural History from the Jacobite Rising of 1745 to Walter Scott

VICCY COLTMAN

University of Edinburgh

CAMBRIDGE
UNIVERSITY PRESS

CAMBRIDGE
UNIVERSITY PRESS

University Printing House, Cambridge CB2 8BS, United Kingdom

One Liberty Plaza, 20th Floor, New York, NY 10006, USA

477 Williamstown Road, Port Melbourne, VIC 3207, Australia

314–321, 3rd Floor, Plot 3, Splendor Forum, Jasola District Centre, New Delhi – 110025, India

79 Anson Road, #06–04/06, Singapore 079906

Cambridge University Press is part of the University of Cambridge.

It furthers the University's mission by disseminating knowledge in the pursuit of education, learning, and research at the highest international levels of excellence.

www.cambridge.org
Information on this title: www.cambridge.org/9781108417686
DOI: 10.1017/9781108278133

First published 2019

Printed in the United Kingdom by TJ International Ltd. Padstow, Cornwall

A catalogue record for this publication is available from the British Library.

ISBN 978-1-108-41768-6 Hardback

Contents

The plate section can be found between pp 142 and 143

Plates

Figures

Acknowledgements

I have accrued many debts in the writing of this book, which has been in various stages of progress and stasis since as far back as 2003. Thank you to those colleagues who generously read earlier drafts of individual chapters and gave feedback, Stuart Allan, Michèle Cohen, Penny Fielding, Margot Finn, Caroline McCracken-Flesher and Kate Teltscher. Margot and Caroline have also written references more times than I care to remember, as have John Brewer and Giorgio Riello. I am indebted to all of them for their continued belief in this project and in me to deliver it even when their enthusiasm was not shared by external funding bodies. Margot, Ludmilla Jordanova and Marcia Pointon have been driving forces behind it in so many ways as mentors, scholars, collaborators and friends. As an external advisor to the Leverhulme-funded 'East India Company at Home' project, I worked with Margot and her team at UCL, Helen Clifford, Kate Smith and Ellen Filor, across a number of years and events; Chapter 3 is my modest contribution to our theme which has been shaped by our collaboration. Margot first put me in touch with Cambridge University Press, where the manuscript has been nurtured with Liz Friend-Smith as editor. I also thank Kathleen Fearn for copyediting the whole manuscript. CUP operates a rigorous peer review system and I would like to thank the readers for their informed interventions and their generous praise for the manuscript at different stages, especially their admiration for the archival work that I have undertaken. This would not have been possible without the support of many archivists and owners and I must mention Alison Rosie, Tessa Spencer and Josephine Dixon at the National Register of Archives for Scotland (NRAS) who have facilitated access to the private collections listed elsewhere in the book. Thank you to those owners who placed their private papers on temporary deposit in Edinburgh; or who allowed me to access them *in situ*, especially Etain Hagart Alexander and Ianthe Alexander who allowed me to work on their family archive when it was unlisted. Visiting these archives, I have travelled the length and breadth of the Highlands, Lowlands and Borders of Scotland, sometimes with the photographer John Mckenzie, who has been endlessly patient as I arranged for objects to be moved and photographed, sometimes for the first time in their history. I have also made extensive use of the papers in the National Records of Scotland; quotations from material on permanent deposit in this repository are with the permission of the following owners: Sir Robert Clerk of Penicuik, Mr Drummond Moray, Thomas Fotheringham, John Home Robertson and the Earl of Seafield. Sir Alastair Gordon Cumming has granted permission for quotations from the National Library of Scotland, Dep. 175.

The following colleagues provided invaluable assistance of one sort or another, so thank you Jane Anderson, John Arthur, Stephen Astley, Adam Budd, Peter Burman, Aude Claret, Pat Crichton, Fintan Cullen, George Dalgleish, Christopher Dingwall, John Fisher, John Getley, Christopher Johns, Sarah Kay, Sarah Laurenson, the late Susan Manning, the late Hamish Miles and Jean Miles, Catriona Murray, Charles Noble, David Patterson, Murray Pittock, Ian Riches, Tracy Smith, Ruth Stewart, Susie West and Lucy Wood; Imogen Gibbon, Sarah Jeffcott, Lucinda Lax and Helen Smailes at the Scottish National Galleries; Elaine MacGillivray, when she was responsible for the Bogle papers at the Mitchell Library, Glasgow City Archives.

The Carnegie Trust of the Universities of Scotland funded a week's research at the British Library in the summer of 2009. Short-term fellowships at the Huntington Library and Colonial Williamsburg followed a three-year term as Head of History of Art, which coincided with the merger between the University of Edinburgh and Edinburgh College of Art. Thanks to the brilliant input of Chris Breward, Tamara Trodd and Heather Pulliam, I survived this period more-or-less unscathed. During my period at the Huntington, Simon Macdonald was my partner-in-crime and Yoga Kingdom Sanctuary my second home. Vincent and Marilyn Harris have allowed me to cat-sit, house-sit and then just sit with my manuscript as it emerged over a number of writing retreats at their home in Eskdalemuir, within easy walking distance of Samye Ling Monastery and Tibetan Centre.

An earlier version of Chapter 2 appeared as 'Scottish architects in eighteenth-century London: George Steuart, the competition for patronage and the representation of Scotland', in Stana Nenadic (ed.), *Scots in London in the Eighteenth Century* (Lewisburg, PA: Bucknell University Press, 2010), pp. 91–108; with thanks to Stana Nenadic and Rick Sher. My article 'Party-coloured plaid? Portraits of eighteenth-century Scots in tartan', *Textile History* 41.2 (2010), pp. 182–216, informed parts of Chapters 1 and 4.

The Moray Endowment Trust, the Pasold Foundation, the Strathmartine Trust and the William Grant Foundation covered the image costs and enabled the inclusion of the colour insert; I could not have delivered this illustrated book without their generous support. Elisabeth Gernerd provided initial input into the sourcing of the images and Emily Goetsch delivered the fiddly task with characteristic grace. Elisabeth is a former postgraduate student whose thesis nurtured my thinking, as has the work of Heather Carroll, Hannah Lund, Maeve O'Dwyer and particularly Freya Gowrley. My current PhD cohort, Sydney Ayers, Joyce Dixon, Lillian Elliott, Anna Myers, Danielle Smith and Georgia Vullinghs ensure that I am forever reading drafts.

As ever in these acknowledgements, you save the best until last. So Stanley Wynd, thank you for everything all the time.

Introduction

Identity is a new term, as well as being an elusive and ubiquitous one.

Philip Gleason, 'Identifying Identity', 1983[1]

This book seeks to map the cultural contours and detours of identity by focussing on the representation of certain Scots as individuals and Scotland as a nation within Britain's global empire, from the middle decades of the eighteenth century to the early 1830s. Its conceptual starting point is a speech, specifically the fourth anniversary discourse delivered by David Stewart Erskine, the 11th Earl of Buchan, at a meeting of the Society of Antiquaries of Scotland on 15 November 1784. The foundation of the society in 1780 has been described as Buchan's most memorable contribution to the cultural identity of Scotland.[2] In it, he informed his fellow antiquarians:

I consider Scotland my native Country as a rude but noble medallion of antient sculpture which ought not to be defaced or forgotten in the Cabinet of Nations because it lay next to one more beautiful & splendid richer and larger, more polished, and elegant, but of less relief. As a Man I felt myself a Citizen of the World, as a friend to Peace to Liberty & to Science which cannot exist asunder I considered myself as an inhabitant of a United Kingdom, but as a Citizen I could not help remembering that I was a Scot.[3]

Buchan's characterisation of his native country as a medallion of ancient sculpture displayed in a 'Cabinet of Nations' casts Scotland into the artefactual territory of material culture. The ensuing narrative is not a history of the Society of Antiquaries of Scotland – a complement to the tricentennial exhibition and publication *Visions of Antiquity: The Society of Antiquaries of London, 1707–2007*, which makes only cursory mention of

---

[1] Philip Gleason, 'Identifying identity: A semantic history', *Journal of American History* 69.4 (1983), p. 910.

[2] R. G. Cant, 'David Steuart Erskine, 11th Earl of Buchan: Founder of the Society of Antiquaries of Scotland', in Alan S. Bell (ed.), *The Scottish Antiquarian Tradition: Essays to Mark the Bicentenary of the Society of Antiquaries of Scotland and Its Museum, 1780–1980* (Edinburgh: Donald, 1981), p. 9.

[3] NLS, Adv. MS. 29.3.14 folio 76.

its younger sister institution which was founded on similar lines later in the eighteenth century. Instead, this cultural history uses identity as an interpretative and analytical concept for getting to grips with the representation of Scots and Scotland in visual and material culture, during a period of well-documented social and economic transformation. Its chronological bookends extend from a defeat – around the period of the latest and what would be the last of the Jacobite uprisings in 1745 – to the death of 'Scotland's darling son', Sir Walter Scott, almost ninety years later in 1832.[4] The narrative posits identity as a discourse that is inherently protean, enjoying shifting degrees of immanence and contrivance, while always subscribing to the view that it 'is not as transparent or unproblematic as we think'.[5] For instance, roughly halfway through the chronological period under consideration, in the early 1780s, the ennobled Earl of Buchan imagined himself as having tripartite identities as a Scot, an inhabitant of a united Britain and a citizen of the wider international world. Following Buchan's lead, Part I of this book looks at Scots in Europe, London and Empire, their exposure to and participation in cosmopolitan, metropolitan and colonial contexts. Part II considers the real and imagined geographies of Scotland as a nation of distinctive tripartite territories: the Highlands, the Lowlands and the Borders, looking in turn at Jacobite visual and material culture, the visit of George IV to Edinburgh in August 1822 and (Sir Walter) Scott and the physiognomy of Romanticism.

Buchan's tripartite formulation of his identities as a Scot, a Briton and a citizen of the world may be seen to conform to a perspectival paradigm of loyalties as promulgated by T. C. Smout in 1994 in which he suggested that Scots might be imagined as having seven concentric rings of territorial identity: working from the centre out, of family, kin or clan, locality, state, nation and supranational.[6] While it would be intellectually facile to seek to apply Smout's prototype for the last decade of the twentieth century teleologically backwards onto the historical period under scrutiny, nevertheless, his 'aid to thought rather than a vigorous model', as he describes it,

---

[4] *Caledonian Mercury*, 17 August 1846. NLS, FB.m.55. [Four volumes of press-cuttings, photographs, engravings &c., relating to the work of Sir John Steell.] See Conclusion: Scott-land for the context of this phrase.

[5] See Stuart Hall, 'Cultural identity and diaspora', in Nicholas Mirzoeff (ed.), *Diaspora and Visual Culture: Representing Africans and Jews* (London: Routledge, 2000), p. 21.

[6] T. C. Smout, 'Perspectives on the Scottish identity', *Scottish Affairs* 6 (1994), pp. 101–113. See also Smout's 'Problems of nationalism, identity and improvement in later eighteenth-century Scotland', in T. M. Devine (ed.), *Improvement and Enlightenment* (Edinburgh: John Donald, 1989), pp. 1–21, esp. p. 19, where he refers to Scots' feelings of national identity as being of the concentric loyalty type.

can be seen as a provocation that has yet to be adequately addressed for the period under consideration. This narrative asks what we were the constituents of identity? And what did it mean to be Scottish during a crucial period that witnessed on the one hand, the latency of the Scottish nation state, while on the other, the growth of Britain's empire with concurrent ideas about nationhood? Despite the usefulness of Smout's orderly concentric rings in showing how identities may be held concurrently, it will propose that they should be imagined as an uneven, messier constellation in which identities are tangled and entangled; wavy and undulating between the real and the rhetorical, or literal manifestation and discursive emblem; being afforded different precedence and weight at particular historical periods and in different contexts; or in the same historical periods in different geographical contexts.

Smout's all too brief account of Scottish identity draws on Benedict Anderson's seminal *Imagined Communities: Reflections on the Origin and Spread of Nationalism* which casts nationality, nation-ness and nationalism as an imagined community or cultural artefacts of a particular kind. Many theorists and historians have echoed Anderson's contention that these terms are notoriously difficult to define, never mind begin to analyse. Even in the face of such obstacles, the study of nation-ness has become an academic industry, notably since the 1990s when there was a renewed interest in response to their political valency throughout parts of the globe.[7] Stressing the importance of historical forces in the evolution, change and continued potency of his subject matter, Anderson is especially interested in two print technologies, which first flowered in eighteenth-century Europe, the novel and the newspaper. These forms of literary imaginings, he argues, provided a mass means for 're-presenting the *kind* of imagined community that is the nation'.[8] Given Anderson's insistence on investing these nebulous terms in material form – as a cultured artefact – it seems surprising that they have not been discussed in relation to visual and material culture in more systematic detail.[9] The Earl of Buchan's characterisation of Scotland as a medallion of ancient sculpture provides

---

[7] Natividad Gutiérrez, 'The study of national identity', in Alain Dieckhoff and Natividad Gutiérrez (eds.), *Modern Roots: Studies of National Identity* (Aldershot: Ashgate, 2001), p. 3.

[8] Benedict Anderson, *Imagined Communities: Reflections on the Origin and Spread of Nationalism* (London: Verso, 1983), p. 25.

[9] There are two volumes of collected essays that deal with Britain: Dana Arnold (ed.), *Cultural Identities and the Aesthetics of Britishness* (Manchester: Manchester University Press, 2004) and Fintan Cullen and John Morrison (eds.), *A Shared Legacy: Essays on Irish and Scottish Visual Art and Culture* (Aldershot: Ashgate, 2005).

one instance in eighteenth-century discourse – an oral lecture, which was later published in pamphlet form – where the nation is explicitly conceptualised as an artefact to be possessed and displayed in a cabinet, where it lies alongside a larger, more polished and elegant medallion with shallower carvings which is England.

In the introduction to her prize-winning *Britons: Forging the Nation, 1707–1837*, the historian, Linda Colley, echoes the Earl of Buchan's 1784 anniversary discourse, where she asserts 'Identities are not like hats. Human beings can and do put on several at a time.'[10] Colley's subtitle captures the ambivalence of the process of identity making as creation and counterfeiting, where both are the productions of material artistry and artifice.[11] Drawing on the formative explorations of Anderson, Smith and Colley, this book seeks to deal with Scottish-ness as a category of identity and as a cultural production. Despite our corresponding time-frames, it is not attempting to do for Scotland what Newman has previously done for England with his *The Rise of English Nationalism: A Cultural History, 1740–1830*. Where my own study hopes to complement that of Newman is in its focus on the visual and material as forms of cultural expression, where his is on the literary. For Newman, 'Nationalism is, at the outset, a creation of writers.'[12] It eschews references to nationalism in either the title or the body of the narrative since, as Kidd has pointed out, it is misleading to apply such a label to historical periods before the doctrinaire nationalisms of the later nineteenth and twentieth centuries.[13] Newman seems to use nationalism and national identity more or less synonymously, much as English and British have been traditionally used by art historians.[14] Scottish art is sometimes marginalised as a subsection of *English*, rather than British art.[15]

[10] Linda Colley, *Britons: Forging the Nation, 1707–1837* (New Haven, CT and London: Yale University Press, 1992), p. 6.

[11] Martin Daunton and Rick Halpern, 'Introduction: British identities, indigenous peoples, and the empire', Martin Daunton and Rick Halpern (eds.), *Empire and Others: British Encounters with Indigenous Peoples, 1600–1850* (London: UCL Press, 1999), pp. 1–9 at p. 3. See also Colley's comments in the second edition to the book (London: Pimlico, 2003), p. xiv.

[12] Gerald Newman, *The Rise of English Nationalism: A Cultural History, 1740–1830* (London: Weidenfeld & Nicolson, 1987), p. 87.

[13] Colin Kidd, *British Identities before Nationalism: Ethnicity and Nationhood in the Atlantic World, 1600–1800* (Cambridge: Cambridge University Press, 1999), p. 6. See too Julian Hoppit (ed.), *Parliaments, Nations and Identities in Britain and Ireland, 1660–1850* (Manchester: Manchester University Press, 2003), p. 2.

[14] William Vaughan, 'The Englishness of British Art', *Oxford Art Journal* 13.2 (1990), p. 11.

[15] Cullen and Morrison, *A Shared Legacy*, p. 4.

Much like identity as it has been characterised by Buchan and Colley – as tripartite or deserving of many hats – the investigator of nation-ness in its cultural manifestations must be prepared to try on many scholarly roles in the course of their study.[16] She also becomes aware of the rich historiographical and theoretical expositions in which the location of identity, its definitions and categories seem highly contested intellectual forces as much as historical ones. Many academic disciplines and individuals have, it would seem, invested their own identity, or a part thereof, in its enunciation.

In Colley's wider account, a sense of mass Britishness – or what she dubs the 'business of being British' – was forged by its civilian population in opposition to the 'Other' beyond their island shores.[17] In an invaluable article supporting her thesis and published the same year as the first edition of *Britons* entitled 'Britishness and Otherness', she asserts that national identity is contingent and relational, positing with characteristic boldness: 'we usually decide who we are by reference to who and what we are not'.[18] Colley's Britain is a nation whose thousands of inhabitants are welded together by a succession of seven wars with France that took place between 1689 and 1815 that is sometimes called 'the second hundred years war'. Colley's Britons, especially those who were poorer and less privileged, she suggests, were united and defined themselves collectively *against* the French enemy.[19] Thus, Colley sees British identity being forged in contradistinction to the enemy France over a period of a hundred and thirty years via various negative constructions which result in a series of binary oppositions in the formation of a collective British identity: Protestantism not Catholicism; constitutional monarchy not absolutism; an economy that was commercial and progressive, rather than agrarian and backward.[20] In material culture terms for manufacturing coins and medals, appropriate to

---

[16] Newman, *The Rise of English Nationalism*, p. 52. [17] Colley, *Britons*, p. 131.

[18] Linda Colley, 'Britishness and otherness: An argument', *Journal of British Studies* 31.4 (1992), p. 311.

[19] Colley, *Britons*, p. 368.

[20] Many critiques of Colley's methodology proliferate. I have found especially useful those cited elsewhere in this chapter, plus Theodore Koditschek, 'The making of British nationality', *Victorian Studies* 44.3 (2002), pp. 389–398; Alexander Murdoch, 'Scotland and the idea of Britain in the eighteenth century', in T. M. Devine and J. R. Young (eds.), *Eighteenth-Century Scotland: New Perspectives* (East Linton: Tuckwell Press, 1999), pp. 106–121; John M. Mackenzie, 'Empire and national identities: The case of Scotland', *Transactions of the Royal Historical Society* 8 (1998), pp. 215–231 and Dror Wahrman, 'National society, communal culture: An argument about the recent historiography of eighteenth-century Britain', *Social History* 17.1 (1992), pp. 43–72.

the forging process referenced in Colley's subtitle, we might say that her non-elite Britons are the design products of a mass-produced obverse die.

Rather than an insistence on a segmentary model of contrast and opposition in which 'self definition depends on antithesis, identity on counter-identity', Chapter 1 highlights the historicity of this dogmatic position.[21] Focussing on painted portraits commissioned by young, elite Scotsmen from the late 1750s to the early 1780s, it demonstrates how such identificatory determinism is an ideology of the later eighteenth-century grand tour of Europe with its partial exposure to men and manners of different nations. Whereas de Seta claims 'it would be dangerous to classify the tourists simply by nationality' due to the essentially cosmopolitan nature of the tour, this opening chapter seeks to demonstrate the contrary – the efficacy of such an approach in recognising how a formative sense of Britishness was inculcated in and among these travelling Scots.[22] *Contra* Colley, Chapter 2 subscribes to Bhabha's contention in which 'The "other" is never outside or beyond us; it emerges forcefully, within cultural discourse, when we *think* we speak most intimately and indigenously "between ourselves"'.[23] This chapter looks at Scots in London in an attempt to understand the sometimes hostile, sometimes convivial, but always processual relationship between Scotland and England, or North Britons and their southern neighbours. It adopts a microhistorical approach to identarian study, focusing on the painter cum architect George Steuart, a Highlander, London-based rival and one-time employee of the architectural empire of the Adam brothers. Refuting the traditional characterisation of the Scots outside Scotland operating as a monolithic, self-serving entity, it demonstrates the extent to which the vagaries of the competitive London marketplace from the 1760s to the 1780s caused conflict between fellow Scots Robert Adam and Steuart in their rivalry for architectural commissions.

In concentrating on the professional animosity between Scottish architects in London, Chapter 2 seeks to shift the emphasis away from prevailing histories of the hostility between English and Scots. Such hostility betrays a distinctly Anglocentric viewpoint since as Kidd notes, Scottish Anglophobia never evolved into anything resembling a coherent ideology.[24] Neither did Englishness according to its historians. 'If you are clearly in charge, you do

---

[21] Peter Sahlins, *Boundaries: The Making of France and Spain in the Pyrenees, 1659–1868* (Berkeley: University of California Press, 1989), p. 272.

[22] Cesare de Seta, 'Grand Tour: The lure of Italy in the eighteenth century', in Andrew Wilton and Ilaria Bignamini (eds.), *Grand Tour: The Lure of Italy in the Eighteenth Century* (London: Tate Gallery, 1996), p. 15.

[23] Homi K. Bhabha, *Nation and Narration* (London: Routledge, 1990), p. 4.

[24] Colin Kidd, 'North Britishness and the nature of eighteenth-century British patriotisms', *Historical Journal* 39.2 (1996), p. 382.

not need to beat the drum or blow the bugle too loudly', writes Kumar, in whose narrative of the making of English national identity, the English were an imperial nation in a double sense, having created a land empire, Great Britain, and an overseas empire, twice: first in North America and the Caribbean; secondly in India and southeast Asia. These two empires, internal and external, 'made meaningless the development of a specifically English national identity', he writes.[25] Kumar's emphasis on Englishness necessarily overlooks the disproportionate role that Scots played in the Scottish-ness of Britain's empire and the imperial-ness of Scotland. Even Colley, in Koditschek's perspicacious review, sees the Scottish participation in the creation of the empire 'as an adventitious excrescence of Britishness run amok'.[26] As Scottish grasp of imperial opportunities is better documented in the Atlantic Empire for this period, so Chapter 3 on Scots in Empire looks at the East Indies, specifically at Claud Alexander, a Scot working for the East India Company in Calcutta between 1772 and 1786, who returned to invest his imperial fortune into the domestic economy in Scotland by establishing a cotton manufacturing village at Catrine in Ayrshire.[27] This chapter celebrates 'the thick particularities of an individual's life' by documenting Alexander's cultural activities alongside the social and economic counterparts that enabled them.[28] Taken together, the three chapters in Part I attempt to respond to Peter Mandler's appeal for more microhistorical study of the specific contexts and situations in which what he styles 'identity talk' takes place.[29] The microhistories of these individuals and the visual and material objects they variously commissioned, produced, transported and displayed, seek to challenge some of the existing and long-held clichés around the subject of Scots beyond Scotland. The chronological concentration of Part I, from the late 1750s to the 1780s, offers a focussed historical sample in which to see alternate identities but most notably Scottishness wax and wane across an expansive geographical landscape.

---

[25] Krishnan Kumar, 'Nation and Empire: English and British national identity in comparative perspective', *Theory and Society* 29.5 (2000), p. 589. See too Krishnan Kumar, *The Making of English National Identity* (Cambridge: Cambridge University Press, 2003), esp. pp. 178–179.

[26] Koditschek, 'The making of British nationality', p. 394.

[27] A. L. Karras, *Sojourners in the Sun: Scottish Migrants in Jamaica and the Chesapeake, 1740–1800* (Ithaca, NY and London: Cornell University Press, 1992); David Hancock, *Citizens of the World: London Merchants and the Integration of the British Atlantic Community, 1735–85* (Cambridge: Cambridge University Press, 1995); Douglas J. Hamilton, *Scotland, the Caribbean and the Atlantic World, 1750–1820* (Manchester: Manchester University Press, 2005). Ten out of the twenty-three London-based merchants in Hancock's study were born in Scotland or to Scots parents.

[28] Francesca Mari, 'The microhistorian', *Dissent* 60 (2013), p. 81.

[29] Peter Mandler, 'What is "national identity"? Definitions and applications in modern British historiography', *Modern Intellectual History* 3.2 (2006), p. 297.

This global canvas simultaneously allows us to revisit the lineaments of Anderson's imagined community via the series of provocative questions latterly posed by exponents of the so-called new imperial history. As the historian Kathleen Wilson asks in relation to Anderson's 'felicitous phrase', whose community it is that is being imagined? Who was imagining it? What was it imagined to consist of?[30] In this, she echoes the pleas of other historians like Partha Chatterjee who have found Anderson's unitary notion of the nation highly problematic in relation to the colonial and post-colonial worlds.[31] Chatterjee posits a distinctly anti-colonial nationalism in Asia and Africa which resides in two domains: the material and the spiritual, or the outside and inner realms. It is worth noting the persistence of 'the material' in both Anderson's and Chatterjee's narratives, which are otherwise seemingly in opposition in their formulations of nation and which this book brings to the fore.

Part II of the book, in contrast, takes a Scottish-centred approach to its subject. It demarcates collective, rather than individual identities, in relation to the tripartite territories of Scotland: moving from north to south, the Highlands, the Lowlands and the Borders. This second part of the book recognises that in attempting to map Scottishness within an imperial panorama between the mid-eighteenth century and the early 1830s, we need to embrace multiple selves and other others, so to speak, beyond the self/other dialectic of colonialism. This enables us to recognise the many and complex interactions and transactions in the enmity and/or allegiances between nations – as in Scotland and England – and subsections of those nations – as in Highland and Lowland. Within Scotland, the line of demarcation between Highland and Lowland was linguistic and geographical, differentiating between Highland Gaelic and Lowland Scots by following the mountainous contours of the land.[32] Withers reminds us that the division between Highlands and Lowlands 'is not an immutable fact of geography' as much as a cultural creation.[33] When one Jacob Pattison undertook a tour from Edinburgh through parts of the Highlands of Scotland during the summer

---

[30] Kathleen Wilson, 'Citizenship, empire and modernity in the English provinces, *c.* 1720–1790', *Eighteenth-Century Studies* 29.1 (1995), p. 72.

[31] Partha Chatterjee, *The Nation and Its Fragments: Colonial and Postcolonial Histories* (Princeton, NJ: Princeton University Press, 1993), chapter 1, 'Whose Imagined Community?', pp. 3–13.

[32] Ian Charles Cargill Graham, *Colonists from Scotland: Emigration to North America, 1707–1783* (Ithaca, NY: Cornell University Press, 1956), p. 2.

[33] Charles Withers, 'The historical creation of the Scottish Highlands', in Ian Donnachie and Christopher Whatley (eds.), *The Manufacture of Scottish History* (Edinburgh: Polygon, 1992), p. 144.

of 1780, he noted: 'The Highlanders [at Fort William] generally speak of the Lowlanders with contempt, & prefer the English – thus every nation is disposed to be at enmity with its neighbours, & a traveller may be pleased when his own is not altogether the subject of detestation'.[34] 'Great caution is to be observ'd in taking the report of the Highlanders and Lowlanders relating to each other [wrote the anonymous author of a tour of Scotland in 1794]: there prevails between them an inveterate & illiberal antipathy'.[35] The chapters in Part I give equal precedence to domestic British tours of the Scottish Highlands such as these and to journals of cosmopolitan grand tours in contemporary Europe. Such travel narratives are more often estranged as a genre by the geographical borders of their separate fields of study. By juxtaposing these accounts of domestic and foreign travel with the colonial correspondence of Claud Alexander, we are able to see what it meant for Scots from the upper and middling social strata to leave home for a variety of economic, social and cultural reasons, on a temporary or permanent basis. Indeed, the concept of Scotland as 'home' seems to have become that more evocative as time passed and geographical distances extended. '[T]he further I am from Bemersyde [in the Scottish Borders] the more I think of it with pleasure', wrote James Haig, a Captain in the 93rd Regiment of Foot, from Paris in June 1783.[36]

In Chapter 4, Jacobitism, with which the Scots were inextricably aligned, posed an internal political threat to the British establishment. At the time of the '45 uprising, the Stuarts and their supporters, the Jacobites, were considered domestic enemies with *all* Scots being tarnished with the seditious brush of Jacobitism. Linda Colley's characterisation of British patriotism as 'a bandwagon on which different groups and interests leaped so as to steer it in a direction that would benefit them', offers an equally apt description of Jacobite support with its pick and mix followers, Scots and English, Catholic and Protestant, from across the social spectrum.[37] The Jacobites were arguably as diverse and dispersed as the movement itself. Chapter 4 looks at examples of Jacobite objects, both visual and material, within a culture of embodied insurrection. Using the body as a synthesising thematic, it suggests that these objects gave Jacobitism a cohesive corporeal identity, albeit one that was clandestine in intent given its seditious currency. It also had an ideological uniform, tartan or plaid, the sartorial apparel of the Scottish Highlands. During the period under discussion, Highland culture became increasingly endangered for its associations with

---

[34] NLS, MS. 6322 folio 77.   [35] NLS, Acc. 8278 folio 52.   [36] NRAS, 105/5/66.
[37] Colley, *Britons*, p. 5.

Jacobitism; dealt a series of deadly blows by the British establishment, including the Disarming Act of 1746, which prohibited the wearing of Highland dress in Scotland. Moving chronologically forwards into the nineteenth century, aspects of the external features of Highland culture were reinvented without their seditious martial charge, most memorably during the twenty-one day visit of King George IV to Edinburgh in August 1822. As documented in Chapter 5, Scottishness was on display during the royal visit as part of a plaided panorama – a scopic event in which Lowland cultural identity was muted into a spectacle of sameness – being overshadowed by its tartanised Highland equivalent. Kidd's contention that ethnic identities are not timeless, but provisional and pliable, with an elasticity that allows a considerable degree of invention and reinvention, is readily applicable here.[38] This chapter demonstrates the efficacy of dress and textiles as a means for reinventing collective identities at a surface level. It discusses a number of visual renderings of the series of events that comprised the royal visit, situating the monarch and the body of Scottish citizens that attended to get a view of their king as subjects and objects in an art historical narrative of nation-ness.

Finally, Chapter 6 reconsiders Sir Walter Scott as 'the architect of cultural Scottishness', as he has been labelled by McCracken-Flesher, by looking again at the vagaries of his relationship with visual and material culture.[39] This chapter traces the identity of Scott's historical physiognomy through the interwoven threads between art, literature and life; considering how they bordered and embroidered upon each other as part of the romantic endeavour. The border as a zone or space is additionally represented through the landscape territory and distinctive dress of the Scottish Borders. Ian Baucom has written of the locations of identity in the pursuit of Englishness as follows: 'They are places where an identity-preserving, identity-enhancing, and identity transforming aura lingers or is made to appear.'[40] Scott's identity as a Scottish Borderer was preserved and enhanced by the location of his house with its manifold collections at Abbotsford near Melrose. He was sometimes transformed into a border's bard by being attired in maud (a Border tartan) in the veritable production line of portraits he sat for during his lifetime. The border figures in the

---

[38] Kidd, *British Identities before Nationalism*, p. 4. See Hugh Trevor-Roper, 'The invention of tradition: The Highland tradition of Scotland', in Eric Hobsbawm and Terence Ranger (eds.), *The Invention of Tradition* (Cambridge: Cambridge University Press, 1983), pp. 15–41.

[39] Caroline McCracken-Flesher, *Possible Scotlands: Walter Scott and the Story of Tomorrow* (Oxford: Oxford University Press, 2005), p. 3.

[40] Ian Baucom, *Out of Place: Englishness, Empire and the Locations of Identity* (Princeton, NJ: Princeton University Press, 1999), p. 19.

illustrations that accompanied his prolific output of verse and prose are also represented enveloped in maud – in an identity that as we shall see, Scott took pains to ensure was characterised by its sartorial realia rather than its pictorial falsehood.

In privileging the visual and material as instruments of identity formation and articulation for Scots and Scotland, this book seeks to complement and to revisit aspects of Dror Wahrman's thesis in his *The Making of the Modern Self: Identity and Culture in Eighteenth-Century England* (2004). Wahrman's influential study focuses on four key categories of personal identity that are understood in his study to be primarily collective rather than individual: gender, class, race and species (the distinction between human and animals); discerning a shift in the last two decades of the century, around 1780 after the American Revolution, in the form of 'a sharp uneasy reversal' where what he designates an *ancien régime* of identity was rapidly transformed into a modern regime of selfhood. According to his account, identity shifted across these categories from being malleable, fluid, assumable and divisible, to an innate, fixed, essential core of selfhood 'stamped indelibly on each and every person'.[41] 'It is easy to see that for some identity categories the story told here is inadequate', concedes Wahrman, referring to religion and nation, which he asserts did not follow the innate, essentialising route of his other identity categories.[42] In focussing on Scotland, the narrative that follows necessarily sifts Wahrman's categories, retaining gender and class, and adding national, occupational and political identities. Part I is especially concerned with gender, class and occupation as categories of identity that pertained to individuals, rather than groups, although the dozen or so grand tourists discussed in Chapter 1 constitutes a diminutive collective of sorts. The book as a whole brings Scottishness to the fore as a manifestation of national identity long eclipsed by studies of Englishness.

The ensuing narrative actively seeks to reify identities for Scots as individuals and as a nation within a global empire via their representation, manifestation and iteration in visual and material culture. Like the *study* of identity, the concept itself is relational and contingent, both inadequate and indispensable. Antoinette Burton makes the latter claim about nation – though it 'may be indispensable, it is also woefully inadequate to the task of representation for which it is apparently historically determined'.[43] While

---

[41] Dror Wahrman, *The Making of the Modern Self: Identity and Culture in Eighteenth-Century England* (New Haven, CT and London: Yale University Press, 2004), p. 128.

[42] Wahrman, *Making of the Modern Self*, pp. 279–280.

[43] Antoinette Burton, 'Introduction: On the inadequacy and the indispensability of the Nation', in Antoinette Burton (ed.), *After the Imperial Turn: Thinking with and through Nation* (London and Durham, NC: Duke University Press, 2003), pp. 1–23.

the nation may be wanting, the task of representation forms the disciplinary sinews of visual culture and to a lesser extent, of material culture, where pictorial meaning can be secondary or complementary to social function. Using an art historical approach to think with and through identity will, it is hoped, invest 'the old epistemology of identity' with a renewed analytic purchase that embraces different regimes of representation and alternative taxonomies.[44] It simultaneously seeks to offer a revisionist account of later eighteenth and early nineteenth-century Scottish history of art as it has traditionally been conceived. That is, as a school of 'profoundly' Scottish painters.

Genre and Gender: The Scottish School of Painters

It is no exaggeration to say that one type of monograph has served Scottish art history in its promulgation of a cohesive painterly tradition as part of a collective national aesthetic spectacularly well: the geography of art survey text. Its evolution began with Robert Brydall's *History of Art in Scotland: Its Origin and Progress* (Edinburgh, 1889), a monograph whose 'aim [writes Brydall in the preface] has been to fill a blank in our national literature, and to place on record the successive steps by which Art in Scotland has attained its present high pre-eminence.'[45] Brydall's volume was superseded in the early twentieth century by James L. Caw's *Scottish Painting Past and Present 1620–1908* (1908) which was in turn, followed almost seventy years later by David and Francina Irwin's *Scottish Painters at Home and Abroad, 1700–1900* (1975), a book which positions itself as 'a deliberate attempt to re-set Scottish painting in its broader context of British and European art', in contrast to Brydall and Caw with their inward-looking explanations of Scottish art as part of a native tradition. According to their introduction, 'The chauvinistic tendency of Scottish writers around 1900 and since to see it [Scottish painting] as an isolated national phenomenon has obscured the truth … Chauvinism not only determined evaluation, but led these writers to lament the emigration of painters from Scotland, as if by so doing, they weakened the cause of

---

[44] Richard Handler, 'Is "identity" a useful cross-cultural concept?', in John R. Gillis (ed.), *Commemorations: The Politics of National Identity* (Princeton, NJ: Princeton University Press, 1994), pp. 27–40; For a more recent, withering critique of the reifying connotations of identity, see Rogers Brubaker and Frederick Cooper, 'Beyond "identity"', *Theory and Society* 29 (2000), pp. 1–47.

[45] Robert Brydall, *Art in Scotland: Its Origin and Progress* (Edinburgh: W. Blackwood & Sons, 1889), p. vi.

painting at home, rather than enhancing Scotland's cosmopolitanism.'[46] A decade after the Irwins, Duncan Macmillan's *Painting in Scotland: The Golden Age* (1986) accompanied an exhibition in London and Edinburgh, followed by his *Scottish Art, 1460–2000* (1990; 2000), and most recently, Murdo Macdonald's *Scottish Art* (2000). With the exception of the Irwins, these texts embrace centuries of the work of (primarily) painters of the 'Scottish School' in tracing its chronological artistic development in a linear narrative sequence.

Despite its appeal to a non-academic audience, the survey text is a highly polemical tool – art history at its most grandiose and at its most political 'reducing cultural and individual differences to questionable hierarchies and generalities'.[47] Both Caw and Macmillan adopted this historiographical model pioneered by Brydall in the later nineteenth-century to contrive a coherent story of Scottish painting up to their (then) presents – 1908 and 2000 respectively. Caw explained the object of his monograph was not so much to recount the history of Scottish painting by providing biographical portraits of the artists, as an attempt to trace its development in their works, to contrast its different phases and analyse its essential characteristics. In other words, to discern 'Scottishness' as a recognisable stylistic category identifiable in a body of painted works produced across almost three centuries between 1620 and 1908. Caw divided his narrative into two unequal parts: The Past: 1620–1820 and The Present: 1860–1908. His contention in the Résumé and Conclusion that 'the key to the art of a nation must needs lie . . . in racial character and in the environment which has helped to shape it and which, in some degree, it has shapen' seems remarkably outdated and smacks of eugenics, as indeed it did to the Irwins in the early 1970s.[48]

In its conception of art as shaped and shapen by immutable climatic and ethnic determinants, rather than political or institutional ones, Caw's thesis anticipated aspects of a classic, mid-twentieth-century study of art and national identity: *The Englishness of English Art*, by the émigré art historian Nikolaus Pevsner.[49] Published in 1956, when studies of national character were extremely popular, Pevsner asserted that a history of style

---

[46] David Irwin and Francina Irwin, *Scottish Painters at Home and Abroad, 1700–1900* (London: Faber, 1975), p. 35, p. 38.

[47] Mitchell Schwarzer, 'Origins of the art history survey text', *Art Journal* 53.4 (1995), p. 24.

[48] James L. Caw, *Scottish Painting Past and Present, 1620–1908* (Edinburgh: T. C. & E. C. Jack, 1908), p. 470.

[49] John Barrell, 'Sir Joshua Reynolds and the Englishness of English Art', in Homi K. Bhabha (ed.), *Nation and Narration* (London: Routledge, 1990), p. 157. Barrell argues that the Englishness of English art was a suggestion first made by Reynolds.

and the cultural geography of nations could only be successful if it is conducted in terms of polarities.[50] The chapters that followed on 'Hogarth and observed life', 'Reynolds and detachment', 'Perpendicular England', 'Blake and the flaming line', 'Constable and the pursuit of nature' and 'Picturesque England' focussed on four of the pictorial protagonists of the eighteenth and early nineteenth centuries in an attempt to divine some of the 'apparently contradictory qualities' of Englishness that produced a native art.[51] Pevsner marshalled a dazzling array of art historical examples, for instance, to support his view of English art as the keen observation and quick recording of nature, from an illuminated manuscript of *c.* 1300 depicting babooneries or monkey-business, to the utilitarians of the nineteenth century and their 'unshakable faith in reason and experience'.[52] His argument is no doctrinaire account of Englishness; as he writes in the introduction, 'the geography of art is by no means nationalism in action'.[53] Rather, he recognises the inherent complexity of a nation's characteristics, their impermanence and also their fluidity, in his suggestion that national character does not at all moments and in all situations appear equally distinct.[54] He returns to this theme in chapter 5, in which in reference to Henry Moore, the Englishness of English art remains a work-in-progress, with Moore being a sculptor whose works seemingly contradict the view of the English as 'not a sculptural nation'.[55] Referencing Moore again in the conclusion, he posits, 'National character is not a procrustean bed. There is nothing stagnant in national qualities, they are in a perpetual flux. New possibilities may at any moment be thrown up and force us to revise our categories.'[56] Two pages later, he reiterates that national character 'is no procrustean bed, so it is no divining-rod either'. In a sentence that surely has underlying autobiographical resonance, Pevsner suggests, 'England has indeed profited just as much from the un-Englishness of the immigrants as they have profited from the Englishing they underwent.'[57] Notions of un-Scottishness and Scottishing could be usefully applied in revisiting those late eighteenth- and early nineteenth-century artists assigned into the hoary canon of Scottish painting.

---

[50] Philip Gleason, 'Identifying identity: A semantic history', p. 926. Nikolaus Pevsner, *The Englishness of English Art* (London: British Broadcasting Corporation, 1956), p. 24.

[51] Pevsner, *The Englishness of English Art*, p. 24.

[52] Pevsner, *The Englishness of English Art*, pp. 46–47.

[53] Andrew Causey, 'Pevsner and Englishness', in Peter Draper (ed.), *Reassessing Nikolaus Pevsner* (Aldershot: Ashgate, 2004), p. 165.

[54] Pevsner, *The Englishness of English Art*, p. 23.

[55] Pevsner, *The Englishness of English Art*, p. 137 and p. 139.

[56] Pevsner, *The Englishness of English Art*, p. 194.

[57] Pevsner, *The Englishness of English Art*, p. 198.

In chapter XIII, the final section of the Résumé and Conclusion of *Scottish Painting Past and Present*, Caw has this to say:

That a small country like Scotland should have produced so much art in little more than a century is notable, but that so large a proportion should be of excellent quality is indeed wonderful. Caring more for the significance and beauty of common things than for the far off or fanciful, it possesses at its best a keen and dramatic perception of character and situation, a profound love of Nature, and a touch of poetic glamour expressed with an instinct for the essentials of expression, whether realism or decoration be in the ascendant, a dexterous and masculine quality of handling, combined with a fine use of paint, and a use of colour which assures it a distinct and honourable place.[58]

It is no wonder that the quality of handling is gendered as discernibly 'masculine', when the painters of the Scottish School between the early nineteenth century and early twentieth centuries ('in little more than a century') are almost exclusively men. Here then the defining characteristics of a national Scottish painterly tradition are elucidated by Caw, where his reference to 'the significance and beauty of common things' is surely indebted to Dugald Stewart's common sense philosophy. As we shall see in more detail in Chapter 6, the concept of the Scottish School of painters first began to be addressed in the Edinburgh press and periodical literature from the 1810s. Writing in the first decade of the twentieth century, Caw could be forgiven for what now seems an outdated, blinkered and impoverished approach to art history in general and to Scottish painting in particular. More worrying is Macmillan, who wrote in 1994 that his own view of Scottish art still coincided with that of Caw 'to an important degree in its essentials'.[59] What these essentials constitute is not explained. Macmillan's *Painting in Scotland* subscribed to a contrived, teleological view of Scottish art – 'the golden age' – from the Union of 1707 to 1843, the year of Disruption in the Church of Scotland.[60] Following Caw's linear outline, Macmillan delineated a Scottish School of painters in their wider cultural context, the essence of which had by now become canonical. Namely, that Scotland as a nation was culturally homogenous and that Scottish art was a coherent national tradition whose features were profoundly and demonstrably 'Scottish'.[61] Macmillan's *Painting in Scotland* was as much

---

[58] Caw, *Scottish Painting Past and Present,* p. 495.

[59] Duncan Macmillan, 'The canon in Scottish art: Scottish art in the canon', *Scotlands* 1.1 (1994), p. 99.

[60] Duncan Macmillan's *Scottish Art, 1460–2000* (Edinburgh: Mainstream, 2000), is his most ambitious survey, covering over six hundred years, to include the Reformation.

[61] See Murdo Macdonald, 'Finding Scottish Art', in Glenda Norquay and Gerry Smyth (eds.), *Across the Margins: Cultural Identity and Change in the Atlantic Archipelago* (Manchester: Manchester University Press, 2002), pp. 171–184.

political manifesto as art history textbook – part of a concerted effort after the 1979 failed referendum on political devolution for Scotland to insist on the singular achievements of this geographically diminutive but culturally precocious nation.[62]

From this introductory overview, it should be apparent that identity has been and continues to be a buoyant area of investigation across a wide range of disciplines at least since the 1970s, when it was imported into the humanities from the social sciences; although it is one that is not without its critics for what they berate as its conceptual elasticity.[63] The same cannot be said for art history in Scotland in the period of the later eighteenth and early nineteenth centuries, which remains wedded to the study of the painterly productions of a discernible national school. Such an approach, pioneered in the early nineteenth century, and subsequently revived and revisited in the early and late 1900s has enjoyed a longevity well beyond its historical shelf life.

This book draws on ongoing debates about identity and nation-ness in disciplines contiguous to art history, applying them to a regime of representation in visual culture and manifestation in material objects, that offers an alternative narrative to the 'Scottish School' of painters. It employs an inclusive, non-hierarchical understanding of what constitutes the stuff of visual and material culture.[64] Chapter 1 starts conventionally enough by focussing on portraits in oil and in miniature – portraits being one of the traditional genres of art historical enquiry. Later in Chapters 4 and 6, the sculpted busts of Prince Charles Edward Stuart and Sir Walter Scott are incorporated into the discussion alongside their painted counterparts. After this first chapter, what constitutes visual and material culture is deliberately capacious, indebted to Bill Brown on 'thing theory' and to Daston's enticing notion of making things 'talkative . . . without resorting to ventriloquism or projection.'[65] The things incorporated into Chapters 2 to 6 include examples of interiors, engravings, ceramics, furniture, sculptures and jewellery. Chapter 5 is a case in point since it looks at the built and natural environment of Edinburgh as a cultural metropolis, at portrait,

---

[62] Tom Normand, '55° North 3° West: A panorama from Scotland', in Dana Arnold and David Peters Corbett (eds.), *A Companion to British Art: 1600 to the Present* (Chichester: Wiley-Blackwell, 2013), esp. pp. 266–268.

[63] Brubaker and Cooper, 'Beyond "identity"', pp. 1–47. They suggest 'category of practice' as an alternative rubric.

[64] For a discussion of the relationship between visual and material culture, see Viccy Coltman, 'Material culture and the history of art(efacts)', in Anne Gerritsen and Giorgio Riello (eds.), *Writing Material Culture History* (London: Bloomsbury, 2015), pp. 17–31.

[65] Bill Brown, 'Thing theory', *Critical Enquiry* 28.1 (2001), pp. 1–22; Lorraine Daston (ed.), *Things that Talk: Object Lessons from Art and Science* (New York: Zone, 2004), p. 21 and p. 9.

landscape, history paintings and engraved satire, in order to explore a variety of scopic domains visible and visualised during the visit of George IV to Edinburgh in August 1822.

Nearly two decades ago, Sankey and Szechi opined that 'research on the material culture of eighteenth-century Scottish society is in its infancy'.[66] The book hopes to assist in its coming of age, while recognising that what is classified under the rubric 'Scottish' may have originally been produced in or commissioned by Scots in Europe, London or across the empire and subsequently dispatched or transported to the Highlands, Lowlands and/or Scottish Borders. Alongside this broad repertoire of objects of material culture are examples of immaterial culture, including Buchan's medallion of ancient sculpture that he conjures up through ekphrasis and Scott's evocative narrative descriptions of artists and works of art in his voluminous literary corpus.

That the book draws on the genre of travel literature, both domestic and foreign, has already been remarked. During the course of his picaresque novel, *A Sentimental Journey through France and Italy* (1782), Laurence Sterne's Mr. Yorick thinks he 'can see the precise and distinguishing marks of national characters more in these nonsensical *minutiae* [in a Paris barbers], than in the most important matters of state'.[67] Such a statement constitutes a rallying cry for the historian of material culture, who gives as much historical import to what some may understand as being 'nonsensical *minutiae*' as a historian of politics would to matters of state. Pevsner quotes Yorick in chapter 1 of *The Englishness of English Art,* in which he 'enumerat[es] the characteristics of the English', while cautioning 'It would be unwise to brush aside such little things as ventilation and queueing as trifles compared with the great and lasting qualities of a nation's character.'[68] For Homi Bhabha the weather is similarly 'the most changeable and immanent signs of national difference', where the heat and dust of India is the 'daemonic double' of the English weather.[69] This is a subject discussed below in Chapter 3 in letters between Claud Alexander and one of his Scottish friends and constant correspondents, David Anderson. Their letters concern the inclement weather at home in Scotland, where they were intent on returning to, while they broiled making fortunes to enable their return in the Indian subcontinent in Bengal. For their mutual

---

[66] Margaret Sankey and Daniel Szechi, 'Elite culture and the decline of Scottish Jacobitism, 1716–1745', *Past and Present* 173 (2001), p. 99.

[67] *A Sentimental Journey through France and Italy*, by Mr. Yorick (London, 1782), I, p. 24.

[68] Pevsner, *The Englishness of English Art*, p. 21.

[69] Homi K. Bhabha, 'DissemiNation: Time, narrative and the margins of the modern nation', in Homi K. Bhabha (ed.), *Nation and Narration* (London: Routledge, 1990), pp. 291–322 at p. 319.

friend George Bogle 'home' was a memory both climactic and domestic. In letters to his sister Bess dated 1771, he wrote of 'the pure air at Daldowie' where the family had a house and estate on the River Clyde; of his longing for a fire in 'a nice clean hearth and a charming sparkling Ingle'.[70] Chapter 3 seeks to elucidate Alexander's Scottishness, while the book as a whole gives equal credence to 'little things' as to 'great and lasting qualities', recognising how historically subjective such statements are.

Erika Rappaport's contention that 'Personal letters are an especially fruitful and yet under-theorised source from which to study the imperial history of the self and the family, and the personal history of empire' is equally applicable to art history as to history.[71] Though her focus is on colonial India in the 1850s and 60s, the same claim might be made of Claud Alexander and George Bogle's letters written from Bengal in the latter decades of the previous century. Similarly, George Steuart's protracted correspondence with his aristocratic patrons the Dukes of Atholl discussed in Chapter 2 is an invaluable resource for studying the professional self and his family (his brother Charles was also a painter) in the mercantile history of the metropolis. This book seeks to position epistolary correspondence as an art form in addition to a repository of historical evidence; art historians could profit from paying attention to the work of their literary counterparts in using the contents of such letters, be they familial or commercial, as primary data. Used throughout the book, the idea of epistolary identities will become a familiar one.

The 'visible envelope of the self' is how Entwistle describes dress, allowing us to segue between the material paraphernalia of epistolary history and to consider its sartorial equivalent.[72] Research by historians, especially during the last two decades, has firmly established identity as a critical component of the sartorial project, where 'dress is both a social and an intimate activity', one begun in private but which generated most meaning when viewed by others in the public domain.[73] Part II of this book situates examples of dress, textiles and accessories within the remit of material culture studies, as part of a detachable corporeal carapace by which identity is manipulated by the wearer and manifest to others. While subscribing to

---

[70] Mitchell Library, TD 1681, bundle 25, 31 August 1771; 29 March 1771.

[71] Erika Rappaport, '"The Bombay Debt": Letter writing, domestic economies and family conflict in colonial India', *Gender & History* 16.2 (2004), p. 235.

[72] Joanne Entwistle, 'Fashion and the fleshy body: Dress as embodied practice', *Fashion Theory* 4.3 (2000), p. 327.

[73] Joanne Entwistle, *The Fashioned Body: Fashion, Dress and Modern Social Theory* (Cambridge: Polity, 2000), p. 35; Susan Vincent, *Dressing the Elite: Clothes in Early Modern England* (Oxford: Berg, 2003), p. 9 and p. 108.

Jones and Stallybrass's view that 'Clothing is a worn world: a world of social relations put upon the wearer's body', it seeks to demonstrate the extent to which these outer layers were especially prominent markers of individual and collective identities within regimes of presentation and their pictorial representation.[74] As in Richard Wrigley's study of the politics of dress in Revolutionary France, it considers how questions of identity were apprehended through what he describes as the 'culturally complex business of the legibility of appearance' in reference to the wearing of Highland dress during the '45 uprising and the 1822 visit of George IV to Edinburgh.[75] On these two occasions, dress was an instrument of insurrection and subsequently of loyalty to the British state in an about-face documented below in Chapters 4 and 5.

******

Later in his 1784 speech to the members of the Society of Antiquaries of Scotland, Buchan offers a well-known simile for the union between the English and Scottish Parliaments of seventy-seven years earlier in which Scotland is conceptualised as a young, healthy and high-born heiress with a Highland estate and England as a rich merchant of advancing age '& beginning through Turtle and Madeira to have more to do then he could excecute'.[76] In this marriage of old and new wealth, youth and age, he is the parasitic partner whose city feasts and 'ill concocted projects of agrandisment' are funded by her land in the Highlands. The sometimes convivial, at other times acrimonious, relationship between Scotland and England, and that between old and new monies, land and commerce, and even these dietary predilections will be addressed below. By being represented and manifest in visual and material culture they act as what Henderson has called 'vehicles for understanding identity [which] can play as large a role as the motives for that understanding in making identity meaningful'.[77] The ensuing chapters ask meaningful to whom and in what ways, to later eighteenth- and early nineteenth-century Scots with their tangled and entangled identities within a nation of culturally distinct territories (Highland/Lowland/Borders) and to us as their contemporary interlocutors.

---

[74] Ann R. Jones and Peter Stallybrass, *Renaissance Clothing and the Materials of Memory* (Cambridge: Cambridge University Press, 2000), p. 3.

[75] Richard Wrigley, *The Politics of Appearance: Representations of Dress in Revolutionary France* (Oxford: Berg, 2002), p. 5 and p. 231, where he writes of 'the semantic import of appearances'.

[76] This notional coupling with Scotland as a bride and England as her suitor is a persistent feature of both pro- and anti-Union pamphlets as Juliet Shields notes in her *Sentimental Literature and Anglo-Scottish Identity, 1745–1820* (Cambridge: Cambridge University Press, 2010), pp. 12–13.

[77] Andrea K. Henderson, *Romantic Identities: Varieties of Subjectivity, 1774–1830* (Cambridge: Cambridge University Press, 1996), p. 5.

PART I

Beyond Scotland

1 | Scots in Europe

'Making a Figure': Painted Portraiture on the Grand Tour

> There is a natural sympathy between people of the same country when
> they meet abroad which draws them irresistibly towards each other.
>
> Sir William Forbes, travel journal, Naples, 1793[1]

According to Mrs Hester Lynch Piozzi, the 'many agreeable Scotch' she
encountered in her marital home of Italy were supported by a 'national
phalanx' formation in which 'every Individual of that respectable country
suffers no Native of it wholly to want regard.'[2] Piozzi's evocative description situates the Scots in Italy within a collective military identity, an
identity that is often understood as being given visual form in Pompeo
Batoni's celebrated, full-length portrait of *The Honourable Colonel William
Gordon* of 1766 (Plate I). Attired in the scarlet tunic of the Queen's Own
Royal Highlanders and swathed in Huntley tartan, the statuesque Gordon
is represented before an elevated, seated statue of Roma with the ruins of
the Colosseum – 'the most stupendous monument of antiquity in Rome' –
in the left background.[3] Art historians have observed how Gordon's uniform evokes the dress of the ancient Romans with the toga-like folds and
pleats of the plaid, especially the section emblazoned across his chest, and
his matching plaid hose, which are rolled down to give the appearance of
buskins, soft leather boots worn by the Romans.[4] When the portrait was
painted, the Disarming Act of 1746 had proscribed the wearing of
Highland dress following its adoption by the Jacobites as part of the
ideological armoury of sedition. More will be said about the Jacobites
later in Chapter 4. The Act was one of a series of legislative measures
instituted by the British government in an attempt to assimilate Scotland
into Britain following the most recently crushed Jacobite uprising.
However, it would be misleading to read this complex image as a portrait

---

[1] NLS, MS. 1542, 204.

[2] Quoted by Basil Skinner, *Scots in Italy in the Eighteenth Century* (Edinburgh: Scottish National Portrait Gallery, 1966), p. 15.

[3] John Moore, *A View of Society and Manners in Italy* (London, 1781), I, p. 416.

[4] Anthony M. Clark, *Pompeo Batoni: A Complete Catalogue of His Works* (Oxford: Phaidon, 1985), no. 298.

of defiance within a visual repertoire of political expression that deliberately flouted the proscriptions of the Act, because the wearing of Highland dress was forbidden only in Scotland and even there, would not apply to a military professional like Gordon. Such a misreading of insubordination sets the Scots in political opposition to the British establishment, when they are in fact shown via Gordon, to be in its military service. The bronze medal secured to Gordon's uniform seems to depict the profile bust of the Hanoverian monarch, King George III; it makes the political currency of the image one of Scottish compliance in Britain's imperial ambitions, far removed from one of rebellious Scottishness. The military persona of the sitter, or rather the poseur, with his 'proprietary swagger and martial sang-froid' only has eyes for the orb the helmeted statue extends towards him.[5] The laurels of victory are out of his reach.

It is important to recognise the quotations from ancient Rome excerpted into this portrait, in the first place for Gordon's sartorial swagger, but rather more crucially, for the Scottish colonel employed in Britain's militia. Gordon stands – his near-profile visage is like an antique cameo – surrounded by the surviving monuments of ancient Roman triumph and civilisation, where Rome is the paradigm of empire. Where the implication is that ancient Rome's empire was being superseded by that of later eighteenth-century Britain precisely through the participation of men like Colonel Gordon. Gordon's Scottish identity is paraded so graphically because one of the outposts of empire that the Romans were *not* able to conquer was the far northern territory of Scotland, of the Highlands and Aberdeenshire.[6] The implication of the portrait being, if Gordon's ancient Caledonian ancestors resisted Roman domination, then Scottish participation in Britain's military machine will create an empire to rival and supplant that of Rome. While notionally mapping the progress of this imperial advance, it is also worth citing the monumental size of Batoni's canvas. At 259 by 187.5 cm, it completely dominates the display of family portraits in the drawing room at Fyvie Castle in Aberdeenshire and is the largest of all the grand tour portraits discussed in this chapter (Figure 1). In light of such an 'imperial' re-reading, Batoni's bravura portrait of Colonel Gordon could equally introduce Chapter 3 on Scots in Empire.

And what of the *artist* who was responsible for this enduring image of Scottish participation in the expansion and consolidation of Britain's late

---

[5] Christopher M. S. Johns, 'Portraiture and the making of cultural identity: Pompeo Batoni's *The Honourable Colonel William Gordon* (1765–66) in Italy and North Britain', *Art History* 27 (2004), p. 385.

[6] Johns, 'Portraiture and the making of cultural identity', p. 394.

Figure 1: Drawing Room, Fyvie Castle. C. F. Kell, Lith.8 Castle St, Holborn, London F. C.; Lumleys, Land Agents & Auctioneers, London, SW. *c.* 1885. © HES.

eighteenth-century global empire? Clearly he was not part of Mrs Piozzi's Scottish phalanx; he was 'the best painter in Italy' so the hyperbolic accounts of contemporary sitters, like the Scot James Bruce of Kinnaird (Plate II) tell us.[7] Looking through the complete catalogues of Batoni paintings it is easy to be overcome by visual fatigue in the one hundred and fifty-four British faces looking back.[8] With this type of catalogue, there is a temptation to see Batoni's portraits as formulaic with their legions of sitters, the contrived 'Roman-ness' of their situations and in their genuflections to antiquity. In the 1940s, the art historian John Steegman began to inventorise the props in some ninety 'English [*sic*] portraits' by Batoni, including that of Gordon (Plate I). 'The majority [of Batoni's English portraits, he writes] perhaps, cannot claim to be more than superlatively good furniture pieces. But like all the best eighteenth-century furniture, they are well mannered and excellently made.'[9] The latter claim could equally be applied to the Scottish sitters represented by Batoni whose inculcated British manners and acquired cosmopolitan polish accrued in the course of a grand tour this chapter will document. Another example of the twenty known portraits of Scots by Batoni will give us a flavour of Steegman's endeavour: Plate III is a whole-length (236.4 × 144.7 cm) portrait representing *John, Lord Mountstuart*, which is signed and dated 1767.[10] The sitter is standing cross-legged, with his right hand on his hip, in front of an elevated sculpture identified as the famous seated *Agrippina* in the Capitoline Museum in Rome. One British visitor to the museum in 1770 described her as 'sedens to the last degree exquisite: such drapery and expression as I [Charles Burney] never saw in sculpture'.[11] This famous statue is cited as being the model for the sedens pose of Roma in Colonel Gordon's portrait (Plate I) which Batoni painted the previous year.[12] James Boswell, whose grand tour portrait we will encounter in due course, met Mountstuart in Rome and described him in a letter to Jean-Jacques Rousseau dated 3 October 1765 as 'a young noblemen who merits his being of the blood of the ancient kings of Scotland. He deserves

---

[7] Clark, *Pompeo Batoni*, no. 257.

[8] Clark, *Pompeo Batoni*; Edgar Peters Bowron, *Pompeo Batoni: A Complete Catalogue of His Paintings* (New Haven, CT: Yale University Press, 2016), 2 volumes.

[9] John Steegman, 'Some English portraits by Pompeo Batoni', *Burlington Magazine* 88 (1946), p. 59.

[10] The number twenty comes from Edgar Peters Bowron and Peter Björn Kerber, *Pompeo Batoni: Prince of Painters in Eighteenth-Century Rome* (New Haven, CT and London: Yale University Press, 2008), p. 42.

[11] H. Edmund Poole (ed.), *Music, Men and Manners in France and Italy, 1770, Being the Journal Written by Charles Burney* (London: Folio Society, 1969), p. 137.

[12] Clark, *Pompeo Batoni*, no. 298.

my drawing his portrait for you ... From each character of our nation of originals I always drew something which I could turn to profit, and I formed friendships with one or two worthy men that will last for the rest of my life.'[13] Boswell adopts an art historical critique to delineate his Scottish countryman, 'drawing his portrait' in the letter to Rousseau and describing him as one of a nation 'of originals', rather than copies or fakes. In Batoni's portrait (Plate III) the young Scottish nobleman in his salmon pink dress with its elaborate silver embroidery and his fur-lined tricorn hat, far outshines the seated sculpture famed for her drapery and expression, whose head and chest are bathed in a golden light.

Basil Skinner's pioneering work on the Scots in Italy provided an overview of the configuration of the Scottish phalanx abroad, particularly in Rome, from the young (most are in their early twenties) aristocratic Scots following a geographical itinerary and pedagogical curriculum on their grand tours; the expatriate antiquaries and dealers Gavin Hamilton, James Byres and Colin Morison; the artists whose tours were often far from grand, including John Brown, John and Alexander Runciman and David Allan; to the Stuart court in exile at the Palazzo Muti from 1719. One of the limitations of Skinner's Scottish focus – for him Batoni's portrait of *Colonel Gordon* (Plate I) 'epitomises the Scot in Italy ... endowed with the strongest pride in his own national identity' – is that it marginalises the Britishness and cosmopolitanism of the tour (grand or otherwise).[14] This chapter offers a survey of a series of 'essays upon snouts' by looking critically and in detail at about a dozen oil on canvas grand tour portraits of aristocratic and gentleman Scots.[15] These were commissioned from Batoni and other portraits painters while their sitters were participating in the ritualised educational pilgrimage that was the grand tour from the late 1750s to the early 1780s. It suggests these portraits – themselves an elite art form – image Scots in Europe as being and having been assimilated into the inclusive project of Britishness, as privileged socio-economic protagonists at the cultural front, rather than rebellious political antagonists at the geographical fringes. Instead of a myopic focus on the physiognomies of their painted faces, it seeks to consider the wider cultural and social implications of what it means to make a figure on canvas on the grand

---

[13] Frank Brady and F. A. Pottle (eds.), *Boswell on the Grand Tour: Italy, Corsica and France, 1765–1766* (London: Heinemann, 1955), p. 9.

[14] Basil Skinner, 'A Scot's-eye view of Rome', *Country Life* 28 July 1966, pp. 218–219 at p. 218.

[15] See Captain John Clerk's letter from Rome of 18 November 1769 referring to his cousin, the artist Anne Forbes who 'has made several good portraits from Nature, and soon intends to make an essay upon my snout'. NRS, GD18/5494/2.

tour; recognising the significance of the Scottish cohort in Italy, while simultaneously moving beyond Mrs Piozzi's constricted phalanx formation.

The term the 'Grand Tour' seems to have been first coined, or at least popularised, by Richard Lassels in his 1670 guidebook, and by the historical period under consideration a century later it was entrenched as what Cohen has called 'a technology of the self', for having an instrumental role in the formation of elite adult male identity.[16] It typically involved a standardised geographical passage from northern to southern Europe, with Italy, and especially Rome, as the culmination of the route. This topographical itinerary was mirrored in a social one, whereby the predominantly male participants moved from one life stage to another (from youth to adulthood) and from one place in the social hierarchy to another: from members of a provincial elite with local attachments, to members of a national and transnational ruling class with a wider set of allegiances and commitments.[17] This, at any rate, was the ideology of the grand tour – to act as a rite of passage, which to quote Richard Hurd's 1764 *Dialogues on the Uses of Foreign Travel; Considered as Part of an English Gentleman's Education*: 'can be taken to polish and form the manners of our liberal youth, and fit them for business and conversation of the world'.[18] The polishing phase as it was known, placed particular emphasis on the cultivation of manners by first-hand exposure to the men and manners of different nations, which according to Bowers helped 'to enact a transformation of personhood'.[19] Although Newman in his *Rise of English Nationalism* asserts that 'No sociological analysis of the touring phenomenon [that was the grand tour] exists', Bourdieu's account of the production of a new man in which 'such store [is set] on the seemingly most insignificant details of *dress, bearing, physical* and *verbal* manners' has particular resonance for the transformative aspect of the later eighteenth-century grand tour.[20] One of the difficulties of studying the grand tour as a cultural institution is that, as Cohen observes, it

---

[16] Michèle Cohen, *Fashioning Masculinity: National Identity and Language in the Eighteenth Century* (London: Routledge, 1996), p. 60.

[17] Terence Bowers, 'Reconstituting the national body in Smollett's *Travels through France and Italy*', *Eighteenth-Century Life* 21.1 (1997), p. 6. Henry French and Mark Rothery, '"Upon your entry into the world": Masculine values and the threshold of adulthood among landed elites in England, 1680–1800', *Social History* 33.4 (2008), pp. 402–422, surveys what its authors term the final fraught formative stage in a son's passage to adulthood (p. 403).

[18] Richard Hurd, *Dialogues on the Uses of Foreign Travel; Considered as Part of an English Gentleman's Education* (London, 1764), p. 8.

[19] Bowers, 'Reconstituting the national body', p. 6.

[20] Gerald Newman, *The Rise of English Nationalism: A Cultural History, 1740–1830* (London: Weidenfeld & Nicolson, 1987), p. 42; Pierre Bourdieu, *Outline of a Theory of Practice* (Cambridge: Cambridge University Press, 1977), p. 94.

was not a coherent story even in the eighteenth century, but was riddled with contradictions and ambiguities.[21] While criticism concerned its *practices*, its defenders referred to its *ideals*, so even the terms of reference were mismatched where a 'dislocation between the project and its outcomes is woven into its discourse'.[22] For the historian of Scotland this muddied situation is compounded by much of the more rigorous existing secondary literature, including Cohen's studies of the construction of the English gentleman, being resolutely Anglocentric in focus, with no separate mention of their North British counterparts. As 'Britishness was not and is not mere Englishness, Englishness writ large', so it would be promiscuous simply to map the defining qualities of Englishness onto their Scottish equivalents on the grand tour.[23]

This chapter asserts that instances of young, elite, male Scots on canvas commissioned during their grand tours provide an entrée for recruiting visual culture into readings about the self and the transformation of personhood during this critical period of geographical and social passage. Marcia Pointon has recently posited 'the idea of portraiture as a tool that makes possible the registering of an identity in relation to the social'.[24] Witnessing the formation and dispersal of Mrs Piozzi's phalanx of Scots, this chapter seeks to elucidate different iterations of 'the social' by considering the commission and display of the grand tour portrait as a means for representing, disseminating and reproducing pedagogical, familial and homosocial relations. In proposing the plurality of social meanings in commissions for grand tour portraits, it is necessary to extend the geographical parameters of Italy to incorporate the rest of Europe. In other words, we need to consider the influences of a wider European context – those 'capitals and . . . courts of Princes' – although only one portrait discussed immediately below was painted outside of Italy in Geneva.[25] The visual evidence will be supplemented by drawing on the unpublished letters and the published journals and diaries of travelling Scots, including that of Dr John Moore, physician and tutor to Douglas, the sickly 8th Duke of

[21] Michèle Cohen, 'The Grand Tour: Constructing the English gentleman in eighteenth-century France', *History of Education* 21.3 (1992), p. 242. See also Cohen's 'Manliness, effeminacy and the French: gender and the construction of national character in eighteenth-century England', in Tim Hitchcock and Michèle Cohen (eds.), *English Masculinities, 1660–1800* (London: Longman, 1999), pp. 44–62 and her 'The Grand Tour: National identity and masculinity', *Changing English: Studies in Culture and Education* 8.2 (2001), pp. 129–141.

[22] Cohen, 'The Grand Tour: Constructing the English gentleman', p. 248.

[23] Krishnan Kumar, *The Making of English National Identity* (Cambridge: Cambridge University Press, 2003), p. 156.

[24] Marcia Pointon, *Portrayal and the Search for Identity* (London: Reaktion, 2013), p. 11.

[25] 'Outlines of a plan for making the Tour of France Italy and Germany. Coltness, 7 June 1769', Highland Archive Centre, D766/1/4/8.

Figure 2: Mattio Bolognini, *Alexander Chapman, John Bargrave and his nephew, John Raymond*, 1647. 13.5 × 10.5 cm. Bargrave collection (Canterbury Cathedral Archive).

Hamilton with whom he made a prolonged grand tour lasting nearly five years.

Take this portrait of 1774 (97 × 75 cm) by the Genevan artist Jean Preud'homme, which depicts Dr Moore with his aristocratic pupil, Douglas, the eighteen-year-old 8th Duke of Hamilton and Moore's son, also John Moore (Plate IV). The threesome is represented in an interior with an Alpine landscape depicted through the window. Standing in the centre, between father and son, Hamilton rests his arm on his tutor's shoulder, while the latter, half kneeling on a chair, points to a globe. On the left of the composition, John, or Jack as he was known, unrolls a map of Scotland to show to the viewer; a book lies on the table next to him. On one level, this image has much of the conventional baggage we have come to expect from grand tour portraiture: the landscape, globe, map and book. In his account of the seventeenth-century English collector, traveller and witness, Dr John Bargrave, Stephen Bann reads our triple portrait along these lines – the figures engaged in what he calls a polite ritual – as a comparison to the triple portrait with Bargrave in the centre that was painted by Matteo Bolognini in Siena in 1647 (Figure 2).[26] Bann notes the similarity of the compositions in these two grand tour portraits separated chronologically by over a century. In Bolognini's portrait, the dominant figure of Bargrave, whose coat of arms hangs behind him, is flanked on the right by his nephew, John Raymond and on the left, by his Kentish neighbour Alexander Chapman. The three figures pore over a map of the Mediterranean with Bargrave pointing to the city of Siena where the three were staying when their portrait was painted.

In a letter from Chatelaine dated July 1773 to his wife Jeanie in Glasgow, Dr Moore describes the Preud'homme portrait with its triangulated composition in more informative detail:

There is a picture of the Duke Jack & I in one Group almost finished. We are at full length one foot & a half high each figure. I lean on a chair & Point at Gr[eat]. Britain on a Globe & look to the Duke as much to say there is the country of all the world whose History & Government you ought to know best & where your affections & attention should be fixed. The Duke leans on me & has his eyes fixed on Britain. Jack looks at the spectator & unrolls a map of Britain. The history of B[ritain]. lies on the table. A view of Geneva & the lake at a distance. The figures are all like. The Duke in Red – White vest & Br[eeches] Jack in white green vest & Br[eeches]. me Blue red vest.[27]

---

[26] Stephen Bann, *Under the Sign: John Bargrave as Collector, Traveler and Witness* (Ann Arbor: University of Michigan Press, 1994), pp. 68–69.

[27] BL Add. MS. 57321 folio 24.

According to Moore's letter, the objects strategically assembled in the painting, the book, map and globe, are not so much the polite accoutrements of a global geography lesson, as pedagogic, political and patriotic tools. They are unequivocally positioned, in this representation of an interior space within a distinctive Swiss landscape, to enable the young *Scottish* aristocrat to learn about and love his native country of *Great Britain*. The fixity of the young duke's projected relationship with Britain invites comparison with a transience imaged in the painting in which the three figures are passing through the landscape in the upper left of the picture plane, as mobile travellers rather than permanent fixtures. In contrast with the travelling canes held vertically by his father and his father's charge, Jack's cane lies on the floor next to him. This suggests the inexperience of youth in that he has not yet learned to handle the responsibility of power as represented by the cane. Moore wrote to his wife from Geneva on 16 September 1774, describing their son Jack as 'realy a pretty youth – his face is of a manly beauty – his person is strong & his figure very elegant'.[28] His is the only portrait on the canvas whose figure is not obscured by the furniture. Moore wrote to the Duchess of Argyll on 31 April 1773 describing her son in artefactual terms – with his student as a precious yet unrefined prototype: 'the materials we have to work upon are excellent and capable of the finest polish, and well worthy of all our care to prevent their being defaced or broke to pieces before they are finished'.[29] The triple portrait by Preud'homme, painted in Geneva where the party stayed for two years, is a visual rendering of this polishing stage in-progress.

'The Duke has made more than one Tour round the Globe', Moore wrote from Geneva to the Duchess of Argyll on 4 July 1772, 'and he is familiarly acquainted with all the Countries of Europe, and the European Settlements in Asia, Africa, and America, and has a pretty good General Idea of the present State of most Countries. We proceed also in Particular History, especially in that of Europe since the Revival of Letters.'[30] One of the duke's surviving exercise books from 1773 reveals the particularities of the pedagogical curriculum that accompanied his grand tour at this date, with brief essays on aspects of classical antiquity, history and statesmanship, including Homer, Louis XIV, the reign of Charles II, Tronchin's death and the 1707 Union between England and Scotland.[31] In one of his many annotations, Moore refers to the book as a 'literary exercise', asking

[28] BL Add. MS. 57321 folio 27.

[29] Duke of Argyll, *Intimate Society Letters of the Eighteenth Century* (London, 1910), II, p. 361.

[30] Duke of Argyll, *Intimate Society Letters*, II, p. 343.   [31] NRAS, 2177/volume 1985.

the Duke to spend half an hour each day answering a question: 'such an exercise does not seem to be intirely unworthy of your attention [explains Moore] because it will tend to fortify your hand of write, to form your stile of language & will compel you in some degree to employ your thinking faculty'.

In a letter to his wife from Paris, Moore complained at the lengthy weekly dispatches such as that cited above from Geneva that he was obliged to write to the Duke and Duchess, which were published in 1910 by the then Duke of Argyll with other so-called *Intimate Society Letters of the Eighteenth Century*.[32] Though far from intimate with his aristocratic employer, Moore's weekly missives still make for instructive reading as they were intended to when they were composed. They subscribe to the ideology of the grand tour as a means for transcending the stereotypical behaviour of national characters by first-hand exposure to them. Despite overblown claims to impartiality, this exposure was far from objective since Britons were repeatedly reassured of their own superiority. As Black puts it, most Britons returned to Britain following a grand tour 'as better-informed xenophobes'.[33] This chapter will show that at the same time, most Scots returned to Britain as better-informed Britons. Writing from Berlin, on 12 June 1775, Moore describes the duke as follows: 'With regard to the first impression, this always is greatly in his favour, for devoid of the Pert vivacity of a French Petit Maître or the Supercilious reserve of an English coxcomb, he possesses all the easy Elegance of a Man of Rank and Fashion.'[34] Projecting the duke's future onto a blank canvas, his letter proceeds to imagine three alternative scenarios, metropolitan, provincial and national:

When he returns to Britain one of these things may happen. He may be Suck'd into the Whirl of London dissipation, pleas'd with the admiration of Girls and imitation of one set of men; he may lead Modes or become one of the most conspicuous figures in the Fashionable Circle, and satisfied with that species of distinction, he may lose all desire for a higher Ambition. Or Pleased with Blind approbation and

---

[32] From Paris, 12 May 1772. BL Add. MS. 57321 folios 11–12.

[33] Jeremy Black, *The British and the Grand Tour* (London: Croom Helm, 1985), p. 186. See Thomas Watkins's letter written to his father, dated 4 April 1782 at Calais as he bid adieu to England: 'I go with the fond hope of returning convinced from experience of thy superior advantages over all countries'. Travels in a series of letters from a gentleman to his father, in the years 1787, 88 and 89, Beinecke Library, Osborn c569 folio 7. Also, James Byres's letter dated 20 February 1773 to Norton Nicholls: 'above all I believe one must sit down more satisfied and happy at home after an impartial examination of the countries sensible of the great advantages our own has at present over them'. Lewis Walpole Library, MSS MISC box 6 folder 69.

[34] Duke of Argyll, *Intimate Society Letters*, II, p. 390.

undisputed precedency he may prefer living in Scotland, surrounded by Hunters and obsequious Retainers,

> Like Cato give his little Senate Laws
> And Sit attentive to his own Applause.

Or, despising the degrading distinction of being a mere man of mode as well as the Dictatorial Pride of an unimportant Chieftain, he may by a Proper exertion of his Talents Shew that he is as able to make a conspicuous figure in the Senate or Cabinet as in the Drawing Room.[35]

Listing Hamilton's possible career trajectories on his return to Britain, Moore's letter locates him geographically, spatially and morally in opposing arenas: dissipated London, surrounded by an obsequious clan in Scotland, or beyond the social confines of the drawing room, as a member of the ruling class in the British Government. We will encounter Hamilton in the drawing room via one of his other painted grand tour portraits in due course.

At the same time as subscribing to an ideology of the grand tour, Dr Moore's letters to the Duchess of Argyll unwittingly reveal the rhetorical representational strategies embedded in its painted portraiture. One of Moore's letters from Geneva recounts 'The Duke, like many people of his age, is fond of Dress. I have endeavoured to convince him that the Duke of Hamilton needs not draw attention of sick importance from that Quarter'.[36] Writing a week later still at Geneva where the portrait was painted, he 'took occasion to Paint the character of a youth we have here whose only sollicitide and study is Dress'.[37] Preud'homme's triple portrait (Plate IV) depicts the duke as a willing pupil, whose attention is focussed on the lessons to be gleaned from Great Britain, rather than his (said to be) undivided attention on a self-directed sartorial curriculum. Bourdieu lists dress first in his account of the production of a new man (followed by bearing, physical and verbal manners) and it was and remains one of the ways in which identity was constituted and performed especially on the transformative grand tour. Wahrman has pointed out that this was not a peculiarity of the eighteenth century although what was specific to the period he designates as the *ancien régime* 'was the possible literalness with which dress was taken to *make* identity, rather than merely to signify its

[35] Duke of Argyll, *Intimate Society Letters*, II, p. 391. The quotation is from Alexander Pope's 'Epistle to Dr. Arbuthnot'.

[36] 12 October 1772. Duke of Argyll, *Intimate Society Letters*, II, p. 351.

[37] 19 October 1772. Duke of Argyll, *Intimate Society Letters*, II, p. 352.

anterior existence'.[38] While in one sense dress was what Wahrman calls an anchor of identity, he identifies the extent to which the opposite is also true, where clothing can be assumed or shed at will in the fashioning of the exterior self. Much more will be said about identity and dress as corporeal carapace in Part II of this book. Coincidentally in this shifting sartorial context, the proposed colours for the clothing worn by our triptych of teacher, aristocratic pupil and teacher's son in Preud'homme's portrait was evidently changed from that which Moore recounted to his wife in his letter of July 1773, as being dominated by a patriotic British palette of red, white and blue.

The Duke of Hamilton's continued passage across Europe and his subsequent residence at Rome was given visual form in two further por-traits painted in a city that was hailed by his countryman Robert Adam as being the 'most glorious place in the Universal World'.[39] The first by Hamilton's distant kinsman Gavin Hamilton dated 1775–7 (183 × 144.7 cm), is particularly celebrated for being the émigré Scottish artist's only known Roman portrait group (Plate V).[40] When James Boswell visited Hamilton at Frascati in April 1765, he rightly predicted that the latter's 'merit as a painter will ever do honour to cold Caledonia'.[41] As in Preud'homme's earlier portrait (Plate IV), Dr Moore and Moore's son accompany the Duke of Hamilton to either side. But in contrast with the Genevan painter's schoolroom scene in which Hamilton literally leans on his tutor, Gavin Hamilton's is a coming of age portrait. Jack both points and gazes towards his father's twenty-one-year old charge, a point of view that is echoed by the dog below. Jack appears to be wearing the uniform his father obtained for him to appear in at the German courts, which he described in a letter to his wife as 'Red faced up with white, white Vest & Britches with a gold shoulder knott'.[42] Shown seated on the left, Dr Moore's outstretched arm is deliberately ambiguous: is he inviting us to view the distance highlights of Rome, that include the Forum, Colosseum and arch of Titus, or the equally admirable, rather more proximate, nearly full-length figure of Hamilton? The group is represented as if on a viewing platform at the back of the Palazzo Senatorio on the

---

[38] Dror Wahrman, *The Making of the Modern Self: Identity and Culture in Eighteenth-Century England* (New Haven, CT, and London: Yale University Press, 2004), p. 177.

[39] 5 March 1755. Robert to Margaret Adam. NRS, GD18/4766.

[40] Brinsley Ford, 'A portrait group by Gavin Hamilton: With some notes on portraits of Englishmen in Rome', *Burlington Magazine* 97 (1955), pp. 372–378.

[41] Ralph S. Walker (ed.), *The Correspondence of James Boswell and John Johnstone of Grange* (London: Heinemann, 1966), pp. 161–162.

[42] Geneva, 16 September 1774. BL Add. MS. 57321, folio 28.

Campidoglio overlooking what had been the Forum but was then a cow market. Moore confirmed the location when he met Eliza Dawson at Hamilton Palace during her 1786 visit with her uncle when the portrait hung in the billiard room facing the door.[43] Following this unscheduled meeting, Dawson confirmed that his works were 'an exact type of himself very entertaining, interesting and eligant'. In one of his publications, *A View of Society and Manners in Italy*, Moore described how 'The beautiful approach to this palace [the Palazzo Senatorio], and all the ornaments which decorate the area before it, cannot detain you long from the back view to which the ancient Capitol fronted. Here you behold the Forum Romanum, now exhibiting a melancholy but interesting view of the devastation wrought by the unified force of time, avarice and bigotry.'[44] The temple included on the right-hand side of the canvas bears the following truncated inscription Senatus Populusque Romanus Incendio Consumptum Restituit ('the Roman Senate and People restored what fire had consumed'). The lapidary inscription on the temple visually echoes that on the dog's collar. Hamilton's canine companion is easily identifiable as a mastiff, a breed that, from the end of the sixteenth century, was especially celebrated as a product of English soil. Ian MacInnes has surveyed the gentrification of the mastiff, 'from tinker's cur to national icon' via aristocratic companion in sixteenth- and seventeenth-century literature, when the breed became emblematic of a particular kind of national masculine identity.[45] Dr Moore draws on this literary trope in his bestselling publication devoted to his travels in France, Switzerland and Germany, where he uses animals as metaphors for national characters, explaining 'For after all his efforts of imitation, a travelled Englishman is as different from a Frenchman or an Italian, as an English mastiff is from a monkey, or a fox: And if ever that sedate and plain meaning dog should pretend to the gay friskiness of the one, or to the subtilty of the other, we should certainly value him much less than we do.'[46] Moore's statement makes one of the subtexts of this portrait, in which the artist and the

---

[43] NLS, Acc. 12017 folio 62.   [44] Moore, *A View of Society and Manners in Italy*, I, p. 437.

[45] Ian MacInnes, 'Mastiffs and spaniels: Gender and nation in the English dog', *Textual Practice* 17.1 (2003), pp. 21–40. See also the essays in Frank Palmeri (ed.), *Humans and Other Animals in Eighteenth-Century British Culture: Representation, Hybridity, Ethics* (Aldershot: Ashgate, 2006) and Ingrid H. Tague, *Animal Companions: Pets and Social Change in Eighteenth-Century Britain* (University Park: Pennsylvania State University Press, 2015), especially pp. 233–234, where she refers to national identity.

[46] John Moore, *A View of Society and Manners in France, Switzerland, and Germany* (London, 1779), I, pp. 74–75. John Brewer discusses the various editions of Moore's travel accounts in his 'Between distance and sympathy: Dr John Moore's philosophical travel writing', *Modern Intellectual History* 11.3 (2014), p. 657.

dominant central figure are related, about the breeding of manly national proclivities and their further inculcation in the course of a grand tour.

'We made a very short stay at Rome on our return from Naples', Dr Moore wrote to the Duchess of Argyll on 24 May 1776, 'and would not have remained as long as we did had it not been for his Grace's sitting to Pompeio [Batoni] for his Portrait for your Grace. It is to be a large full length. The face only was finished when we left Rome. He is to be paid as he proceeds, and therefore there is Reason to believe he will not delay so very much as is his custom.'[47] In Moore's letter, we see the social prestige of the famous Italian portrait painter – Hamilton's face being 'captured' by Batoni is said to have altered the party's planned itinerary – and also his much-commented-on dilatoriness. A letter dated 12 April 1758 by a fellow English traveller, George Lucy, demonstrates how Italian artists inverted the conventional hierarchies of artistic patronage by demanding that *they* be flattered by the patron rather than the other way round:

I have shown my face and person to the celebrated Pompeo Battoni [he explained], to take the likeness thereof; I have sat twice, and am to attend him again in a day or two. These painters are great men and must be flattered; for 'tis the custom here, not to think themselves obliged to you for employing them, but that they oblige you by being employed. When I asked my operator what time he would require, his answer was, a month or five weeks, and that he would not undertake to do me in less time, so I was forced to comply with him.[48]

On this occasion, Lucy's completed portrait was ready to be dispatched by 2 June, making it only weeks overdue. In September 1764, the Scot Sir Thomas Kennedy paid half the price (twenty-five sequins) upfront for a completed portrait, which was finally despatched to Livorno to be shipped to London some *four years* later.[49] John Moore's letter to the Duchess of Argyll confirms Batoni's continued tardiness into the 1770s. It also reveals that Hamilton's full-length (246.4 × 165.1 cm) portrait (Figure 3) was commissioned for her, his mother. It still hangs in the saloon at Inveraray Castle opposite Thomas Gainsborough's portrait of Henry Seymour-Conway, the son-in-law of the 4th Duke of Argyll, which was enlarged to mirror the considerable height of Batoni's canvas (Figure 4).

Clark has previously noted the social dynamic in Batoni's portraits, as in a pair of half-lengths representing James Moray, the 13th Laird of Abercairny (Figure 5) and his eldest son James Francis Edward Moray (Figure 6), both of which he assumes to have been painted in Rome in the early 1760s.[50]

[47] Duke of Argyll, *Intimate Society Letters*, II, p. 413.   [48] Clark, *Pompeo Batoni*, no. 212.
[49] NRS, GD25/9/29/2/18. 16 September 1764; 5 March 1768. NRS, GD25/9/38.
[50] Clark, *Pompeo Batoni*, nos. 259 and 260.

Figure 3: Pompeo Batoni, *Douglas, 8th Duke of Hamilton*, 1776. 246.4 × 165.1 cm. By kind permission of the Duke of Argyll, and with credit to the photographer, Nick Hugh McCann.

Figure 4: East end of the saloon at Inveraray. Gill/Country Life Picture Library.

Previously unpublished epistolary correspondence concerning Batoni's portrait of the son shows that this was not the case and adds a further arterial branch to the formation of the elite family's portrait gallery – in the commissioning of grand tour portraiture as a means for mapping affective relationships with temporarily separated family members. In a letter written at Rome and dated 26 November 1762, James wrote to his father at Abercairny: 'tell her [his aunt, Lady Frances Montgomerie] that I have got a half length Picture done which I send her hoping that she wont refuse it a place over some door or chimney in Argyle Square which will not a little flatter her most affectionate and grateful Nephew … tell her that I should have sent her a full-length, but that would have cost me sixty guineas … this one has only sixteen, but is admirably well done.'[51] Batoni's portrait of Moray was commissioned to be hung in the interior of his aunt's home. Its execution had been projected since his stay at Nice in the summer of 1759 and revisited three years later when Moray was at Pisa. He wrote to his father on 2 April 1762, 'There is nothing

[51] NRS, GD24/1/390/58.

Figure 5: Pompeo Batoni, *James Moray, 13th Laird of Abercairny*, before 1762. 73.7 × 62.2 cm. Private collection.

I desire so much as to make a Present of something to Lady Fanny . . . God knows it is my Duty to study to please her in every thing, even in the most minute Trifles, it is the only recompense I can make her for the infinite trouble she has been at, for the welfare of your family for many years . . . I shall allways think myself happy in having an occasion to show her my gratitude for the many obligations I ly under to her.'[52]

---

[52] NRS, GD24/1/390. When Moray's mother, Lady Christian, died in 1748, her sister, Lady Frances Montgomerie, had helped to bring up her nieces and nephews.

Figure 6: Pompeo Batoni, *James Francis Edward Moray*, 1762. 74.3 × 62.2 cm. Private collection.

Among the surviving family papers is a note confirming that Moray paid the sum of thirty Roman zechins to Batoni for his portrait in the early 1760s.[53] As he wrote to his father at the time the half-length portrait was commissioned, this figure corresponds to about sixteen guineas or sixty scudi. Though scholars of Batoni are right to caution against making generalisations about the prices of his canvases, for portraits they were standardised by fixed sizes: a head and shoulders or bust portrait, a half-

---

[53] NRS, GD24/1/627/10.

length or kit-kat, a three-quarter-length and the largest, a full-length, for which sizes expanded exponentially.[54] Moray claimed a full-length portrait would have cost him sixty guineas in the early 1760s. Batoni increased his prices at different points in his career, from £25 for a full-length in the 1760s, to £50 twenty years later. Even with such staggered rises, Batoni's 1780s prices were still a quarter of what Joshua Reynolds was charging for an equivalent size portrait in London.[55] Paying half the sum in advance, as Thomas Kennedy did for his three-quarter-length portrait in 1764, was part of the standard transaction between painter and sitter in both urban centres. Once the face had been executed, the rest of the portrait could be completed in the sitter's absence, as was the case with the Duke of Hamilton's portrait by Batoni whose 'face only was finished when we left Rome', as Moore recounted in a letter to his mother.

Hamilton's full-length portrait (Figure 3) offers material testimony of the ongoing filial/maternal bond between the sitter typically in the final throes of a grand tour in Rome and his mother back home in Britain. To fully enact the transformation from youth to man, it was necessary to first deracinate the youth from the maternal realm and travelling parties of Britons in Europe that included mothers inevitably attracted criticism. 'I think Lady Glasgow would have done better if she had not gone [abroad] with her son [wrote the 3rd Earl of Breadalbane], a motherly fondness is very proper for daughters, but not for sons.'[56] While a grand tour initiated the necessary separation between sons and mothers, it also provided the opportunity for sons to instigate commissions of maternal regard. In addition to sitting to Batoni for a full-length portrait intended for his mother, Hamilton is said to have purchased from Gavin Hamilton for the vast sum of £500 an ancient statue of Venus to 'remain after ages the model of his mother'.[57] Such seamless equivalence between eighteenth-century individuals and antique sculptures is a characteristic of many of Batoni's canvases, including his portrait of Hamilton (Figure 3), where the sitter adopts an informal cross-legged pose, an attitude of 'careless gracefulness' reminiscent of a bronze *Mercury* in the Farnese collection (Figure 7).[58] As Arline Meyer explains, 'No matter how inauthentic, misidentified, or misunderstood, antique statuary

---

[54] Clark, *Pompeo Batoni*, p. 41.

[55] David Mannings, 'Notes on some eighteenth-century portrait prices in Britain', *Journal for Eighteenth-Century Studies* 6.2 (1983), p. 191.

[56] NRS, GD112/74/3. 4 November 1780.

[57] Bowood archive, AA3. 16 January 1776. George Taylor to Lord Grosvenor. MS. of the Duke of Westminster, Eaton Hall.

[58] The phrase 'careless gracefulness' is from a letter of John Moore's describing the duke's pose at a ball held at Geneva. Duke of Argyll, *Intimate Society Letters*, II, p. 248.

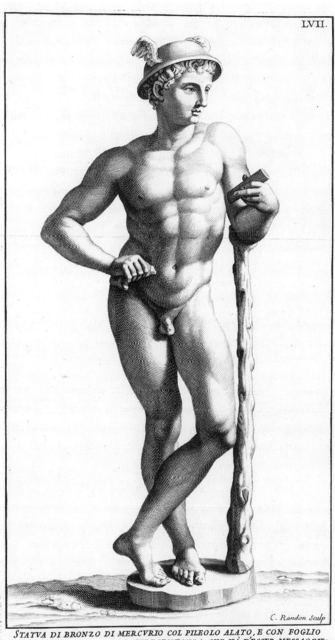

Figure 7: Farnese *Mercury*; plate LVII from Domenico de Rossi, *Raccolta di statue antiche e moderne* (Rome, 1704). 31.5 × 15.8 cm. © The University of Edinburgh.

molded England's [*sic*] pictorial imagination'.[59] The mastiff in Gavin Hamilton's triple portrait (Plate V) may similarly allude to the Vatican *Meleager*, an ancient marble sculpture of the young huntsman who is accompanied by a Molossian, the ancestor of the modern mastiff. Framed in a wooded landscape with the Temple of Sibyl beyond, the Duke of Hamilton stands in Batoni's canvas (Figure 3) with another dog at his feet against a large marble pedestal carved with a relief of a weeping woman in profile and surmounted by a statue of Roma seated frontally. It may be overexploiting the evidence to read the multiple female figures, the Sibyl, weeping woman and female personification of Roma, as additional allusions to the sitter's absent mother for whom the portrait was commissioned.

In his published guidebook *A View of Society and Manners in Italy* (London, 1781), Dr Moore describes Batoni as 'the best Italian painter now at Rome', explaining

His chief employment, for many years past, has been painting the portraits of the young English, and other strangers of fortune, who visit Rome … [he is] seduced from the free walks of genius, and chained, by interest, to the servile drudgery of copying faces. Beauty is worthy of the most delicate pencil; but gracious heaven! Why should every periwig-pated fellow, without countenance or character, insist on seeing his chubby cheeks on canvas?[60]

Because of Batoni's widely known reputation for dilatoriness, not all periwig-pated Scots on the grand tour were prepared to wait to see their chubby cheeks emerge on his canvases. One such example is the Hope brothers, James and Charles; the former writes to their father Lord Hopetoun from Vienna in October 1763 of leaving

the Care of paying for my portrait to my Brother, it is done by the same Person who did his, one [Nathaniel] Dance, an Englishman, whom we preferr'd to Pompeo Batoni, because he is reckoned equal in Genious & Battoni has as many Portraits for English gentlemen on hand that we could not expect one for two or three years to come. He has severals begun two or three years ago … Dance makes good likenesses & will certainly make a figure when he returns to England. He has sent one home for [fellow Scot] Lord Strathmore, which was much admired, for the likeness & Painting; I expect it will not be inferior in any Respect.[61]

In correspondence like this, the commissioning of portraits is inscribed into the ritualised itineraries of the grand tour. Hope's criteria, concerning

---

[59] Arline Meyer, 'Re-dressing classical statuary: The eighteenth-century "hand in waistcoat" portrait', *Art Bulletin* 77.1 (1995), p. 47.

[60] Moore, *A View of Society and Manners in Italy*, II, p. 73.

[61] 8 October 1763. NRAS, 2171/bundle 879.

the likeness of the sitter and the technical proficiency of the artist, are typical of the later eighteenth-century British portrait sitter-subject. His brother, Charles, wrote to their father in a letter he received on 28 March 1763: 'My pretty person I have had painted by a young man of great merit whose name is Dance they tell me it is strikingly like & a very well painted portrait.' Charles Hope's full-length (247 × 173 cm) portrait (on the right-hand side of Plate VI) shows the sitter pausing on a tree trunk after a shooting expedition near an aqueduct in the Roman campagna, accompanied by a setter and a spaniel with the spoils of the hunt on his left-hand side. Charles died three years after the portrait was painted by Dance and at least one visitor to Hopetoun House who saw it there commented on his prognostic appearance – how his resting pose was 'beautifully expressive of a languid and ill state of health'.[62] His brother's pendant portrait (on the left-hand side of Plate VI) is the same size and depicts James standing, right hand-on-hip, dressed in the red military coat of the 3rd Regiment of Foot Guards, with the Temple of the Sibyl at Tivoli in the right background. 'I have made almost no Cloaths but Regimentals [Hope wrote to his father] as I find it both the genteelest & cheapest dress I can wear in these Countrys I have been in.'[63] James Hope's uniform affords him a collective military identity far removed from the frivolous fashions of the grand tour to which travellers including the Duke of Hamilton succumbed. One Scottish Major goes so far as to describe military dress as being as 'sacred to a soldier as his pontifical to a priest'.[64]

In his Italian travel journal for 30 April 1793, the Scottish banker and author, Sir William Forbes, inventoried the portraits by Batoni in Scotland whose sitters were 'of my own acquaintance'.[65] Along with the portraits of the Duke of Hamilton at Inveraray (Figure 3), Lord Haddo at Haddo House, Aberdeenshire, Colonel Gordon at Fyvie (Plate I) and Lord Bute and Mr Boswell at Auchinleck House (which is untraced), Forbes misattributed the portraits of the Hope brothers at Hopetoun House (Plate VI) as being by Pompeo Batoni, rather than by Nathaniel Dance. Although Batoni did not invent the grand tour portrait, his name had become synonymous with the subgenre in which he was the leading proponent of his generation (he died in 1787) and for generations to come. Forbes also recorded that at a time when Batoni was charging twenty zechins or ten guineas for a head in Rome,

[62] NLS Acc. 12017 folio 22: 'A tour through part of England and Scotland by Eliza Dawson in the year 1786'.

[63] 8 October 1763. NRAS, 2171/bundle 879.

[64] NRAS, 783/140/2/25. Major Patrick Ferguson to his sister, Elizabeth. Paris, 7 October 1766.

[65] NLS, MS. 1544, 179.

Reynolds was getting thirty-five guineas for the same size in London. But as he explained 'I do not mean to say that Pompeio was a painter of equal merit with Sir Joshua for I am clearly of opinion there was no comparison ... I really believe [Reynolds was] the best since the time of Vandyck'.[66] A number of portraits of Scots on the grand tour demonstrate an indebtedness to van Dyck, as will become apparent in due course.

The Hope brothers commissioned a third canvas from Dance, which is a significantly smaller (90 × 70 cm) triple portrait in which they are shown at full-length accompanied by their grand tour tutor, William Rouet, who was Professor of Ecclesiastical History at the University of Glasgow (Plate VII). Signed and dated 1763, Dance shows the travelling companions with Charles again in repose, seated on the right of the canvas. His brother James in the centre, still wearing his military jacket, rests his right hand on Rouet's shoulder, as their tutor points towards a cropped bust shown in profile and upraised on a pedestal. Both brothers look at the unidentified bust he gestures towards in this representation of a pedagogic encounter in the environs of Rome. Between the brothers is a Bacchic krater with St Peter's in the distant left background beyond a lush, watery landscape. In one of his letters to his mother, the Scot Robert Adam offered a striking analogy for St Peter's in the context of this chapter on grand tour portraiture as being 'like the Face of a Man or woman, which has something pleasing, well proportion'd and sweet in it, in spite of some bad features, pock pitts and other little failings. It has some gross faults, many small ones, fine on the whole though without the grandeur, or nobility of the Antique.'[67] Adam will feature in the next chapter devoted to Scots in London where he based himself after the completion of his continental tour and his immersion into antiquity.

For now, if we revisit Pointon's 'idea of portraiture as a tool that makes possible the registering of an identity', then the grand tour portrait was arguably as, if not more, important for the professional *artist* as it was for its aristocratic Scottish sitter-subjects, like Charles and James Hope, shown with and without their tutor in their individual pendant and group portraits (Plates VI & VII).[68] James's letter to their father dated October 1763 offers a positive projection of Dance's incipient career, writing he 'will certainly make a figure when he returns to England'. Dance himself described embarking on Charles Hope's portrait in a letter to his father, 'I have this day [6 February 1763] begun a whole length as large as life of

---

[66] NLS, MS. 1544, 179–180. Forbes was a friend of Reynolds and sat for him twice, in *c.* 1776 and a decade later, for a portrait (now SNPG 1296) that cost him fifty guineas.

[67] 1 March 1755. NRS, GD18/4765.   [68] Pointon, *Portrayal and the Search for Identity*, p. 11.

Lord Hope, another Scotch nobleman who is very much pleased with that I did for Lord Strathmore. I assure you it is a very good thing to be well with the Scotch.'[69] Here we see Mrs Piozzi's description of the 'national phalanx' favoured by the Scots in Italy take formation, in which a commission for a portrait of the Scottish aristocrat the 7th Earl of Strathmore, which is now lost, leads to the English artist Dance being patronised by other Scottish peers in Rome.[70] Dr. Moore's criticism of portraiture as 'the servile drudgery of copying faces' is confirmed in an earlier letter written by Dance to his father in which he describes

hav[ing] not yet quite freed myself from the disagreeable task of copying the Conversation Picture, tho' I believe it will not now be long before I shall. It has taken me up a good deal of time, as I was obliged to make 4 copys . . . Yet I could not refuse doing it as it was the means of making me acquainted with my Lord Grey and the other gentlemen who have given me commissions for pictures. Besides it was done on the footing of friendship, & I am convinced these gentlemen will do me all the service that lyes in their power. I hear already that Mr. Robinson has recommended me to the Duke of Marlborough.[71]

Dance's letter reveals the professional investment he made in the prospect of continued patronage for historical paintings, rather than portraits, that necessitated him undertaking the 'disagreeable task' of producing four copies of the conversation piece (96.5 × 123.2 cm) for each of the sitters, James Grant, John Mytton, Thomas Robinson and Thomas Wynn (Plate VIII).[72] In this image of companionable Britishness, a Scot (Grant), a Welshman (Wynn), a Yorkshireman (Robinson) and a native of Shropshire (Mytton) are depicted before the ruins of the Colosseum on the left. On the right, an urn whose figural decoration derives from an ancient relief known as the Borghese Dancers, is elevated on a pedestal. 'Just as the four dancers visible to the viewer on this urn are frozen in their sinuous frieze, so the four sitters are artfully arranged into a subtle and rhythmic composition.'[73] The seated Robinson holds a drawing of the

---

[69] Quoted by B. C. Skinner, 'A note on four British artists in Rome', *Burlington Magazine* 99 (1957), p. 238.

[70] An autograph half-length portrait survives at Glamis Castle; it is reproduced in Francis Russell, 'Notes on Luti, Batoni and Nathaniel Dance', *Burlington Magazine* 130 (1988), p. 854, figure 49.

[71] 17 December 1760. RIBA, MSS DA FAM/1/3. See B. C. Skinner, 'Some aspects of the work of Nathaniel Dance in Rome', *Burlington Magazine* 101 (1959), pp. 346–349.

[72] Subsequent commissions for historical paintings, which were forthcoming, are beyond the scope of this chapter.

[73] Richard Dormont, *British Painting in the Philadelphia Museum of Art from the Seventeenth through the Nineteenth Century* (London: Philadelphia Museum of Art in association with Weidenfeld & Nicolson, 1986), p. 91.

elevation of the Temple of Jupiter in Rome, taken from plate 51 of the third volume of Giacomo Leoni's edition of Palladio's architectural tome, *Quattro Libri dell'Architettura*. James Grant's countryman, the Scottish artist, David Allan, defined 'the small domestic and conversation style' of portrait painting as 'the means of everlastingly joining frends together on the canvace'.[74] In having the artist replicate the canvas four times, for each of the sitters depicted on it, the Roman friendship of these native Britons is given material form in painted portraiture. The replicated canvases are also testimony to the grand tour as a shared social experience among members of the elite ruling class. As Bowers has written, the grand tour unified the nobility by helping to create that class and construct the social order than assigns them the dominant position within it.[75] We might recall Boswell writing to Rousseau in October 1765 of how during the course of his grand tour he has 'formed friendships with one or two worthy men that will last for the rest of my life'.

Although Dance's group portrait gave a visual dimension to the grand tour as a shared social experience for young, elite, male Britons, this reading takes at face value the eighteenth-century ideologies that informed debates about and around its educative usefulness. The private correspondence between Scottish tutors and parents, in contrast, reveals a persistent anxiety during the polishing phase about the appropriateness of their young traveller's unmediated exposure to the citizens of different nations. And repeatedly in such accounts, the main constituent to be avoided is their fellow Britons: the English. A couple of examples will suffice concerning the sitters in grand tour portraits already discussed and to follow. For instance, in a letter dated 3 August 1772, Dr Moore wrote to the Duchess of Argyll: 'The worst circumstance in this place [Geneva] is the English, but there are so many advantages to counterbalance that we must put up with them.'[76] The extended grand tour of John Campbell and his brother Colin involved a stay at Morges, where it was said they could learn French in the absence of any English travellers before proceeding to Lausanne.[77] Dr Thomas Dundas recommended to James Moray that after a brief trip to Tuscany, his sickly son, also James Moray (Figure 6), should return to Nice to improve his French. He and his travelling

[74] 3 December 1780. Allan to the Earl of Buchan. Centre for Research Collections, The University of Edinburgh, Laing MSS, LA.IV.26.
[75] Bowers, 'Reconstituting the national body in Smollett's *Travels through France and Italy*', pp. 6–7.
[76] Duke of Argyll, *Intimate Society Letters*, II, p. 201.
[77] Bedfordshire Archives and Records Service, L30/9/17/251.

companion Archibald Menzies would 'mess with the officers of the Swiss regiment now quartered there, by far the best people in the country, they speak very good French, and are very sober', Dundas reassured him.[78]

Three years later, Moray wrote to his father from Pisa estimating that 'three months in France will be sufficient to brush it [his French language] up again, as to the English Language I never could have any opportunity of forgetting that, as it is what I never had and I believe before I return to England I shall be able to talk both French and Italian with greater propriety than it.'[79] Linguistic competency was one of the lessons the grand tour sought to inculcate and for some Scottish travellers, including James Moray, the English language was as much of a foreign tongue as its French or Italian counterparts. It has been said that there was no subject about which Scots were more sensitive than their speech, although such a summary statement requires clarification in reference to variegated class distinctions.[80] When George Dempster returned to Edinburgh via London after a truncated tour of Europe, he wrote to his former travelling companion on 5 December 1756 of how he 'labour[ed] to tone myself down like an overstrained instrument to the low pitch of the rest about me'.[81] Speech rather than writing provides the most potent metonym for national identity in the mother tongue.[82] Yet incriminating traces of Scottish dialect were still apparent in the latter; writing to Mrs. Campbell, the 3rd Earl of Breadalbane complained 'I found some Scotticisms in it [a letter from her son Colin from the continent] which I was in hopes seven years of Westminster school would have worn off'.[83] Even as Scots sought to avoid the swarms of fellow Britons conversing with each other in English enclaves on the continent, their mother tongue was the preferred linguistic idiom to an increasingly marginalised and debased Scots. In light of such concerns articulated and constraints implemented on social intercourse and linguistic competency, Dance's conversation piece (Plate VIII) accrues an additional cache for the representation of convivial sociability between Britons in Rome in the early 1760s.

---

[78] 28 March 1759. NRS, GD24/1/389/6.   [79] 19 April 1762. NRS, GD24/1/390.

[80] John Clive and Bernard Bailyn, 'England's cultural provinces: Scotland and America', *William and Mary Quarterly* 11.2 (1954), p. 210.

[81] Ibid.

[82] Penny Fielding, 'Writing at the North: Rhetoric and dialect in eighteenth-century Scotland', *The Eighteenth Century* 39.1 (1998), p. 27.

[83] 10 August 1779. NRS, GD112/74/2. On Scotticisms, see Richard W. Bailey, 'Scots and Scotticisms: Language and Ideology', *Studies in Scottish Literature* 26 (1991), pp. 65–77; J. G. Basker, 'Scotticisms and the problem of cultural identity in eighteenth-century Britain', *Eighteenth-Century Life* 15.1 & 2 (1991), pp. 81–95.

In a letter dated 2 February 1768, the Scottish artist James Clark wrote to a Mr Dalrymple that he had seen one of the quartet of canvases by Nathaniel Dance (Plate VIII) at Thomas Robinson's London townhouse. His letter describes the composition in some detail, beginning with the figure of James Grant on the far left, who was one of his aristocratic Scottish patrons and who had provided an introduction to the son of Lord Grantham:

Mr Grant stands in the fore ground in an easy careless manner with one hand in his breast and t'other in his breeches pocket. His shape is very fine & quite exact, and the face too a striking likeness but I think an unfavourable one. He is drest in a suit of light blue and silver, silk stockings, and a very bad old hat. Beside Mr. Grant is Mr. Robinson sitting in a light coloured suit broad gold lace, hat on – and behind him stands a gentleman in scarlet very much in shade. Another gentleman in green & gold stands by Mr. Robinson and leaning on his chair. The scene is supposed to be within doors. This picture as well as that at Sir Alex.^rs [Grant's] was done at Rome when Mr. Grant & these his companions were there. I think the whole is very natural and vastly well painted.[84]

Clark's description of the 'manner' and 'shape' of Grant's pictorial representation offers a critique of portraiture in which the viewer familiar with these aspects of the sitter is not solely determined by myopic issues of physiognomic likeness. These aspects that relate to the sitter's physical bearing are especially applicable to portraits commissioned on the grand tour which, as we have seen, was an institution intended to inculcate manners 'as helping to enact a transformation of personhood' – a transformation seemingly enshrined in oils on canvas.[85] Although there are some discrepancies between the portrait and Clark's description, this is otherwise an accurate epistolary account of the depiction and ordering of the sitters, if not the scene. Clark writes that the background is supposed to be 'within doors', which seems improbable for a subgenre than prized the specificity of its external pictorial location, notably the Colosseum (as in Plate I) or the Roman campagna (on the left-hand side of Plate V).

Clark's letter additionally records that he was given an annual allowance of £50 by James Grant to study portrait painting in Italy. He arrived in Rome later that year and subsequently spent thirty years working as a painter and an antiquary in Naples. In 1782, he was commissioned to produce a coming of age portrait for another aristocratic Scotsman on his grand tour, John Campbell, 4th Earl of Breadalbane. When the portrait was

[84] NRS, GD248/839.

[85] Bowers, 'Reconstituting the national body in Smollett's *Travels through France and Italy*', 6.

despatched in December 1783, Clark wrote an accompanying explanation of how the initial proposal for representing the sitter in Highland dress had not been realised. Fellow Scottish émigré, the antiquarian James Byres in Rome had reportedly not been able to procure the required clothing:

> In the meantime [writes Clark] Mr. Ramsay the Painter came here [Naples], and I consulted him about it – he assured me that from a mere Description without a Model to copy after, it would be impossible for me to produce anything tolerably good, besides that the Highland Dress could never appear to advantage except in a full-length figure where the more picturesque parts could be introduced – therefore he warmly disswaded me from attempting it at all.[86]

In Clark's epistolary account, members of the Scottish cultural phalanx in Italy assisted in attempting to style Breadalbane in his Highland dress for his grand tour portrait. Breadalbane's coming of age and his inheritance of the title from his uncle coincided chronologically with the repeal of the Disarming Act. Almost forty years after it had been banned in Scotland, tartan was not readily accessible in Europe, even in its cosmopolitan urban centres. 'As to Highland tailors, we have none here', Baron Grant wrote from Paris in 1782.[87] Colonel Gordon seems to have deliberately brought his tartan uniform with him to Rome for Batoni to copy in the studio (Plate I).[88] James Boswell's grand tour diary entry for 18 April 1765 records 'Yesterday morning I saw Batoni draw Gord. Drapery'.[89]

Clark's passing reference to a studio prop in the form of a 'a mere Description' may be associated with an earlier letter from Campbell in Rome to his mother, dated 10 March 1782, in which he acknowledges receipt of 'the highlander though I wish you had sent me a better however I believe with the description of the adjustment and what with the figure we may be able to make it out'.[90] What the highlander 'figure' consisted of remains unclear. What is patently unambiguous, however, is the 'warm' advice of Allan Ramsay, a fellow Scot, veteran portrait painter and traveller, then on the fourth of his visits to Italy, who insisted that Clark was insufficiently accoutred to execute the portrait as planned. Ramsay also advocated a full-length figure for such a portrait – as in Batoni's Colonel William Gordon (Plate I) – not the three-quarter length that had been agreed upon. Clark's letter to Breadalbane recounts that he had produced a preliminary sketch from the material sent from Rome, but when the sketch did not equal his expectations, he altered the sitter's

---

[86] NRS, GD112/20/1/36.   [87] William Fraser, *The Chiefs of Grant* (Edinburgh, 1883), II, p. 549.
[88] Steegman, 'Some English portraits by Pompeo Batoni', p. 55.
[89] Brady and Pottle, *Boswell on the Grand Tour,* p. 69.   [90] NRS, GD112/74/3/21.

dress into 'the Vandyke Dress as your friend Mr de Saussure first proposed to me'. Louis de Saussure was the Swiss tutor of John Campbell and his younger brother, Colin, during their extended grand tour of Europe lasting four and a half years. He 'is a very polite man, having been in best company at Paris, & is very much like a French man, with all the vivacity and genteel behaviour of that nation ... he seems well qualified to introduce a youth into the world, & to conduct him thro it', wrote the 3rd Earl of Breadalbane to his daughter.[91] Having appointed him as tutor to his young nephews, Breadalbane was compelled to recommend the Swiss in such glowing terms. It is worth noting how de Saussure's contrived and commendable Frenchness ('all the vivacity and genteel behaviour of that nation') could be negatively recast, by John Moore for instance earlier in this chapter, as 'the Pert vivacity of a French Petit Maître' with its incriminating accusations of vanity and other notably female failings.

In proposing van Dyckian dress as an alternative to Highland plaid, de Saussure was superintending his young companion's portrait representation, in much the same way that a governor or tutor oversaw a pedagogical and social curriculum while on the course of an extended grand tour. An oil on canvas portrait commissioned in Italy and preferably from Batoni was habitually regarded as visual confirmation of the completion of the grand tour and its syllabi via that accrued social polish. In Redford's account it was 'a way of proclaiming accomplishments, articulating allegiances, and consolidating status' even if they were fabricated to a degree – an aspect of the rhetoric of painted portraiture that Redford seems unaware of.[92] The executed canvas was duly dispatched from Italy. Clark records its dimensions as being 102.87 × 76.2 cm and it cost Breadalbane thirty Neapolitan ounces. The portrait in question survives but has been misattributed to Angelica Kauffmann who often attired her male sitters in this distinctive fancy dress (Plate IX).[93] It shows the sitter seated in a three-quarter pose looking to the right with Mount Vesuvius smoking ominously through the window in the distance. The sitter's right elbow rests on a book; his other arm lies across his lap. He is dressed in a distinctive buff-coloured van Dyckian jacket with split sleeves, lace collar and cuffs and

---

[91] Taymouth, 16 July 1778. Bedford Records Office, L30/9/17/245.

[92] Bruce Redford, *Venice and the Grand Tour* (New Haven, CT and London: Yale University Press, 1996), p. 81.

[93] Kauffmann also painted sitters in Highland dress: see her portrait of *Alasdair Ranaldson MacDonell, 15th Chief of Glengarry, c.* 1790, Museum of the Isles PD/CU/015; and her *Archibald, Lord Montgomerie*, 1800, on loan to the Black Watch Castle & Museum, A3588.1.

wears his brown hair long in generous curls. In recommending van Dyckian dress as an alternative to Highland plaid, de Saussure was advocating a change of clothes that was both fanciful and fashionable in its cosmopolitanism, rather than niche and hereditary in its Scottish Highlandism. Its popularity in portraiture in Britain from around 1730 has been related to the contemporary fashion for masquerades. Horace Walpole described one such social occasion hosted by the Duchess of Norfolk in February 1742 at which 'There were quantities of pretty Vandykes and all kinds of old pictures walked out of their frames'.[94] While the fashion for early seventeenth-century dress brought art to life from the canvases of van Dyck and his contemporaries, many eighteenth-century portrait sitters were painted and reframed in their masquerade dress. Although there are more female sitter-subjects in portraits so attired in Britain, Clark's portrait of the Earl of Breadalbane provides one example of a recently ennobled Scotsman on canvas executed by a fellow Scot in Naples in the early 1780s.[95]

Anton Raphael Mengs's portrait of John Viscount Garlies (99.5 × 72 cm), signed and dated 1758, is another (Figure 8). It represents its Scottish sitter at three-quarter length in a right hand-on-hip pose and attire that is indebted to van Dyck's portrait of Petrus Stevens. His dress consists of a white collar edged with lace over a buttoned black and bronze-coloured doublet; the cuffs of the sleeve are trimmed with lace. Garlies's illuminated face is shown in three-quarter view, while his left-hand gestures towards the edge of the canvas with an upraised palm. Terry Castle's description of such fancy masquerade dress with its 'voluable costumes, at once digressive and feigning' has implications for the supposed veracity of painted portraiture.[96] Hers is also a more provocative reading and more in keeping with the identity play that was the 'essence of the masquerade' than the suggestion raised in a recent catalogue entry that such van Dyckian

---

[94] Cited by Aileen Ribeiro, *The Dress Worn at Masquerades in England, 1730 to 1790, and Its Relation to Fancy Dress in Portraiture* (New York and London: Garland, 1984), p. 183. On the vogue for van Dyckian dress, the following are also useful: J. L. Nevinson, 'Vandyke dress', *Connoisseur* 157 (1964), pp. 166–171; J. L. Nevinson, 'Vogue of the Vandyke dress', *Country Life Annual* 1959, pp. 25–27; Deborah Cherry and Jennifer Harris, 'Eighteenth-century portraiture and the seventeenth-century past: Gainsborough and Van Dyck', *Art History* 5.3 (1982), pp. 287–309.

[95] Aileen Ribeiro, *The Art of Dress: Fashion in England and France, 1750 to 1820* (New Haven, CT and London: Yale University Press, 1995), p. 204.

[96] Terry Castle, *Masquerade and Civilization: The Carnivalesque in Eighteenth-Century English Culture and Fiction* (London: Methuen, 1986), p. 60.

Figure 8: Anton Raphael Mengs, *Portrait of John Viscount Garlies, Later 7th Earl of Galloway, as Master of Garlies*, 1758. 99.38 × 71.44 cm. Los Angeles County Museum of Art, M.2001.21.

dress alluded to the northern origins of the portrait's Scottish sitter-subject.[97]

[97] Wahrman, *The Making of the Modern Self*, p. 159; Edgar Peters Bowron and Joseph J. Rishel (eds.), *Art in Rome in the Eighteenth Century* (Philadelphia, PA: Philadelphia Museum of Art, 2000), no. 253.

Thus far, portraits of elite Scotsmen have been described as offering visual testimony of the differing social relations encountered and maintained in the course of a grand tour – as tools for imaging the various pedagogical, fraternal and homosocial relationships between men that were understood as making accomplished men. That is, between tutors and pupils, between brothers and other male travelling companions, and between sons and their absent family members, especially their mothers from whom they had been separated. The reproduction of oil on canvas grand tour portraits into other artistic media and their geographical exportation, as so-called ambulant portraits, provided a further means for mapping the intimacy and sociability of affective relationships.[98] Batoni's half-length canvas of James Bruce of Kinnaird (Plate II) was copied for his fiancée in Scotland 'by the best painter of miniatures in Italy', one Veronica Stern.[99] A head and shoulders portrait of James Grant, his face in a three-quarter view by Gavin Hamilton, was serially reproduced in miniatures by Maria Felice Tibaldi, by Mengs's daughter and by Colin Morison.[100] In an indication of professional rivalry between painters in Rome, the Abbé Peter Grant, the Roman agent for the Scottish Catholic Mission, recounted in a letter to the sitter that Gavin Hamilton was unhappy with the original portrait being dispatched to Mengs's house 'for he is persuaded that gentle man will criticise it too much and that his criticizing may do him prejudice.'[101] In the event, it was too late to withdraw the commission, which was due to be dispatched to Thomas Wynn in Florence; Wynn was already in receipt of the much-admired copy by Tibaldi and both sitter and recipient (Grant and Wynn) are included in the convivial conversation piece by Dance which he replicated four times (Plate VIII). The Abbé Peter Grant had extensive dealings with many Scots during their sojourns in Rome, which were often prolonged after they had departed in a voluminous cavalcade of correspondence. In a letter to Sir Archibald Grant dated 5 December 1767, he wrote 'Altho I have been more than two thirds of my life at such an immense distance from my country and relations, yet I have their prosperity at much at heart as if I had been constantly among them, and never had pass[d] the [River] Tweed'.[102]

---

[98] The term 'ambulant portraits' is Marcia Pointon's and refers to miniatures. See her
'"Surrounded with brilliants": Miniature portraits in eighteenth-century England', *Art Bulletin*
133 (2001), pp. 48–71.

[99] Clark, *Pompeo Batoni*, no. 257.

[100] 5 July 1760. NRS, GD248/99/3/3. On Tibaldi, see Peters Bowron and Rishel, *Art in Rome in the Eighteenth Century*, no. 288.

[101] 14 June 1760. NRS, GD248/99/3.   [102] NRS, GD345/1171.

A third, better documented, example of a portrait miniature being copied from a grand tour oil on canvas precedent is James Boswell's portrait by the Edinburgh-born artist George Willison (Plate X). Boswell's life has been described as 'a search through a range of roles and *personae* for an identity' – and his painted portraits should necessarily be recruited into such a reading.[103] His grand tour journal for May 1765 refers to his sittings for Willison from 4 May 'This day at nine, Willison's, and sit, a plain, bold, serious attitude' – note the emphasis on 'attitude' – and two days later, record his consultations with fellow Scots, Andrew Lumisden and Gavin Hamilton 'over scheme, whether head or owl &c.'[104] The entry for 7 May reads 'Yesterday began half-length at Willison's earnest desire' and for 10 May 'sat to Willison all day'. In the completed oil on canvas portrait (135.2 × 96.5 cm) that the American Boswellian scholar Frederick Pottle identified in the late 1920s, Boswell is shown seated against a tree and rocks wearing a fur-lined green coat in what is unusually a nocturnal portrait with the sea in the near distance (Plate X).[105] Skinner suggests the Roman night owl may be a dual comment on Boswell's wisdom and his nocturnal pursuits.[106] The owl's yellow eyes seem to echo the golden colour of Boswell's brocade richly embroidered on his waistcoat and breeches. Pottle described the portrait as a 'visual embodiment of the idea of Boswell he has tried to present through words: odd, eager, egotistical, boyish, sensual – and attractive' – prescribing a traditional view of portraiture as the visual counterpart to biography.[107] At the end of May 1765 and on into June, Boswell's journal makes the following more elliptical allusions: 'This morning send to Alves', 'Yesterday morning sat to Alves'.[108] A letter written to John Johnstone of Grange, dated 19 July 1765, explains further,

Before I left Rome I took care to execute your Commission of having my Picture done in miniature. I had it painted by a Mr [James] Alves an Inverness Lad who is studying in Italy. It is thought like and well-painted. I wish it may please you. It has been sent off some weeks ago to Mr [Robert] Strange the Engraver, who is to convey it to Mr Thomas Boswell [Accountant in Edinburgh Post Office], from whom you will receive it upon asking for it. I left it at Rome to the care of a very worthy exile [Andrew Lumisden], who is Secretary to a Scots Gentleman of a very

103 Kenneth Simpson, *Protean Scot: The Crisis of Identity in Eighteenth-Century Scottish Literature* (Aberdeen: Aberdeen University Press, 1988), p. 117.
104 Brady and Pottle, *Boswell on the Grand Tour*, p. 78.
105 Pottle's correspondence is in the Scottish National Portrait Gallery file on the painting.
106 Skinner, *Scots in Italy*, p. 12.
107 Frederick A. Pottle, *James Boswell: The Earlier Years, 1740–1769* (New York: McGraw-Hill, 1966), p. 222.
108 Brady and Pottle, *Boswell on the Grand Tour*, p. 90.

ancient Family who is obliged to live abroad for particular reasons. You see there is something romantic in the history of this same miniature.[109]

Boswell's letter confirms that he commissioned a miniature portrait from Alves on behalf of his absent friend John Johnstone. His patronage of both Willison and Alves in Rome demonstrates his adherence to the cultural ranks of the Scottish phalanx in Italy, demonstrating what Forbes in his travel journal dubs a 'national partiality' in the grand tour portrait commissions he awarded.[110] The history that Boswell describes as 'romantic' is on account of this same miniature being left in Rome with Andrew Lumisden, the private secretary of the exiled James VIII and III. Note that Boswell does not explicitly name Lumisden and his employer; their identities are referred to obliquely via their Jacobite status and lineage. More will be said about the Jacobites, including Lumisden's brother-in-law, the engraver Robert Strange in Chapter 4. With Lumisden acting as an intermediary between Boswell and Johnstone via Strange, the 'like and well painted' object that is the miniature by Alves accrues a politicised connection with the exiled Jacobite court in Rome. Elsewhere in correspondence between Italy and Scotland, the Abbé Peter Grant wrote to Sir James Grant, who was one of the sitters in Nathaniel Dance's conversation piece (Plate VIII), of the attention shown by his 'dearest young chief' in the English travellers in Rome, William Weddell and the Revd William Palgrave. The Abbé insists, 'your interesting yourself so warmly for them, engages me as strongly in their behalf as if the whole house of Common's of Great Britain had recommended them to me'.[111] In the juxtaposition of these two letters, reference is made to the political establishment of Britain, the House of Commons and to the source of political unrest to its ruling body, the exiled Stuarts.

The Scot, Gordon Cumming, nicely summed up an ideology of the grand tour in his travel journal for 1770–1, as follows: 'The more I see of different countries, Laws & religion, the happier do I think myself in being born and bred a Britton and subject only to its equitable laws'.[112] Throughout the eighteenth century, liberty became an 'emblem of Britishness' to the point where it is said to be 'the single most important ingredient of an imperial identity in Britain and the British Empire'.[113]

---

[109] *The Correspondence of James Boswell and John Johnston of Grange* (London, 1966), pp. 174–175.

[110] NLS, MS. 1544, 178.   [111] 3 October 1764. NRS GD248/99/3/16.

[112] NLS, Dep. 175/Box 175.

[113] Jack P. Greene, 'Empire and identity from the Glorious Revolution to the American Revolution', in P. J. Marshall (ed.), *The Oxford History of the British Empire: Volume II, the Eighteenth Century* (Oxford: Oxford University Press, 1998), pp. 212 and 228.

Chapter 3 considers an alternative narrative of imperial identity in relation to the colonial career of a sojourning Scot in Bengal, Claud Alexander. Meanwhile, this chapter has proffered readings of a number of grand tour portraits and miniatures commissioned by aristocratic and gentleman Scots in Europe during the later 1750s to the early 1780s. Elaborating on the work of Skinner, it has sought to expand the geographical territory and national formation of Mrs Piozzi's Scotch phalanx in Italy. Rather than a myopic canvas of Italy and an isolationist view of the elite Scots therein, it has explicitly reinstated cosmopolitan Europe and notions of *British* identity into the critical field, where Britishness as a form of social polish has been shown to be a concatenation of nations – in theory if not in practice. We have seen aristocratic Scots as patrons of Scottish, English, German and Italian artists in Europe, where the phalanx of Mrs Piozzi's metaphor is repeatedly formed, disbanded and re-formed in a number of different configurations. The preferred way in which to conceptualise Scots in Europe is not to be too prescriptive. In other words, to witness, where relevant, the tight social networks between members of Mrs Piozzi's Scottish phalanx, but not to impose this as a reductive template for the cultural activities of *all* elite Scots travelling abroad. The painted grand tour portrait has been shown to be invested and associated with multiple layers of historical meaning: cultural, social, economic and even, in the case of the passage of Boswell's miniature portrait by James Alves, political.

Aside from Batoni's bravura portrait of Colonel Gordon (Plate I), which has been re-read here as an image of the martial Scot assimilated into Britain's imperial endeavour, only one other grand tour portrait seems to reference the sitter's Scottishness via a carefully contrived accessory (Plate XI). The inscription on the reverse of the canvas (76.2 × 65.5 cm) helpfully identifies the sitter, artist and date as Archibald Menzies by Anton von Maron painted at Rome in 1763; on this occasion, there is no need to question its veracity. We already know Menzies as the travelling companion of James Moray, who sat to Batoni for a portrait for his aunt in 1762 (Figure 6); both Scots were from the County of Perthshire. In his portrait by von Maron, Menzies's substantial torso seems to fill the canvas. He 'is fully as fat as ever', James Moray wrote to his father when the two were reunited at Florence in August 1762.[114] In the portrait by von Maron, he is represented slightly off-centre, wearing a white shirt with ornate lace cuffs, a fashionable waistcoat that seems to restrain his protruding stomach and a fur-lined jacket. His chubby face with its ruddy complexion recalls a comment made by Frances Gordon, Lord Gardenstone in his

[114] NRS, GD24/1/390.

Figure 9: Pompeo Batoni, *Adam Fergusson of Kilkerran*, 1757. 76.2 × 65.5 cm.

Travelling Memorandums Made in a Tour upon the Continent of Europe in the Years 1786, 1787 and 1788, regarding a portrait by van Dyck with 'what we significantly call, in Scots, the apple cheek'.[115] In his left hand, Menzies holds a small leather-bound book, although his gaze is directed straight out at the viewer and is not inclined downwards towards its open pages. The inclusion of books like this one are part of the habitual baggage of the studious traveller as represented in his grand tour portrait – Clark's portrait of John Campbell, 4th

[115] Francis Garden Gardenstone, *Travelling Memorandums Made in a Tour upon the Continent of Europe in the Years 1786, 1787 and 1788* (Edinburgh, 1795), III, p. 246.

Earl of Breadalbane (Plate IX) is one example; Batoni's half length of the Scot Adam Fergusson of Kilkerran in Ayrshire is another (Figure 9). Ferguson's grand tour accounts record him paying £6 6s for his portrait on 27 August 1757, followed by the outstanding half payment of £6 on 7 October.[116] The following month, a further 9s 8d was paid to the artist 'for altering the ruffles and book of my portrait'. In contrast with the portrait of Fergusson, in which the small leather-bound book held in his left hand faces outwards, with the spine resting on the sitter's chest, an inscription on the visible spine of the book in the portrait of Menzies (Plate XI) identifies the volume as 'Fingal', published by James Macpherson in December 1761 as (to give it its full title) *Fingal, an epic poem in six books, together with several other poems published by Ossian, the Son of Fingal, translated from the Gaelic language.* More will be said about Ossianic painted schemes in visual culture in the Highlands and Lowlands of Scotland in the next chapter. By the time Menzies sat to von Maron in 1763, the volume was reputed to be 'a literary conversation piece, a highly controversial document' whose authenticity of the so-called translations from the Gaelic, was publicly and passionately disputed.[117] In choosing to be represented accompanied by this volume for his grand tour portrait, Menzies appears to be displaying his Highland Scottishness as well as himself as a fashionable talking point in cosmopolitan circles. Given that the initial reception of the poems focussed so much on their authenticity, a related reading of the portrait might be asking us to scrutinise it for its verisimilitude: is this portrait a truthful facsimile of the sitter, or a fictional imposter? Much like Boswell who in drawing Mountstuart's epistolary portrait found him to be one of a nation 'of originals', rather than copies or fakes, is Menzies's painted portrait an authentic portrayal?

Travelling South from Rome to Naples in December 1762, James Moray and Archibald Menzies met James Bruce of Kinnaird who sat to Batoni for a portrait that same year (Plate II), 'what makes me mention this more particularly [Moray wrote to his father] is that three Scotsmen should meet on St. Andrews Day without having a drop of liquor to drink prosperity to their Country. I am affraid you'll think that the present up coming Generation is sadly degenerate.'[118] Far from 'sadly degenerate', the upcoming generation of aristocratic and gentlemen Scots were poised to make

---

[116] The Fergusson archive is closed to researchers. I obtained these references from Antony Dufort.

[117] George R. Brooks, 'A Portrait by Anton von Maron in the Busch-Reisinger Museum', *Gazette des Beaux Arts* 67 (1966), p. 115.

[118] 4 December 1762. NRS, GD24/1/390/59.

a figure on their return home – at least according to a literal reading of their grand tour portraits – where the ideology of the grand tour for inculcating a sense of Britishness is brilliantly enunciated in the visual rhetoric of painted portraiture.

Where does all this grand tour posturing leave *Scottish* identity? Superseded by the cosmopolitan polish of Britishness? Not entirely. While its negative traces (the tell-tale accent; incriminating Scotticisms) had preferably been erased in the course of a grand tour, in two of the portraits discussed above – three had James Clark had access to Highland textiles in Naples – Scottishness is valorised through its dress and its attendant objects. For Jones and Stallybrass in their discussion of Holbein's *Ambassadors* in their study of Renaissance clothing, identity is 'clearer in the case of the objects than of the subjects. And the objects refer us back to the *making* of identities . . . through which subjects and objects alike come into being.'[119] This chapter and those that follow, especially in Part II, situate dress, textiles and accessories as items of material culture and as vehicles for reifying facets of identity both in and out of pictorial representation. Portraits are themselves part of this objectscape, implicated into the promulgation of an individual's pictorial identity, albeit one fabricated to a greater or lesser degree. Two of our portraits were commissioned when their young male sitter-subjects came of age in Italy, as markers of this rite of passage while engaged in another rite of passage that was the transformative grand tour. The next chapter continues to focus on the cultural contours and detours of identity. Gender remains a governing category of identity, but in terms of class, the narrative moves further down the social hierarchy from the upper to the professional classes, and geographically from cosmopolitan Europe to the commercial metropolis. 'Scots in London' pursues the notion of occupational identity via the microhistory of George Steuart, a painter cum architect, a Highlander patronised by the Dukes of Atholl throughout his London-based career and a one-time employee and subsequent rival of the Adam brothers, the eponymous Adelphi.

---

[119] Ann R. Jones and Peter Stallybrass, *Renaissance Clothing and the Materials of Memory* (Cambridge: Cambridge University Press, 2000), p. 46.

2 | Scots in London

'The Means of Bread with Applause': George Steuart's Architectural Elevation

A Painter can enrich his canvas without any other limit than his own merit but the Architect must be honored with Patronage and that not the patronage of the vulgar wealthy, but of the Great and the enlightened.

James Playfair to Lord Findlater, 14 March 1788[1]

In a chapter 'On the character of the English' in his *A View of England towards the Close of the Eighteenth Century* (London, 1791), the German traveller, Gebhard Wendeborn, wrote of finding it 'rather curious' that the English 'who pride themselves on the name of Britons, which they bear in common with the Scotch, are, notwithstanding more averse to them, than even to a foreigner'.[2] Contemporaneous English xenophobia towards their North British neighbours is given visual form in two satires produced in London in the 1790s by the artist Richard Newton.[3] In one entitled 'A Flight of Scotchmen' and dated 1796 (Plate XII), hordes of Scots are shown literally descending like a plague of insects from the skies onto the rooftops of London. This airborne diaspora continues onto the territories in the right middle ground that are delineated Ireland, the West Indies, America and Germany. Ostensibly an image about the Scottish invasion of near and distant lands, the company in closest proximity to the viewer is depicted raining down on the capital city. The signpost in the bottom right-hand corner points towards London as 'The best road for a Scot', a directive that recalls Samuel Johnson's well-known dictum, 'the noblest prospect which a Scotsman ever sees, is the high road that leads him to England!' And what a motley crew these Scotsmen are, all cast as Highlanders in their plaid dress and bonnets; some attired with bagpipes or broomsticks; others with a noticeable lack of shoes, stockings and underwear. Newton produces a stereotypically negative image of Scots, as brawny Highlanders, rugged

---

[1] NRS, GD248/591/2/87.

[2] Gebhard Friedrich August Wendeborn, *A View of England towards the Close of the Eighteenth Century* (London, 1791), I, p. 374.

[3] David Alexander, *Richard Newton and English Caricature in the 1790s* (Manchester: Whitworth Art Gallery, 1998), colour plates 44 and 23.

and ugly: an uncouth clan descending uninvited and mostly empty-handed (a minority bring their inheritance in treasure chests) onto the urban metropolis.[4]

In another image (Plate XIII), Newton embellishes the parameters of the narrative by showing a Scotsman before and after his flight to London. In 'Progress of a Scotsman' published in 1794, the generic Scot, barefoot – a certain sign of impoverishment – and bare-buttocked, heads from the Highlands to Edinburgh, where he performs a couple of futile exertions for paltry financial remuneration – running 'two miles for a halfpenny' and 'sweep[ing] hell for a farthing' – before heading south to London. Once in the capital, he gains work by clannish sycophancy: 'Booing to a Scots servant to get him a place'. Decked out in his new livery and powdered wig, an extraordinary social apotheosis takes place, as our Highlander rises through the ranks, from nobleman's porter, to steward, to husband of a rich widow, to a corpulent Member of the British Parliament. The final image in the sequence of fifteen shows the Scotsman wearing a baron's coronet in an armchair whose back and arms are similarly ennobled. The progress of the Scotsman in the title of Newton's image is both geographical and social. His transferable native skills of sycophancy, cruelty and opportunism, transform him from an impoverished specimen, indigenous to the margins of Britain, into one of the privileged socio-political establishment in the capital city of London. These images by Newton attack Scots with an arsenal of insults, many of which had been first manifest thirty years previously during the wave of anti-Scottish propaganda directed towards the first Lord of the Treasury and royal favourite, John Stuart, the 3rd Earl of Bute. By the 1790s beggary, infestations and bare-buttocked impoverishment had become standard accusations that continued into the early nineteenth century.[5]

While Newton represents the invasion and accession of Scots in London in graphic form, the allure of the capital city to an enterprising eighteenth-century Scot is articulated in personal correspondence from the architect, Robert Adam. Unlike Newton's Scotsman, Adam was not a Highlander by birth, but a member of a Scottish architectural dynasty from Lowland Fife. Like Newton's Scotsman, he was elected as a Member of Parliament for

---

[4] See Michael Duffy, *The Englishman and the Foreigner* (Cambridge: Chadwyck-Healey, 1986), pp. 18–20.

[5] Eric Rothstein, 'Scotophilia and *Humphry Clinker*: The politics of beggary, bugs and buttocks', *University of Toronto Quarterly* 52 (1982–3), pp. 63–78; Paul Langford, 'South Britons' reception of North Britons, 1707–1820', in T. C. Smout (ed.), *Anglo-Scottish Relations from 1603–1900* (Oxford: Oxford University Press, 2005), p. 148; Gordon Pentland, '"We speak for the Ready": Images of Scots in political prints, 1707–1832', *Scottish Historical Review* 90.1 (2011), pp. 64–95.

Kinross-shire in 1768. During the course of his grand tour in Italy from 1755 to 1757, Adam's letters to various family members at home in Scotland reveal him devising ambitious plans for the Adam brothers to become 'the sovereign architects of the United Kingdom'.[6] Rather than throwing away his 'genius' on such a 'narrow place' as Scotland, Adam proposes in a letter to his brother James that he should adopt 'a more extensive & more honourable scene I mean an English Life'.[7] Adam's letters contrast an English, which appears to be a euphemism for a London life, with that offered by Scotland and Edinburgh. In a letter to one of his sisters from Rome, dated 23 October 1765, Adam bemoans the fickleness of the Scotch in general and the Edinburgers in particular, for whom 'No player, no singer, no preacher, no Architect, tho' a Lacey, a Storer, a Whitefield or an Adam will please them above a season, their great heat is changed into shivering Coldness, their furious affection into disgust & Discontent. And their ill timed Elogiums into bitter & malicious invectives.'[8] Note his emphasis on occupational identities across a range of professions, which is a major preoccupation of this chapter. Janet Adam Smith quotes from these and other fragments of Robert Adam's grand tour correspondence in her often-cited account of 'Some eighteenth-century ideas of Scotland'.[9] While her conclusion that 'Scotland' was a composite notion of ideas is entirely convincing, her reading of the sources is partial in that she fails to recognise the extent to which Adam's *idea* of Scotland in the mid-1750s was determined by the experience of foreign travel in Italy. In other words, the strongly anti-Scottish sentiment in his letters needs to be re-viewed in the wider context of his exposure to the men and manners of cosmopolitan Europe – an ideology of the grand tour documented in the previous chapter. In contrast with the reported fickleness of the Scots in Scotland, Adam's letters to his family describe being 'caressed & courted by all' the English in Rome; writing 'I believe I shall (as conceited Allan [Ramsay – a fellow Scot in Italy] says of himself) be as well known as Marcus Aurelius in the Capitol, or the Laocoon in the Belvidire'.[10] Having become something of a landmark in cosmopolitan Rome (if we subscribe to Adam's self-mocking delusions of grandeur), Adam seeks 'a new scene of life amongst people more immersed in Business' in London, rather than

---

[6] 12 July 1755. NRS, GD18/4779.

[7] 18 April 1755. NRS, GD18/4770. To James Adam from Naples.   [8] NRS, GD18/4823.

[9] Janet Adam Smith, 'Some eighteenth-century ideas of Scotland', in N. T. Phillipson and Rosalind Mitchison (eds.), *Scotland in the Age of Improvement* (Edinburgh: Edinburgh University Press, 1970), pp. 107–124.

[10] 18 December 1756. NRS, GD18/4827.

among 'the undistinguishing scum of People, sans gout et sans charité; who in a narrow place are more listen'd to than those of true merit, & real taste'.[11] Adam's fashionable French parlance is in marked contrast to an earlier portion of the same letter, where he adopts the inflected Scots vernacular to parody the parochial mindset of his uncle Archibald Robinson: 'In short if you have only a necessary house to build, they [the Scots] would look for a St Peters church, & on finding that Commodity (which if invented by the great Architect of Heaven) would be something but a simple stinking closet, they wou'd turn on their Healls, & like Bauldy or his friend the Doctor, exclaim Hi Hi Hi Is that all he's learn'd abroad I think I've seen just as good . . . Houses, & better too built by Our Archie Handyside that ne'er was out of Fisheraw [a fishing village in East Lothian] a the Days of his Life.'[12]

If Scotland is, in Adam's phrase, a 'narrow place' furnished with ungenerous architectural critics, then it is not as straightforward as London being the binary opposite – an expansive utopia crammed with compliant patrons. Adam's letters from Italy offer as much of a negative *idea of London* as they do of Scotland. Casting the capital as a 'great city', but one crammed with 'boisterous Lords', 'rich and senseless squire[s]' and 'proud and overbearing noble[s]'. To survive in this 'bustling' metropolis, Adam proposes his emigrant family play along in the social charade of refinement. Suggesting that they should adhere to what he calls an 'English essay, where House, Exterior & Interior appearance must be such as to blind the world by dazzling their eyesight with vain pomp'.[13] It was precisely the construction of these sorts of exterior and interior appearances that brought the Adam brothers a measure of commercial success in the competitive metropolis.

Newton's images and Robert Adam's correspondence offer alternative constructions of Scotland and London and Scots in London in eighteenth-century visual and epistolary discourse. Both parody the sights and sounds of Scottish identity – including their dress and accent – from the perspective of an Englishman (a fellow Briton and a foreigner) and a native Scot. Though Newton deliberately plays on these polarities, the dichotomy indigenous/foreign is as problematic as the binary juxtapositions Scotland/England and Edinburgh/London in our reading of Robert

---

[11] NRS, GD18/4823.

[12] Penny Fielding, 'Writing at the North: Rhetoric and dialect in eighteenth-century Scotland', *Eighteenth Century* 39.1 (1998), p. 34, notes that written dialect can be more subversive than spoken.

[13] 4 September 1756. NRS, GD18/4816.

Adam's grand tour correspondence from Rome. The Union of Parliaments in 1707 meant that politically the Scots and English were united as fellow Britons, even if the satirical image was divided into agonistic English/Scottish factions. Robert Adam's own invective towards Scots and Scotland in letters composed in Italy in the mid-1750s might also be contrasted with the poetic eulogies of his brother James; writing in 1762 of 'the genius of Caledonea', of Scotland 'the mother of so many great men' present and past, including David Hume and Fingal (the hero of James Macpherson's Ossianic poetry) whose published volumes James was anxious their sister Janet should procure and despatch to him in Rome.[14] The Scot Archibald Menzies is shown with a volume inscribed Fingal in his grand tour portrait by Anton von Maron painted at Rome the following year (Plate XI).

This chapter focusses on George Steuart, a fellow Caledonian who relocated to London in the second half of the eighteenth century. Like Newton's Scotsman in the 'Progress' (Plate XIII), Steuart was a Highlander, from Blair Atholl in Perthshire on the southern edge of the Grampian Highlands. He had extensive business dealings with the Adam brothers during what Robert Adam in the 1750s called their English life. These dealings, as we shall see, were far from convivial, when Steuart, who was initially a painter by trade, established an architectural practice in the capital. While the Adam brothers have taken their place in the pantheon of notable Scots, alongside Fingal and Hume, Steuart remains largely obscure. It is not my intention however to recover his place in a visual or architectural canon of Scottish masters and masterpieces.[15] Rather, this chapter discusses the content and context of Steuart's correspondence with his aristocratic Scottish patrons, John Murray, the 3rd and John Murray, the 4th Duke of Atholl (who succeeded in 1774). The first half of the chapter focusses on the precarious social and economic landscape in which Steuart and other professional Scots like the Adam brothers operated in in London. Discussion of the client–patron relationship between Steuart and the Dukes of Atholl is extended into an examination of the

---

[14] NRS, GD18/4923. Richard J. Finlay, 'Caledonia or North Britain', in Dauvit Broun, Richard J. Finlay and Michael Lynch (eds.), *Image and Identity: The Making and Re-Making of Scotland through the Ages* (Edinburgh: John Donald, 1998), p. 149, refers to the vernacular poetry of Ramsay, Fergusson and Burns as 'Caledonianism'.

[15] Existing bibliography on Steuart's architectural commissions in England stress his obscurity, see M. M. Rix and W. R. Serjeant, 'George Steuart, Architect, in the Isle of Man', *The Journal of the Manx Museum* 6 (1962–3), pp. 177–179. Sally Goodsir, 'George Steuart and Robert Adam: A professional relationship revealed', *Georgian Group Journal* 18 (2010), pp. 91–104, seeks to reinstate Steuart as an interior painter for the Adam's building empire.

wider social networks of Scottish patronage in London that were facilitated by introductions from the dukes. In terms of economic history, Steuart's letters are loaded with information on the financial crisis of 1772 – itself facilitated by the bankruptcy of a Scot – and its detrimental effects on the business empire of the Adam brothers. Continuing to draw on Steuart's correspondence, the second half of the chapter shifts from the metropolitan centre, to the Highlands, and the so-called discovery of Scotland by English travellers in the second half of the eighteenth century. Here, the narrative revisits the contentious relationship between centre and periphery. It does so by dealing to an extent in the currency of the satirists, in juxtaposing London with the Highlands, the urban townhouse with the Scottish estates and the exterior landscape of the country house with its interior spaces. Yet the chapter proceeds by casting the modes of cultural exchange between the Highlands and London as in some instances, reciprocal, rather than always predatory, at least in the field of design history. Despite the allure of a notion of Scots in London, my discussion argues that they were far from the homogenous community portrayed in graphic satire. Using George Steuart as a case study, it attempts to show the extent to which London, Scotland and Scots in London were culturally constructed in a heterogeneous web of eighteenth-century discourses.

George Steuart's surviving correspondence with the Dukes of Atholl constitutes about a hundred letters dating from the 1760s into the early nineteenth century. Their content shows him to be writing to his patrons on a wide range of topics, as a professional London business man and a source of metropolitan news and gossip, as well as their architect. In 1764, the year the third duke succeeded to the title, Steuart was busy building and decorating a townhouse for him on the east side of Grosvenor Place, near Hyde Park Corner, in the fashionable area of Belgravia in London's West End (Figure 10). There was 'such desire for that spot' by 1771 that the last three houses were reported to have been sold before they had even been built.[16] Research into the London townhouse has begun to establish the historical significance of this architectural entity in the urban environment, which has been long eclipsed in the existing literature by its country counterpart.[17] That said, the country house/townhouse configuration is

---

[16] 6 December 1771. NRAS. 234/54/2/179.

[17] M. H. Port, 'West End palaces: The aristocratic town house in London, 1730–1830', *The London Journal* 20 (1995), pp. 17–46; Julie Schlarman, 'The social geography of Grosvenor Square: Mapping gender and politics, 1720–1760', *The London Journal* 28 (2003), p. 8; Rachel Stewart, *The Town House in Georgian London* (New Haven, CT and London: Yale University Press, 2009).

distinctly Anglocentric and fails to embrace the veritable satellite of properties that constituted even an English estate.[18] Rachel Stewart's findings
have demonstrated that that there was no single governing principle for
patrons choosing to come to London or to occupy a West End house.[19]
Like their better-documented English counterparts, Scots' London town-
houses were market commodities, enabling them to participate in the
capital's political and social institutions during the season that lasted
from November to June. Once the Atholl's Grosvenor Place house was
completed, they sold their other London property in South Audley Street,
Mayfair. Following the 3rd Duke's death, Steuart found a house in Old
Bond Street for his widow to rent, later renting the Grosvenor Place house
on an annual lease to Lord Ossory.[20] Steuart 'is always indefattigable
whenever he can be of any use to any of the family', Colonel James
Murray wrote to the 4th Duke.[21] By the late 1780s and into the early 90s,
the 'indefattigable' Steuart was attempting to procure another London
house for the family to rent. These urban, metropolitan properties both
owned and rented in London's West End were in addition to Atholl House
(now Blair Castle) in Blair Atholl. The family seat was twenty miles away
from their other Highland home and winter residence, Dunkeld House on
the banks of the River Tay to the north of Dunkeld.[22] As we shall see, the
Dukes of Atholl's patronage of George Steuart and Steuart's younger
brother Charles appears to derive from their shared Highland descent.
When focussing on the cultural contours and detours of Scottish identity in
cosmopolitan, metropolitan and colonial contexts, we should not lose sight
of its enduring significance at a regional and local level.

Although a native Highlander by birth, in a letter to the Duke of Atholl
of 1769, Steuart described having been an inhabitant of London for over
twenty years.[23] In 1766, he was appointed Painter to the Board of
Ordnance for North Britain, while continuing to oversee progress on the
Atholl property in Grosvenor Place (Figure 10).[24] His letters are littered

---

[18] See M. H. Port, 'Town house and country house: Their Interaction', in Dana Arnold (ed.), *The Georgian Country House: Architecture, Landscape and Society* (Stroud: Sutton, 1998), pp. 117–138.

[19] Stewart, *The Town House in Georgian London*, '"Tired of worsted" – reasons for coming to London', pp. 28–40.

[20] 29 November 1774. NRAS, 234/54/5/240.

[21] 29 November 1774. NRAS, 234/54/5/240; 6 May 1780. NRAS, 234/65/4/4.

[22] The distance between the two properties of twenty miles is cited in a letter from the Duchess of Atholl to her sister, 9 July 1776. NLS MS. 16004 folio 17. Christopher Dingwall, 'Gardens in the wild', *Garden History* 22.2 (1994), p. 143, describes Dunkeld House as the family's winter quarters.

[23] NRAS, 234/49/8/150.   [24] 22 April 1766. NRAS, 234/49/5/60.

Figure 10: View of Grosvenor Place, London, 1955. Photographed as demolition was in progress. By permission of Historic England Archive.

with scraps of information about the (now demolished) townhouse. We learn it was 'small', but at the same time 'an Excellent Family House, and extreamly convenient'.[25] At a cost of £10,000 it was reckoned by Steuart to be 'very cheap'.[26] One of his letters reports that Mr. Douglas paid £16,000 for his London townhouse, while the projected budget for Sir Watkin Williams Wynn's new three-bay terrace house at 20 St James's Square built between 1771–5 was around four times that of Atholl at Grosvenor Place.[27] Once largely completed by March 1772, Steuart gave a guided tour 'from the cellar to the leads' to a select group of Scottish visitors, the Duke and Duchess of Gordon, Lord Adam Gordon and the Dowager Duchess of Atholl.[28] As a result of which, Lord Adam Gordon wrote commending the duke on 'Your ceilings & finishing & furniture, [which] I think uncommonly light & elegant – & every thing, what the French call unie, a perfection, I admire = in English one would translate it – all of a piece.'[29] This *unie* interior included a painting of Flora executed by Cipriani for the breakfast room ceiling.[30] A portrait of the royal family hung over the chimney-piece in the drawing room. Elsewhere, were a series of family portraits of the Atholls by the Italian artist Angelica Perotti: 'there is not in England the paralele', Steuart wrote to the duke in December 1771, 'every viewer congratulates your Grace on the numerous Noble Family. Sig.ᵃ has acquit herself very well, took great pains with the draperys, and fixing them on frames properly.'[31] The 3rd Duke fathered eleven surviving children – a prodigious family even by eighteenth-century standards.

The Dukes of Atholl's prolonged patronage of Steuart over a period of forty years exceeded the conventional client–patron relationship. As is typical for an eighteenth-century architectural commission, much of their professional dealings were conducted on paper rather than what another of Steuart's letters describes as by 'continual attendance in the field'.[32] Their content reveals Steuart to be also acting as a London agent for the dukes. They, in turn, helped to engineer the longevity of Steuart's independent architectural business, rather than the transient subcontracts of his painterly career, by facilitating a number of introductions to their aristocratic peers who were usually fellow Scots. In June 1772, Steuart was overseeing the transport by sea from London to Perth of imported luxury commodities,

[25] 27 August 1769. NRAS, 234/49/8/103.   [26] 7 March 1772. NRAS, 234/54/3/49.
[27] 20 June 1772. NRAS, 234/54/3/119. £40,000 is cited by Rachel Stewart for Sir William Watkins Wynn's house: *The Town House in Georgian London*, p. 65.
[28] 5 March 1772. NRAS, 234/54/3/47.   [29] 5 March 1772. NRAS, 234/54/3/47.
[30] 15 August 1772. NRAS, 234/54/3/165.   [31] 23 December 1771. NRAS, 234/54/2/189.
[32] 20 March 1802. NRAS, 234/48/3/54.

oranges and stockings.[33] In January 1774, he resolved to procure drawings, rather than 'letting the pictures out of the [Grosvenor Place] house' so that the Staffordshire potter, Josiah Wedgwood, could reproduce the views on his yellow stoneware pottery.[34] Soon after, he was negotiating with Wedgwood's London-based partner, Thomas Bentley and with Mr Duesburg of the Derby and Chelsea porcelain manufactories, for trials on Dunkeld earth for producing china.[35] On this and other occasions, we see how Steuart was acting for the profit of the duke and for the benefit of the industry on his Highland estate, being involved in business negotiations that were organised more effectively via London. One of Steuart's letters refers to spending time in the Herald's Office to furnish authenticated copies of the duke's pedigree.[36] Another recounts a consultation on Atholl's behalf with a German doctor, Mr Geisler, for a remedy for 'schinn cancer'.[37] Via Steuart's representation, we see how the Atholl family had continued access to London's luxury commodities and her specialist personnel.

While representing the duke's interests in all variety of endeavours, Steuart's letters comment on the social and political machinations of what his architectural rival, Robert Adam, called an English life. In a letter dated 21 January 1772, 'the tongue of scandal is never silent'.[38] In contrast to idle gossip concerning the affairs of aristocratic married women ('Towns talk'), Steuart's letters offer eyewitness accounts of contemporary political events and reproduce conversations held in the public, masculine domain of the London coffeehouse.[39] Many of these letters read like newspapers in their quotation from speeches in Houses of Lords and Commons, which in some cases, provide the number of Members who voted for and against a particular motion.[40] By 1773, John Wilkes is losing his political influence: 'Several proselytes', writes Steuart 'will find their suffrages sold for valuable considerations by their Idol'.[41] Epistolary updates on the 'Yankys', the fall of East India stock and the 'Denmark affair' situate the city of London in a network of debates of global, as well as national, significance.[42]

The Duke of Atholl is reported to have found Steuart's letters 'entertaining'.[43] In the late 1760s and into the early 1770s, progress on the Grosvenor Place house is dealt with in an increasingly perfunctory

---

[33] 26 June 1772. NRAS, 234/54/3/131; 12 June 1772. NRAS, 234/54/3/111.

[34] 10 January 1774. NRAS, 234/54/5/6.   [35] 3 June 1774. NRAS, 234/54/5/95.

[36] 6 May 1780. NRAS, 234/65/4/4.   [37] 11 January 1774. NRAS, 234/54/5/6.

[38] NRAS, 234/54/3/9.   [39] 17 May 1772. NRAS, 234/54/3/97.

[40] 13 November 1769. NRAS, 234/49/8/150.   [41] 4 December 1773. NRAS, 234/54/4/230.

[42] 8 October 1774. NRAS, 234/54/5/198; 28 May 1769. NRAS, 234/49/8/73; 4 February 1772. NRAS, 234/54/3/22.

[43] 6 December 1771. NRAS, 234/54/2/179.

manner. We need to view the content of the letters as part of Steuart's business strategy. Entertaining one's patron, or being sufficiently socially adept to know what would entertain them, was a vital part of the success of eighteenth-century businesses in such a competitive field, for all professionals, whether they were architects, sculptors or painters, English or Scots. Steuart's letters enabled him to continually petition the patron he described as 'my best Friend', to assist him in securing new architectural commissions in the overcrowded marketplace that was London.[44]

The Dukes of Atholl's patronage of Steuart as revealed in his surviving correspondence is closely aligned with the animosity of his professional architectural rivals and fellow Scots in London: Robert and James Adam, a fraternal partnership known as the Adelphi, after the ancient Greek for brothers. The building of the Grosvenor Place townhouse for the 3rd Duke of Atholl is said to have 'created a jealousy' of Steuart, that while 'flatter-[ing] to my vanity', simultaneously worked against him in making him a professional rival, rather than a sometime employee of the Adam's. Steuart's letters recount at least three awkward professional encounters with Robert Adam, of which two will be referred to. Having promised Steuart work as a painter at Luton Park, Bedfordshire, where the Adams were employed by the Scottish Minister, Lord Bute, Adam appointed someone else on the grounds that Steuart's work as an architect was taking bread out of their mouths. 'I have no great loss in their pretended attachment to me', Steuart wrote to Atholl in August 1769.[45] But Steuart was to lose out again two years later, when he was excluded from work as a painter on another Adamic project, the London townhouse of Sir Watkin Williams Wynn. One of Steuart's letters recounts a meeting with Adam in which he castigated his more prominent architectural rivals than Steuart, William Chambers and James Wyatt, for plagiarism: 'picking a bitt here, and a bitt there, from the Labour of our studys and converted them to designs of our own. Mr Chambers when I came here made such ridiculous Ornaments placed close to the eye that ought to be at 18 or 20 feet distance; run down my manner till he found it wou'd not do; and now coppys me as much as any body, Mr Wyat at the Pantheon still closer as he draws better; is this not the same as putting their hands in my pocket and taking out my money.'[46] Although most professional Scots in London exploited their Scottish connections, in the Adam/Steuart standoff, we see how they were also locked into professional rivalries and animosities with each other – rivalries that

[44] 10 June 1771. NRAS, 234/54/2/104.   [45] 27 August 1769. NRAS, 234/49/8/103.
[46] 10 June 1771. NRAS, 234/54/2/104.

are in marked contrast to the satirical image of Scots outside Scotland as
markedly insular in their personal and professional loyalties. The Adam
brothers were no longer able to employ Steuart on a contractual basis as
a painter in their architectural empire. Once he established his own
architectural practice, his shared national identity as a fellow Caledonian
was quickly superseded by an occupational one – a professional threat.

Such animosity between professional rivals is in marked contrast to the
protectionist client–patron relationship. 'I must ever eye your favour as the
source of my success', Steuart wrote to the 4th Duke when he succeeded in
1774 – no doubt anxious for a smooth transfer of patron.[47] The Grosvenor
Place townhouse, which he built for the 3rd Duke, became a showcase for
Steuart's architectural talent. At the visit of the Scottish aristocrats, the
Duke and Duchess of Gordon, Lord Adam Gordon and the Dowager
Duchess of Atholl in March 1772, Steuart described to Atholl exhibiting
examples of his architectural designs in an attempt to secure new commissions. It took a further two years for a commission from the Duke of
Gordon to materialise and tellingly, it wasn't until Steuart was, in his
own phrase, 'enter'd into the bustle of business' having already secured
a commission from the Duke and Duchess of Buccleuch to build a nursery
at Richmond House and via the Buccleuchs, being introduced to the Duke
and Duchess of Montague.[48] Steuart wrote triumphantly to Atholl at the
time, 'All this [aristocratic patronage] flatters my vanity much! will it not
stir the spleen of the Adelphi! that I have the Honour to serve so many
noble Dukes? Happy! very happy shall I be in acquitting myself to occasion
these noble personages.'[49] In the intervening years, Steuart had been in
pursuit of financial remuneration *and* social recognition as an architect:
what he describes in one of his letters as the 'double pleasure in having the
means of bread with applause'.[50]

The Duke of Atholl had also acquitted himself on Steuart's behalf –
writing letters of recommendation to the Duke of Argyll, the Chief
Commissioner of the army in Scotland to help Steuart retain his position
as painter to the Board of Ordnance and to Sir Charles Frederick when
Steuart was angling for a position as an artillery painter in the Office of
Works at the Tower of London, when he assumed (wrongly it turned
out) that the then incumbent had died.[51] Another letter of recommendation from Atholl saw Steuart received and entertained by the Duke of
Buccleuch at Richmond in May 1774. He recounts in a letter to Atholl of

---

[47] 20 April 1774. NRAS, 234/54/5/60.   [48] 3 July 1774. NRAS, 234/54/5/120.
[49] 20 May 1774. NRAS, 234/54/5/86.   [50] 17 May 1772. NRAS, 234/54/3/97.
[51] See NRAS, 234/54/3/74; 54/3/55.

having 'the hon.[r] of a seat at Dinner, I mention this, knowing the genteel reception was owing to your Grace's letter, altho there was not the least hint from the Duke of receiving one'.[52] Steuart's elevated social status on this occasion – when he was invited to dine at home with potential aristocratic patrons – might be contrasted with an event four years earlier when following the auction of the contents of Sir Watkin William Wynn's old London townhouse in June 1770, he dined with those much further down the social hierarchy, Sir Watkin's steward and the auctioneer, surrounded by the debris from the house sale.[53] Steuart explicitly asks for the Duke of Atholl's advice on more than one occasion. From navigating the social minefield that was the polite rituals of aristocratic patronage – should he make an unsolicited overture to Mr Douglas, whom he saw at a Christie's sale in March 1772? – to undertaking a speculative investment by building a house near Cavendish Square and renting it to the Duke of Gordon.[54] The Duke did not endorse the latter scheme. In a letter of 8 October 1774, Steuart thanked him for his advice and offered the following assurance: 'the example of my Bro.[r] Architect [Robert Adam] will not in haste induce me to covet a seat in St. Stephens, build babel or puff of tickets – the seat is now annihilate; the Building a monument of sheer Folly'.[55]

Steuart's denunciation of his estranged 'brother architect', Robert Adam, makes elliptical but topical reference to a speculative London development that almost bankrupted the Adam brothers. The main points of this business venture are worth revisiting since they highlight the precarious economic climate in which expatriate, professional Scots like George Steuart and the Adam brothers operated in London.[56] In 1768, the same year that Robert Adam was elected MP for Kinross-shire, the property developing company that he set up with his brothers under the name of William Adam & Company leased for ninety-nine years at a ground rent of £1,200 a year a prime site in central London from the trustees of the impoverished 3rd Duke of St. Albans.[57] Covering just over three acres (or 400 by 360 feet), the site lay between two of the capital's key routes: the River Thames and the Strand (Figure 11). It was known as the Durham House Estate, after property

[52] NRAS, 234/54/5/86.   [53] NRAS, 234/54/2/104.   [54] 7 March 1772. NRAS, 234/54/3/49.
[55] NRAS, 234/54/5/198.
[56] The account that follows is based on Alistair J. Rowan, 'After the Adelphi: Forgotten years in the Adam brothers' practice', *Journal of the Royal Society of Arts* 122 (1974), esp. pp. 661–667; Margaret H. B. Sanderson, *Robert Adam and Scotland: Portrait of an Architect* (Edinburgh: HMSO, 1992), pp. 67–70. See too Jerry White, *London in the Eighteenth Century: A Great and Monstrous Thing* (London: Bodley Head, 2012), 'Robert Adam's London, 1754–99', pp. 49–58.
[57] John Slater, 'The Strand and the Adelphi', *Journal of the Royal Society of Arts* 71 (1922), p. 28.

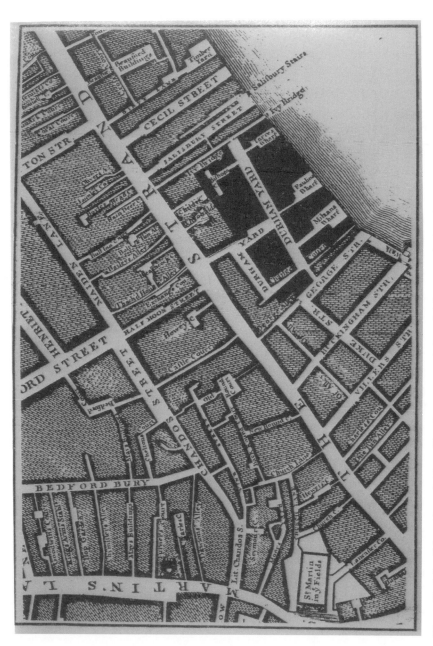

Figure 11: A detail from Roque's Map of London, 1746, with the Adelphi site marked in black. After Alistair J. Rowan, 'After the Adelphi: Forgotten years in the Adam brothers' practice', *Journal of the Royal Society of Arts* 122 (1974), figure 2. © The British Library Board, Maps. Crace XIX.

of the Bishop of Durham that had stood there in the sixteenth century. The Adelphi development transformed the site, which sloped forty feet vertically from the river to the Strand, into a combination of luxury urban housing and commercial storage (Figure 12). The plan was to lease the warehouses and vaults on which the terraces of the houses were built to the Ordnance Board. When William Adam & Company sought licences to embank the Thames, opposition from the city was overruled by the support of the government, Lord North and the king. The Act permitting the development was passed by Parliament in 1771 and the sixty-nine houses that were built on the site became the London residence for the Adam brothers themselves, as well as others of fashion and fortune, including the actor David Garrick.

Then in 1772, there was a financial crisis when the London banking house of Neale, James, Fordyce and Downe went bankrupt.[58] Fordyce was another member of the emigrant Scottish community in London. He had arrived in the capital from Aberdeen as a hosier and made his fortune by gambling on hops. After the stock market slump of 1770, he continued banking using fictitious bills. George Steuart's letters to the Duke of Atholl for June 1772 refer to the 'fatale effects at Edinburgh' of Fordyce absconding; his fears for 'Scotch credit (which has been in no great repute for some time past) be[ing] in a manner anihilate' and the subsequent fate of Fordyce's associates, with two Scots committing suicide and another being confined to a madhouse.[59] The failure of the Fordyce Bank had less fatal, but still devastating financial consequences for William Adam & Company. Having funds in at least two companies affected by the Fordyce crash, work on the riverside development stopped. Steuart's letters evoke the general post-bankruptcy confusion among the mercantile class in London and in particular, how the knock-on effect of the Adam brothers' failure was diffused down the social hierarchy – among the labouring classes their business empire employed, the actual figure for which varies from an extraordinary 2,000 to 3,000 men.[60] To put these figures in perspective: Steuart had 36 to 40 men working on the Atholls' Grosvenor Place townhouse in May 1769.[61] Having been excluded from Adam commissions on more than one occasion, Steuart was predictably smug, writing to Atholl, 'I

---

[58] Julian Hoppit, *Risk and Failure in English Business, 1700–1800* (Cambridge: Cambridge University Press, 1987), p. 136; Julian Hoppit, 'Financial crises in eighteenth-century England', *Economic History Review* 2nd series, 39.1 (1986), p. 54.

[59] 12 June 1772. NRAS, 234/54/3/111. 26 June 1772. NRAS, 234/54/3/131.

[60] These are figures quoted by Alistair J. Rowan, 'After the Adelphi: Forgotten years in the Adam brothers' practice', *Journal of the Royal Society of Arts* 122 (1974), p. 667, as being cited by the *Scots Magazine* and David Hume.

[61] NRAS, 234/49/8/73.

Figure 12: Benedetto Pastorini, *A View of the Adelphi Terrace: late Durham Yard*, June 1771. 46.5 × 85 cm. © Museum of London/Benedetto Pastorini.

Figure 13: Adelphi lottery ticket, signed by William Adam, 1774. Royal Society of Arts (RSA/AD/MA/305/10/73).

am affraid from the multiplicity of great affairs they carried on never can recover their fortune; the Adelphi cannot answer the too sanguine expectations they had form'd; it was ever my opinion, and now confirms by the general opinion, the fable of the Dog & pice of flesh is too Applicable in this case.'[62] The Adams expended every effort to recover their pound of flesh. In February 1773, they held a five-day sale at Christie's of their collection of paintings and antiquities. Another common recuperative financial strategy was what one of Steuart's letters already quoted referred to as the 'puff of tickets'. This was a lottery sanctioned by Parliament (of which Adam was a member) when William Adam & Company sold 4,370 tickets at £50 each (Figure 13) and raised sufficient funds by March 1774 to free their business from its immediate debt. Prizes in the lottery included leases on properties in the fated Adelphi development, which the Government had declined to lease for fear of flooding.[63] For the Duke of Atholl advising George Steuart about another speculative scheme in 1774, the Adelphi became a cautionary model of the pitfalls of such an investment project.

George Steuart's correspondence with the Dukes of Atholl provides a compelling example of the professional career of an émigré Scot in London in the second half of the eighteenth century. What is significant about the content of Steuart's letters is the degree to which his national identity as a Scot is implicit, rather than ever being explicitly stated. In a letter dated 13 October 1769, Steuart was sympathetic towards 'Poor John Bull [who] has strong passions, in Imagination very often, but he's an honest

---

[62] 26 June 1772. NRAS, 234/54/3/131.   [63] The Adelphi was redeveloped in 1936.

fellow for all that.'[64] An account of the explosion of the powder mills and the stories circulated concerning the extent of the damage are reckoned to 'shew how inventive Londoners are'.[65] Steuart's characterisation of John Bull as the personification of England and his mention of Londoners suggest that he saw himself as distinct from these communities.[66] In contrast with these passing references to non-Scots, Steuart's letters as we have seen are loaded with information on members of the Scottish community in London. They enforce its social diversity, rather than its cultural homogeneity, as propagated in satires like Plates XII and XIII. What one of Steuart's letters describes as 'the bustle of business' took many forms for Scots in London. His letters document the urban affairs he managed for his aristocratic patrons, the Dukes of Atholl. From citing members of the aristocracy who co-located to London, they also deal with enterprising Scots from the middling classes, a contingent which included the Adam brothers and the banker, Fordyce, in addition to George Steuart and his brother, Charles, who we will meet in due course. While the Scottish Highland dimension seems crucial to understanding the Atholls' prolonged patronage of Steuart, the same cannot be said of the animosity from Robert Adam, with which it coincided and contrasted. Having been offered contract work by the Adam brothers as a painter, Steuart's subsequent architectural ambitions led to his being blackballed by his Scottish competitors and former employers. This reminds us of the cut-throat marketplace that was later eighteenth-century London. Steuart's letters reveal the course of their professional estrangement: from Adam recommending Steuart to his own Scottish patrons, Sir Laurence Dundas, Henry Drummond and Lord Mansfield, to their 'pretended attachment' by 1769 which continued to disintegrate until 1774, when 'every new acquisition on my [Steuart's] part is a fresh stab that widens the breach'.[67]

Though one of Steuart's letters of 1769 reveals his having relocated to London over twenty years previously, elsewhere they retain a palpable sense of his continued attachment to the Highland landscape of the Dukes of Atholl. In a letter to the 3rd Duke, dated 14 January 1772, Steuart explained,

M^r [Thomas] Pennant has published his tour [of Scotland of 1769], without two Views he intended one of Taymouth [Figure 14], and the other of Dunkeld [Figure 15], which He intends for the next Edition: I think him a Curious Observer, and admire his Erse quotation I am surpris'd at his knowledge of the

---

[64] NRAS, 234/49/8/118.   [65] 14 January 1772. NRAS, 234/54/3/5.

[66] Miles Taylor, 'John Bull and the iconography of public opinion in England, *c.* 1712–1929', *Past and Present* 134 (1992), pp. 93–128.

[67] 10 June 1771. NRAS, 234/54/2/104. 27 August 1769. NRAS, 234/49/8/103. 8 October 1774. NRAS, 234/54/5/198.

Figure 14: 'View from Taymouth of Kinmore and Loch-Tay', Thomas Pennant's 1776 edition of *A Tour in Scotland and Voyage to the Hebrides*, plate IV. 19.1 × 12 cm. © The University of Edinburgh.

Figure 15: 'View of Dunkeld, Birnam Wood, and Dunsinane at a distance', Thomas Pennant's 1776 edition of *A Tour in Scotland and Voyage to the Hebrides*, plate VI. 19.1 × 12 cm. © The University of Edinburgh.

Language, I suspect some highland Friend helpt him out. I have been always taught that our knowledge of the polite Arts came from Greece & Room [Rome].[68]

While ambitious Scots had been invading the political, social and economic institutions that punctuated the London landscape since the Union of 1707, Englishmen were discovering Scotland for the first time in the wake of the Government defeat of the Jacobites in the '45. In many ways, the so-called 'discovery of Scotland' thesis as it is known is a misleading rubric as the territory of the Lowlands was far from foreign. Nor was it the whole of the Highlands that was being 'discovered' in the eighteenth century, but particularly the southwest and central region.[69] In June 1755, John Campbell, the 3rd Earl of Breadalbane wrote to his daughter, Jemima Yorke prior to her visiting him at Taymouth in Perthshire, 'wish[ing] this rejected Countrey may answer your expectation. If it does not in being pretty, I'm sure it will in being new & very different from any you ever saw'.[70] Just four years later, the prospect looked very different, as Campbell informed Yorke, 'It has been the fashion this year to travel into the Highlands, many have been here this summer from England, I suppose because they cant go abroad'.[71] Foreign travel to the continent was interrupted from 1759 during the Seven Years' War with France. Even after the 1763 Treaty of Paris, English and foreign tourists continued to visit the Highlands, especially in the months of June and July. In the summer of 1763 Breadalbane recounts receiving the Duke of Portland, Colonel Barre, the Napiers, Sir Thomas Cave, Lord Hyde and the Mackenzies at Taymouth. Later complaining in a letter to his daughter how during one week in the summer of 1765 forty-seven beds had been 'lain in at once, including servants, in the house and over the stables'.[72] He subsequently built an inn in the village to ease the social and economic burden of entertaining the 'glut of company ... who came rather from curiosity than for a visit'.[73]

Among the visitors who stayed at Taymouth in 1769 was Thomas Pennant who one of Breadalbane's letters describes as being 'a very ingenious man, Author of the British zoology, who is going thro the most

---

[68] NRAS, 234/54/3/5. Pennant was assisted with Gaelic by Dr. Joseph Macintyre, minister of Glenorchy. Thanks to Nigel Leask for this information.

[69] Charles Withers, 'The historical creation of the Scottish Highlands', in Ian Donnachie and Christopher Whatley (eds.), *The Manufacture of Scottish History* (Edinburgh: Polygon, 1992), p. 147.

[70] Bedfordshire Archives and Records Service, L30/9/17/5.

[71] Bedfordshire Archives and Records Service, L30/9/17/23.

[72] Bedfordshire Archives and Records Service, L30/9/17/92.

[73] Bedfordshire Archives and Records Service, L30/9/17/206.

remote & desart parts of this Island in search of curiosities'.[74] Pennant's *Tour in Scotland* (published in 1771) was one of a number of travel accounts that began to colonise the hitherto uncharted territory of the central Highlands.[75] As Samuel Johnson famously wrote in his *A Journey to the Western Islands of Scotland* (1775), a tour whose paths and pages overlapped with those of Pennant, to Lowland Scots like his travelling companion James Boswell, the condition of the Highlands and Islands was as unknown as that of Borneo or Sumatra.[76] George Steuart alluded to Johnson's tour in a letter to the Duke of Atholl of 27 August 1783, referring to a Madame Birchine who was en route for Scotland for reasons of her health: 'This Lady brings in her train Dr Johnson every Highlander is fully revenged ... poor pomposo! pray Lett the Lady see him!'[77] These tourists encountered a Scotland that was in the process of being radically transformed by social and economic improvements following the Jacobite defeat at Culloden; the pro-Union Pennant noted that the town of Perth 'as well as all Scotland, dates its prosperity from the year 1745'.[78] In an account of his second, extended, 1772 tour of Scotland and voyage to the Hebrides, Pennant described the country's accelerated metamorphosis from lawlessness to refinement in less than thirty years, from when 'the whole was a den of thieves' into 'security and civilisation possess[ing] every part'.[79]

'It is with great impatience I wish to make another visit to N. Britain & to ramble thro those parts that I did not see in 1769', Pennant wrote to the

---

[74] Bedfordshire Archives and Records Service, L30/9/17/134.

[75] In 1769, Pennant travelled 920 miles in three months; his *Tour* was published in five editions between 1771 and 1790. See Ralph E. Jenkins, '"And I travelled after him": Johnson and Pennant in Scotland', *Texas Studies in Literature and Language* 14.3 (1972), pp. 445–462; Paul Smethurst, 'Peripheral vision, landscape and nation-building in Thomas Pennant's tours of Scotland, 1769–72', in Benjamin Colbert (ed.), *Travel Writing and Tourism in Britain and Ireland* (Basingstoke and New York: Palgrave Macmillan, 2012), pp. 13–30 and the essays in Mary-Ann Constantine and Nigel Leask (eds.), *Enlightenment Travel and British Identities: Thomas Pennant's Tours in Scotland and Wales* (London: Anthem Press, 2017). On English tourists to Scotland in the second half of the eighteenth century, see John R. Gold and Margaret M. Gold, *Imagining Scotland: Tradition, Representation and Promotion in Scottish Tourism since 1750* (Aldershot: Scolar Press, 1995); Richard W. Butler, 'Tartan mythology: The traditional tourist image of Scotland', in Greg Ringer (ed.), *Destinations: Cultural Landscapes of Tourism* (London: Routledge, 1998), pp. 121–139.

[76] Samuel Johnson, *A Journey to the Western Islands of Scotland*, Ian McGowan (ed.) (Edinburgh: Canongate, 1996), p. 77. Alan Chalmers, 'Scottish Prospects: Thomas Pennant, Samuel Johnson and the possibilities of travel narrative', in Lorna Clymer and Robert Mayer (eds.), *Historical Boundaries, Narrative Forms: Essays on British Literature in the Long Eighteenth Century in Honor of Everett Zimmerman* (Newark: University of Delaware Press, 2007), p. 199.

[77] NRAS, 234/65/4/126.   [78] Thomas Pennant, *A Tour in Scotland* (Chester, 1771), p. 70.

[79] Thomas Pennant, *A Tour in Scotland and Voyage to the Hebrides* (Dublin, 1775), II, p. 400.

Duke of Atholl on 20 December 1771, sending him a copy of his published tour with the hope his engraver had done justice to the drawings.[80] What is distinctive about Pennant's published tours of Scotland that he undertook in 1769 and again in 1772 is that the text of his literary journeys is accompanied by engraved topographical views. The view from Taymouth of Kinmore and Loch Tay (Figure 14) and that of Dunkeld, with Birnam Wood and Dunsinane at a distance (Figure 15) that Steuart mentions in the letter to the Duke of Atholl previously cited are reproduced as engraved plates IV and VI in the 1776 publication of the second, more extended *Tour*, where they are ascribed to a Stewart – which must be either George Steuart or, more likely, his brother, Charles. A landscape painter 'is essential to my scheme', insisted Pennant prior to embarking on his second, extended tour of Scotland.[81] The English artist, William Tomkins, wrote to one of his Scottish patrons, Sir James Grant of Grant, that he had been invited to accompany Pennant on this second tour.[82] Tomkins represents his refusal (he was replaced by the Welsh topographical artist, Moses Griffiths) as an opportunity to complete Grant's outstanding commission for views of and around his estates in Strathspey. An overture from the Duke of Atholl was similarly postponed: 'I will not show my face in Scotland till I have done all your [Grant of Grant's] Pictures', Tomkins maintained, after asking Grant if he had seen 'Mr Pennants Book of his tour of Scotland where there is a few print of some of my Views only as a tryal to see how they would sell. They have sold amazeingly and I have got much credit by them'. In this, we see how the landscape of Scotland was packaged in travel literature accompanied by engraved views for the purposes of mass-consumption beyond its borders – including in the metropolitan centre.

James Grant's former grand tour travelling companion, Thomas Wynn – they are shown with two other male friends in the Roman group portrait by Nathaniel Dance (Plate VIII) – wrote to him on 8 February 1772: 'By our fireside in Grosvenor Square [London] we [he and Lady Catherine] have much admir'd the Beauties of the Northern part of Britain'.[83] His letter elucidates that it was Pennant's published tour that 'has made us well acquainted with every circumstance relative to N. Britain; excepting the happiness we both should enjoy in making a visit to Mrs Grant & yourself,

[80] NRAS, 234/54/2/187.

[81] 13 May 1772. Pennant to George Paton. Quoted in James Holloway and Lindsay Errington, *The Discovery of Scotland: The Appreciation of Scottish Scenery through Two Centuries of Painting* (Edinburgh: National Gallery of Scotland, 1978), p. 57.

[82] 29 May 1772. NRS, GD248, 678/5/5.   [83] NRS, GD248, 179/1/82.

in that Ancient Chatteau [Castle Grant near Forres] that I wish much to see'. John Campbell, the 3rd Earl of Breadalbane, who received Pennant at Taymouth as part of a party of visiting British tourists in August 1769, wrote to his daughter in December 1771: 'Pray get Mr Pennant's Tour into Scotland just publish'd by Dodseley, where you will see Taymouth finely puff'd. Mr. Pennant has sent me a book. Some of the best views about Taymouth were not ready for engraving, it being necessary first to contract the scale of the original Pictures which are pretty large, into a very small compass. The cascade, fine in itself, is ill represented in the book [Plate III – Figure 16].'[84] The published engraving records the original painting of the cascade near Taymouth was executed by William Tomkins. This domestication of the Scottish landscape in the text of Pennant's first tour and in the images that accompanied it was a shared professional endeavour by English and Welsh travellers and artists. The Highland estates they described and delineated in topographical views had recently been improved by planting and design schemes initiated by notable aristocratic Scottish landowners like Sir James Grant, the Earl of Breadalbane and the Dukes of Atholl. 'Improvement meant changing the economy, agricultural as well as industrial, and also the landscape', explains Mitchison in her class-inflected account of national identity in eighteenth-century Scotland.[85]

George Steuart's correspondence with the Dukes of Atholl has then wider historical and cultural significance than the professional activities of émigré Scots in the social and economic context of the metropolis. His letters allude to the discovery of the Highlands of Scotland by English tourists: its colonisation in the genre of domestic travel literature and its visual codification in topographical images. Steuart's letters further describe the reproduction and dissemination of an idea of Highland Scotland in material form. One of his letters to the Duke of Atholl mentions a meeting with Thomas Bentley, the London-based partner of the Staffordshire potter, Josiah Wedgwood.[86] Bentley been delayed in London as a result of the exhibition in Greek Street, Soho of the so-called Frog Service, some 680 items for dinner, 264 pieces for dessert for fifty people ordered 'for the Empress of Russia whereon is painted all the Views in Great Britain they cou'd collect [actually 1222]; among the number is several from your Graces'.[87] Catherine the Great's dinner and dessert

---

[84] Bedfordshire Archives and Records Service, L30/9/17/167.

[85] Rosalind Mitchison, 'Patriotism and national identity in eighteenth-century Scotland', in T. W. Moody (ed.), *Nationality and the Pursuit of National Independence* (Belfast: The Appletree Press, 1978), p. 77.

[86] 3 July 1774. NRAS, 234/54/5/120.   [87] NRAS, 234/54/5/120.

Figure 16: 'Cascade near Taymouth', Thomas Pennant's 1769 edition of *A Tour in Scotland and Voyage to the Hebrides*, plate III. 19.1 × 12 cm. © The University of Edinburgh.

service in Wedgwood's Queen's Ware pottery was, as Steuart's letter recounts, decorated with topographical views consisting primarily of landscape gardens and ancient Gothic buildings in Britain. The engravings published in the first edition of Pennant's *Tour* and in preparation for the later volume, furnished the Wedgwood firm with a pattern book of views in Scotland, including the estates of the Duke of Atholl.[88] Thus, plate IV 'A view from the King's seat near Blair' (Figure 17) appears on one side of the cover of an oblong dish by Wedgwood in the Russian royal collection (Figure 18).[89]

Catherine the Great's commissioning of the Frog Service from Wedgwood has been described as an act of cultural politics.[90] Catherine's Anglophilia was distinctly ideological, in its adopting the political structure of Britain as a model on which she hoped to base her reforms of the Russian constitution. When the Scottish aristocrat Charles, 9th Baron Cathcart, was exported to St Petersburg as British Minister in 1768, he wrote: 'Russia, to my predecessors . . . appeared under French influence, from inclination, custom and education. Russia is now, by the Empress's firm determined and declared options, and will be more so by all her institutions *decidedly* English.' The dinner and dessert service by Wedgwood provides material evidence of Catherine's adherence to British manufacturing institutions. Its painted illustrations affirmed a view of Britain's liberty and democracy, with an allegiance to the country via the land. The Gothic buildings punctuating the landscape bespoke a glorious national past and a shared national identity, much of which was highly rhetorical; as Raeburn shrewdly observes, the service offered 'a remarkably unified, unclouded version of the national myth'.[91] We can begin to discern cracks in the myth by looking again at Pennant's plate IV 'A view from the King's seat near Blair' (Figure 17), which was reproduced on the cover of a dish in the Frog Service (Figure 18). Peter Mazell engraved the view of part of the Duke of Atholl's Highland estate after a painting by Paul Sandby whose images of

---

[88] Hilary Young, *The Genius of Wedgwood* (London: V&A, 1995), G242. See also G237.

[89] Michael Raeburn, Ludmila Voronikhina and Andrew Nurnberg (eds.), *The Green Frog Service* (London: Cacklegoose Press, 1995), view 1188. Thomas Pennant, *A Tour in Scotland* (London, 1776), p. 64, explains that the title of the engraving is incorrect in earlier editions as the King's seat is near Dunkeld, not Blair.

[90] Michael Raeburn, 'Catherine the Great and the image of Britain', in Raeburn, Voronikhina and Nurnberg, *The Green Frog Service*, pp. 42–56 at p. 42. My discussion derives from Anthony Cross, 'Cultural relations between Britain and Russia in the eighteenth century', in Brian Allen and Larissa Dukelskaya (eds.), *British Art Treasures from Russian Imperial Collections in the Hermitage* (New Haven, CT and London: Yale University Press, 1996), pp. 16–35.

[91] Raeburn, 'Catherine the Great and the image of Britain', p. 55.

Figure 17: Engraved by Peter Mazell after a painting by Paul Sandby. 'A view from the King's seat near *Blair*', Thomas Pennant's 1769 edition of *A Tour in Scotland and Voyage to the Hebrides*, plate IV. 19.1 × 12 cm. © The University of Edinburgh.

Figure 18: Covered rectangular dish ornamented with *View near Blair, Scotland*. The Frog Service. Wedgwood Manufactory, Staffordshire, Great Britain, 1773–1774. Inv. no. ZF-20849. The State Hermitage Museum, St Petersburg. Photograph © The State Hermitage Museum. Photo by Alexander Lavrentyev.

Scotland offered an alternative act of cultural politics to Catherine's pottery service.[92] Sandby was the official draughtsman of the Military Survey of Scotland; one of a team of artists and surveyors employed by the Board of Ordnance, a branch of the Army, to map for the first time after the '45, the uncharted territory of Scotland. He is credited with having travelled more extensively in North Britain than any other artist before him.[93] But Sandby's delineations were prescribed by politics, not aesthetics. The survey was designed first and foremost to render accessible the inaccessible parts of Scotland to Government troops, rather than tourists: a systematic survey of Jacobite territory after the '45 uprising. Thus, Sandby's view of the Highland landscape from the King's Seat can be read as a form of military intelligence. This is the landscape panorama as a form of

[92] See Michael Charlesworth, 'Thomas Sandby climbs the Hoober Stand: The politics of panoramic drawing in eighteenth-century Britain', *Art History* 19 (1996), pp. 247–266.

[93] Jessica Christian, 'Paul Sandby and the military survey of Scotland', in Nicholas Alfrey and Stephen Daniels (eds.), *Mapping the Landscape: Essays on Art and Cartography* (Nottingham: University Art Gallery, 1990), p. 22.

coloniser's tool for visually recording the terrain of the enemy, which was in this case domestic as opposed to foreign.[94] By the 1770s, however, Sandy's military images were no longer intelligible in the same way. They had become commodified within a culture of domestic tourism; reproduced on mass-produced Wedgwood ware as part of a packaged landscape aesthetic; served-up as images on an imperial dinner service.

In both the London townhouse and at Dunkeld, George Steuart was responsible for pictorially representing and reproducing aspects of the Duke of Atholl's improved Highland landscape. In a letter dated 15 August 1772, Steuart describes how Cipriani had put up the painting of Flora in the ceiling of the breakfast room in the Grosvenor Place townhouse. Steuart wanted something 'of the India kind' to furnish the rest of the room that would be consistent with its entirely 'historical' parts: 'wish[ing, he writes] to preserve that Idea which nothing can do but paintings either oil or water. this mode is more expensive but how becoming a propriety in dress! may I introduce some Ornamental copartments being places for some historical pieces either figure or Landscape to be introduced at Leisure of the kind alluded to at the Hercules.'[95] Steuart's opaque reference to 'the Hercules' alludes to a design precedent in the garden at Atholl House (now Blair Castle), the gist of which he wished to imitate in the furnishing of a room in the interior of the family's London townhouse. 'The Hercules' takes its name from a life-size lead copy of the colossal ancient marble sculpture of the *Farnese Hercules* that was purchased in 1743 from the London workshop at Hyde Park Corner of the sculptor John Cheere (Figure 19). The statue formed the focus of the eastern half of an extensive formal landscape covering nine acres around Atholl House, the ten-year creation of James Murray, the 2nd Duke of Atholl and his gardener, John Wilson. It lent its name to a series of exterior spaces: the Hercules Walk, a riverside walk along the banks of the Tilt, the Hercules Wilderness, Park and Garden. Steuart's letter seems to refer to the Hercules Garden, which consisted of a traditional Scottish walled garden containing a mixture of styles and ideas borrowed from the French and Italian landscaping traditions and the exotic architectural vocabulary of Chinoiserie.[96] The 2nd Duke combined a new garden with

---

[94] Charlesworth, 'Thomas Sandby climbs the Hoober Stand', p. 263. John Bonehill and Stephen Daniels, 'Designs on the landscape: Paul and Thomas Sandby in North Britain', *Oxford Art Journal* 40.2 (2017), pp. 223–248.

[95] NRAS, 234/54/3/165.

[96] Christopher Dingwall, 'The Hercules Garden at Blair Castle, Perthshire', *Garden History* 20 (1992), pp. 153–172.

Figure 19: John Cheere, *Farnese Hercules,* 1743. © HES.

a remodelling of the Hercules pond with its series of islands and peninsulas. A miscellany of sculptures were displayed in the garden, including allegorical figures (the Seasons and Time supporting a sundial), birds (an Eagle) and some seventeen statues bought off Cheere in 1754 of classical, rustic and theatrical subjects, all painted to simulate life. In August 1772, Steuart asked the 3rd Duke's permission to emulate in landscape or figure paintings executed in watercolour or oils for the breakfast room in London, the display of the eclectic sculptural programme in the Hercules Garden at Atholl House in the Highlands. What we are dealing with here is the transference of design precedents in projects executed at the Highland property to the London townhouse, between schemes in the exterior and interior landscapes and between the art historical media of sculpture and painting. Reminding us that in this documented instance, the rural Highlands is the model, with the metropolitan centre, London, the receptacle. This is just one example of the traffic of cultural exchange between the Highlands and London, which as we shall see in due course, was multi-directional, rather than the unidirectional manpower resource that the satires (Plate XII & XIII) suggest, from the culturally impoverished periphery to the rich spoils of the metropolitan centre.

Further evidence of the blurring of exterior and interior categorisations and between landscape and artefact is witnessed in the painted decoration of the dining room at Blair Castle (formerly Atholl House). Amid the carnival of carved stucco that was completed about 1751 (Figure 20), are five large painted wall panels representing local topographical views: *Black Lynn Fall on the Bran*, 1766 (Figure 21), the ruins of *Dunkeld Cathedral*, 1767, Perthshire valley with mountains in the background, *Craig a Barns & Craig Vinian from Torrvald*, 1768, the *Upper Fall at Bruar*, 1777 and the *Lower Fall*, 1778. George Steuart's brother, Charles, was commissioned to execute this suite of painted scenes as early as 1764, when the Duke of Atholl wrote to his brother, 'The Hermitage is very fine at present I have gott a landskip painter from London who is to take a View of the Cascade and all the other fine prospects here I believe you saw him at London it is Stuart's younger brother and he seems to be doing very well.'[97] Unlike his architect brother, George, Charles Steuart has retained a passing mention in traditional surveys of Scottish historical art.[98] The Hermitage the Duke's 1764 letter refers to as being 'very fine' that July was a summer retreat created by the 3rd Duke in 1757–8 as a view house overlooking the Black Lynn Fall on the banks of the River Braan near Dunkeld. It was the culmination of a riverside walk which 'enchanted' Jane Cathcart, the Duchess of Atholl in July 1776 with its 'variety of fine cascades among the Rocks'.[99] The Duchess wrote to her sister, 'by the time I came home I was quite tired of admiring [these views]; as it w.^{d} have required a much longer time to satisfy one self with examining the different prospects w^{h} succeeded one another so quick'. The wall panels by Charles Steuart captured a succession of these 'most beautiful & Romantick' views on canvas and installed them into the interior of the dining room at Atholl House.

---

[97] 14 July 1764. NRAS, 234/49/3/217.

[98] David Irwin and Francina Irwin, *Scottish Painters at Home and Abroad, 1700–1900* (London: Faber, 1975), pp. 129–130. Duncan Macmillan, *Scottish Art, 1460–2000* (Edinburgh: Mainstream, 2000), pp. 133–134.

[99] 9 July 1776. NLS MS. 16004 folio 17.

Figure 20: View of the dining room at Blair Castle, from the south. © HES.

Figure 21: Charles Steuart, *Black Lynn Fall on the Bran*, 1766. © HES.

Steuart's painting of the Black Lynn Fall represents the view up the valley showing the cascade from the vantage point of the Hermitage, with torrents of water pouring over the immense outcrop of rocks at various angles (Figure 21). A diminutive Highland figure and his seated female companion on the left bank give the forty-foot waterfall a suitably gigantic scale.

In 1782–3, the Hermitage overlooking the Black Lynn Fall was remodelled for the 4th Duke of Atholl. The interior of this riverside view house was transformed into a stateroom for the Highland Homer, a third century

Gaelic bard, and became known as Ossian's Hall. The poems of Ossian, the son of Fingal, had been rediscovered by James Macpherson during a sponsored tour of the West Highlands and Islands and published in 1761. They affected a cultural rehabilitation of the Highlands, by reinstating a native poetic pedigree as ancient as that of the cradle of western civilisation, the Greeks and Romans. As George Steuart wrote to the Duke of Atholl (quoted above), 'I have been always taught that our knowledge of the polite Arts came from Greece & Room [Rome]'.[100] Ossian was a Highland Homer whose translated poems seemed to contradict the prevailing external view of Highlanders as uncivilised barbarians: a view still endorsed in Richard Newton's graphic satires (Plate XII & XIII). With a notable lack of geographical specificity in the poems, Ossian was relocated in a variety of topographical sites in the Highlands and Islands of Scotland – and even in the Lowlands.[101] One of the most famous, or arguably better-documented, visual representations of Ossian in the later eighteenth century, was the painted ceiling formerly at Penicuik House outside Edinburgh.[102] The Edinburgh artist, Alexander Runciman produced a monumental Ossianic narrative for the coved ceiling of Sir John Clerk of Penicuik's drawing room in 1772. According to *A Description of the Paintings in the Hall of Ossian at Pennycuik, near Edinburgh* (Edinburgh, 1773), 'of all poets, Ossian is perhaps the most difficult to be exhibited by the pencil'.[103] Runciman translated the Ossianic poems into pictorial form, producing seventeen compositions in a room twenty-four by thirty-six feet. The central oval extended twenty-four feet on its long axis, with representations of life-sized figures including the poet playing his harp on the seashore and singing to an audience that included Malvina who was betrothed to his dead son, Oscar (Figure 22).[104] While the clouds in the sky assumed the shapes of ghosts of departed heroes, the four corners of the room contained gigantic river gods personifying the Clyde, Tay, Tweed and Spay. These human and divine figures were located in what has been identified as containing the natural and man-made features of a specifically Scottish landscape – with a waterfall, a pier with a tower reminiscent of that formerly at Leith and

---

[100] NRAS, 234/54/3/5.   [101] Gold and Gold, *Imagining Scotland*, p. 55.

[102] J. Duncan Macmillan, '"Truly national designs": Runciman's Scottish themes at Penicuik', *Art History* 1 (1978), pp. 90–98; Martin Myrone, *Bodybuilding: Reforming Masculinities in British Art, 1750–1810* (New Haven, CT and London: Yale University Press, 1995), pp. 145–162. The painted scheme was lost in the fire of 1899.

[103] *A Description of the Paintings in the Hall of Ossian at Pennycuik, near Edinburgh* (Edinburgh, 1773), p. 8.

[104] Elizabeth Isabella Spence, *Letters from the North Highlands during the summer 1816* (London, 1817), p. 31.

Figure 22: Alexander Runciman, *The Blind Ossian singing and accompanying himself on the harp, c.* 1772. Oval 46.6 × 59.9 cm. National Galleries of Scotland. David Laing Bequest to the Royal Scottish Academy transferred 1910.

hills visible over the water as across the Firth of Forth.[105] The eye was said to be dazzled by the brilliant gold and colour scheme of the Penicuik ceiling.[106]

Ossian's Hall on the banks of the River Braan at Dunkeld (Figure 23) lacked the monumental scale of its Lowland counterpart, but was no less dazzling for its technical ingenuity, rather than its painted brilliance.[107] Part of the 4th Duke's programme of redecoration involved the installation of internal mechanisms into the existing fabric of the structure. Sketches by Revd John Sime in 1806 (Figure 24) confirm that the interior consisted of two rooms, the entrance comprising a circular vestibule, which led into the viewing room. Sime's longitudinal section shows the viewing room as a rectangle with apsidal ends, the furthest of which was a bay window overlooking the falls. On entering the vestibule, visitors encountered a painting opposite them of Ossian by Charles or George Steuart. The

---

[105] Macmillan, "Truly national designs", p. 94.

[106] *A Description of the Paintings in the Hall of Ossian at Pennycuik, near Edinburgh*, p. 21.

[107] On the Hermitage, see David Irwin, 'A 'picturesque' experience: The Hermitage at Dunkeld', *The Connoisseur* 187 (1974), pp. 196–199; Christopher Dingwall, 'Ossian and Dunkeld: A hall of mirrors', *Scotlands* 4.1 (1997), pp. 62–70.

Figure 23: 'Ossian's Hall near Dunkeld'. Engraved plate from Robert Heron's *Observations made in a journey through the western counties of Scotland* (Perth, 1799), volume I. 16.2 × 10.5 cm. © The University of Edinburgh.

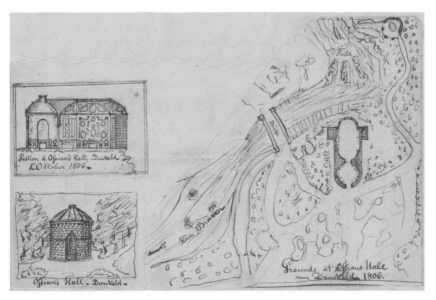

Figure 24: Sketches by Revd John Sime showing the 'Grounds of Ossian's Hall near Dunkeld 1806' and on the left, a longitudinal section and elevation. © HES.

Figure 25: Attributed to Luciano Borzone, *Blind Belisarius receiving the alms*, 1640s. 208.2 × 226.3 cm. © Devonshire Collection, Chatsworth. Reproduced by permission of Chatsworth Settlement Trustees.

composition was recorded by at least two visitors as being based on *Blind Belisarius receiving the alms*, a painting purchased by Richard Boyle, the 3rd Earl of Burlington from the Melfort collection in Paris in 1715 as a van Dyck, which is now attributed to Luciano Borzone and dated to the 1640s (Figure 25).[108] The former general of the sixth century AD Byzantine

---

[108] The visitors were Warren Hastings in 1787 and Alexander Campbell in 1802. The acquisition of the Borzone from the widow of the Jacobite Earl of Melfort is referred to by Edward T. Corp, 'Lord Burlington's clandestine support for the Stuart Court at Saint-Germain-en-Laye', in Edward T. Corp (ed.), *Lord Burlington, the Man and His Politics: Questions of Loyalty* (Lewiston, NY: Edwin Mellen Press, 1998), pp. 7–26 at p. 11. For Burlington's Jacobite inclinations, see the start of Chapter 4 below. On the iconography of Belisarius, Klaus Weschenfelder, 'Belisar und sein Begleiter: Die Karriere eines Blinden in der Kunst vom 17. bis zum 19. Jahrhundert', *Marburger Jahrbuch für Kunstwissenschaft* 30 (2003), pp. 245–268.

emperor, Justinian, Belisarius is represented in reduced social and economic circumstances. Having led Rome's reconquest of the West, with
victories against the Persians, Huns, Vandals and Goths, the disgraced
Belisarius was blinded and forced to beg for a living. Steuart transposed this
late antique subject into a Caledonian context, with the blind Ossian
playing his harp and singing to the maidens of Morvern.[109] When the
guide operated a secret pulley, the painting split vertically into two halves
that slid into apertures in the opposite walls. This motion exposed the
circular viewing room which was described by one female visitor as 'an
elegant saloon, more appropriate to the fashionable females of a midnight
city ball, than to such a rural place'.[110] At the far end of the viewing room
were three large front windows whose painted and gilded side walls and
ceiling, as we see in outline in Sime's monochrome section (Figure 24),
were covered in mirrors containing red, green and colourless glass; that in
the ceiling was of concave form. These mirrors reflected the waterfall on
either side and above the viewer who was seemingly enveloped in the
torrents of water and foam. 'you feel as if encircled by a cataract of water,
a lava of liquid verdigrease, and a torrent of fire', recounted James McNayr
in his *A Guide from Glasgow, to Some of the Most Remarkable Scenes in the
Highlands of Scotland* (Glasgow, 1797).[111]

The reflection and refraction of the waterfall in the coloured and colourless mirrors positioned the viewer in a virtuoso trompe l'oeil, in which the
heightened visuality of the actual experience was contrasted with the
blindness of the painted representation of the poet, Ossian. Indeed,
the experience at Ossian's Hall was as much oral as visual, sonic as scenic,
from imagining the musical strains emanating from Ossian's painted harp
to hearing the roar of the waterfall above and around you – the cadence of
the cascade. For the former Governor-General of India, Warren Hastings,
who visited in September 1787 prior to his protracted impeachment trial,
Ossian's Hall was 'a place of enchantment' that actually disoriented the
senses, where the cascades of water reflected in the concave mirror on the
ceiling 'gave it the appearance of a white smoke ascending with great
velocity through an opening above, instead of an object reflected'.[112]
Simultaneously, the reflected water crashed over the rocks 'with an

---

[109] Steuart's painting was destroyed by a gunpowder explosion in 1869.

[110] Elizabeth Isabella Spence, *Sketches of the Present Manners, Customs and Scenery of Scotland*
(London, 1811), II, p. 22.

[111] James McNayr, *A Guide from Glasgow, to Some of the Most Remarkable Scenes in the Highlands
of Scotland* (Glasgow: Courier Office, 1797), p. 98.

[112] NLS, MS. 19200 folio 12.

Impetuosity and weight & turbulency wch confounded ye sights, & a noise that deprived us of the power of hearing our mutual exclamation of astonishment'. Hastings's party during his fourteen-day tour of the Highlands included David Anderson and his wife and the brother of the late George Bogle. Both Anderson and Bogle were part of Hastings's phalanx of 'Scotch guardians' as he called them during his Governor-Generalship; we shall encounter them in the next chapter with a fellow Scot in India, Claud Alexander.[113]

Accounts of visits to Ossian's Hall at Dunkeld feature prominently in later eighteenth-century domestic travel literature.[114] Ossian was both a stimulus and telos to travel in the Highlands and Islands of Scotland: a reason for going and a summation of what you would find; the high point of the Ossianic tour was Fingal's cave on the island of Staffa.[115] Like the versified extracts from Ossian which were carved onto Ossian's cave (as it was known) half a mile from the Hall at Dunkeld, these touristic accounts inscribed Ossian into the cultural geography of the Highlands. A visit to Ossian's Hall offered an opportunity to experience first-hand the sublime features of the Scottish landscape.[116] Edmund Burke's *Inquiry into the origin of our Ideas of the Sublime and the Beautiful* (1756) codified power, vastness, light, colour, sound, loudness and suddenness as sublime qualities – all of which were experienced at Dunkeld. One such Ossianic traveller in pursuit of the natural sublime of the Highlands was Elizabeth Montagu who in August 1766, made a four-week jaunt as far north as Inveraray. Ian Ross has demonstrated how for Montagu the poetry of Ossian was the primary storehouse of the rhetorical sublime and directly associated with the natural sublime of the Scottish Highlands.[117] She carried the *Fingal* (1762) and *Temora* (1763) volumes in her post chaise, read the passages *in situ* and quoted directly from them in her letters, including the following to Elizabeth Carter:

[113] John Riddy, 'Warren Hastings: Scotland's benefactor', in Geoffrey Carnall and Colin Nicholson (eds.), *The Impeachment of Warren Hastings: Papers from a Bicentenary Commemoration* (Edinburgh: Edinburgh University Press, 1989), pp. 30–57 mentions both Bogle (36) and Anderson (39, 49).

[114] Gold and Gold, *Imagining Scotland*, 'In search of Ossian', pp. 53–57.

[115] Paul Baines, 'Ossianic geographies: Fingalian figures on the Scottish tour, 1760–1830', *Scotlands* 4.1 (1997), p. 45.

[116] Dingwall, 'Gardens in the wild', pp. 133–156.

[117] Ian Ross, 'A bluestocking over the border: Mrs Elizabeth Montagu's aesthetic adventures in Scotland, 1766' *Huntington Library Quarterly*, 28.3 (1965), p. 227. For her itinerary in 1766, see pp. 232–233. For a more recent account which does not mention Montagu, see Nigel Leask, 'Fingalian topographies: Ossian and the Highland tour, 1760–1805', *Journal for Eighteenth-Century Studies* 39.2 (2011), pp. 183–196.

I travell'd by Lough Loman to Inveraray. I was much pleased with the Lake, but transported with the Mountains. Here I enter'd Classick ground. I dined in the Glencrow by the streams of Cona & wanted nothing to compleat my happiness but that Ossian's Ghost would have sung in my ear *the tales of other times*, but memory did this for me. I heard Ghosts on the blast of the desart, & saw Malvina weeping in the mist . . . [Lord Kames] carried me to Stirling Castle, & to see the Iron works at Caron. I look'd here for the sad Comala, *pale she lies at the rock, & the cold winds lift her hair*; but I could not find her.[118]

While Ossian's hall at Dunkeld is firmly embedded in eighteenth-century poetic and aesthetic debates, it is further implicated into our discussion of the cultural traffic between Scotland and London, the Highlands and the metropolis. We have already seen that one of the Steuart brothers executed the painting of Ossian singing on the partition wall in the early 1780s. In June 1783, George Steuart was additionally responsible for 'compleating the packages containing Ossians furniture' to be sent via sea to Perth. His letter to the 4th Duke of Atholl explains,

the few [packages] that have view'd are high in commendation. it will give me pleasure to find all pleasing at Dunkeld . . . These paintings are framed to fitt the sides of the room between the return glass Pillasters and a space left in the Centre pannels to screw the convex glass to the light is revers'd on the painting to suit the light from one end. the circular end at the door is form'd by 3 pannells of Glass, on each side the door and I think Gentle [the carpenter] will find no difficulty in pulling them neatly up. The south side is Hospitality supported by Justice and Fortitude on the North Harmony attended by Temperance and Prudence and the <u>Logia Vaticans</u> is not fairer than these Lady dress but you shall judge.[119]

The interior fittings and furnishings for Ossian's Hall at Dunkeld were evidently made in London and then shipped to their intended Highland venue.[120] The Revd John Sime's 1806 sketch (Figure 24) shows the suite of Ossianic furniture *in situ* in the vestibule and viewing room. It consisted of eight lyre-backed, rush-seated chairs and a matching settee (Plate XIV) made by the London firm of Chipchase and Lambert, who were upholders (or upholsterers) and cabinet-makers.[121] Carved in softwood, the frames are japanned in green with added painted decorations. The lyre-backs of

---

[118] 14 September 1766. Quoted in Ross, 'A bluestocking over the border', p. 228.

[119] 28 June 1783. NRAS, 234/65/4/103.

[120] In the archives at Blair Castle is a document of goods dispatched from London to Perth by George Steuart. Dated 23 July 1782, it lists the large historical painting of Ossian on the door, as well as parcels and cases from Chipchase. I owe this reference to Christopher Dingwall.

[121] Anthony Coleridge, 'The 3rd & 4th Dukes of Atholl and the firm of Chipchase, cabinet-makers', *Connoisseur* 161 (1966), pp. 96–101.

the chairs invoke Ossian's painted harp and contribute to the interplay between the oral and visual spectacle that viewers experienced at Ossian's Hall. Steuart's letter also recounted the provision of framed paintings of female personifications of the Virtues. These images, presumably executed by him or his brother, Charles, were tailored to fit in the sides of the temple interior.[122] Steuart's boast that 'the <u>Logia Vaticans</u> is not fairer than these Lady dress', offers a highly inflated pictorial precedent – Raphael's scheme in Rome, the cultural centre of cosmopolitan Europe. 'what a performance immortal Raphael you will live in all ages,' extolled Patrick Home during his second visit to the Vatican in October 1772.[123]

In an often-quoted letter, dated 12 September 1819, the Edinburgh portrait painter Henry Raeburn wrote to his fellow artist and Scot, the émigré David Wilkie, entreating him to write at least annually with news of the commercial London art scene.[124] Examples of works by both artists will be discussed later in Chapters 5 and 6, but in concluding the present chapter, Raeburn's letter evocatively conveys a sense of his isolation from the metropolitan centre and its cultural institutions in the form of exhibitions and newspaper reviews. Although Raeburn takes our discussion into the early decades of the nineteenth century, he is a noteworthy conclusion as an example of a professional Scot who remained at home; who never joined the Scottish diaspora in embarking on a precarious social and economic move to the British capital, either temporarily or permanently. Professing to know as little about London artists as if he 'were living at the Cape of Good Hope', Raeburn's letter also introduces a global dimension to our discussion that foregrounds that to come. How one Scot participated in the British empire in India, which was accessed via the Cape of Good Hope, forms the focus of the next chapter.

This chapter has tried to argue *against* the notion of Scots in London as a monolithic entity, by privileging their professional differences, rather than their ethnic sameness. It has suggested that the opposing factions in our discussion should not be solely dictated by matters of national identity (Scottish/English), but at least in George Steuart and the Adam brothers' case, by the competitive business of occupational rivalry. London and Scotland in the later eighteenth century have been shown to be as much constructed ideas as actual places; in Scotland's case, at least two distinct and contrasting places: the Lowlands and the Highlands. Rather than the agonistic prejudices delineated in the images by Richard Newton, the

---

[122] As recorded in 'A Tour through part of England and Scotland by Eliza Dawson in the year 1786'. NLS, Acc. 12017 folio 39.

[123] NRS, GD267/33/2.   [124] NLS, MS. 1003 folio 74.

invasion of London by professional Scots can be more usefully situated as part of a reciprocal traffic of cultural exchange. Where aristocratic Scots in the Highlands were in receipt of luxury commodities and specialist services from London, so English travellers came to discover first-hand the Ossianic riches of the Scottish Highlands.

3 | Scots in Empire

'Good Fishing in Muddy Waters': Claud Alexander in Calcutta
and Catrine

Scotchmen always stick together in a strange country
Antony Maxtone, Barrackpoor, 26 February 1800[1]

In a letter dated 14 February 1772, one John Russell wrote from Edinburgh
to Claud Alexander in London proffering advice prior to the latter's
imminent departure for India. 'you will find it extremely difficult to keep
yourself out of debt for some years', his letter to the twenty year-old Scot
begins and proceeds to advocate 'frugality and industry'; the judicious
saving of money, rather than liberal spending, except with regard to
'good cloaths and a genteel outward appearance [which] has a good
effect'.[2] Dress was both highly discernible and easily detectable as a form
of social passport. For the prolonged sea passage of approximately six
months, Russell recommended Alexander learn French and take instruction in navigation 'to amuse you and stop you gaming'. Following his
projected arrival, Russell encouraged Alexander to further broaden his
linguistic competency by learning Persian 'the surest road to preferment,
as it is the language of the great'. Persian was the official language of the
English East India Company, a community of investors who by 1772, the
same year that Alexander was recruited, had become a political power
when it assumed direct rule of Bengal. John Russell's final instruction to the
young Scot was to write to his father at every opportunity, but to always be
cautious as to the content of letters as they might be read by a third party.
The safest way to send letters was by 'Company Pacquett', rather than
private individuals, who could not always be trusted and might fail to
deliver them.

Almost three years later, when writing from Calcutta to his uncle, Robert
Nielson, in Paisley, Alexander recalled the usefulness of Russell's prescient

---

[1] NRS, GD155/874/16.

[2] NRS, GD393/63. Typed transcriptions of the bulk of Claud Alexander's correspondence are
catalogued as NRS, GD393. Various correspondents are listed under GD393/63; letters to his
brother Boyd are GD393/64; the original letters to David Anderson are British Library Add. MS.
45424 folios 1–147; transcriptions of them are NRS, GD393/6. Some of the original letters
remains in private hands, although the great portion of the archive was recently donated to the
NRS (GD540). While revising this chapter for publication, it remained unavailable.

advice. His letter provides an introduction to a discussion of Scots in Empire on account of its signalling the commencement of Alexander's East Indian sojourn with his departure from the metropolis, the gateway to that empire. Russell's letter also assists in demarcating the pivotal role of correspondence in articulating and facilitating the imperial experience during the eighteenth century. Kate Teltscher has established the importance of what she designates the colonial archive – of letter writing as a form of literary production, mediating, as she sees it, between the periphery and the metropolis, exotic and domestic, and the spheres of work and home.[3] Teltscher looked at the multiple epistolary identities in the letters of George Bogle, a fellow Scot from a prominent Glasgow tobacco trading family and a friend of Alexander's in Bengal. Alexander co-erected a memorial to his friend in Calcutta's Park Street cemetery after his premature death in 1781 and was one of the guardians of Bogle's illegitimate Tibetan daughters.[4] Extracts from Bogle's letters to family members in Scotland will be cited again here; he is also cast in an unspeaking 'walk on' part in Claud Alexander's epistolary correspondence.

Drawing on Teltscher's formative research into Bogle, but simultaneously seeking to resist the reductive binaries favoured by colonial regimes (periphery/metropolis, exotic/domestic, work/home) and 'by which imperialist ideology becomes hegemonic, establishing itself as an apparently natural and inevitable authority', this chapter begins by offering an account of Claud Alexander as a colonial correspondent in Bengal in the 1770s and first half of the 1780s.[5] A close reading of his letters reveals his overlapping epistolary identities as a colonial servant and a private trader, a European in Bengal and a Scot with many personal and professional links with fellow Scots. Interwoven with the narrative of the protean nature of colonial identity is another related narrative, concerning the investment of Alexander's economic fortune made in India into land and industry back home in Scotland. In weaving together these two narrative trajectories, this chapter attempts to situate Claud Alexander the colonial correspondent within the contexts that determined the getting and spending of his fortune

---

[3] Kate Teltscher, 'Writing home and crossing cultures: George Bogle in Bengal and Tibet, 1770–1775', in Kathleen Wilson (ed.), *A New Imperial History: Culture, Identity and Modernity in Britain and the Empire, 1660–1840* (Cambridge: Cambridge University Press, 2004), p. 282.

[4] H. E. Richardson, 'George Bogle and his children', *Scottish Genealogist* 29 (1982), pp. 73–83.

[5] Tim Fulford and Peter J. Kitson, 'Romanticism and colonialism: Texts, contexts, issues', in Tim Fulford and Peter J. Kitson (eds.), *Romanticism and Colonialism: Writing and Empire, 1780–1830* (Cambridge: Cambridge University Press, 1998), pp. 1–12 at p. 12.

in both Calcutta and Scotland.[6] Key individuals and events in the social and economic histories of 1770s Scotland, like the so-called mercantile monarch of the Glasgow tobacco traders, Alexander Speirs and the Ayr Bank crash, which rarely figure within existing accounts of Scots in Empire, will here be introduced. Later, the constitution of Claud's colonial identity will be extended beyond the epistolary domain into the visual, with a discussion of two oil on canvas portraits commissioned in India and shipped back home to Scotland. According to one of the leading historians of the genre of portraiture it is 'an art form that is in many ways an index of changing concepts of selfhood and social significance', a statement that is readily applicable to Alexander's colonial portraits.[7]

In Spivak's memorable pithy phrase, 'empire messes with identity'.[8] While her statement is usually taken to mean that colonialism disrupts, distorts and deforms the identities of the colonised (in readings that are uniformly negative), the responsibility of empire can equally 'mess up' the cultural identity of a colonising nation.[9] This chapter considers a Scot from one such colonising nation whose identity was not so much disrupted by empire as consolidated. If it seeks to disrupt, or mess up the messiness of identity, it does so by revisiting Dror Wahrman's discussion of identity and culture in later eighteenth-century England. In this much-lauded and influential narrative, Wahrman looks at gender, race, class and species as what he terms the personal (as opposed to the political or national) categories of identity. He discerns in the last two decades of the century, around 1780 after the American Revolution, a shift in the form of a sharp retreat or reversal where (what he designates) an *ancien régime* of identity was rapidly transformed into a modern regime of selfhood. In the microhistory of Claud Alexander, his national identity as a Scot perdures; the personal and the political are not easily disentangled, while his other categories of identity will be seen to remain markedly porous during the entirety of his imperial service in Bengal from 1772 to 1786. Wahrman's

---

[6] John M. Mackenzie and T. M. Devine (eds.), *Scotland and the British Empire* (Oxford: Oxford University Press, 2011), p. 27, note that more research is needed 'on Scottish cultural activities, both in the colonies and in Scotland, in preserving the identities of Scottish people as a nation during the period when the Scottish state was in abeyance'. This chapter attempts to address these lacunae with its microhistory of Alexander.

[7] Marcia Pointon, *Brilliant Effects: A Cultural History of Gem Stones & Jewellery* (New Haven, CT and London: Yale University Press, 2009), p. 49.

[8] Gayatri Chakravorty Spivak, *Outside in the Teaching Machine* (New York and London: Routledge, 1993), p. 226.

[9] Ian Baucom, *Out of Place: Englishness, Empire and the Locations of Identity* (Princeton, NJ: Princeton University Press, 1999), p. 14; Simon Gikandi, *Maps of Englishness: Writing Identity in the Culture of Colonialism* (New York: Columbia University Press, 1996), p. 31.

narrative, as he concedes, 'only rarely marshals forth the self-aware, articulate reflections of contemporaries on the topics of identity, categories of identity, or self'.[10] Claud Alexander's eloquent letters by contrast are on occasion, both implicitly and explicitly, concerned with such issues.

In London in January 1772, Alexander was about to embark on a fourteen-year sojourn with the East India Company, working first as an assistant in the Account's Office at Calcutta and later, following a series of accelerated promotions in Warren Hastings's administration, as Paymaster-General for the Company in Bengal, with by 1780 some thirty writers working under him. Prior to the receipt of Russell's letter, he had already been concerned with money and dress when his father had advanced £400 for his outfit and passage. His, however, is not a 'rags to riches' social and economic apotheosis, however seductive that narrative might at first appear and appear to be endorsed by the persistent moaning in letters to his father, mother and sister of another Scot in India, the Hon. Frederick Stuart. For over a year from 1772 to 1773, Stuart wrote from Bombay, 'this inhospitable shore' and later from Calcutta, of how for a man of noble birth like himself competing against his social inferiors – 'the son of a Grocer or a ship chandler' – for preferment was inconceivable for a man 'better qualified' for Parliament than 'for the weighing of iron & the sorting of Cloths'.[11] As historians have pointed out, those eighteenth-century Scots who went to India were, like Stuart, largely derived from the upper and middling classes with transferable educational and occupational skills.[12] Many were younger sons of landed gentry looking for independent wealth, or heirs trying to resuscitate flagging family fortunes.[13] These young men possessed a network of social contacts, since considerable influence in the form of patronage was required to get a foot in the door of the East India Company whose Court of Directors were responsible for nominating individuals to posts at all levels.[14] Alexander was recruited into its hierarchical and competitive ranks through the influence of an uncle, James Alexander and his aunt Rebecca, who married

---

[10] Dror Wahrman, *The Making of the Modern Self: Identity and Culture in Eighteenth-Century England* (New Haven, CT and London: Yale University Press, 2004), p. xv.

[11] A photocopy of Stuart's letter book is contained in NLS, Acc. 9260/30.

[12] Andrew Mackillop, 'Europeans, Britons and Scots: Scottish sojourning networks and identities in Asia, *c.* 1700–1815', in Angela McCarthy, *A Global Clan: Scottish Migrant Networks and Identities since the Eighteenth Century* (London: Tauris Academic Studies, 2006), p. 19.

[13] G. J. Bryant, 'The Scots in India in the eighteenth century', *Scottish Historical Review* 64 (1985), p. 28.

[14] Bryant, 'The Scots in India in the eighteenth century', p. 30.

a Governor of Madras.[15] His petition for the post of writer was backed by the Directors Frederick Pigou and Thomas Walpole; the latter was in business with a collateral branch of the Alexander family, a Scottish banking firm.

Claud Alexander fits the typical profile of a Scottish career emigrant being an educated, young unmarried man from a large family from Renfrewshire. He was the third of five brothers Robert, Alexander (Sandy), Boyd, John and four sisters. Like many Scottish families during the eighteenth century, the brothers were dispersed throughout Britain's global empire, with in December 1775, Robert planning to relocate to the West Indies, Sandy already in Jamaica, Boyd 'shin[ing] as a patriot in Maryland' and little Jock at Lanark School. Boyd left Maryland after the outbreak of war between Britain and the American colonies and joined his brother in India by the Autumn of 1776. Sandy died two years later. In 1779, Claud recounted how the eldest of the brothers, Robert, had left Antigua having failed to get the controllership with debts of £800. After losing his father's estate and drifting around Europe, there is word of him in Dublin by 1781. Writing to his younger brother Boyd on 11 & 15 April 1779, Claud recalled one of Robert's misguided entrepreneurial schemes: a 'partnership with a druggist who he acknowledged had no money but that he was clever and would not ask him to give any attendance. In short, all he was to do was to pay the piper, and when the money was out he would have left Bob in the lurch'. Robert's debt-ridden return to Scotland demonstrates the precarious nature of colonial ventures – not all Scots were to return home flushed with the economic success of imperial profiteering like Claud Alexander. According to Alexander, their brother Robert's ruin was written all over his letters to him: 'his writing and spelling shews he has idled his time'. Like dress, letter writing was a potent sign of gentility, or its lack – Lowenthal describes it as the 'theatrical costuming of the self in various languages and styles'.[16] Elsewhere, sister Peggy gets an epistolary thrashing for her poor spelling and grammar, in an episode where Alexander fears for his own reputation as her brother, seemingly neglectful of her basic educational provision. He writes, 'Good God was your letter to fall into any persons hands in this Country [India] they would imagine that I had sprung from a Dunghill to see my sister so destitute of learning'.[17] Eve Tavor Bannet has coined the term 'letteracy' to refer to the

---

[15] George K. McGilvary, *East India Patronage and the British State: The Scottish Elite and Politics in the Eighteenth Century* (London: Tauris Academic Studies, 2008), p. 172.

[16] Cynthia Lowenthal, *Lady Mary Wortley Montagu and the Eighteenth-Century Familiar Letter* (Athens and London: University of Georgia Press, 1994), p. 21.

[17] This unpublished letter is in a private collection in Scotland.

'collection of different skills, values, and kinds of knowledge beyond mere literacy that were involved in achieving competency in the writing, reading and interpreting of letters'.[18] Claud Alexander's criticism of his brother and sister's 'illetteracy' left his own proficiency in such matters in no doubt.

Letters, suggests one historian of epistolarity, 'were a genre that allowed the borders of self to be renegotiated', shaping a self separate from a fractured family, by alleviating many of the pressures of geographical distance and temporal separation.[19] During his fourteen years in the service of the East India Company in Bengal, Claud Alexander maintained a global correspondence with members of his family in Scotland, including his widowed mother, Joanna (his father died in January 1772 after funding his son's outfit and passage), his uncle Robert Neilson, his aunt and uncle and Cuninghame cousins and his former tutor, the Librarian and Chaplain to the College of Glasgow, Professor Archibald Arthur. He had a number of correspondents in London, as well as Sandy in Jamaica. Over the course of eight years, from 1776 to 1784, he regularly wrote to his brother Boyd who had by then left the American colonies and followed him to India. Alexander the professional company servant and constant colonial correspondent should be situated at the centre of a satellite of contacts internally in India and across oceans and continents to Britain and her empire. In a letter dated 7 November 1779, Claud wrote to Boyd who was a Deputy-Paymaster to the Garrisons at Patna, although not in a much-coveted post of covenanted Company servant, describing his preoccupation with Company business: 'There is not an hour from 8 in the morning until past two [dinner was served at two] that I have not 15 or 20 hircarahs and sircars in waiting with chits and Bills on the service. Not a man in the Army understands the New Regulations, so that I must act just now as a Commissary-General, Paymaster-General, Paymaster to the Garrisons and to the 3rd Brigade.' Alexander emphasises his unrelenting colonial schedule and his tripartite professional occupations.

---

[18] Eve Tavor Bannet, *Empire of Letters: Letters, Manuals and Transatlantic Correspondence, 1688–1820* (Cambridge: Cambridge University Press, 2005), p. xvii. The following texts about epistolarity have been invaluable: Amanda Gilroy and W. M. Verhoven, *Epistolary Histories: Letters, Fiction, Culture* (Charlottesville and London: University Press of Virginia, 2000); Clare Brant, *Eighteenth-Century Letters and British Culture* (Basingstoke: Palgrave Macmillan, 2006); Sarah M. S. Pearsall, *Atlantic Families: Lives and Letters in the Later Eighteenth Century* (Oxford: Oxford University Press, 2008); Susan E. Whyman, *The Pen and the People: English Letter Writers, 1660–1800* (Oxford: Oxford University Press, 2009).

[19] Brant, *Eighteenth-century Letters*, p. 214; Pearsall, *Atlantic Families*, p. 243. Chapter 1 is entitled 'Fractured Families: The perils and possibilities of Atlantic distance', pp. 26–55.

The dispatch of letters overseas was, like their receipt, seasonal, the season being determined by favourable weather for undertaking the passage of around six months' duration to or from Britain.[20] A voyage from London to Asia usually began between December and April, with a ship leaving Calcutta for Britain every four to six weeks during the sailing season from September to April. Chaudhuri explains how the complete operational cycle of sending a letter and receiving a reply took a minimum of sixteen months to cover a round voyage from London to Asia and back and a distance of over 6,000 miles.[21] Writing to Thomas Brown in London on 26 March 1776, Alexander informed him that George Bogle had returned to Calcutta from his diplomatic mission to Bhutan and Tibet. His letter remembered the visual spectacle of Bogle's arrival 'clad in furrs, with his whiskers & Chinese cap after the manner of the Tartars' some nine months previously. He may have overestimated the speed of the printing press, but not the slowness of the post from India in his supposition 'you will have an acco^t of his [Bogle's] travels in print before you receive this letter, it is therefore needless to say anything about the Wonders he mett with'. While the transport of letters was always prolonged and sometimes precarious, the act of composition was highly repetitive. In 1782, Claud was answering more than forty letters with replies sent in triplicate and quadruplicate to Europe under the care of Captain John Gordon from Banffshire.[22] Colonial correspondence had this distinctive annual rhythm and a social etiquette not confined to the colonies – Claud advised his brother Boyd to keep business letters separate from personal correspondence and not to keep copies of the personal letters sent to him.

'[T]his inhospitable shore' is how Fredrick Stuart dubbed unhomely India in February 1772, in a characterisation all too familiar from contemporary correspondence.[23] Remarks in other letters from eighteenth-century Scots show them to be similarly unimpressed with their new domiciles; trapped in a self-imposed exile in far from congenial circumstances: 'I'd almost as soon live in Hell as in India', opined Alexander Campbell in 1748.[24] What incentives drove these young, educated Scots to temporarily relocate across the globe to India is communicated in letters

[20] H. V. Bowen, *The Business of Empire: The East India Company and Imperial Britain, 1756–1833* (Cambridge: Cambridge University Press, 2006), p. 154.

[21] K. N. Chaudhuri, *The Trading World of Asia and the English East India Company, 1660–1760* (Cambridge: Cambridge University Press, 1978), p. 74.

[22] BL, Add. MS. 45421 folio 99.   [23] NLS, Acc. 9260/30.

[24] Quoted by Bryant, 'The Scots in India in the eighteenth century', p. 27. See also P. J. Marshall, *East Indian Fortunes: The British in Bengal in the Eighteenth Century* (Oxford: Clarendon Press, 1976), p. 214.

from Stair Dalrymple to his brother, Sir Hew Dalrymple, the Baronet of North Berwickshire.[25] Stair was another well-connected Scot. Appointed as a writer to the East India Company in 1752, he wrote at the time that he expected to spend at least fifteen to twenty years in India during which 'I may be made Governour if not that, I may make a Fortune which will make me live like a Gentleman'. When he arrived at Bengal, the 'melancholy truth' hit hard. 'I have built many castles in the Air', he realised, since 'everything' was double the price that it was in Britain and though he had letters of recommendation, so did every other young Company servant.

We are unable to follow Stair Dalrymple in his pursuit of money and power – his narrative cannot precede that of Claud Alexander – since he died in India in 1757 in hostilities between the East India Company and Nawab Siraj-ud-Daula that saw the trading station at Calcutta razed to the ground. Mortality was the harsh reality of what for many was far from a sojourn in the sun; the estimated lifespan of a Briton in India was two monsoons.[26] Marshall has calculated that out of 645 civil appointments to the East India Company in Bengal between 1707 and 1775, some 368, or 57 per cent died in India.[27] Claud Alexander's earliest surviving consignment of letters written on 17 January 1774 to his brother Sandy in Jamaica, his aunt in Scotland, one William Fleming in Glasgow and a Dr Brown in London refer to his having been ill following his arrival in Calcutta with a liver disease common in Madras, one of the three main settlements of the East India Company, the others being Fort William (Calcutta) and Bombay. While his other correspondents received a short notice of the disease, its duration and Alexander's incipient recovery, Dr Brown was privy to a more detailed diagnosis (an occupational hazard):

the liver was a more serious matter [than the bile], and had it not been at a favorable time of the year I perhaps would not have got so well over it. As soon as the Doctors were convinced that my complaint was the liver, I was ordered to be

---

[25] J. G. Parker, 'Scottish enterprise in India, 1750–1914', in R. A. Cage (ed.), *The Scots Abroad: Labour, Capital, Enterprise, 1750–1914* (London: Croom Helm, 1985), p. 195, cites Stair Dalrymple as a typical Scot of good connection in Bengal. His letters to his brother are NRS, GD110/1021.

[26] A. L. Karras points out that sojourner is a sociological term, referring to migration and remigration. See *Sojourners in the Sun: Scottish Migrants and the Chesapeake, 1740–1800* (Ithaca, NY and London: Cornell University Press, 1992), p. xi and p. 4.

[27] Marshall, *East Indian Fortunes*, pp. 217–218. See also Robert Travers, 'Death and the nabob: Imperialism and commemoration in eighteenth-century India', *Past and Present* 196 (2007), pp. 83–124; Mark Harrison, '"The Tender Frame of Man": Disease, climate and racial difference in India and the West Indies, 1760–1860', *Bulletin of the History of Medicine* 70.1 (1996), pp. 68–93; Philip D. Curtin, *Death by Migration: Europe's Encounter with the Tropical World in the Nineteenth Century* (Cambridge: Cambridge University Press, 1989).

blooded, and took two tablespoonfulls of the disolution of mercury every day. This, with a good deal of physick, perfected my care in about 5 weeks, and I am now thank God pretty well.

Like Stair Dalrymple arriving in Bengal twenty years previously, Alexander found the cost of imported goods, exorbitant: 'Everything from Europe is so extravagant here that it almost ruins me', he wrote, describing Calcutta as 'a Devilish extravagant place', where the cost of living far exceeded his income from the East India Company. Calcutta was the political and mercantile centre of Bengal; according to a letter of William Young to his Uncle, General Hon. James Murray, it was 'the grand Stage of Politicks and Business in this part of the world'.[28]

In Alexander's initial consignment of letters written from India, his identity as a Scot is formative in terms of the shared social networks and relationships he forged with his countrymen. In the first instance, in the form of his landlord, a Mr Ferguson, a free merchant from Ayr and the nephew of Provost Ferguson there, who had been in India for seven or eight years and with whom Alexander was living in Calcutta. Bengal, it would seem, was saturated with Scots. 'There are now so many of my Countrymen here [Calcutta] that I am, every now and then, meeting with some old Acquaintance', George Bogle wrote to his brother Robin and sister Mary in letters of February 1771, and again a year later to Mary, 'There are lately a great many Scotchmen come out here'.[29] Statistics so beloved by some historians would seem to endorse this demographic picture. Riddy suggests that of some 249 writers appointed by the Directors of the East India Company to serve in the last decade of Warren Hastings's administration, 119 (or 47 per cent) were Scots.[30] Of 116 cadets for the officer cadres of the Company's Bengal army recruited in 1782, 56 per cent or 49 per cent were Scots (the differential of 7 per cent is not explained). In the nine years between 1776 and 1785, almost 60 per cent (about 211) of the free merchants given permission by the Company to reside in Bengal and northeastern India were Scots. Those unable to secure a coveted appointment with the East India Company

---

[28] 6 March 1778. Arthur C. Murray, *The Five Sons of 'Bare Betty'* (London: John Murray, 1936), pp. 185–186.

[29] 4 February 1771; 24 February 1771; 20 April 1772. Mitchell Library, TD 1681, bundle 25.

[30] John Riddy, 'Warren Hastings: Scotland's benefactor?', in Geoffrey Carnall and Colin Nicholson (eds.), *The Impeachment of Warren Hastings: Papers from a Bicentenary Commemoration* (Edinburgh: Edinburgh University Press, 1989), p. 42. Andrew Mackillop advocates caution and provides some alternative figures in 'Locality, nation and empire: Scots and the Empire in Asia, *c.* 1696–*c.* 1813', in Mackenzie and Devine (eds.), *Scotland and the British Empire*, esp. pp. 64–71.

could become free merchants once given a licence to trade by the Company (like Alexander's landlord, Mr. Ferguson).[31] More than half the assistant surgeons recruited were also Scots. These figures represent the many branches of the East India Company which were infiltrated by expatriate Scots: civil, military, mercantile and medical.[32] The same pattern is true throughout the colonies, not just in India, suggests Richards, although compared to the profusion of recent work on Atlantic empire, the coverage of Scots in India is still relatively modest.[33]

While the figures cited above require further explanation and exploration, such statistics, as Rothschild notes, 'provide only a partial view of the different respects in which the exterior world of the Indies extended into the interior of the British empire'.[34] Rothschild's pursuit of the inner lives of Empires via the connected micro and macrohistories of the seven brothers and four sisters that comprised the Scottish Johnstone family, provides a precedent for my own discussion of Claud Alexander whose attachment to his homeland is manifest in other ways in his earliest consignment of letters home. Beyond lodging in Calcutta with a fellow Scot from Ayrshire, Alexander asks for copies of the Glasgow papers. Instructing William Fleming to send them via India House, the East India Company's London headquarters in Leadenhall Street and assuring him they will be better utilised than as 'bum' paper. Historian Kathleen Wilson has noted the 'obsession with the moveable products of empire and commerce' in the printed pages of English provincial newspapers, from the progress of wars, to advertisements for luxury goods, seemingly overlooking that such newspapers (English and Scottish) were themselves moveable products across that empire.[35]

In Alexander's initial surge of correspondence from Calcutta, Scotland is referred to explicitly and repeatedly. Not as a country that he had recently left, but as a 'home' that he was intent on returning to in the future.[36]

---

[31] Parker, 'Scottish enterprise in India', p. 198.

[32] Bowen, *The Business of Empire*, pp. 272–273.

[33] Eric Richards, 'Scotland and the uses of the Atlantic Empire', in Bernard Bailyn and Philip D. Morgan (eds.), *Strangers within the Realm: Cultural Margins of the First British Empire* (Chapel Hill and London: University of North Carolina Press, 1991), p. 96. Works published since 1991 on Scots in India are cited in the footnotes above and below; see too the essays in T. M. Devine and Angela McCarthy (eds.), *The Scottish Experience in Asia c. 1700 to the Present: Settlers and Sojourners* (Cham, Switzerland: Palgrave Macmillan, 2017).

[34] Emma Rothschild, *The Inner Life of Empires: An Eighteenth-Century History* (Princeton, NJ: Princeton University Press, 2011), p. 186.

[35] Kathleen Wilson, 'Citizenship, empire and modernity in the English provinces, c. 1720–1790', *Eighteenth-Century Studies* 29.1 (1995), p. 72.

[36] For a discussion of the different resonances of home in an imperial context, see Catherine Hall and Sonya O. Rose, 'Introduction: Being at home with the Empire', *At Home with the Empire: Metropolitan Culture and the Imperial World* (Cambridge: Cambridge University Press, 2006),

Observe his resolve when writing to his Aunt Cuninghame to 'scrap[e] together a small pittance in the course of twenty or thirty years to enable me to spend my old days comfortably at home'. At this point at which he embarked on his career in India, 'home' was a pervasive idea than becomes all the more palpable as his career progressed and his fortune increased. Andrew Mackillop has suggested that the prospect of returning home was a crucial factor in perpetuating a sense of Scottishness in Asia.[37] Yet a letter from one such Scot who never made it home, George Bogle, suggests that many Britons in Bengal, not just Scots, were intent on returning home: 'there is not one of us that has not his Heart fixed on his native Land, and buoy ourselves up with the Hopes of returning to it – This strong desire for home that possesses all of us is however sometimes productive of evil fore now and then it tempts a man to make use of any means to get a fortune, and he hopes that by the Time he arrives in old England, all his faults will be forgotten or gilded over.'[38] The contemporary anxiety around the relentless pursuit of fortunes by whatever nefarious means will be discussed in due course.

Having looked at the content of the earliest consignment of Alexander's letters dated January 1774, rather than considering the rest in chronological order by date of composition, pertinent themes will be extrapolated that elucidate Alexander's overlapping epistolary identities in colonial Calcutta – as a Scot, a Briton, a European, a company servant, a private trader, and even an unmarried man. In a letter to his former tutor, Professor Arthur, dated 26 March 1776, Alexander announced his promotion from an assistant in the accounts office to assistant to the Commissary-General, 'whose business is to audit and check the accounts of the whole army, and the muster of the troops'. Arthur, in turn, described his former pupil's many accomplishments when he left Scotland as 'profitable commodities in any part of the world'.

In addition to his official commission business with the East India Company, Alexander traded in all manner of profitable commodities. This was a high-risk undertaking: in his own words, 'a lottery' and in those of his friend, George Bogle, 'good fishing in muddy waters'.[39] Soon after Alexander's arrival in Bengal, he recounted in a letter to his uncle, Robert Neilson how 'a young person coming to India certainly ought to be

---

pp. 1–31, esp. pp. 23–25; Ranafit Guha, 'Not at home in Empire', *Critical Inquiry* 23.3 (1997), pp. 482–493.

[37] Mackillop, 'Europeans, Britons and Scots', p. 36.
[38] Mitchell Library, TD 1681, bundle 25. 10 April 1771, to Mrs Brown.
[39] Mitchell Library, TD 1681, bundle 25. 20 December 1770, to Robin.

very cautious in entering into any trade whatever, the Black Gentry are so knowing that we ought to have an eye in our neck, I believe I know them, & will take care . . . I will be an Importer & Exporter which I am sure I have no business with'.[40] The East India Company's regulations gave their employees freedom in trading with the rest of Asia in all commodities except for their own stalwarts of calicoes and pepper.[41] Trade with Europe was only permitted if individuals could secure part of the limited space available for private goods in one of the Company's ships. Alexander had no need to worry about his counterfeit role as an importer and exporter: his position as paymaster meant that he handled large sums of public money which could be diverted for his private use.[42] As long as the amounts borrowed were repaid as and when required, such a system of private profiteering was not considered illegal although it was coming under increasing scrutiny by the British Parliament in the 1770s. Later when Boyd was in India, Claud addresses him as 'the Schemer General' for his reckless pursuit of contracts for textiles and opium, advising him not to 'meddle with them unless on commission: they are deceitful things, cloths'. On his eventual return to Scotland, Claud would conquer his reservations about 'cloths' by establishing a cotton manufacturing village at Catrine in Ayrshire – placing material culture at the nucleus of Alexander's microhistory within this cultural history of Scotland. His letter to Boyd continues, 'Don't have it said of you when you go home that you was merely a shroff, and do not, I advise, have so many irons in the fire: some of them must cool . . . I have a regard to fame. I wish to have it said that I have excelled my predecessors and that I have been of real service to my employers.' In this passage, Claud represents his occupational identity as the defining feature of his career with the East India Company. His understanding of what constitutes 'a regard to fame' was predicated first and foremost on outstanding service in company affairs – a lesson he no doubt hoped to inculcate in his younger, ambitious sibling. On another occasion, he follows his covenants with the Company to the letter, recounting his refusal to participate in politics and even to discuss them with his friend and correspondent David Anderson – a subject on which he felt they were not able to agree. Only the latter is privy to Claud's criticism of Warren Hastings via a maritime metaphor: '[he] would make a damnd good Governor if he was not so clever, that is, he has <u>too much sail</u> and <u>no ballast</u>, he deceives people by his writings and he is a great <u>schemer</u>'.[43]

[40] NRS, GD393/92/1.   [41] Marshall, *East Indian Fortunes*, pp. 18–19.
[42] Marshall, *East Indian Fortunes*, p. 201.   [43] 13 November 1784. BL, Add. MS. 45421 folio 144.

We have seen that in his first consignment of letters home in January 1774, Alexander imagined his return to Scotland with 'a small pittance' twenty or thirty years hence. One of his numerous Scottish colleagues and correspondents in India, a Captain D. H. McDowall at Kisnagur, summed up the situation many company servants found themselves in by which 'next to making money, the getting it home is the greatest point'. Alexander's career of 'real service' in Calcutta was prolonged on at least two occasions. In August 1782, he resolved to remain in India until the end of 1783 on account of his having 70,000 rupees still at Bencoolen. Complaining in a letter to Anderson: 'I make little or nothing just now. My expences are very high owing to the vast number of people I had recommended to me & my house being in so public a part of the town. I must turn over a new leaf.'[44] Then in June 1783, he was instructed to audit the military accounts as far back as 1760. In a further indication of his professional responsibility, he wrote to Anderson 'I am determined to do [this arduous task] before I go home'.[45] The correspondence that Claud dispatched and received from early 1780 onwards reveals his determination to invest his remitted money in terra firma in Scotland prior to his departure and never to have to return to India.

The articulate images the letters have already conveyed of 1770s Calcutta – the heat, diseases, exorbitant prices and commodity trading – are now complemented by a series of epistolary constructions of Scotland, specifically the counties of Ayrshire and Renfrewshire, in a period of economic instability and war with the American colonies, where it is represented as a land of inclement weather with a population predisposed to excessive drunkenness. In 1775, the former estate of Alexander's father of Newton-on-Ayr, having been on the market for almost a year, was sold to one of the leading Glasgow tobacco merchants, Alexander Speirs, for £7,700. Speirs was the son of an Edinburgh merchant family who had made a fortune as a plantation owner in Virginia.[46] He returned to Scotland in the 1740s, and by the 1770s was reputed to be 'the mercantile god of Glasgow'. As Devine has shown, in the twenty year period between 1755 and 1775, the estimated value of imports from America ranged from a third to a half of all Scottish imports; the vast proportion of which was tobacco shipped by merchant firms like that of Speirs.[47] The perceived impact of

[44] BL, Add. MS. 45421 folio 93.   [45] BL, Add. MS. 45421 folio 109.

[46] My account of Speirs is based on T. M. Devine, *The Tobacco Lords: A Study of the Tobacco Merchants of Glasgow and Their Trading Activities, c. 1740–90* (Edinburgh: Donald, 1975), p. 30.

[47] Devine, *The Tobacco Lords*, esp. pp. 107–109.

the war between Britain and her American colonies on the highly profitable trade between Glasgow and North America was said by Professor Arthur in a letter to Alexander dated 1 March 1775, to be 'the principal subject of conversation for some time past', much as it was in the letters exchanged between them.

Prior to the outbreak of war with the American colonies, in the earlier 1770s, Speirs had acquired several estates in Renfrewshire, including Elderslie for £6,000. Uncle Robert Neilson wrote to his nephew that Speirs 'is boundless in his purchases', of how he had faced no competition in the form of rival bidders. Neilson thought the sum realised was less than what the estate was reckoned to be worth when his nephew left Scotland for Bengal three years previously. This portfolio of land, a traditional marker of social distinction and source of economic security through rents 'now make[s] him a great Laird in this County [Renfrewshire]', reported Neilson. Speirs consolidated his smaller estates into a landed empire that over the course of the next decade included properties in Stirlingshire and Lanarkshire.[48] His new found social status via the acquisition of land might be contrasted with that of Claud Alexander's brother Robert who lost his father's estate and who, so Claud relates to Boyd, 'expected to be a Laird, forsooth. That was the rank he first split on; he thought he was born to a fortune and therefore had nothing to mind. And I firmly believe that he looked as anxiously for his Father's death as ever an old Jew did for the death of an old annuitant on which depended a large sum of money.'[49]

According to Devine's calculations, by 1773 the estates Speirs had bought in Renfrewshire were valued at over £48,000. That same year, aged fifty-nine, he was worth £153,000.[50] These staggering but bald figures start to become more meaningful when we consider the sums cited by Alexander – that in 1782, he expected to return to England worth £50,000, of which £36,000 had already been remitted. When in 1780, David Anderson offered his friend a part in his Dutch remittance, Alexander was unable to commit more than a modest amount on account of wanting to invest his money in terra firma – with the incipient sale of a number of estates back home in Ayrshire and in the neighbouring counties.[51] These sales had been necessitated by the failure of the Ayr Bank in June 1772,

---

[48] See Devine, *The Tobacco Lords*, p. 21, table 5, showing land purchases of Alexander Speirs, 1760–80.

[49] Here, as elsewhere in the eighteenth century, Jews were associated 'with roguery ... malignant villainy, contemptible meanness'. Michael Ragussis, 'Jews and other "Outlandish Englishmen": Ethnic performance and the invention of British identity under the Georges', *Critical Inquiry* 26.4 (2000), p. 790, quoting a review of 1814.

[50] Devine, *The Tobacco Lords*, p. 10 & p. 21.   [51] BL, Add. MS. 45421 folio 60.

which as we know from the previous chapter, had devastating financial consequences for William Adam & Company. It has been described by the economic historian, Henry Hamilton, as a major catastrophe for Scotland.[52] Commonly known as the Ayr Bank, Douglas Heron and Company was established in 1769 during a period of unprecedented economic progress in Scotland that has been traced back to the 1740s. In the two decades following the '45, the increased activity in manufacturing and investment created a demand for capital in the form of short and long-term loans. The purpose of the Ayr Bank was to keep the wheels of the economic machine turning – to facilitate the supply of finance and so expand investments in agriculture and industry. Branches were opened at Dumfries and Edinburgh; much of the capital being supplied by the counties of Ayr, Dumfries and Kirkcudbright and with landowners prominent among the Bank's shareholders. Then a bad harvest in 1771 saw prices rise and the failure of the banking house of Neale, James, Fordyce and Downe with whom the Ayr Bank had extensive dealings, led to the shutting down of other merchant and banking houses in Edinburgh. As customers rushed to cash their notes, the Bank was forced to suspend payment. Many influential Scots, both landed and mercantile, were shareholders or customers. In the wake of the Bank's collapse, they were forced to sell their estates to reach a financial settlement. Writing to George Bogle on 14 April 1774, William Scott projected a recuperative economic plan: 'were two or three Nabobs to take up their residence amongst [us], matters would soon revive, but it seems there is something in the air of that Country which repels the precious metals'.[53] What was an economic catastrophe for Scotland was to prove a lucrative opportunity for Claud Alexander in Calcutta, when he bought the estate of Sir John Whitefoord at Ballochmyle near the village of Mauchline in East Ayrshire. Whitefoord was one of the Scottish lairds broken like crockery in the aftermath of the Ayr Bank crash – to quote a simile invoked by Alexander in a letter to his cousin Cuninghame of November 1782.[54]

---

[52] Henry Hamilton, 'The failure of the Ayr Bank, 1772', *Economic History Review* 8.3 (1956), p. 412. My discussion that follows derives from Hamilton. See also Frank Brady, 'So fast to ruin: The personal element in the collapse of Douglas, Heron and Company', *Ayrshire Archaeological and Natural History Society* 11.2 (1973), pp. 27–44.

[53] Quoted by Bryant, 'The Scots in India in the eighteenth century', p. 39.

[54] 'it is owing to the extravagence of living in Scotland that so many estates are now at market. I was sorry to see in a late letter from Edinburgh to a friend of mine "that it was as common now a days for a Scotch laird to break as it was for crockery". The simile is not a very good one, however, I am affraid it is too true.'

Prior to the acquisition of Ballochmyle in 1782, Alexander had had his eye on other estates in Renfrewshire, including that at Houston, which had previously belonged to his mother's grandfather and which bordered the estate of his cousin Cuninghame at Craigends. Its acquisition would have been a sign of recouping the family's fortunes lost in previous generations and consolidating the extended family's influence in the local area. While Alexander was anxious David Anderson should also settle in Renfrewshire, his friend had specific misgivings based on climate and community pastimes: 'they say it rains there almost incessantly, and the people in the towns are greatly addicted to praying and drinking – neither of which do I excel or wish to excel in'. Alexander replied that his friend was misinformed about Renfrewshire's weather – that the rain was at Port Glasgow and Greenock: 'but near the middle of the Country we have not more rain than you have & a better society is no where – as for the Drinking I hear it is much left off but I wont drink with them I'll be as jovial as they can be for their souls & keep perfectly sober'.[55] In September 1781, the estate of Blackhouse and Craigie House and its estate in Ayr came on the market. According to the further particulars dispatched to Alexander, the coal-rich land of Craigie consisted of four to five hundred acres, with about one hundred and sixty acres around the house. He wrote to his cousin that Craigie House with its thirteen or fourteen bedrooms was too big for him, later saying the same of Ballochmyle after he had acquired it, and how he would have been happy with a house half the size. Ballochmyle was built by one of the Adelphi – Robert Adam's brother John – for the Whitefoord family in the 1760s. An elevation and ground plans for the attic storey, principal floor and ground storey published in *Vitruvius Scoticus* show a central block with five bays linked to either side by two-storey, three bay pavilions (Figure 26). It has undergone many alterations since, including plans drawn up but apparently not executed by David Hamilton in 1813 and a major remodelling in 1888 by Hew Montgomerie Wardrop (Figure 27). Having bought the Ballochmyle house and estate in Scotland for £27,000 based on valuations he did not fully comprehend, Alexander reckoned himself 'not old enough to bury myself in the country' and looked towards the metropolis and a Directorship in the East India Company. At the same time, he still hankered after his maternal grandfather's Houston estate on the River Gruffe, where he refers for the first time in a letter dated 27 September 1783 to his 'plan of making the town a place of great industry'.

---

[55] BL, Add. MS. 45421 folio 62.

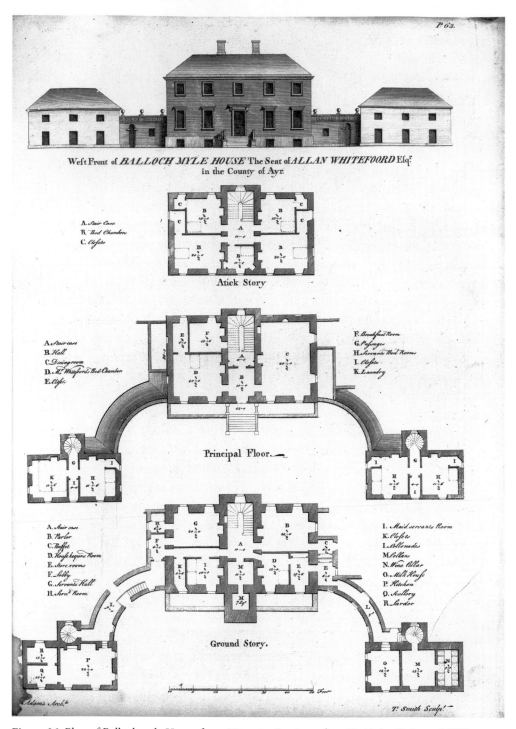

Figure 26: Plan of Ballochmyle House from *Vitruvius Scoticus*, plate 63. 48.4 × 32.3 cm © HES.

Figure 27: View of Ballochmyle House. Private collection. Photograph by John McKenzie.

Figure 28: Catrine Mill, view of entrance block from northwest. © HES.

Alexander finally returned to London in August 1786. 'I find it devilish cold', he shivered, 'I shall never be able to bear the Winter.' As he left India, so his youngest brother John arrived at Madras as a Lieutenant in the 73rd Regiment; his commission seems to have been purchased by Claud. 'I hope you have given over all thoughts of becoming one of the <u>old foggies</u> of Leadenhall Street', McDowall wrote to Alexander, 'leave them to pore over their worm-eaten records and musty cloths, and apply yourself to such pursuits as will improve the country where you have taken up your residence.' The following year, he would realise the plan devised in India for a manufacturing village in Scotland, going into partnership with David Dale in a pioneering cotton spinning factory at Catrine on the banks of the River Ayr, near Ballochmyle (Figure 28).[56] The cotton industry had begun in

---

[56] Anthony Cooke, *The Rise and Fall of the Scottish Cotton Industry, 1778–1914* (Manchester: Manchester University Press, 2010), p. 176, notes that multiple partnerships like that between Alexander and Dale were especially prevalent in Scotland.

Scotland the previous decade in 1778 at Penicuik in Midlothian.[57] That same year, the first cotton mill opened at Rothesay processing raw cotton imported from the West Indies. On 16 April 1791, Claud Alexander wrote to his friends in India, Francis (Frank) Redfearn and Miss Sarah Touchet (the habit of writing multiple letters on the same day appears to have remained with him from Calcutta), describing the mills he had built the previous summer, with the waterwheel of thirty feet diameter turning a great number of lesser wheels spinning at 5,000 spindles a time and preparing the cotton for spinning by carding and roving it. A ton of yard was apparently being spun and sent to market each week by what was the largest manufacturing establishment in Ayrshire.[58] This was one occasion when Scotland would welcome precious metals from Asia a decade after Scott wrote this to Bogle; providing a hitherto unexplored case-study in how a private fortune amassed in the East India Company service was invested in local industry back home in Scotland.[59]

Alexander's letters to his friends in India also mention building a nursery at Ballochmyle House for his two boys in a retired part of the property, which was evidently no longer too big for him now that he was married with children.[60] For his 'large family', the population of 1,000 in the new village and factory complex, he described how he was building a house for a Sunday school and raising a subscription for a church. Once a year he attended the India Club in Edinburgh. Alexander's identity, so one of his letters suggest, had become a matter of public scrutiny in Scotland: 'They say [he wrote] . . . that a cotton spinner is not the employment of a gentleman. But I am satisfied in my own mind that I am doing good. Therefore I do not mind what they say.' His identity as a gentleman or a manufacturer was much more contentious in Scotland than it previously had been in India, where social distinctions of class and profession were far less rigid.

One of Alexander's letters from India is emphatic in respect of an oppositional identity that he is not under any circumstances prepared to

---

[57] John Butt, *The Industrial Archaeology of Scotland* (Newton Abbot: David & Charles, 1967), p. 64. See also Butt's 'The Scottish cotton industry during the industrial revolution, 1780–1840', in L. M. Cullen and T. C. Smout (eds.), *Comparative Aspects of Scottish and Irish Economic and Social History, 1600–1900* (Edinburgh: Donald, 1977), pp. 116–128.

[58] John Strawhorn, 'The background to Burns. Part II: Industry and commerce in eighteenth-century Ayrshire', *Ayrshire Collections* 4 (1958), p. 188. See also Ian Donnachie and George Hewitt, *Historic New Lanark: The Dale and Owen Industrial Community since 1785* (Edinburgh: Edinburgh University Press, 1993), p. 13, p. 15, pp. 30–31.

[59] See the remarks by Bowen, *The Business of Empire*, p. 288.

[60] Claud married Helenora, the eldest daughter of Sir Maxwell Springkell in 1788.

countenance on his return to Britain: that of nabob. Here he is writing to his cousin Alexander Cuninghame in November 1782:

in the first place I mean to have nothing Indian about me except my brown face, which I cannot help. No, Sandie, I shall do as other lairds do, and shew the world that we Company's servants are not all the people that they take us to be. Plain roast and boiled is good enough for me with a little East India Madeira to wash it down. And in place of setting at the bottle, pouring punch into my guts and destroying my bowls, I would prefer walking out or retiring to the drawing room to drink tea or coffee and enjoy the agreeable conversation of the ladies. As for gambling and horse-racing, I know nothing about them, and am determined never to spend more than a thousand a year.

In this letter to his cousin, Alexander projects an identity for himself on his return to Scotland as a laird, rather than a nabob.[61] Although he does not use the latter term explicitly, it is apparent that it is nabobs who he intends to mould himself in opposition to. The term itself is an Anglicised corruption of the Persian *nawab*, a title that was used to refer to a regional governor under the Mughal Empire of the Indian subcontinent. From around 1760, it was also used disparagingly to describe former employees of the East India Company who had returned to Britain. They were castigated in print and in Parliament, in graphic satires and on stage for all manner of reportedly despicable crimes, from their lowly origins, which their economic fortunes attempted to conceal through social pretensions; to the unscrupulous, often desperate, measures by which they has amassed those private fortunes through speculation or trading in frivolous luxuries

---

[61] There is a growing literature around the nabob, of which I have consulted Philip Lawson and Jim Phillips, '"Our Execrable Banditti": Perceptions of nabobs in mid-eighteenth century Britain', *Albion* 16.3 (1984), pp. 225–241; Renu Juneja, 'The Native and the Nabob: Representations of Indian experience in eighteenth-century English literature', *Journal of Commonwealth History* 27.1 (1992), pp. 183–198; James Raven, *Judging New Wealth: Popular Publishing and Responses to Commerce in England, 1750–1800* (Oxford: Clarendon Press, 1992), esp. pp. 221–248; Stephen H. Gregg, 'Representing the nabob: India, stereotypes and eighteenth-century theatre', in Tasleem Shakur and Karen D'Souza (eds.), *Picturing South Asian Culture in English: Textual and Visual Representations* (Liverpool: Open House, 2003), pp. 19–31; Tillman W. Nechtman, 'Nabobs revisited: A cultural history of British Imperialism and the India Question in late eighteenth-century Britain', *History Compass* 4.4 (2006), pp. 645–667; Tillman W. Nechtman, 'A Jewel in the Crown? Indian wealth in domestic Britain in the late eighteenth century', *Eighteenth-Century Studies* 41.1 (2007), pp. 71–86; Christina Smylitopoulos, 'Rewritten and reused: Imaging the nabob through "Upstart iconography"', *Eighteenth-Century Life* 32 (2008), pp. 39–59; Tillman W. Nechtman, *Nabobs: Empire and Identity in Eighteenth-Century Britain* (Cambridge: Cambridge University Press, 2010); Christina Smylitopoulos, 'Portrait of a nabob: Graphic satire, portraiture and the Anglo-Indian in the late eighteenth century', *Revue d'art canadienne* 37 (2012), pp. 10–25.

Figure 29: 'The Unhappy Contrast', published by Henry Brookes, 1791. 20.3 × 36.3 cm. © The Trustees of the British Museum. All rights reserved.

like silks and calicoes.[62] A graphic satire published as late as 1791 highlights 'The Unhappy Contrast' (Figure 29) between the paltry financial rewards given to a military Captain 'serving the King' on half pay – with a double amputation of his right lower arm and leg and an empty purse – in contrast with the surfeit of riches available to Captain Lions 'serving the Crown' working for the East India Company militia and supplanting his salary through the lucrative channels of mercantile trading. The luxury products of India, including shawls, silks and muslins are baled awaiting export, with boxed crockery and a distinctive blend of tea – 'Fine Military Gun powder' – piled unthinkingly on the nabob's neglected India Company affidavit, and resulting in his custom house oath (a proverbial expression for something of little consequence) being torn. The nabob with his protruding belly stands colossus-like on his boxes poised in profile like a statue, elevated and surrounded by the fruits of India and the global commodities on which he made his fortune. In contrast with the captain's empty purse, his three smaller sacks at the end of his left hand are inscribed £40,000 and bulse, a specific type of package containing diamonds – the nabob's preferred social ornament.

---

[62] Andrew Mackillop, 'The Highlands and the returning nabob: Sir Hector Munro of Novar, 1760–1807', in Marjory Harper (ed.), *Emigrant Homecomings: The Return Movement of Emigrants, 1600–2000* (Manchester: Manchester University Press, 2005), p. 237.

In a letter to his cousin of 16 March 1784, Claud Alexander invoked a stereotypical view of nabobs as *Asiatic plunderers* to cite the subtitle of Richard Clarke's satirical and denunciatory poem (1773). Not only were they plunderers of Asia's riches, but even murderers of her inhabitants in their avaricious pursuit of wealth: 'we [writes Claud] are remarked by our sallow complexions. And then again, we have such a stare, that everyone whispers "There, there's a fellow for you, a Nabob; one of the lofty plunderers of Asia. Many is the poor native he has killed for the sake of his money"'. Their ill-gotten, imported wealth would be expended on their return to Britain in as corrupt a manner as it had been acquired – to buy land and to infiltrate their way into in the heart of the British political establishment. Many nouveau nabobs did sit in the House: in 1761 there were twelve nabobs in Parliament, with nineteen by 1768, twenty-two in 1774 and twenty-seven by 1780, so more than double in almost twenty years.[63] This co-ordinated influx of nabobs into Westminster was a cause of further consternation as it was feared that they would rule Britain as they had India – as unruly despots. Their corrupt and corrupting infiltration into the government would signal the erosion of all things British – its constitution, even its diet. The fear being, that nabobs would refashion the traditional institutions at the political heart of the empire according to the unregulated mercantile practices by which they have made their bloated fortunes at its geographical margins.

As cultural historians have observed, nabob became shorthand for a returning parvenu, with nabobish wealth a scapegoat, implicated in wider contemporary debates about Britain's transformation into an imperial power during the ongoing tussle between commercial innovation and socio-political tradition.[64] Claud Alexander's career in India began shortly after the Regulating Act of 1773 and ended two years after the East India Act of 1784, in a year that witnessed the start of the impeachment of Warren Hastings. His letter of 1782 to his cousin taps into a series of anxious topoi concerning the vilified figure of the nabob, specifically the predilections of his palate and his preferred (anti)social behaviour. Instead of the exotic flavours of Asian cuisine beloved by nabobs, Alexander's meat would be 'Plain roast and boiled', rather than curried.[65] He eschews the dissolute male-dominated pastime of drinking punch, for the polite taking

[63] These figures are cited by Lawson and Phillips, '"Our Execrable Banditti"', p. 228.

[64] Nechtman, 'A Jewel in the Crown?', p. 72.

[65] Troy Bickham, 'Eating the Empire: Intersections of food, cookery and imperialism in eighteenth-century Britain', *Past & Present* 198 (2008), p. 103, notes that curry was universally associated with India.

of tea or coffee in female company – although tea and coffee were still the products of British mercantile trade and colonial expansion.

Alexander's professed preference for polite female conversation over the homosocial pursuits of drinking and gambling introduces a crucial gender and age dimension into the social history of this career emigrant and the contours and detours of his identity in India – his status as an unmarried man. Among the European emigrant population of Calcutta, there was a conspicuous shortage of eligible women and those that were eligible were resoundingly criticised.[66] 'The Ladies here, are in general so low bred', George Bogle opined in a letter to his sister Bess dated February 1771.[67] One William Fairlie, who lived with and worked as a clerk for Mr Ferguson in Calcutta, wrote to his sister Margaret almost a decade later:

We were told that several Towns and among them Glasgow are likely to have a trade to this country. In that case I expect soon to see a colony of Scots lassies out here. We have by every fleet a great many female fortune hunters to India and I assure you they hunt not in vain and often from one or two gowns and washing lace or milliners shops they step into their chariots with settlements of £5,000 or £10,000.[68]

Fairlie's letter makes a pointed comment about the social and economic apotheoses in Calcutta of these former shop girls, while elsewhere in his correspondence he notes the 'matches' being made back home by 'Scots lassies' of his acquaintance. Outside of the busy marriage market in Kilmarnock, East Ayrshire, Alexander wrote to his aunt of his 'astonish [ment] that none of my sisters, or the Castlesemple, Duchall and Finlaystone ladies get married. Men are much wanted in Renfrewshire; here we want women.'[69] Notwithstanding the meagre quantity and impoverished quality of the eligible women in Calcutta as he approached and turned thirty, Alexander's thoughts turned to matrimony. He writes to David Anderson on 21 August 1784 of a Martha Redfearn who was 'not a beauty but a devilish good natured Buxom lass' and a Mary Lewis whose picture he possessed – 'she is really a smart looking girl if the painter does not very much flatter her'.[70] Three months later, he wrote again to Anderson of Lewis's portrait which 'not being a small miniature I could not send it up to Moorshedabad . . . it hangs in my Drawing room and is admired by all the Ladies'.[71] The commissioning or gifting of portraits was

[66] P. J. Marshall, 'The white town of Calcutta under the rule of the East India Company', *Modern Asian Studies* 43 (2000), p. 311.
[67] 24 February 1771. Mitchell Library, TD 1681, bundle 25.
[68] 12 October 1780. NRAS, 905/11.   [69] 5 January 1778. NRS, GD393/92.
[70] BL, Add. MS. 45421 folio 142.   [71] BL, Add. MS. 45421 folio 144.

often part of the social ritual of courtship. Like the women themselves, their portraits were regarded as commodities, part of a system of exchange traded between men, although how Alexander came to acquire that of the 'smart looking' Miss Lewis for the social space that was the drawing room of his house in the public part of Calcutta remains unknown.

Alexander's letters also recount a family scandal involving a female cousin, Anne Porterfield. Early signs were not portentous for this young woman; she 'writes rather like a Covent Garden Girl than a virtuous lady' complained Claud in a letter to Boyd written in April 1780. Porterfield had spent a summer with a maiden aunt of the brothers at Craigends, where she met and fell in love with a Lieutenant James Turnbull in the East India Company's militia. She married him privately and against the wishes of her parents, only to follow him to Calcutta. Once there, Claud ensured they were married again, but she later claimed to have fallen in love with him![72] The couple separated soon after and Alexander recounted to Anderson 'at that time [when the couple met] Capt McDowall tells me he was a brisk looking fellow, but now he is such a looking man that as they say in my Country I would not Ca him oot o a kale yeard.'[73] Claud's recourse to Scottish parlance and dialect makes clear Lieutenant Turnbull's unhappy state. It also demonstrates the persistence of his national identity as a Scotsman ('my Country'), and his close associations with fellow Scots in India, Anderson and McDowall, after a decade of service with the East India Company in Bengal.

By December 1784, having finally resolved to leave India, with the disgraced Mrs Turnbull who would be returned to her father, Alexander arranged the shipment of his own portrait. Writing in quadruplicate to members of his extended family that 'I have sent my picture which I request you will get out of the India House as soon as possible as it is a capital painting and I should be sorry if it got any damage; as it was painted by Zoffany a member of the Academy'. In contrast with Mary Lewis's portrait that hung in Alexander's drawing room in Calcutta and whose painter is unknown, Claud's letter refers to the artist of his portrait by name – Zoffany – and invokes his professional credentials – a Royal Academician. The German-born Zoffany arrived in India in 1783 and

---

[72] The Turnbulls' constitutes what is termed an irregular marriage, see Leah Leneman, *Promises, Promises: Marriage Litigation in Scotland, 1698–1830* (Edinburgh: NMS Enterprises Ltd, 2003), pp. 29–38.

[73] BL, Add. MS. 45421 folio 141.

spent six years there, returning to London in 1789.[74] In a letter of introduction to William Dunkin in Calcutta, dated 23 August 1783, Lord Macartney, the Governor of Madras described Zoffany as the greatest painter that ever visited India 'unless Alexander brought Appelles with him in order to draw the Porus family'. Zoffany does not conform to the conventional socio-economic profile of other expatriate British artists in India, some of whom like George Willison (who was responsible for Plate X – the portrait of James Boswell in Rome in 1765) and James Wales were Scottish and many of whom were young. By the time Zoffany arrived in India, he was fifty years old; he had been a member of the Royal Academy since 1769 and the recipient of royal patronage earlier in his career. The half decade spent in India was necessitated by a turn in his fortunes that by the time he left were revived, although his health was said to have been much impaired. Like the free merchants in India (including Alexander and William Fairlie's former landlord, Mr Ferguson from Ayr), artists needed a licence from the Company to practice. In the later eighteenth century, Calcutta was a major centre for the production of portraiture and second only to London in Britain's empire.[75]

An unusually large (227.5 × 195.5 cm) and unlined oil on canvas double portrait of Claud and Boyd Alexander was reproduced by Manners and Williamson in their pioneering 1920 monograph on Zoffany (Plate XV).[76] Painted slightly under life-size, Claud is the focal figure in a three-quarter view in the centre turning to the right. He is easily identifiable on account of his substantial girth, an issue to which his letters repeatedly refer. 'Exercise is much recommended to me [Dr Brown was informed in January 1774]. I am rather inclined to be fat and as I have been quite tyed to my desk since I came to the country, I believe that may be the occasion of my disorder.' Similarly, writing to William Fleming, of the expansive effect of his rich colonial diet given his sedentary occupation, 'I

---

[74] This paragraph is culled from Mildred Archer, *India and British Portraiture, 1770–1825* (London: Philip Wilson, 1979), pp. 130–177 and Victoria Manners and G. C. Williamson, *John Zoffany, R.A.* (London: John Lane, 1920), pp. 80–113.

[75] Marshall, 'The white town of Calcutta', p. 326.

[76] Manners and Williamson, *John Zoffany*, p. 111. In the 1980s, the portrait was reattributed by Archer to Arthur William Devis and dated *c.* 1785: *India and British Portraiture*, pp. 242–243; this was accepted by Beth Fowkes Tobin, *Picturing Imperial Britain: Colonial Subjects in Eighteenth-Century British Painting* (Durham, NC and London: Duke University Press, 1999), p. 262 n. 37. Tobin describes the servant's look as 'somewhat bored', a view contradicted by Webster's enthusiastic description: 'his face is carefully modelled as he looks out with oriental inscrutability and the accuracy of his lovingly painted dress combines a naturalness that contributes to one of Zoffany's finest portrayals of an Indian': Mary Webster, *Johan Zoffany, 1733–1810* (New Haven, CT and London: Yale University Press, 2011), p. 480. The painting was sold at Sotheby's 8 December 2010, lot 42 as a Zoffany.

now sit too close to my desk . . . we feed upon nothing in Bengal but the best'. The most arresting reference to Alexander's expanding waistline is in a letter to his cousin, Camilla Porterfield, where the perceptible impact of his rich colonial diet demarcate him as 'English': 'we will be now about the same size in point of fatness [he writes in a letter to her dated 10 October 1773] – living in good English hospitality, has filled up all the spare Chinks, & coverd the high cheekbones, so much the Characteristick of our country, in short they will persuade me I am an Englishman.'[77] A skeletal face was part of the distinctive physiognomy of Scots signifying their impoverished diet in a visual trope favoured by graphic satirists. In contrast with Alexander's protruding stomach (shared by Captain Lions in the 'Unhappy Contrast', Figure 29), the portrait shows no sign of his nabobish sallow complexion that his letters mention as much as his physical expansiveness.[78] His skin has been strategically etiolated to demarcate his European descent, in strident opposition to the black skin of his Indian servant standing on the far left of the composition, holding his master's cane and tricorn hat. The latter's face turned in a three-quarter view towards the external viewer contrasts with the interlocking gazes of the brothers and the profile, upturned look of the pointer dog in between master and servant. The right-hand figure of Boyd leans on his stouter sibling in a relaxed informal pose in which his bent left arm mirrors his bent right leg opposite. Our gaze follows that of the expectant dog towards the paper in his master's hand. Manners and Williamson suggested a date of *c.* 1768 and identified the composition as Alexander reading a letter from his wife to his brother Boyd announcing his successful acquisition of the Ballochmyle estate.[79] While the content of the letter is correct, both the suggested date and Claud's marital status are premature.

The index finger of Claud's right hand points to the letter, which is dated 22 December 1782 at Glasgow, should we be in any doubt as to its significance. Notice the cover of the letter discarded as if in a hurry on the ground between the feet of the brothers. Allowing for the six-month passage of the post to India, this would provide a date for the execution of the portrait between the middle of 1783 and its despatch from Calcutta in December 1784, the same year Boyd returned to Scotland. It is a striking image of affection,

---

[77] This letter is in a private collection in Scotland.

[78] Such whitewashing was common practice in colonial portraits, see Viccy Coltman, 'Sojourning Scots and the Portrait Miniature in Colonial India, 1770–1780', *Journal for Eighteenth-Century Studies* 40.3 (2017), pp. 421–441; Viccy Coltman, 'The aesthetics of colonialism: George Chinnery's portrait of *Gilbert Elliot, 1st Earl of Minto*, 1812', *Visual Culture in Britain* 17.2 (2016), pp. 1–26.

[79] Manners and Williamson, *John Zoffany*, p. 172.

Figure 30: Photograph showing the Zoffany portrait (Plate XV) *in situ* at Ballochmyle House. Private collection. Photograph by John McKenzie.

obedience and loyalty – fraternal, servile and canine. These various social relationships are framed, literally and metaphorically, by Alexander's parallel relationship with his employer, the East India Company. The image also attests to the centrality of the receipt and dispatch of letters in colonial India, a theme which has recurred throughout this chapter; from the introductory letter of advice composed by John Russell in February 1772 before Claud Alexander had left London, to the instructions he wrote in quadruplicate to family members regarding the shipment of the portrait by Zoffany in December 1784. The portrait commemorates the receipt of news concerning Alexander's successful acquisition of a house and estate at Ballochmyle: a purchase made possible by economic failure and fortune in a financial banking crisis in Scotland and by imperial profiteering in Bengal. It was seemingly commissioned to hang in the property whose procurement it announces by letter (Figure 30). It is 'almost as dangerous to purchase an estate as to chuse a wife, for a man in his absence', James Macpherson cautioned his cousin, Colonel Allan Macpherson who like Alexander was estate-hunting at a distance – looking at land and property in Scotland while working in the military branch in India in the early 1780s.[80]

A second, previously unpublished portrait of Alexander remains in a private collection. Here attributed to Tilly Kettle, it represents the sitter at half-length in a three-quarter view of his face looking to the left (Plate XVI). He wears a plain-coloured jacket and matching waist-coat, which may be the English broad cloth that Bogle describes the Europeans wearing in a letter of 1771.[81] Kettle is recognised as being the first British portrait painter of consequence to go to India. Mildred Archer's summary description of his style of 'polished elegance. Here are "nabobs" with resolute faces, smartly but not brashly dressed and without a trace of the domineering vulgarity that had so affronted their countrymen in England', is certainly applicable to Alexander's portrait, which must date to his early years in Calcutta, as Kettle left the Indian subcontinent in March 1776.[82] As with Zoffany, Warren Hastings was a patron of and sitter to Kettle, so Alexander followed his Governor's cultural patronage if not his politics – recall the letter to Anderson in which he described Hastings as being too clever. These two portraits of Alexander seem to bookend the duration of his career in Calcutta and to document his socio-economic elevation there, from a half-length of the assistant in the Account's Office (Plate XVI), to a full-length, slightly under life sized portrait of the Paymaster General for the East India Company in Bengal (Plate XV) with his brother and one of his servants; an incipient Laird with an estate and property in Scotland.

The shipment of the portrait by Zoffany on the Southampton vessel in December 1784 was not the first occasion that Claud had dispatched his colonial possessions in expectation of his return home to Scotland. Writing to his mother on 7 December 1777, he anticipated the delivery of china ware that he commissioned the previous year and that he intended to ship on to her in Scotland.[83] Rather than the two months that he envisaged, an invoice from Canton is dated a belated five years later. Claud's letter to his mother also describe sending twenty-five gold *mohurs* and a diamond ring of no significant value to be unevenly distributed to his sisters, Peggy, Wilhelmina and Lockhart, with two pieces of muslin for her. Like the traffic of goods between the Highlands and London explored in the previous chapter, that between Britain and India was reciprocal. For instance, in December 1779, Wilhelmina sent her brother Boyd a 'very fashionable'

---

[80] 25 August 1781. NRAS, 2614, bundle 157.   [81] 26 November 1771. ML TD1681, bundle 14.
[82] Archer, *India and British Portraiture*, pp. 67–69.   [83] NRS, GD393/92.

chain for his watch, that she explained was made in London from plaited strands of her hair (Figure 31).[84] The use of hair jewellery was widespread in Anglo-Indian material culture during the later eighteenth and early nineteenth centuries.[85] According to a sociology/anthropology of hair, it is a powerful symbol of individual and group identity, both symbolising the self and '*is* the self since it grows from and is part of the physical human body'.[86] Enclosed in rings and brooches or braided into necklaces or chains, ornamental hairwork – a non-commodifiable commodity – formed part of an interwoven material and emotional bond between family members separated by distance including the siblings Wilhelmina and Boyd Alexander.[87] Wilhelmina's letter helpfully blurs the binary and hierarchical division between centre and periphery in casting Bengal, not London, as the centre of refinement for luxury goods. She writes, 'you are all such elegant people and has with yourselves everything that is pretty' – asking that Boyd might wear the hair chain and think of his devoted sister 'who thinks of you ten times in a day'. As Lester reminds us in 'Constructing colonial discourse', 'Colony and metropole, periphery and centre, were, and are, co-constituted.'[88]

Writing to his sister, Martha, on Christmas day 1770, George Bogle characterised the structure of society at Calcutta as follows:

whenever a few persons are together and secluded from society with the rest of the world they are naturally attracted to one another ... The natives are so different in their Manners, Language & Religion, that it was impossible to have any intercourse with them but in Business ... if they had been willing I believe few Europeans would have liked to dine upon rice and fish currie and drink goats milk and water.[89]

---

[84] NRS, GD393/102/6.

[85] See Margot C. Finn, 'Colonial gifts: Family politics and the exchange of goods in British India, *c.* 1780–1820', *Modern Asian Studies* 40.1 (2006), pp. 203–231. The existing literature on hair jewellery makes (too?) much of its associations with death. See Deborah Lutz, 'The dead still among us: Victorian secular relics, hair jewelry and death culture', *Victorian Literature and Culture* 39 (2011), pp. 127–142; Christiane Holm, 'Sentimental cuts: Eighteenth-century mourning jewelry with hair', *Eighteenth-Century Studies* 38.1 (2004), pp. 139–143; Marcia Pointon, 'Wearing memory: Mourning, jewellery and the body', in Gisela Ecker (ed.), *Trauer tragen – Trauer zeigen: Inszenierungen der Geschlechter* (Munich: Fink, 1999), pp. 65–81.

[86] Anthony Synnott, 'Shame and glory: A sociology of hair', *British Journal of Sociology* 38.3 (1987), pp. 381–413.

[87] Helen Sheumaker, '"This Lock You See": Nineteenth-century hair work as the commodified self', *Fashion Theory* 1.4 (1997), pp. 421–445.

[88] Alan Lester, 'Constructing colonial discourse: Britain, South Africa and the Empire in the nineteenth century', in Alison Blunt and Cheryl McEwan (eds.), *Postcolonial Geographies* (New York and London: Continuum, 2002), p. 29.

[89] ML, TD1681, bundle 25.

Figure 31: (a) Watch chain or guard chain of woven hair with central silver mount and terminals, part of the Hunter Collection of mourning jewellery. K.2001.886.101. (b) Watch chain or guard chain of woven brown hair with central yellow metal mount and terminals, part of the Hunter Collection of mourning jewellery, K.2001.886.100. Both probably mid-nineteenth-century British-made. © National Museums Scotland.

Once again, diet is invoked as an index of identity, where the predilection for certain foodstuffs and beverages determines the social politics of inclusion or exclusion. Indeed, we might add diet to Cohn's description of the British in India who in their 'dress and demeanor ... constantly symbolized their separateness from their Indian superiors, equals, and inferiors'.[90] In his letter to Martha, Bogle isolates the 'natives' collectively, where their distinctive 'Manners, Language & Religion' are part of the cultural glue of sameness and/or difference. While he employs the reductive binary logic of colonial power inculcated by the regime he served, work by historians on British encounters with indigenous peoples from 1600 to 1850 has established the extent to which this encounter for both British colonisers and colonised indigenes involved a constant interplay between their identities and a process of mutual redefinition. Kupperman notes in her study of the cultural encounters between native Americans and the English along the Atlantic coast in the late sixteenth and early seventeenth centuries: 'As colonists and native peoples observed each other, they also thought in novel ways about their own identities.'[91] To which we might add Hall's discerning observation, 'Colonizer and colonized were themselves unstable categories with multiple forms. There were many different colonizers and many different colonized.'[92]

This chapter has focussed on Claud Alexander as a coloniser in colonial Bengal in the 1770s and early 1780s. The seasonal consignments of letters that he despatched and received ensured that he was not wholly 'secluded from society with the rest of the world', to cite Bogle's letter again. In another of his letters, Bogle uses 'European' as a synonym for 'English', which is itself used interchangeably and as if synonymous for British.[93] These national and supranational identities likewise characterise his friend and fellow Scot, Claud Alexander, although his Scottishness was always more prominent than his interpenetrating British- or European-ness. It was manifest in his professional and recreational dealings, conducted in person and on paper from colonial Calcutta, and as represented on canvas

---

[90] Bernard S. Cohn, *Colonialism and Its Forms of Knowledge: The British in India* (Princeton, NJ: Princeton University Press, 1996), p. 111.

[91] Karen Ordahl Kupperman, *Indians & English: Facing Off in Early America* (Ithaca, NY: Cornell University Press, 2000), p. 4.

[92] Catherine Hall, 'William Knibb and the constitution of the new Black subject', in Martin Daunton and Rick Halpern (eds.), *Empire and Others: British Encounters with Indigenous Peoples, 1600–1850* (London: UCL Press, 1999), p. 303.

[93] See, for instance, ML, TD1681, bundle 25, 31 August 1771: 'All the Europeans in this Country (I mean English) are very much courted by the black People'. Also, Stephen Conway, 'War and national identity in the mid-eighteenth-century British Isles', *English Historical Review* 116 (2001), pp. 872–873.

by Zoffany. Alexander was a son and a brother from Renfrewshire, Scotland; a friend and correspondent and a young unmarried man; a company servant and a private trader, who later expended his fortune made in India to become an improving laird rather than an indolent nabob, by acquiring property and overseeing industry in Ayrshire. In adopting a microhistorical approach to Scots in Empire, this chapter has sought to edit and refine what Wahrman identifies as the key categories of personal identity in eighteenth-century England to highlight alternative identity categories that were enumerated by Alexander. According to the findings of this chapter, Wahrman's 'sharp uneasy reversal' from one mutable identity regime into another fixed one around 1780, or the shift from identity as 'identicality' to identity as uniqueness, itself appears contingent and unreliable in respect of national identities – a claim he makes for the 'identity problematics' of the American War which occasioned the shift as he discerns it.[94] In the palimpsest of colonial identities in later eighteenth-century India, Alexander's national identity – his Scottishness – endured while his other personal identities proliferated in and alongside it.[95]

---

[94] Wahrman, *The Making of the Modern Self*, p. 40, p. 255.

[95] In this respect, Alexander's imperial career contrasts with that of Sir James Mackintosh in early nineteenth-century Bombay, whose 'performance of a British imperial identity relied upon distancing himself from the Scottish Highlands'. See Onni Gust, 'Remembering and forgetting the Scottish Highlands: Sir James Mackintosh and the forging of a British Imperial identity', *Journal of British Studies* 52 (2013), pp. 615–637.

PART II

Within Scotland

4 | The Prince in Scotland

'Daubed with Plaid and Crammed with Treason': The Visual
and Material Culture of Embodied Insurrection

From Copper here you Veiw my outward part
But to Oblige Engrave me on your Hart

Inscription accompanying an anonymous mezzotint
portrait of Prince Charles Edward Stuart[1]

In October 1723, the Scottish-born artist William Aikman wrote from
London, to his cousin, Sir John Clerk of Penicuik, that he was gainfully
employed painting for money – producing portraits of members of the
political and social elite for the price of eight guineas a head. The emigra
tion of Scotland's artistic professionals to the metropolitan marketplace
was previously discussed in Chapter 2, so this one opens with a double
portrait that Aikman painted that Autumn of Lord and Lady Burlington
(Figure 32). Describing in his letter to Clerk how it 'had givn extreme
contentmt, so that I now have his Lop[h] for another Padron and he is
reckon'd the best in England being himself a great virtuoso and master of
an estate of 25 thousand per annum'.[2] The following month, Aikman wrote
again to Clerk of the 'great applause' he had garnered for the portrait of the
Burlingtons, for which he had been paid the generous total sum of twenty
guineas, adding 'I have been told of it by severall of the first quality who
have seen it that they like it extremely and make no doubt when winter
comes on [the London season began in November] that I shall have my full
share of business'.[3] The double portrait in question is now in the Harris
Museum and Art Gallery in Preston, Lancashire. Of horizontal orientation
(96.5 × 116.8 cm), it depicts Lord and Lady Burlington at half-length and
was painted two years into their marriage. He on the left, the more
proximate figure to the external viewer, is dressed in a velvet cap and
jacket, holding a compass on a seemingly blank sheet of paper and looking
out beyond the edge of the canvas to the right. His wife next to him looks
directly out from the canvas holding with one hand and indicating with the
other a part-rolled scroll of similarly blank paper. Her dress, turban and
scroll are pregnant with art historical precedence in their reference to

---

[1] British Museum, 2010,7081.3670.   [2] NRS, GD18/4588.   [3] NRS, GD18/4589.

Guercino whose many painted sibyls (Phrygian, Persian, Samian, Libyan and Cimmerian) testify to the popularity of this enigmatic, classicising subject in seventeenth-century visual culture. The image by Aikman has been classed as a 'virtuoso portrait' (Aikman used the same appellation for the sitter in his letter to Clerk) and discussed with the dozen documented portraits of Burlington who was, as the painter of this double portrait of him and his wife was patently aware, a prodigious patron of the arts in the early decades of the eighteenth century.[4] The provenance of the painting is uncertain, although it appears to have been commissioned by an unnamed third party, who, so Aikman also informed Clerk, wanted 'a fine frame from Paris'. While the surviving correspondence securely establishes the identity of the artist and the sitters, the precise meaning of the iconography of the double portrait remains elusive. How are we to read the significance of the blank sheets of paper that both figures gesture to so prominently? Is the compass in Burlington's left hand an indication of his penchant for architectural pursuits, or an artefactual metaphor? The portrait seems loaded with elliptical and possibly prophetic meanings in its sibylline allusions that are no longer intelligible to us, but that would have been apparent to the sitters and the third unidentified party who commissioned the painting from Aikman in the autumn of 1723.

Since the mid-1990s, the historiography of Richard Boyle, the 3rd Earl of Burlington has undergone a dramatic shift from cultural pursuits to cultural politics; from the then prevailing view of Burlington as an enlightened patron of the arts, to the radical suggestion propagated by the historian Jane Clark that he might have been a Jacobite sympathiser.[5] In pursuit of this seditious subtext, Clark re-reads the itineraries of Burlington's grand tours in Europe from 1714 to 1715 and again in 1719, beyond his learned exposure to cosmopolitan travel and tastes, to his strategic encounter with 'forts and forces'. According to this reading, Burlington's acquaintance with Palladio's architectural villas in Vincenza and on paper via the drawings he collected, is less significant than his stays at the Jacobite hotspots of the Austrian Netherlands and Holland. Clark's interpretation of Burlington's neopalladian villa, Chiswick House in southwest London, recruits the symbols of Freemasonry and its associations with the Stuart cause to re-cast the

---

[4] John Wilton-Ely, 'Lord Burlington and the virtuoso portrait', *Architectural History* 27 (1984), pp. 376–381.

[5] Jane Clark, 'Lord Burlington is here', in Toby Barnard and Jane Clark (eds.), *Lord Burlington: Architecture, Art and Life* (London: Hambledon, 1995), pp. 251–310. See also Edward T. Corp (ed.), *Lord Burlington, the Man and His Politics: Questions of Loyalty* (Lewiston, NY: Edwin Mellen Press, 1998).

Figure 32: William Aikman, *Richard Boyle, 3rd Earl of Burlington and his wife, Lady Dorothy Savile,* 1723. 96.5 × 116.8 cm. Harris Museum and Art Gallery, Preston.

architecture, the ceiling paintings, even the colour scheme (the red of the Red Velvet Room is linked to the Royal Arch whose ritual theme is resurrection and restoration) as the various shades of Jacobitism.

The Aikman double portrait (Figure 32) is similarly marshalled into the surviving body of circumstantial evidence. Regarding Lady Burlington's Sibylline representation, Clark reminds us that it was the Cumean Sibyl who led Aeneas into the Underworld in book VI of Vergil's *Aeneid*, where the future of Rome was revealed to him. The Jacobites, as is well known, adopted the myth of Aeneas as a metaphor for their own enforced exile and projected restoration to the British throne. It was crucial to their concept of monarchical authority and the sacramental status of that authority, as Pittock explains.[6] Clark identifies the compass held by Burlington in the portrait by Aikman as

[6] M. G. H. Pittock, 'The *Aeneid* in the Age of Burlington: A Jacobite text?', in Barnard and Clark, *Lord Burlington*, pp. 232–233.

the attribute of the Master of a Masonic lodge, placed on a blank piece of paper which is inscribed in invisible or white ink. She characterises invisible ink as a metaphor for Jacobitism, pointing out that we would be naïve to expect to find direct or explicit references to Burlington's loyalty to the Stuart cause when such loyalty was a treasonable offence.

This chapter employs Aikman's double portrait (Figure 32) as a starting point, because while aspects of it may elude a definitive reading, there is a significant body of material that is recognisably and defiantly 'Jacobite' in its content and intent. In scrutinising specific objects from this hetero-geneous group of formerly clandestine material, the ensuing narrative seeks to investigate the ideology of Jacobitism through surviving examples of its visual and material culture. It privileges the objectscape about and around Prince Charles Edward Stuart, as the figurehead for the 1745 rebellion which he led on behalf of his father, James VIII and III, and which was initiated and crushed on Scottish soil. The chapter seeks to make Jacobite objects 'talkative . . . without resorting to ventriloquism or projec-tion' now that the threat of recrimination is passed; an idea that would not have been wholly implausible to a contemporary audience, since the so-called literary It-narratives of the eighteenth-century are populated with a range of speaking objects.[7] Since Jacobitism was part of a culture of dissent – in Pittock's phrase, a 'criminalised world' – so the language its objects speak is one of subterfuge: 'a protective code or quotation, not a manifestation of transparency'.[8]

Secondary literature into the cultural productions of Jacobitism exists in a plentiful supply: as Paul Monod observed in a review of twenty-five years of Jacobite studies published in 2013, 'no other political movement of the 18th century has been so thoroughly documented'.[9] Monod identified Jacobite culture as one of six major fields of existing research on Jacobite studies with plots and conspiracies; rebellions and uprisings; Irish Jacobitism; Jacobite diaspora; and the Stuart court in exile. Examples of visual and material culture are pertinent to and pervade all these fields of study. The literature to which Monod refers on Jacobite culture was

[7] Lorraine Daston (ed.), *Things that Talk: Object Lessons from Art and Science* (New York: Zone, 2004), p. 21 and p. 9.

[8] Murray Pittock, 'Treacherous objects: Towards a theory of Jacobite material culture', *Journal for Eighteenth-Century Studies* 34.1 (2011), p. 41; Murray Pittock, *Material Culture and Sedition, 1688–1760: Treacherous Objects, Secret Places* (Basingstoke: Palgrave Macmillan, 2013), p. 15.

[9] Paul K. Monod, 'A Restoration? 25 years of Jacobite studies', *Literature Compass* 10.4 (2013), p. 318. Since Monod wrote this, two single-author books were published on Jacobite material culture as follows: Neil Guthrie, *The Material Culture of the Jacobites* (Cambridge: Cambridge University Press, 2013); Pittock, *Material Culture and Sedition*.

Plate I: Pompeo Batoni, *The Honourable Colonel William Gordon*, 1766. 259 × 187.5 cm. National Trust for Scotland, Fyvie Castle.

Plate II: Pompeo Batoni, *James Bruce of Kinnaird*, 1762. 72.4 × 62.2 cm. National Galleries of Scotland. Bequeathed by Mary Hamilton Campbell, Lady Ruthven, 1885.

Plate III: Pompeo Batoni, *John, Lord Mountstuart*, 1767. 236.4 × 144.7 cm. The Bute Collection at Mount Stuart.

Plate IV: Jean Preud'homme, *Dr. John Moore, Douglas, 8th Duke of Hamilton and John Moore*, 1774. 97 × 75 cm. © National Museums Scotland.

Plate V: Gavin Hamilton, *Douglas Hamilton, 8th Duke of Hamilton and 5th Duke of Brandon, with Dr. John Moore and John Moore*, 1775–7. 183 × 144.7 cm. National Galleries of Scotland. Purchased with the help of the Heritage Lottery Fund and the Art Fund 2001.

Plate VI: View of the red drawing room at Hopetoun House, showing Nathaniel Dance's portraits of the Hope brothers to either side of the chimney-piece by Michael Rysbrack and flanking a central portrait of the Doge of Venice, attributed to Jacopo Palma, 1612–15. 247 × 172 cm (James); 247 × 173 cm (Charles). In the care of the Hopetoun House Preservation Trust at Hopetoun House. Photograph by John McKenzie.

Plate VII: Nathaniel Dance, *Charles, Lord Hope, the Hon. James Hope and William Rouet*, 1763. 96 × 70 cm. In the care of the Hopetoun House Preservation Trust at Hopetoun House. Photograph by John McKenzie.

Plate VIII: Nathaniel Dance, *James Grant, John Mytton, Thomas Robinson and Thomas Wynn, c. 1760. 98.1 ×123.8 cm.* Yale Centre for British Art, Paul Mellon Collection.

Plate IX: James Clark, *John Campbell, 4th Earl of Breadalbane*, 1782–3. 102.87 × 76.2 cm. Bridgeman Images.

Plate X: George Willison, *James Boswell*, 1765. 135.2 × 96.5 cm. National Galleries of Scotland. Bequeathed by Captain James Wood 1912.

Plate XI: Anton von Maron, *Archibald Menzies*, 1763. 76.2 × 65.5 cm. Harvard Art Museums/Busch-Reisinger Museum. Gift of Robert Rantoul Endicott, BR57.147. Photo: Imaging Department © President and Fellows of Harvard College.

Plate XII: Richard Newton, 'A Flight of Scotchmen!', 1796. 32.1 × 45.3 cm.

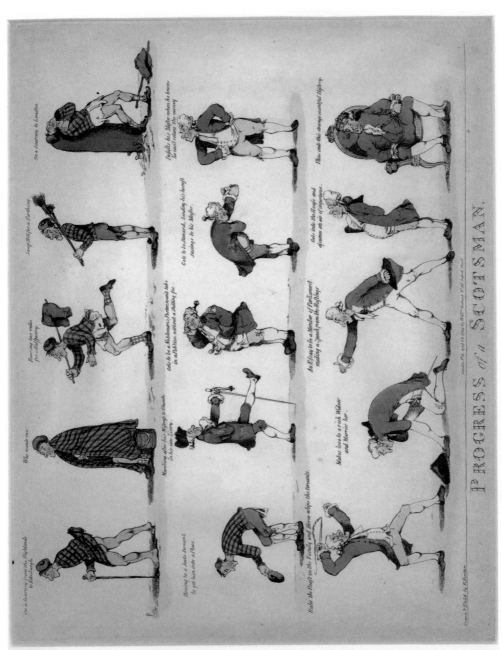

Plate XIII: Richard Newton, 'Progress of a Scotsman', 1794. 40.4 × 52.3 cm. © The Trustees of the British Museum. All rights reserved.

Plate XIV: 'Ossian's furniture': part of the suite made by the London firm of Chipchase and Lambert for Ossian's Hall in the early 1780s. Photograph by John McKenzie.

Plate XV: Johann Zoffany, *Claud and Boyd Alexander with an Indian servant*, early 1780s. 227.5 × 195.5 cm. Richard Green. Photography courtesy of the Richard Green Gallery, London.

Plate XVI: Tilly Kettle, *Claud Alexander*, mid-1770s. 74 × 61.5 cm. Private collection. Photograph by John McKenzie.

Plate XVII: Allan Ramsay, *Prince Charles Edward Stuart*, 1745. 26.8 × 21.8 cm. Scottish National Galleries.

Plate XVIII: Staffordshire salt-glazed teapot, *c.* 1775. 9 cm (height) × 10.5 cm (diameter) × 18 cm (length; spout to handle). Image courtesy of The Potteries Museum and Art Gallery, Stoke-on-Trent.

Plate XIX: Tin-glazed earthenware punch bowl, 1749, exterior (a) and interior (b). Diameter 26 cm, height 10.1 cm. © The Trustees of the British Museum. All rights reserved.

Plate XX: Snuffbox. Height 3.2 cm; diameter 6.5 cm. © National Museums Scotland.

Plate XXI: Inside of the front cover of 'Lyon in Mourning', 18.5 × 22.5 cm. © National Library of Scotland. Licensor www.scran.ac.uk.

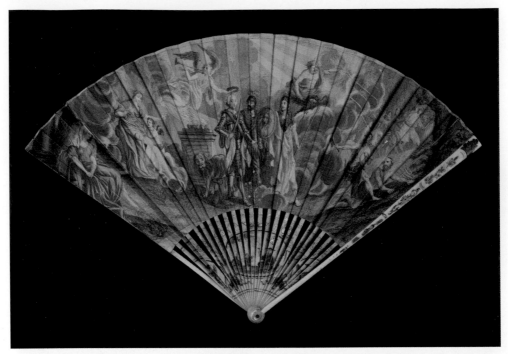

Plate XXII: Robert Strange, Jacobite fan of paper mounted on ivory, with its original case, depicting Prince Charles Edward Stuart surrounded by classical gods, c. 1745. 26.5 cm (height) × 41.5 cm (width) × 2.5 cm (depth). © National Museums Scotland.

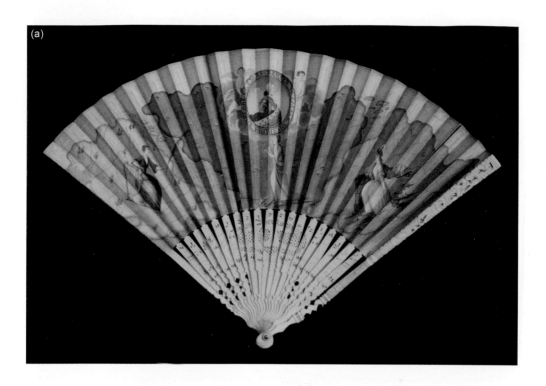

Plate XXIII: Fan. Mid-eighteenth century or slightly later. 29.5 cm (height) × 45 cm (width) × 3 cm (depth). © National Museums Scotland.

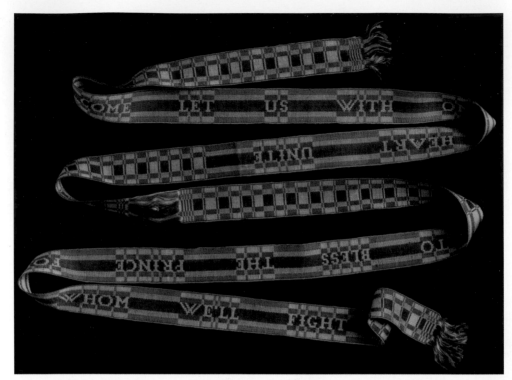

Plate XXIV: Silk garters, *c.* 1745. © National Museums Scotland.

Plate XXV: J. W. Eubank, *The Entry of George IV into Edinburgh from the Calton Hill*, 1822. 150.5 × 240 cm. City Art Centre, City of Edinburgh Museums & Galleries.

BONNIE WILLIE.

Plate XXVI: George Cruickshank, 'Bonnie Willie'. 35.3 × 25 cm. © The Trustees of the British Museum.
All rights reserved.

Plate XXVII: Henry Raeburn, *Colonel Alastair Ranaldson Macdonell of Glengarry*, exhibited RA 1812. 241.9 × 151.1 cm. National Galleries of Scotland.

Plate XXVIII: David Wilkie, *George IV*, 1829. 279.4 × 179.1 cm. Royal Collection Trust/© Her Majesty Queen Elizabeth II 2019.

Plate XXIX: Highland dress accoutrements of George IV: dirk, knife and fork, 1822. Royal Collection Trust/© Her Majesty Queen Elizabeth II 2019.

Plate XXX: David Wilkie, *The Entrance of George IV at Holyroodhouse*, 1822–30. 126 × 198.1 cm. Royal Collection Trust/© Her Majesty Queen Elizabeth II 2019.

Plate XXXI: James Northcote, *Self-portrait of the artist painting Sir Walter Scott*, 1828. 96.52 × 124.46 cm. © The Royal Albert Memorial Museum and Art Gallery, Exeter City Council.

Plate XXXII: Sir William Allan, *Sir Walter Scott, 1st Bt.*, 1831. 81.3 × 63.5 cm. © National Portrait Gallery, London.

variously produced by historians, curators and collectors, who often have their own distinct material specialisms (glass is a case in point) and sometimes conflicting intellectual agendas. This chapter will attempt to highlight these agendas and to integrate the material they deal with into a more holistic discussion of Jacobite material and visual culture as it proceeds.

One of the primary obstacles in studying Jacobitism, even before we get on to the visualisation and materialisation of its ideology in artefactual culture, is that there is no consensus among historians about the precise nature of the movement; or indeed, if it can even be designated a movement with its 'loosely-knit, faction-ridden, internationally-dispersed promoters'.[10] Whether Jacobitism was a minor dynastic squabble or a major political, military and religious threat remains open to interpretation dependent on the point of view of the historian says Daniel Szechi and if they are an optimist, a pessimist or a rejectionist.[11] In a 1999 essay 'In search of Scottish Jacobitism', Macinnes entered the semantic battleground questioning whether it should be designated a movement or a cause when in his opinion it 'cannot unequivocally be said to have demonstrated structured organization, strategic coherence or even ideological uniformity'.[12] All this may be true when we look for organisation, coherence and uniformity within the disorganised ranks of Jacobite support within Scotland, never mind beyond its borders to Europe where the court was in exile and even further, across the British Empire to the American colonies. Jacobitism was 'a global phenomenon', according to three of its leading historians, Monod, Pittock and Szechi.[13] For my immediate purposes what is significant is not so much what Jacobitism lacked, or is perceived to have lacked by its later historians. While it may not have had ideological uniformity, as Macinnes suggests, this chapter asserts that its visual and material culture articulated an ideology that gave the criminalised cause a cohesive identity, albeit one that was on occasion necessarily opaque in form and function given its seditious currency. It also had an ideological uniform: tartan or plaid, the sartorial apparel of the Scottish Highlander.

---

[10] Thomas E. Kaiser, 'The drama of Charles Edward Stuart: Jacobite propaganda and French political protest, 1745–1750', *Eighteenth-Century Studies* 30.4 (1997), p. 366.

[11] Daniel Szechi, *The Jacobites: Britain and Europe, 1688–1788* (Manchester: Manchester University Press, 1994), p. 1.

[12] Allan I. Macinnes, 'Scottish Jacobitism: In search of a movement', in T. M. Devine and J. R. Young (eds.), *Eighteenth-Century Scotland: New Perspectives* (East Linton: Tuckwell Press, 1999), p. 70.

[13] Paul Kleber Monod, Murray Pittock and Daniel Szechi (eds.), *Loyalty and Identity: Jacobites at Home and Abroad* (Basingstoke: Palgrave Macmillan, 2010), p. 7.

In a chapter on the Scottish Episcopal clergy and the ideology of Jacobitism, Lenman identifies the former as the most significant single group of men responsible for creating and transmitting an articulate Jacobite ideology, since their congregations produced the vast majority of active participants in every Jacobite rebellion over half a century, from 1689 to 1746.[14] Lenman differentiates between active Jacobites and those we might call armchair Jacobites; writing 'one of the problems facing anyone who tries to recreate the mental values of active Jacobites is that, by and large, those who wrote most did not act, and those who acted wrote little, if anything'. The study of material culture has been posited as providing access to what Lenman dubs the 'mental values' of Jacobites. It has been described as 'fundamentally a quest for mind, for belief', as 'a rather undisciplined substitute for a discipline' in which objects can make accessible aspects of culture that are not always present or detectable in other modes of cultural expression.[15] Within the existing historiography of Jacobitism some historians refer to objects as active/passive, exclusive/inclusive and to elite and popular, patrician and plebeian as organising social categories, without a coherent explanation of what constitutes either grouping.[16] Seeking to avoid such dichotomies and methodological minefields, this chapter adopts the Jacobite body as material culture, 'a thing among things' and a synthesising thematic across a disparate group of objects, the majority of which are in the collection of the National Museums Scotland.[17]

'The nature and contents of the history of the body, and the methods whereby it should be pursued, are themselves bones of contention', writes Porter in a 'skimming survey' in which he situates the history of the body as one limb of material culture study.[18] Recognising that 'Bodies are messy, fluid, and under-determined', as well as socially produced and culturally

---

[14] Bruce Lenman, 'The Scottish Episcopal clergy and the ideology of Jacobitism', in Eveline Cruickshanks, (ed.), *Ideology and Conspiracy: Aspects of Jacobitism, 1689–1759* (Edinburgh: Donald, 1982), p. 36. Thanks to Sarah Heaton for this reference.

[15] Jules D. Prown, 'Mind in matter: An introduction to material culture theory and method', *Winterthur Portfolio* 17.1 (1982), p. 15 and p. 20; Daniel Miller, *Stuff* (Cambridge: Polity Press, 2010), p. 1.

[16] Guthrie, *The Material Culture of the Jacobites*, p. 42, makes this point in relation to court/popular. See Roger Chartier, 'Culture as appropriation: Popular cultural uses in early modern France', in Stephen Laurence Kaplan (ed.), *Understanding Popular Culture: Europe from the Middle Ages to the Nineteenth Century* (Berlin and New York: Moulton, 1984), p. 229, for the minefield that is defining the boundaries between elite and popular.

[17] Bill Brown, 'Thing Theory', *Critical Enquiry* 28.1 (2001), p. 4.

[18] Roy Porter, 'History of the body', in Peter Burke (ed.), *New Perspectives on Historical Writing* (Cambridge: Polity, 1991), pp. 207–208.

constructed, so in the narrative that follows, the trope of the body is afforded multiple registers of meaning.[19] The body as what Porter elsewhere terms 'an expressive medium' is situated as a site of insurrection in which the body clothed in Jacobite colours is aligned with a politics of dress and its prostheses, in the form of material artefacts, with a politics of possession.[20] The individual human body that defined itself as Jacobite through personal items of dress and accessories is located as part of a wider Jacobite body politic through the surviving material traces of its clandestine sociable interactions, including drinking and snuff-taking. In other words, the Jacobite body is here situated as a locus of individual and collective identities within a mid-eighteenth-century culture of dissent. The represented body in visual and material culture must also be distinguished from its physical counterpart – the flesh and blood it seeks to imitate. Mirzoeff has coined the term 'bodyscapes' to delineate the complex of signs that constitute the body in representation; writing in his study of the fragmented body as being 'assembled from various modes of identity and completed with a rage of prosthetic devices, [it] has been a staple of Western modernity'.[21] This chapter encounters the represented body in its entirety and in parts thereof, as corporeal fragments typically on a vertical axis in which according to the conventions of the genre of portraiture, the face of the sitter is privileged.

By reinstating the body as a thematic and a trope, an articulated bodyscape embodying the objectscape that is Jacobite material culture, it is hoped that it will go some way to alleviating certain historians' unfortunate distrust of objects as ideological weapons or even artefacts of agency. A 'Pretender whose remembrance was preserved by emblematic drinking glasses, buckles, bracelets and garters, more than by musket and bayonet, was unlikely to prove much of a threat', writes Langford, differentiating between the efficacy of genteel artefacts versus bellicose weaponry in a polite/impolite distinction that has been pursued in a recent essay by Jennifer Novotny.[22] Describing the minor, subsidiary economy that

---

[19] Christopher E. Forth and Ivan Crozier (eds.), *Body Parts: Critical Explorations in Corporeality* (Oxford: Lexington Books, 2005), p. 12, 'Introduction: Parts, wholes and people';
Katharine Park, 'Was there a Renaissance body?', in Walter Kaiser and Michael Rocke (eds.), *The Italian Renaissance in the Twentieth Century* (Florence: Olschki, 2002), p. 322.

[20] Roy Porter, *Bodies Politic: Disease, Death and Doctors in Britain, 1650–1900* (London: Reaktion, 2001), p. 35.

[21] Nicholas Mirzoeff, *Bodyscapes: Art, Modernity and the Ideal Figure* (London and New York: Routledge, 1995), p. 3 and p. 28.

[22] Paul Langford, *A Polite and Commercial People: England, 1727–1783* (Oxford: Oxford University Press, 1989), p. 201; Jennifer Novotny, 'Polite war: Material culture of the Jacobite

resulted from the sociability and exclusiveness of Jacobite society, Szechi classes inscribed glassware, brooches with hidden symbols, tartan waistcoats and even the white roses worn on the Old Pretender's birthday as 'knick-knacks' – a pretty desultory classification.[23] Even Monod, who devotes a chapter of his book on *Jacobitism and the English People* to images of the Stuarts, undermines his own insightful reading in his limited understanding of visual culture as 'fossilising family loyalty'.[24] He casts medals, glassware, fans and other artefacts as tangible reminders of the allegiance of one's forefathers, seemingly ignoring the bodies of those family members that wore, utilised and transported these objects and for whom to do so carried latent criminal consequences. It is to be hoped that the reinsertion of a Jacobite body simultaneously embodies and emboldens the objects of material culture listlessly inventorised and underplayed by these historians – much as it embodied and emboldened the cause for eighteenth-century Jacobites.

Monod's image of Jacobitism as a fossil – another object of material culture if we include naturally occurring examples alongside their man-made counterparts – is arguably less applicable to the artefacts themselves and more useful when considering the romanticised strata of historical enquiry. It is these layers that historians are forced to wade through to encounter Jacobitism on its own terms, rather than through the rose-tinted spectacles of later nineteenth-century neo-Jacobitism. On the bicentenary of the Revolution in 1888 a major exhibition devoted to 'The Royal House of Stuart' was held in London at the New Gallery on Regent Street. Its 1,159 items spanning three hundred years from the end of the fifteenth century included fifteen locks of Prince Charles Edward Stuart's hair and eleven pieces of his plaid, from small thumb-sized fragments, to complete outfits. Viewing the portraits of the early Stuart kings in the exhibition, a review noted: 'how thickly, as one gazes at them, come the recollections of the earlier monarchs of the ill-starred race as told to children's ears by the great Wizard of the North'.[25] Another review posited 'The ecstasy of Sir Walter Scott . . . surpasses conjecture. One may say that the spirit underlying its [the exhibition's] conception has sprung a good deal from his writings. Scott made historical romance out of these rusts of the past'.[26] Chapter 6

era', in Allan I. Macinnes, Kieran German and Lesley Graham (eds.), *Living with Jacobitism: The Three Kingdoms and Beyond, 1690–1788* (London: Pickering & Chatto, 2014), pp. 153–172.

[23] Szechi, *The Jacobites*, p. 25.

[24] Paul Kleber Monod, *Jacobitism and the English People, 1688–1788* (Cambridge: Cambridge University Press, 1989), p. 7.

[25] 'The Royal House of Stuart', *All the Year Round*, 9 February 1889, p. 134.

[26] *The Leeds Mercury*, 4 April 1888.

looks at the so-called 'great Wizard of the North', Sir Walter Scott, tracing the empirical form and character of his romantic physiognomy, rather than the 'ecstasy' of ahistorical speculation. For now, these retrospective constructions of the Jacobites as an ill-starred race, codified in the historical fictions of Sir Walter Scott, are embedded in the historiography of Jacobitism. This chapter will demonstrate through analysis of a series of objects that what Cheape has termed the 'mythogenic filter of the Romantic movement' was not so much part of a later Victorian process that sought to obfuscate Jacobitism, but was rather a fundamental part of articulating its rhetoric in the eighteenth-century; a rhetoric that drew in an audacious and opportunistic fashion, on various cultural discourses.[27] It is with the House of Stuart exhibition in the later nineteenth century, that objects of Jacobite material culture emphatically became reminders of the allegiance of one's forefathers, indicative of a type of passive Jacobitism that Monod identifies as early as 1722, after the collapse of the Atterbury plot.[28]

The ensuing section considers the represented body, specifically that of Prince Charles Edward Stuart, as he came to embody the cause of a projected Stuart restoration for which he was the figurehead. According to a literal reading of the medallic propaganda produced in its wake, the Prince's birth in 1720 heralded the dawning of a new golden age. A silver medal by Ottone Hamerani (4.1 cm diameter) in the National Museums Scotland commemorates the providential arrival of the Stuart heir and celebrates his propitious future (Figure 33). On the obverse is a conjoined bust portrait of his parents, James VIII and III and Queen Clementina shown in profile to the right. The reverse is inscribed with the Prince's name and date of birth in Latin at the foot of the coin. Its pictorial tondo depicts a female figure holding a baby and standing in front of a column. The figure is identified from the accompanying inscription as a personification of Providentia Obstetrix, the midwife at the birth of the Prince whose eventual restoration to the united three kingdoms is foretold by the globe marked with maps containing abbreviations for England, Scotland and Ireland, which she points to on her right.[29] The symbiotic relationship between the obverse and reverse of this and other medals should be noted; as should the relationship between their truncated Latin mottoes and shorthand images. On the reverse of another bronze

[27] Hugh Cheape, 'The culture and material culture of Jacobitism', in Michael Lynch (ed.), *Jacobitism and the '45* (London: Historical Association Committee for Scotland and the Historical Association, 1995), p. 47.

[28] Monod, *Jacobitism and the English People,* p. 77.

[29] Noel Woolf, *The Medallic Record of the Jacobite Movement* (London: Spink & Son Ltd, 1988), no. 38.

Figure 33: Ottone Hamerani, silver medal on the birth of Prince Charles, the Young Pretender, 1720. 4.1 cm. © National Museums Scotland.

Figure 34: Otto Hamerani, bronze medal, 'Micat inter omnes', 1729. 4.1 cm. © The Trustees of the British Museum. All rights reserved.

medal designed by Ottone Hamerani and issued in 1729, Prince Charles is shown facing right dressed as a warrior in armour and flanked by a six-pointed star (Figure 34), which situates him in a similarly lustrous constellation as Alexander the Great and Jesus Christ.[30] The Latin inscription from Horace's *Odes* (I. xii) 'MICAT INTER OMNES', translates as 'he shines among all', an ardent forecast that he would restore the fortunes of his ill-fated family line. On the reverse is a profile bust of Prince Henry, his younger brother by five years, facing left, with the inscription ALTER.AB.ILLO 'The next after him'. Neither of the young Princes – the heir and the spare – is mentioned in the accompanying inscriptions on these circular, less than palm-sized objects (4.1 cm) by their incriminating name or title.[31] The oblique inscriptions on a range of Jacobite artefacts, not only medals, are frequently in Latin, the shared language of the clergy and the educated of cosmopolitan Europe, that was itself a form of encrypted code to the unlearned. Mobile and manifold, medals had formed part of the material output of a European court since the Renaissance, albeit one in flight as the Jacobites were, with a veritable production line of diminutive objects that articulated through highly formulaic images and phrases, the hyperbole of the cause.

Between the ages of fifteen and thirty-two, from 1735 to 1752, some seven different medallic portraits of Prince Charles Edward Stuart are said

---

[30] Monod, *Jacobitism and the English People, 1688–1788*, p. 80.
[31] Woolf, *The Medallic Record of the Jacobite Movement*, no. 43.

Figure 35: Jean-Baptiste Lemoyne II, *Plaster bust of Prince Charles Edward Stuart,*
c. 1748. 49.53 cm. The Drambuie Collection, Edinburgh, Scotland/Bridgeman Images.

to have been issued as the Young Pretender grew up, came of age, entered
manhood, led an uprising and survived a bloody defeat.[32] All the obverses
depict a profile bust of the perpetually youthful Prince with short curly
hair and undraped shoulders, in a formulaic representation that relates to
a portrait bust by the sculptor Jean-Baptiste Lemoyne (Figure 35). One

[32] H. Farquhar, 'Some portrait-medals struck between 1745 and 1752 for Prince Charles Edward
Stuart', *British Numismatics Journal* 17.7 (1923–4), p. 183.

Dr William King entertained the Prince during his incognito visit to London in 1750, later recording in his memoirs that 'his busts, which about this time were commonly sold in London, are more like him that any of his pictures which I have yet seen'.[33] King's subjective statement speaks to the verisimilitude of portrait busts as a genre of representation existing in three-dimensions rather than two, as in medals, oil on canvas portraits and prints after them.

On an initial view, Allan Ramsay's portrait of Prince Charles Edward Stuart, 1745 (Plate XVII) retains many of the features common to his earlier portraits on canvas and in miniature painted in Rome by leading court artists such as Antonio David, Jean-Etienne Liotard and Louis-Gabriel Blanchet. In the output of these cosmopolitan artists, the portrait of Prince Charles is often one of a pair, the other pendant showing his younger brother, Prince Henry. In Ramsay's portrait the Prince is shown at half-length in a three-quarter view, wearing court dress and powdered hair, with a cloak of velvet and ermine over his left arm, the fabric and fur of royalty. A paper trail in the form of a letter to Ramsay from Holyrood Palace dated 26 October 1745 confirms that he painted this portrait in Edinburgh during the Jacobite occupation of the Scottish capital. It is the only known image of the Prince to be painted from life when he was in Britain.[34] Both its small size (26.8 × 21.8 cm) and the sitter's dress and accessories seem to have been deliberately contrived for the purposes of reproduction in engravings to be disseminated to an English audience as the Jacobites marched south towards London. Wearing formal court dress, rather than Highland plaid, the Prince sports the blue sash and star of the English Order of the Garter, with no sign of the equivalent Scottish Order of the Thistle that often accompanied it. Charles's father, James VIII and III, had made the wearing of the two orders compatible in 1716, so the absence of the thistle suspended from a green ribbon worn around the neck is telling and is in marked contrast to the portraits produced in Rome.[35] The process of engraving enabled once static and singular objects like Ramsay's portrait of the Prince (Plate XVII), to become serial and mobile, as in Robert Strange's engraving after Ramsay's portrait into which the Prince's image is incorporated (Figure 36). While most eighteenth-century

[33] Quoted in Robin Nicholson, *Bonnie Prince Charlie and the Making of a Myth: A Study in Portraiture, 1720–1892* (Lewisburg, PA: Bucknell University Press, 2002), p. 83.

[34] Bendor Grosvenor, 'Bonnie Prince Charlie returns to Edinburgh', *Country Life* 11 May 2016, pp. 122–125.

[35] Edward T. Corp, 'Maurice Quentin de la Tour's portrait of Prince Charles Edward Stuart', *Burlington Magazine* 139 (1997), pp. 322–325.

Figure 36: Robert Strange, *Prince Charles Edward Stuart*, 1745. 25.7 × 18.4 cm. © National Library of Scotland.

engravers and print publishers are said to 'elude partisan identification', the Edinburgh printmaker Strange was a Jacobite who fought for the Prince at Culloden.[36]

---

[36] Richard Sharp, *The Engraved Record of the Jacobite Movement* (Aldershot: Scolar Press, 1996), p. 53.

In the engraving by Strange (Figure 36), Ramsay's portrait of Prince Charles (Plate XVII) is reproduced in a round architectural frame which is swathed by a fringed curtain. This mode of representation makes the Prince appear like one of the miniatures portraits of him that proliferated in a genre that 'actually turned the sitters into jewels'.[37] The pedestal of the frame below is inscribed with another Jacobite motto in Latin, 'EVERSO MISSUS SUCCURRERE SECLO', with the Prince's weapons, a sword, a targe bearing a gorgon's head and a plumed helmet to the right. An oak branch also forms part of this martial still life. Long a generic symbol of British patriotism, the oak tree became a potent sign in Jacobite iconography that referred to an earlier episode in British history when, following his defeat at the Battle of Worcester in 1651, Charles II hid in an oak tree to elude capture. His successful restoration to the throne nine years later in 1660 served as a concrete precedent for the projected restoration of the exiled Stuarts. The oak as an encoded emblem signalled support for the exiled Stuart, in much the same way that its arboreal rival, an orange tree, was appropriated by the supporters of William and Mary.[38] In the war of images, such emblematic ciphers were part of the armoury of the Jacobite protagonists and their antagonists; at least until the middle of the eighteenth century, when the cause came to be embodied by Prince Charles and his literal military opponent and metaphorical princely hero, the Duke of Cumberland.[39] Colours were similarly partisan, with the Whigs associated with orange in commemoration of William of Orange and the Glorious Revolution, and the Jacobites with white, after their emblem of a white rose.[40]

The inscription in the pedestal on the print, 'EVERSO MISSUS SUCCURRERE SECLO' derives from near the end of book I of Vergil's *Georgics* in a passage that refers to the loss of Julius Caesar and the resultant civil war. The narrator prays that the gods, including Romulus, one of the deified ancestors of the Julian family, should add Augustus to their ranks and suffer the young Prince to restore a ruined age. Such instances of

---

[37] Ann R. Jones and Peter Stallybrass, *Renaissance Clothing and the Materials of Memory* (Cambridge: Cambridge University Press, 2000), p. 41.

[38] Eirwen E. C. Nicholson, '"Revirescit": The exilic origins of the Stuart oak motif', in Edward T. Corp (ed.), *The Stuart Court in Rome: The Legacy of Exile* (Aldershot: Ashgate, 2003), p. 25; Eirwen E. C. Nicholson, 'The oak v. the orange tree: Emblematizing dynastic union and conflict, 1600–1796', in Bart Westerwell (ed.), *Anglo-Dutch relations in the Field of the Emblem* (Leiden: Brill, 1997), pp. 227–251.

[39] Danielle Thom, '"William, the Princely Youth": The Duke of Cumberland and anti-Jacobite visual strategy, 1745–46', *Visual Culture in Britain* 16 (2015), pp. 269–286.

[40] Elaine Chalus, 'Fanning the flames: Women, fashion and politics', in Tiffany Potter (ed.), *Women, Popular Culture and the Eighteenth Century* (Toronto and London: University of Toronto Press, 2012), p. 98.

historical mirroring between antiquity and modernity are a common feature of Jacobite ideology, where the Old Pretender is the counterpart to the deceased Caesar and Prince Charles Edward Stuart to Augustus. Lelièvre has pointed out that while the divine origin and future divinity of Augustus are not strictly applicable to the Stuarts, they are not wholly out of keeping with ideas of the Divine Right of Kings.[41] Such historical obfuscation is characteristic of the idiomatic language of Jacobitism.

It is this engraved portrait by Strange (Figure 36) that is thought to have occasioned the famous outburst by William Pitt the elder in the House of Commons on 26 November 1754:

he saw and heard, but this last Summer, several persons of rank and standing in the University [of Oxford], walk publicly along the streets singing, God bless Great J our King &c &c ... He also saw the Pretender's picture (or Print) in the print-shops' windows &c. This indeed he did not know at first, never having been at Rome to see the original as some others had, but he soon found it out by the civility of the Master of the shop and a latin line and a half at the bottom &c. The very streets were paved with Jacobitism, &c.[42]

Pitt's statement that he was not familiar with the portrait of the Prince provides an apt realisation of the Jacobite motto 'Cognoscunt Me Mei', which is sometimes inscribed on objects of material culture.[43] His reported invective took place some eight years *after* the Battle of Culloden, when Jacobitism is traditionally thought to have become an impotent political force.[44] On this occasion it was a still contentious issue raised by a senior statesman in the heart of the British political establishment. In addition to its communication in oral culture in the form of songs, support for the Jacobites was given a visual presence in the city of Oxford via the Young Pretender's portrait on display in print shop windows. Though London was the nexus of the print trade in Britain, arterial lines of distribution ensured prints were available throughout England, variously sold in specialist shops, distributed more informally or given away. The attitude of the authorities to such contraband items was surprisingly relaxed, with instances of print sellers being taken into custody, although with no serious repercussions.

The mutability of engraved portraiture and the transatlantic dissemination of this example by Strange (Figure 36), is demonstrated in its

[41] F. J. Lelièvre, 'Jacobite glasses and their inscriptions', *The Glass Circle* 5 (1986), p. 70.

[42] Quoted in Sharp, *The Engraved Record of the Jacobite Movement*, p. 57.

[43] For instance, on a wine glass in the British Museum (1889,1015.1) where it accompanies an engraved portrait of the Old Pretender.

[44] Guthrie, *The Material Culture of the Jacobites*, p. 143.

subsequent publication as a portrait of General James Wolfe (Figure 37). With the addition of a tricorn hat and military uniform, what had been the Young Pretender's court portrait taken from life accompanied an obituary of the British military hero which appeared in the *London Magazine* for 1759. The faux portrait was then copied in Germantown, Pennsylvania, and sold there as a portrait of Wolfe.[45] Wolfe fought for the government at the Battle of Culloden – *against* the Prince whose likeness was later to become the basis for his own feigned portrait.

The inscription from Vergil's *Georgics* that occurs on the pedestal in the engraving by Robert Strange (Figure 36) enjoyed widespread currency across Jacobite material culture; as did the Prince's portrait with some notable amendments to the rendering of his dress. It appears on a glass tumbler (9.5 cm high) now in the National Museums Scotland (Figure 38) followed by his latinised initials, and forms a lapidary border or frame for an engraved portrait in which the Prince is shown wearing tartan with the Order of the Garter and the Thistle; his ensemble topped with a bonnet and a cockade. Below the rim of the tumbler is a crown flanked on either side by the exultation LONG LIVE P C and underneath and to either side of the Prince, Scottish thistles and roses and the date 1745. While historians have identified different phases or waves of Jacobite activity, with the major risings in 1689–91, 1715–16, 1745–6 and the minor scuffles in 1708 and 1719, such precision dating is not always applicable to the production of artefacts that accompanied and/or commemorated them, even when they are dated with memorable years from the Jacobite calendar (as in Figure 38).

The study of Jacobite glasses like this one is a distinct subsection of glass history, which is a veritable academic industry with its own collectors, catalogues, circle and periodical. Of their more recent publications, G. B. Seddon's *The Jacobites and their Drinking Glasses* (Woodbridge, 1995) places emphasis on the artistic production of these contraband objects, rather than their consumption – on their use as receptacles in the promulgation of a heady concoction of homosociability and dissent. Seddon identified the handiwork of some five 'major engravers' of Jacobite glass (designated from A to E) from careful, first-hand scrutiny of 487 surviving examples in museums and private collections in Britain, including his own collection. Noting that the number of principal London glass-sellers coincided with that of major Jacobite engravers, Seddon tentatively speculated that Engraver A might be Jerome Johnson and B, Benjamin

---

[45] Alan McNairn, *Behold the Hero: General Wolfe and the Arts in the Eighteenth Century* (Liverpool: Liverpool University Press, 1997), p. 193, figure 11.10.

Figure 37: Unknown, *James Wolfe*, 1759. Plate: 17.8 × 11.8 cm. John Clarence Webster Canadiana Collection, New Brunswick Museum – Musée du Nouveau-Brunswick, www.nbm-mnb.ca. W1868.

Figure 38: Jacobite tumbler. 1745. Height 9.5 cm, mouth 7.6 cm. © National Museums Scotland.

Payne. Seddon considers all the 'treasonable artefacts' of Jacobite glass to have been made in London, with the thirty-five Amen glasses, the most famous class of Jacobite glass, listed in his study as being produced there by one engraver in the 1740s.[46] This group of glasses is so-called from a design that incorporates two to four verses of the Jacobite anthem engraved in diamond point on the exterior of the trumpet-shaped bowl (Figure 39).

---

[46] Geoffrey B. Seddon, *The Jacobites and their drinking glasses* (Woodbridge: Antique Collectors' Club, 1995), p. 174.

Figure 39: Amen glass, 1740–50. Height 18.5 cm, diameter 8.7 cm. Victoria & Albert Museum C. 117–1984.

The anthem – which may have been that which William Pitt heard sung in Oxford in the summer of 1754 – prays for a Jacobite restoration, asking God to save and 'bliss' the unnamed King 'Soon to reign over us', the 'true-born' Prince of Wales, the Church 'Against all heresie/And Whig's hipocrasie' and their subjects 'both great and small/In every station'.[47] The protagonists of Jacobitism are often identified in material culture through their monograms and on the Amen glasses, the cypher JR, a shorthand for Jacobus Rex, is engraved directly or in reverse above a small figure of eight for the Old Pretender who would have been James VIII of Scotland. Sometimes the foot of the vessel carries an additional inscription, as shall be seen in due course on an example in the collection at Dunvegan Castle on the Isle of Skye. Seddon classified the early phase of Jacobite glass manufacture as *c.* 1745–6, with the second passive and sentimentalised phase in the 1750s. In this, he subscribes to a teleological view of Jacobitism as a lost cause by the decade following the defeat at Culloden. Monod too, discussing the Amen glasses, suggests that the 'simple game' of guessing the identity of the King was designed to encourage Jacobite feelings, but not promote human intervention in the process of restoration.[48] It was, in his phrase, a prayer for divine action, rather than a rousing battle cry – the product of a *vita contemplativa* not a *vita activa*; a mobilisation of emotions rather than arms.[49]

The identification of the styles of individual engravers and the classification of Jacobite glass into chronological phases is symptomatic of one type of art historical methodology: connoisseurship, which as Pittock has recently suggested, is more descriptive than analytic, antiquarian rather than historiographic.[50] As a result of this type of empirical research, Jacobite glass has become a valuable commodity in the collector's market, with a record of £66,000 being paid by the Drambuie Liqueur Company for the Spottiswoode Amen glass (21 cm high) at Sotheby's in 1991. Predictably for the collector Seddon, it is the engravings on glass that 'have something to say about the history of the times. They reveal aspects of the true perspective of Jacobitism in the eighteenth century'.[51] This is an

---

[47] The Jacobite anthem is reproduced in B. J. R. Blench, 'Symbols and sentiment: Jacobite glass', in Robert C. Woosnam-Savage, *1745: Charles Edward Stuart and the Jacobites* (Edinburgh: HMSO, 1995), p. 89. It was adapted by Thomas Arne in 1745 and later adopted as the British national anthem.

[48] Monod, *Jacobitism and the English People*, p. 77.

[49] Lorraine Daston, *Biographies of Scientific Objects* (Chicago and London: Chicago University Press, 2000), p. 3.

[50] Pittock, *Material Culture and Sedition,* p. 13.

[51] Seddon, *The Jacobites and their Drinking Glasses*, p. 175.

overly simplistic view of what was in Britain a criminalised movement given a cohesive identity in an embodied artefactual culture. Much Jacobite glass was faked in the later nineteenth-century neo-Jacobite revival, which further obfuscates the apparent veracity of its engraved perspective.

With a dearth of archival evidence concerning the consumption of Jacobite glass in the form of bills, letters, account books and advertisements, a letter from the staunch Jacobite 5th Duke of Perth to Thomas Drummond of Logie, dated 10 April 1750, is particularly prized: 'I have sent by the beairer a Materia Glass [he writes] which is the more valuable that it came from Manchester it is adorned with the Princes figure with a suitable moto & the rose and thistle this fancie I thought would be agreable to you which I hope excuse my sending such a trifle to you'.[52] What Perth means by 'materia' is unclear; 'trifle' is similarly ambiguous; with Manchester uncertainly positioned as either the urban centre where the glass was produced or the city from where it was dispatched to the duke. What the letter does reveal is that the glass accrued a value in being designated 'from Manchester', that it contained a portrait of Prince Charles, a motto and Jacobite flora with a rose and thistle. Even more than the thistle or oak, the rose proliferates in Jacobite iconography. Often with six outer petals and six inner petals around a seeded centre, the rose sometimes represents the Old Pretender James VIII and III, with its unopened buds, signifying the Princes Charles and Henry. Seddon inventoried the recurrent symbols on Jacobite glass, including the rose, oak, star, thistle, feathers, butterflies, birds and compass. Aware of 'the need to find some hidden meaning' in these luxury vessels of transparent material if not meaning, Seddon suggests the butterfly is more than a floral theme and may represent the return of the soul in the form of Prince Charles Edward Stuart.

Jacobite portrait glasses all appear to derive from the same prototype: the Ramsay portrait of the Prince (Plate XVII) engraved by Robert Strange (Figure 36) in which he is dressed in what would become the uniform of the Young Pretender in his transformation from cosmopolitan Prince in exile to Scottish hero – wearing the Orders of the Garter and the Thistle, now over the tartan garb of the Highlanders and topped off with a bonnet and a cockade. This was to become the iconic portrait of Prince Charles Edward Stuart in terms of its widespread adoption and adaptation in material culture in Britain. It appears on the tumbler in the National Museums Scotland (Figure 38) and presumably accompanied the rose, thistle and

---

[52] NRS, GD121/1/104. Quoted and discussed by Eirwen E. C. Nicholson, 'Evidence for the authenticity of portrait-engraved Jacobite drinking-glasses', *Burlington Magazine* 138 (1996), pp. 396–397.

motto on the glass the Duke of Perth dispatched to Thomas Drummond in 1750. Robin Nicholson has exhaustively surveyed the sartorial circumstances that preceded the Disarming Act of 1746 by which tartan came to be adopted as part of the armoury of Jacobitism; viewing the Prince's portraits in tartan as part of a 'cultural dynamic' in which the leader of a military campaign was elevated into an iconic symbol as part of a contrived personality cult. Nicholson adduces from eyewitness accounts documented instances when the Prince actually wore plaid, first in Rome and later after his arrival in Scotland. His narrative, which adopts a sweeping chronological sequence from 1720 to 1892 suggests that the earliest pictorial representation of the Prince in tartan was produced not by his Scottish supporters, but his opponents, in an image by the Edinburgh engraver Richard Cooper produced prior to the Jacobite capture of the city (Figure 40).[53] This representation occurs in an image known as the 'wanted' poster since it accompanied a reward of £30,000 for the capture of the fey-looking Prince dressed in tartan breeches and plaid, a chequered ensemble topped off with a feathered bonnet – a pink parody of the Prince of Wales feathers. The Prince's apparent disinterest in his physical appearance – note his unbuttoned jacket and the chaotic fashion in which his plaid cloak spools over and under his belt shifting the sporran to one side – is apparently mirrored in his lack of conviction to his own cause as his father's printed manifesto falls from his right hand. In his left hand he fingers the hilt of his broadsword in a contorted action that is less fearsome Highland warrior as foppish plaided puppet.

The surface iconography of these objects is one aspect of the meaning and message of the ideology of Jacobite material culture, in which the body of its figurehead Prince Charles Edward Stuart is represented in its entirety, often enveloped in tartan plaid, or as corporeal fragments on a vertical axis that privilege his portrait. Another essential material dimension of Jacobite material culture, with which the Prince's bodyscape often intersects, is the form and function of the objects themselves. In other words, their enduring and sometimes obdurate object-ness in two- and three-dimensions – as material prostheses that are appended to the body of the Jacobite supporter in a corporeal culture of display and concealment. In the case of glass, the Jacobite body that is projected as having used these types of receptacles is gendered as masculine and is a collective, rather than individual one, in its subversive sociability. For the historian of material culture there is a significant disparity between the mass of surviving material examples

---

[53] Nicholson, *Bonnie Prince Charlie and the Making of a Myth*, p. 65.

Figure 40: Richard Cooper, *Prince Charles Edward Stuart* ('Wanted Poster'), 1745. 33 × 19.1 cm. National Galleries of Scotland.

(Seddon accumulates nearly 500 glasses in his study) and the lack of information regarding their use, which due to the risk of prosecution should be understood within a clandestine culture of dissent. Typically associated with lost or secret drinking societies, Jacobite glasses resist wider comprehensive analysis for the same reasons that made them successful in the first place: as a culture and a means of communication which were designed to avoid prosecution for the very thing that later historians seek to identify.[54] The material record is less covert and the profusion of glasses with their accompanying engravings, both pictorial and textual, seem to imply a dynamic ritual interaction between Jacobites and their possessions, when supporters of the Stuart restoration would drink the King's health, passing their glasses over water to signify his exile and kissing the star often engraved on the exterior of the bowl. These Jacobite toasts were 'gestures of defiance' as part of a repertoire of political expression but they need to be uncoupled from the oppositional convivial activities of the Lancashire plebeian radicals in the early nineteenth century for whom drinking was a form of popular politics with which the Jacobite toasts are often associated.[55]

On one side of a diminutive (9.5 cm high) Staffordshire salt-glazed teapot is a representation painted in overglazed enamels of a Jacobite shown in profile kneeling to the left on a platform from which is hung a banner adorned with the word KING (Plate XVIIIa). Wearing the Order of the Garter, tartan breeches and sporting a portly belly that mirrors the squat shape of the pot, the figure is shown drinking wine from a glass vessel held in his right hand; a large corked decanter is positioned in front of him. In his left hand he holds a tricorn hat. On the right behind his back and below a rose with six petals, a second figure with his arms outstretched emerges from behind the platform – he may be identified as the Old Pretender, James VIII and III. On the reverse side of the teapot (Plate XVIIIb) is another kneeling figure holding a glass of wine upraised in his right hand. The platform on which he is kneeling is inscribed JOB – an acronym used in toasting three prominent Jacobites: **J**ames VIII and III, the Tory peer the Duke of **O**rmond, who was accused of supporting the 1715 uprising and the pro-Jacobite Viscount **B**olingbroke, one of Queen Anne's principal ministers.[56] Dated to c.1750, the teapot appears to retrospectively reference an earlier period of eighteenth-century Jacobitism;

---

[54] Pittock, *Material Culture and Sedition*, p. 94.

[55] See James Epstein, 'Radical dining, toasting and symbolic expression in early nineteenth-century Lancashire', *Albion* 20.2 (1988), pp. 271–291.

[56] Seddon, *The Jacobites and their Drinking Glasses*, p. 60.

offering a highly atypical association of James, the Old Pretender, rather than his son, with the Jacobite politicisation of Highland plaid.

The visual and textual embellishment on the spherical sides of this teapot offer a representation of the restoration of the King that the Jacobite toasts symbolically enacted through an intoxicating concoction of rhetoric, gesture and alcohol. Karen Harvey has drawn attention to the strong associations between the type of beverage and the material of the vessel in which it was served; finding that the less refined and more traditional materials of glass, stoneware and the rougher delftwares were used for the alcoholic drinks of ale, wine and spirits and the finer ceramics, for hot drinks like tea.[57] The decoration of the salt-glazed teapot juxtaposes its own liquid contents (tea in a ceramic pot) with that which the Jacobites on its exterior are shown consuming (wine in a glass). In what has been described by the anthropologist Arjun Appadurai as a 'methodological fetishisation' of things we sometimes forget that they were once containers holding all manner of consumables with which to re-enervate the eighteenth-century body, Jacobite or otherwise.[58]

The symbiotic relationship between Jacobite objects as vessels and their decoration in the form of images and mottoes with a body invigorated by those (now empty) contents is manifest on a delftware punch bowl dated 1749 on the base, probably from Liverpool and now in the British Museum (Plate XIX). The dimensions of the bowl (26 cm diameter and 10.1 cm high) imply its communal use as a vessel for punch, a liquid that combined spirit, fruit, sugar, spices and water and which could be made from many different recipes.[59] Painted on the exterior of the bowl are prosaic peonies and other flowers loosely based on the motifs found on Chinese porcelain which echo the foreign ingredients of punch (Plate XIXa). The interior of the bowl (Plate XIXb), in contrast, is embellished in blue paint with a full-length portrait of Prince Charles Edward Stuart dressed in tartan holding an unsheathed sword in his right hand and gesturing across his body with his left hand towards a suspended crown; a targe lies on one side of his feet, crossed pistols on the other. The Prince's poised stance – indicating the instrumentality of his drawn sword in gaining access to the crown – contrasts with that of the ineffectual leader in the 'wanted poster' by

---

[57] Karen Harvey, 'Ritual encounters: Punch parties and masculinity in the eighteenth century', *Past & Present* 214 (2012), p. 176.

[58] Arjun Appadurai, 'Introduction: Commodities and the politics of value', *The Social Life of Things: Commodities in cultural perspective* (Cambridge: Cambridge University Press, 1986), pp. 3–63 at p. 5.

[59] Karen Harvey, 'Barbarity in a teacup? Punch, domesticity and gender in the eighteenth century', *Journal of Design History* 21.3 (2008), pp. 205–221.

Cooper (Figure 40), in a resolution that is echoed in the accompanying text.[60] Opening above him like parted curtains are swags inscribed in Latin and English, 'AUDENTIOR IBO' and 'ALL OR NONE'. The Latin motto is taken from book VI of the *Aeneid* where Aeneas goes to consult the Sibyl who once in a trance-like state, predicts the fighting to come, urging him not to give in to affliction, 'but to go forth against it with greater daring'; the imperative *ito* becoming *ibo* in the future tense. Once more, Vergil's *Aeneid* is the preferred textbook for Jacobitism, with Prince Charles repeatedly cast as an eighteenth-century Aeneas. The translation as 'I will go more boldly' may be read as the portrait of the Prince 'speaking' these words. The motto could additionally refer to the user of the punch bowl, who having fortified himself with its alcoholic liquid contents, adopts its message and is ready to go more boldly with the Prince – 'all or none'. As the bowl emptied of its coloured liquid contents, the tartan-clad body of the emboldened Prince would be revealed to the community of drinkers alternatively fortified by alcohol.

Like the delftware punch bowl in the British Museum, the snuffbox was recruited into the material arsenal of Jacobite prostheses as part of a corporeal culture of seditious sociability. So 'far as Britain was concerned, [the eighteenth century was] a century of snuff taking', recounts McCausland and one where 'the snuff box took its place as an essential part of the equipment of every man of social standing'.[61] Actually, snuffing was a pastime common to both genders for its conspicuous fashionability – a ritual that is implicitly gendered as female in its equivalence to taking tea or manipulating a fan. We have already encountered a Staffordshire teapot; examples of Jacobite fans are imminent. An advertisement in the *Spectator* for 8 August 1711 offered instruction in London in the exercise of the snuffbox whereby various recipients would be initiated into the 'rules for offering snuff to a stranger, a friend, or a mistress, according to the degree of familiarity or distance, with an explanation of the careless, the scornful, the politic, and the surly pinch, and the gestures proper to each of them'.[62] Though satirising the affected social rituals in its delineation of four fashionable typologies of snuff taking, the 'politic' pinch would have been especially apt for sharing snuff from a circular box which is twice as wide as

---

[60] For the engraved source, see 'The Pretender' *Prints, Drawings and Watercolors from the Anne S. K. Brown Military Collection*. Brown Digital Repository. Brown University Library. https://repository.library.brown.edu/studio/item/bdr:227242/

[61] Hugh McCausland, *Snuff and Snuff-boxes* (London: Batchworth, 1951), p. 17 and p. 22.

[62] Cited in J. T. McCullen, 'Tobacco: A recurrent theme in eighteenth-century literature', *The Bulletin of the Rocky Mountain Modern Language Association* 22.2 (1968), p. 32.

it is deep (6.5 diameter × 3.2 cm high) now in the National Museums Scotland (Plate XX). On opening the lid, it seems innocuous enough as a receptacle for storing an expensive commodity; one which was carried close to the body to remove 'the chill . . . [from the tobacco and] to bring out its bouquet'.[63] Careful handling demonstrates that concealed within the outer lid is a second interior 'lid' on which there is a miniature enameled portrait of Prince Charles Edward Stuart after Strange's engraving (Figure 36) of the portrait by Ramsay (Plate XVII) shown dressed in tartan wearing the Orders of the Garter and the Thistle, a bonnet and cockade. At least two boxes have miniature portraits of the Prince contained inside their inner lids, yet this example takes the subterfuge even further by concealing the portrait within the interior architecture of the box.[64] The second lid would enable the possessor of the box to choose to hide or disclose the Prince's portrait to a fellow snuff taker in a proximate encounter that was not only on a social spectrum 'according to the degree of familiarity or distance' (to quote the *Spectator*), but also a politically partisan one in their Jacobitism.

Another Jacobite snuff box survives only as an ekphrasis – a way of conjuring up images through verbal description – in an account of it as published in the *Lyon in Mourning*, the compendium of Jacobite material assembled after the '45 uprising by the Episcopalian minister, the Revd Robert Forbes, later Bishop of Ross and Caithness. Forbes conforms to Lenman's description of an armchair Jacobite who wrote extensively about the cause but did not act during it due to his imprisonment in Stirling Castle. His creation of this exceptional archive, from his release in May 1746 up to his death in 1775, constituted what he calls 'a strict and impartial examination' of recent events 'that truly may be termed PRODIGIES'.[65] Forbes collected and meticulously copied into ten octavo volumes of over two hundred pages first-hand accounts of *Speeches, Letters, Journals, etc, Relative to the Affairs, but more Particularly the Dangers & Distresses, of* . . . to quote the subtitle in its entirety, including the concealed name of Prince Charles Edward Stuart (Plate XXI). As part of the accumulation of primary sources both prodigious in extent and prodigious in substance, Forbes acquired material fragments of the dress worn

---

[63] G. Bernard Hughes, *English Snuff-boxes* (London: MacGibbon and Kee, 1971), p. 20.

[64] David Forsyth (ed.), *Bonnie Prince Charlie and the Jacobites* (Edinburgh: National Museums Scotland, 2017), catalogue nos. 162 and 165.

[65] See Forbes's letter to John Macpherson. Robert Forbes, *The Lyon in Mourning*, Henry Paton (ed.) (Edinburgh, 1895–6), II, p. 44. The original manuscript volumes are NLS, Adv. MS. 32.6.16–25.

by the Prince and the accessories used by him during his escape after the Jacobite defeat at Culloden. These are attached with wax into the inside covers of volumes three to five with an extended explanatory 'label' by Forbes as to their provenance, which is further expanded upon in the text they accompany. Thus the inside front cover of volume 3 (1747) contains four fragments of textiles (Plate XXI): including a piece of the Prince's garter, which Forbes describes elsewhere in his text as 'French, of blue velvet, covered upon one side with white silk, and fastened with buckles', a swatch of the printed gown – 'stamped Linen w a purple sprig' – worn by the Prince for four or five days when he was disguised as Flora Macdonald's Irish maidservant, Betty Burke and a sample of Burke's apron string, which Flora Macdonald gave to Forbes.[66] A piece of red velvet from the Prince's sword hilt was added by Robert Chambers who later purchased the volumes and published about a third of the letters in his *Jacobite Memoirs of the Rebellion of 1745* (Edinburgh, 1834). On the inside back cover of volume 3 are pieces from the outside and inside of the scarlet waistcoat which Macdonald of Kingsburgh gave to the Prince as part of 'a sute of Highland Cloaths', but which he later discarded on the grounds that it was too fine for his disguise as a servant.[67] The back cover of volume 4 (1748) once held two splinters of wood (one is lost) from the eight-oared boat by which the Prince fled from Boradale to Benbecula and at the rear of volume 5 (also 1748), are 'pieces of one of the lugs of those identical Brogs' which the Prince wore when disguised as Betty Burke.[68] The conscientious salvage and precise identification of these scraps of textile, wood and leather represent the transformation of objects explicitly associated with the Prince in Scotland – his possessions, his dress and disguise – from quotidian bits and pieces into precious non-corporeal relics.[69] 'The relic functions synecdochically [explains Sanger]: it stands for the whole (body) from which it derives.'[70]

Though Forbes's editor uses the term 'relics' for the material shards associated with the Prince in his explanatory preface of 1895, it is essential to recognise the extent to which a corporeal relic is ontologically different

---

[66] Forbes, *The Lyon in Mourning*, I, p. 112; NLS, Adv. MS. 32.6.16, 152.

[67] NLS, Adv. MS. 32.6.16, 143.   [68] Forbes, *The Lyon in Mourning*, II, p. 43.

[69] George Dalgleish, 'Objects as icons: Myths and realities of Jacobite relics', in J. M. Fladmark (ed.), *Heritage and Museums: Shaping National Identity* (Shaftesbury: Donhead, 2000), pp. 91–102.

[70] Alice E. Sanger, 'Sensuality, sacred remains and devotion in Baroque Rome', in Alice E. Sanger and Siv Tove Kulbrandstad Walker (eds.), *Sense and the Senses in Early Modern Art and Cultural Practice* (Farnham: Ashgate, 2012), p. 201.

from a representation of that body, or an object appended to the body.[71] Walsham provides the most succinct account to date of the historiography and methodology of relics.[72] Identifying the 'slippery, elastic, and expansive nature of this concept and category', she relates the renewal of academic interest notably by medievalists in the last thirty years to two closely related frames of reference both of which comprise the conceptual architecture of this chapter: the study of material culture and the history of the human body. According to a brief history of secular relics in Britain, these are conjoined when death turns people into things. As part of the afterlife of lives, the subject becomes object. 'The relic makes apparent the terrible poignancy of the body becoming object [Lutz recounts]: it can reenact that moment, again and again.'[73] A hierarchical sequence exists with a first-class relic being loosely defined as the venerated remains of a venerable person.[74] This is followed by second-class relics, the non-corporeal items the venerated person once owned or physically came into contact with. In the Middle Ages, they were called contact relics as they referred to the physical traces that were not the venerated body or parts thereof, but which had once touched it.[75] The material relics that Forbes included in the *Lyon in Mourning* were all non-corporeal items in the form of fragments of dress or accessories that were once possessed or handled by Prince Charles Edward Stuart. We might refer to their inclusion in the *Lyon* as part of the afterlives of these objects. By 1888 and the Royal House of Stuart exhibition in London, these types of relics were further fetishised in their collection, enumeration, display and cataloguing.

Forbes's volumes house other objects of material culture within the black-edged pages of the body of the text. Of these, an octagonal snuffbox described as being in the possession of Donald MacLeod of Gualtergill on Loch Dunvegan in Skye, is notable in its detail.[76] Forbes recounts how the snuffbox was given to Macleod by his friend, John Walkingshaw of London and characterises it as another type of material object already encountered – as 'an excellent medal' – since the history of his involvement with

[71] Forbes, *The Lyon in Mourning*, I, p. xviii.

[72] Alexandra Walsham, 'Introduction', *Relics and Remains* (Oxford: Oxford University Press, 2010), pp. 9–36.

[73] Deborah Lutz, 'The dead still among us: Victorian secular relics, hair jewelry and death culture', *Victorian Literature and Culture* 39 (2011), p. 135.

[74] Lindsay Jones (ed.), *Encyclopedia of Religion* (Detroit and London: Thomson/Gale, 2005), 2nd edition, volume 11, p. 7686.

[75] Caroline Bynum, 'Why all the fuss about the body? A medievalist's perspective', *Critical Inquiry* 22.1 (1995), p. 11.

[76] Forbes, *The Lyon in Mourning*, I, p. 183.

Prince Charles Edward Stuart was engraved in a series of images on the box accompanied by Latin mottoes. On the lid was a representation of a boat with Donald at the helm transporting the Prince and Flora Macdonald as they fled from Skye to Benbecula where they landed on Long Isle. Above the boat, low and heavy clouds were represented with rain falling. There were three Latin inscriptions on this object: on the edge of the lid by the hinge was the first from Vergil's *Aeneid* 'OLIM HÆC MEMINISSE JUVABIT' and the date, 26 April 1746; the second on the edge by the opening, read 'QUID NEPTUNE, PARAS? FATIS AGITAMUR INIQUIS'. On the bottom of the box Donald was named as the faithful Palinurus with the date again, below which was a dove with an olive branch in its bill. The first inscription derives from the *Aeneid* book I, line 203, from the speech of Aeneas to his crew during the storm on their journey to Italy. MacLeod's identification as Palinurus is similarly Vergilian – he was the helmsman of Aeneas' ship – making these references from the *Aeneid* appropriate accompaniments to a representation of the Prince's maritime flight from the government frigates. MacLeod's snuffbox, a gift from Walkingshaw, was always an object of memory rather than utility; he recounted to Forbes that he would not use the box for 'sneeshin' until the King had been restored, then he would go to London and invite him to take a pinch. A damaged Amen glass at Dunvegan Castle carries the inscription 'Donald Macleod of Gualtergil in The Isle of Skye. The Faithful PALINURUS. ÆT.69. Anno 1747'. Seddon finds it quite possible that the inscription on the glass was copied from that on the snuffbox, only a year later, which once again testifies to the reproductive dialogue between Jacobite objects of different media.[77] These two examples – the snuffbox which no longer survives and the foot of the broken Amen glass – highlight the limitation of studying Jacobite artefacts strictly typologically, as glass or ceramics, without recourse to the repetition of their portraits, mottoes and symbols in and across other media. At the risk of using terms anachronistically, we might describe Jacobite material culture as inherently multi-media.

Within an eighteenth-century corporeal culture that oscillated between the extremities of ornament and use, concealment and display, the 'fanciest of all artifice' were fans.[78] Unlike snuffboxes, which seem to have been common to both genders, fans presuppose a body gendered as female, used by women as a prosthetic extension of their arms and a portable

---

[77] Seddon, *The Jacobites and their Drinking Glasses*, p. 215.
[78] Angela Rosenthal, 'Unfolding gender: Women and the "secret" sign language of fans in Hogarth's work', in Bernadette Fort and Angela Rosenthal (eds.), *The Other Hogarth: Aesthetics of Difference* (Princeton, NJ and Oxford: Princeton University Press, 2001), p. 122.

instrument in social discourse. Two language systems existed by which fans could 'speak' in a form of cryptic conversation.[79] By significant positioning, such as raising the fan to the lips or the brow, they spelled out letters which could make a word. Less arduously, a single dexterous movement of the fan could proclaim an entire word or phrase – one example being carrying the fan in the right hand before the face which translates as follow me. While fans served a pragmatic function, protecting their carrier against the light and the heat, they were also part of the fashionable female armoury of eighteenth-century accessories. A judicious flick of the wrist would result in the rapid folding or unfolding of the fan's pictorial plane on which a seditious Jacobite message could be printed and painted. The last of their tripartite meanings as a social marker, a gestural prosthesis and a pictorial bearer of folding pictures becomes especially potent when we look hard at examples of Jacobite fans. In the National Museums Scotland is a paper fan mounted on ivory whose printed design is traditionally attributed to Robert Strange (Plate XXII). Prince Charles Edward Stuart is shown at full-length in the centre of the crowded composition which is a veritable assembly of allegorical figures and those from the classical Greek and Roman pantheon. Charles, wearing full battle armour with the Order of the Garter and holding an upraised sword, is attended on his left by the Roman god and goddess of wars, Mars and Bellona. She holds a long spear and a shield with a gorgon's head as seen in the engraving by Strange (Figure 36). Fame blowing a trumpet flies above the Prince and crowns him with a laurel wreath, while a shaft of light containing a star illuminates the Prince directly from the heavens above. Once again, he shines among all (as in Figure 34). On the other half of the pictorial plane, grey thunderclouds open to reveal Jupiter with the eagle, sending a thunderbolt to earth to destroy the emaciated and half-naked figures of Envy and Discord scrabbling on the scorched earth. In the far right-hand corner, members of the House of Hanover are shown in retreat. The pictorial composition borrows from the iconography of the ancient Greeks and Romans, with allegorical figures of love and war, to suggest with a hyperbole characteristic of much Jacobite propaganda that the restoration of Prince Charles and the concomitant destruction of the House of Hanover are divinely ordained by members of the classical pantheon.

[79] A. G. Bennett, *Fans in Fashion: Selections from the Fine Arts Museums of San Francisco* (Rutland: Fine Arts Museum of San Francisco, 1981), pp. 10–11. See also Avril Hart and E. Taylor, *Fans* (London: Victoria & Albert Museum, 1998) and Edith A. Standen, 'Instruments for agitating the air', *Metropolitan Museum of Art Bulletin* 23.1 (1965), pp. 243–258.

In a satirical essay on the 'Exercise of the Fan' published in the *Spectator* for 27 June 1711, Joseph Addison characterised it as a weapon; the female counterpart of a sword.[80] Addison relates having set up an academy to train the members of his female regiment in the proper arming of 'that little modish machine' with twice-daily martial exercises dedicated to the closed fan, its unfurling, discharge (with a pop like a pistol), grounding, disarming, recovering and fluttering. Addison notes that it was the unfurling of the fan that 'pleases the spectators more than any other, as it discovers on a sudden an infinite number of Cupids, garlands, altars, birds, beasts, rainbows and the like agreeable figures, that display themselves to view, whilst every one in the regiment holds a picture in her hand'. Armed with a Jacobite fan like that now in the National Museums Scotland (Plate XXII), a woman could unfurl a visual declaration of political allegiance, making women active participants in the machinations of the extra-parliamentary nation through the fashionable prosthetic accessories available to them.[81]

Another folding fan in the National Museums Scotland is made of paper mounted on ivory (Plate XXIII) and painted on both sides. The centre of the leaf on one side (Plate XXIIIa) is hand-painted with a half-length portrait in profile to the right of Prince Charles Edward Stuart encircled in a gold frame inscribed with a Biblical phrase: RENDER TO CAESAR THE THINGS THAT ARE CAESARS. The directive comes from the Gospels of Mark and Matthew where Christ orders the tribute money to be paid to Caesar, having identified him from his portrait on a coin – much like those medallic portraits of the Jacobite figureheads (as in Figure 34). Prince Charles is shown wearing armour, the Order of the Garter and a cloak of velvet, ermine and tartan. His representation on the fan reminds us of the less-than-palm-sized miniatures of him which proliferated and which were secreted on the Jacobite body in pockets or appended to chains as jewellery; and off the body, housed in discreet cases or in hidden lids of snuff boxes (as in Plate XX). On the fan leaf, Prince Charles's image is held aloft in the clouds by two putti floating above maps of England, Scotland and Ireland. The geographical territories separated by a channel representing the Irish sea are demarcated by female personifications with their defining attributes, from left to right, a harp for Ireland, a St George's red cross on a white background for England, who holds a crown and a thistle for a tartan-clad and bonnet-wearing Scotland. Like the medallic

---

[80] Rosenthal, 'Unfolding gender', pp. 129–130.
[81] Rosenthal, 'Unfolding gender', p. 123. See Chalus, 'Fanning the flames', pp. 92–112.

record, this fan has a connective relationship between the obverse and reverse. On the centre of the otherwise undecorated reverse (Plate XXIIIb) is a red brick gatehouse with a dove flying overhead carrying an unfurling banner on which is inscribed the text 'My House shall be called the House of Prayer'. The image projects to a time when St James's Palace would once again be occupied by the Stuarts. This would also see the resulting union of England, Scotland and Ireland as ideologically represented on the obverse. Hugh Cheape has pointed out that the sequential phrase to 'My House shall be called the House of Prayer' in the Gospels of Matthew, Mark and Luke, is 'But you have made it a den of thieves'.[82] This is a piece of invective directed at the Hanoverian interlopers. On this occasion, the intertext is not Vergil's *Aeneid*, but the Bible; the true force of the Jacobite subtext being inferred rather than quoted directly.

These fans in the National Museums Scotland may be associated with the social events that took place at Holyrood Palace in Edinburgh after it was occupied by Prince Charles Edward Stuart following the Jacobite capture of the Scottish capital. A print produced in London and entitled 'Scotch Female Gallantry' shows Charles in an inner chamber containing a bed surrounded by a group of nine adoring Scottish women (Figure 41); an ante room beyond is crammed with people, most of whom are women. The Prince's representation in tartan is indebted to Richard Cooper's satirical portrait in his wrinkled plaid stockings and a top-heavy profusion of cerise feathers sprouting from his bonnet (Figure 40). The verse in rhyming couplets that accompanies the image at its foot recounts how 'Charley's' visit to Edinburgh had 'set the Scottish Nymphs on Flame'. The so-called nymphs of various shapes and sizes are described and pictured kissing different parts of the Prince's fissiparous form – Susannah his eyelids, Marg'ry his nose, Nancy his 'gaudy Ribband' (his Order of the Garter hand-coloured a dirty yellow) and 'waddling Jennet', his finger. An unnamed woman to the left of the Prince holds a furled-up fan which shows how discreet and innocuous an object it was when closed. The verse extorts all English nymphs to 'the Pest beware/ For Poison lurks in secret there'. In contrast with the 'base-born wretch' Prince Charles, the 'Pride and Darling of our Land' is William, the Duke of Cumberland, where once again the two sides of the Jacobite challenge to the Hanoverian regime are reduced to their respective leaders. The Jacobite Prince was often accused by his adversaries of being under petticoat patronage and this image shows him as an object of adoration being courted and caressed by 'foolish'

---

[82] Cheape, 'The culture and material culture of Jacobitism', p. 41.

Figure 41: Anonymous, 'Scotch female gallantry', 1745–6. 21.3 × 28.7 cm. © The Trustees of the British Museum. All rights reserved.

Scottish women, as the verse dubs them. The image also provides a precedent in eighteenth-century visual culture of the body of the Jacobite figurehead as a corporation of fragments and parts, a thematic and a trope pursued throughout this chapter.

It draws to a close with the lower swathes of the Jacobite body in a state of undress – relieved of its material prostheses and enveloping drapes of tartan – with garters. These were thin strips of material worn above or below the knee by both men and women to keep their upraised stockings in place. Since the early eighteenth century, garters had been used to carry political slogans designating the partisan preferences of the wearer.[83] In the Victoria and Albert Museum, for instance, is a garter woven with the inscription 'GEORGE LEWIS BY THE GRACE OF GOD KING OF GREAT BRITTAIN FRANCE AND IRELAND DEFENDER OF THE FAITH 1714', which was made for a supporter of the 1688 Revolution and the Protestant succession. From the opposite side of the political spectrum is a pair of garters in woven silk which are inscribed with mottoes in rhyming couplets: 'GOD BLESS THE PRINCE AND SAVE THE KING', 'WHILE WHIGGS AND RUMPS IN HALTERS SWING'; a halter being another kind of ligature, specifically a hangman's noose. The precise identity of the aforementioned 'Rumps' remains ambiguous. The phrase Rump Parliament referred to that in 1648 when members supporting the proposed Treaty of Newport, which would have reinstated Charles I with limitations on his powers, were arrested or prevented from entering the House. Rumps may also refer to Henry Pelham's Prime Ministership from 1743 to 1754 which was dubbed the Broad Bottom Administration; it is as likely to be a collective insult against the Whigs, Hanoverians and Presbyterians. Predictably (by now), derogatory reference to the Rumps occurs across Jacobite material culture, incised and painted on ceramic vessels, as well as stitched on textiles.[84] An uncut pair of garters in the National Museums Scotland declares 'IN GOD ALONE WE PUT OUR TRUST', 'OUR PRINCE IS BRAVE OUR CAUSE IS JUST'; and a third, 'COME LET US WITH ONE HEART UNITE' 'TO BLESS THE PRINCE FOR WHOM WE'LL FIGHT' (Plate XXIV). Though these garters exist as pairs and were worn by individuals, their rhyming mottoes 'speak' with a collective voice as to the surety of the cause and the wearer's unwavering commitment to it.

---

[83] Rosa López, 'The garter: Function and seduction', *Datatèxtil* 13 (2005), pp. 4–19.

[84] See the stoneware mug and jug in the British Museum (2007,8083.1 & 2004,1222.1); the former with the inscribed toast 'Prince Charles/is Good Helth/And Down with/The Rump/1752'.

A contributor to the *Gentleman's Magazine* for 1748 wrote that he heartily 'disapprove[d] when the garter is made the distinguishing badge of party. It ought to be like the caestus of Venus, and not daubed with plaid and crammed with treason. I am credibly informed that garters of this sort were first introduced in the late rebellion by some female aid-de-camp's'.[85] Whether garters were indeed introduced by female supporters of the Jacobites at the time of the '45 cannot be substantiated; certainly women's perceived lack of political capacity made them safer from prosecution than male Jacobites.[86] On this occasion, the satirical equivalence being drawn between the girdle of Venus and Jacobite garters genders them as female and invests them with an erotic potency through the reference to the ancient goddess of love. Concealed on the body under layers of outer garments, garters would have been made visible and their mottoes legible only to intimates of the wearer, where their disguise was a form of encoded display.

The garters now in London and Edinburgh (Plate XXIV) are woven in a brightly coloured red, blue, yellow, green and white palette, in a chequer pattern that resembles the distinctive warp and weft of Highland plaid; with the accompanying text rendered in white silk. Manchester has been put forward as their place of their production from a single passage in the *Manchester Magazine* for 30 December 1746 that explicitly refers to the weaving of inscribed Jacobite garters there: 'Several looms have been lately employed to furnish garters, watch strings, etc. with this elegant motto "God preserve P.C. and Down with the Rump".'[87] Manchester was also mentioned in connection with the portrait glass that the Duke of Perth sent to Drummond of Logie in April 1750. The production of these objects in an emphatically Highland Scottish idiom in the English manufacturing hub that was Manchester in the months and years following the defeat at Culloden merits further scholarly investigation.

In examining how the ideology of Jacobitism was invested and manifested in visual and material culture, this chapter has notionally traversed the individual and collective Jacobite body on a vertical axis. From its upper parts as represented by the bust portraits of Prince Charles Edward Stuart, to the median where the torso is swathed in plaid and appended with a repertoire of artefactual prostheses, including glasses, snuffboxes and fans, to the garters strung below the rump above the knee. For William

---

[85] Quoted in Michael Darby, 'Jacobite garters', *Victoria and Albert Museum Bulletin* 2.4 (1966), pp. 157–158.

[86] Pittock, *Material Culture and Sedition*, pp. 16–17.

[87] Quoted in Darby, 'Jacobite garters', p. 162.

Pitt in the House of Commons in November 1754, the built environment of Oxford that previous summer was charged with insurrection: he recounts that its very streets were 'paved with Jacobitism' eight years after the Battle of Culloden. While historians are unable to agree on many matters pertaining to Jacobitism – was it a movement or a cause? sustained political threat or episodic storm in a teacup? – there is some loose consensus that post-Culloden it was already an impotent political one, that had withdrawn into sentimental drinking clubs and passive commemoration.

Adopting 'a corporealist critique', this chapter has attempted to refute such a lacklustre characterisation.[88] It has done so by demonstrating the extent to which the Jacobite body politic was 'daubed with plaid and

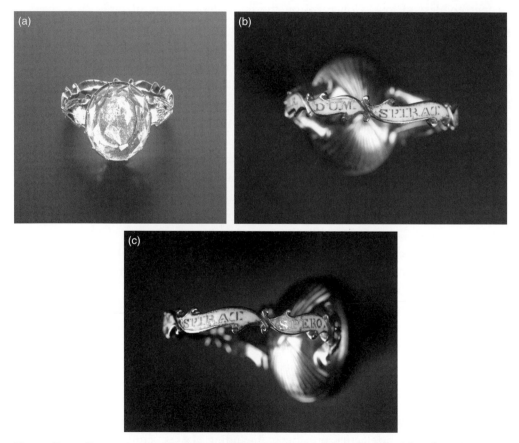

Figure 42a–c: Cameo ring inscribed 'DUM SPIRAT SPERO' [while he breathes I hope], *c.* 1750. Diameter 2.2 cm. © National Museums Scotland.

[88] Dror Wahrman, 'Change and the corporeal in seventeenth- and eighteenth-century gender history: or can cultural history be rigorous?', *Gender & History* 20.3 (2008), p. 601.

crammed with treason' as the *Gentleman's Magazine* for 1748 put it, even after the most recent military defeat. Agreeing with Forth and Crozier that the body was never simply a biological entity, the sum of its physiological processes, this chapter has proposed a cultural politics of the historical body as a means for studying Jacobite objects in which the cause is embodied by its Prince in the regime of representation and emboldened by being sported on the bodies of his loyal supporters in an objectscape of politicised possessions.[89] One tiny item of jewellery previously worn on the extremity of the Jacobite body and now in the National Museums Scotland actually invokes the Prince's animate corpus as a marker for the longevity of the cause. The gold cameo of the ring (2 cm diameter) contains a bust portrait of the Prince in profile (Figure 42), much like those found in the medallic record and in the sculpture by Lemoyne (Figure 35). It is thought to have been made by the exiled Edinburgh goldsmith Adam Tait in Paris, *c.* 1750. On the hoop, after the Prince's latinised initials is a Latin inscription executed in white enamel, C.P.R/DUM/SPIRAT/SPERO: 'while he breathes I hope'. An optimistic message certainly, but an obdurate one.

---

[89] Forth and Crozier, *Body Parts: Critical Explorations in Corporeality*, p. 4.

5 | The Monarch in the Metropolis

A Scopic Spectacle: George IV's Visit to Edinburgh, August 1822

> There may be something delusive in all this – but the delusion is a lofty
> one; and without imagination there can be neither loyalty or patriotism.
>
> Blackwood's Magazine, September 1822[1]

'All is bustle here [Edinburgh] at present among a certain class preparing for
his Majesty', wrote Alexander Gordon, in a letter dated 23 July 1822, to the
artist Hugh Irvine.[2] Gordon proceeded to bemoan the lack of advance warn-
ing for the royal visit of George IV – 'To a Capital who has not seen its
Sovereign for 180 years or thereby, some notice should have been rendered' –
and its unseasonable timing, with the country families being out of town and
those, like his own, with children at school only waiting for the vacation to
depart the city. 'The Royal visit will give neither pleasure nor satisfaction here
[he predicted] ... How his Majesty is to be received entertained or heated I
know not'. Attempts by the Provost and Baillies of Edinburgh to procure a
subscription of five to ten guineas from each member of the citizen body, had
reportedly failed. For Gordon, the prospect for the royal visit was markedly
bleak: 'Poor Caledonia will make a most shabby figure, & but for the gaping
idlers who flock from all quarters to see anything or nothing, I almost presume
a general dissatisfaction will be experienced. The expence attending a bungled
business will be the chief point of criticism and irritation.'

Almost five weeks later, the king's twenty-one day visit to Edinburgh
was over. And despite Gordon's pessimistic prognosis, it was judged to be
far from a 'bungled business', rather a resounding success for the king and
the Scottish capital alike. 'All accounts agree, that his Majesty is delighted
with Scotland', wrote one G. L. Meason to the Revd Buchanan, minister of
Kingarth.[3] In turn, Scotland was said to have delighted in the king.
According to *A Historical Account of His Majesty's Visit to Scotland*
(Edinburgh, 1822), the entry of the British monarch to Edinburgh was
witnessed by no fewer than 300,000 people – about a seventh of the entire

---

[1] *Blackwood's Magazine*, September 1822, p. 259.   [2] NRAS, 1500/715.

[3] 23 August 1822. NRAS, 1948/4.

population of Scotland.[4] Other reported statistics were similarly buoyant: a Drawing Room at Holyrood Palace, the ancient palace of the kings of Scotland, was attended by about 500 society women; a military review on Portobello sands, watched by about 50,000 spectators and a banquet in Parliament House given by the Provost, magistrates and town council of Edinburgh seated 295 invited guests.[5] The émigré Scottish artist, David Wilkie, who travelled from London specifically to witness the royal visit, subsequently wrote to Perry Nursey of the unprecedented crowds: 'Edinburgh was never known to be so full either in the memory of man or in history, people of every rank both savage and sage, who could afford the time or the money came to have an eager look of His Majesty.'[6] In much the same way that his Scottish subjects had turned out to have what Wilkie dubbed 'an eager look', or as Gordon would have it, to gape, at their monarch in their hundreds of thousands, so the king was said to have had an 'Eye full' of Scotland. George IV's private secretary and physician, Sir William Knighton, wrote to the Lord Chief Commissioner of the Scottish Jury Court, William Adam on 28 September 1822, 'Every thing relative to Scotland we look at with an Eye full of the most pleasing & endearing Recollections, the name of a Scotchman will ever be dear to his Majesty.'[7]

These optical references in Gordon, Wilkie and Knighton's correspondence serve to locate the royal visit to Edinburgh of August 1822 in what the cultural historian, Peter de Bolla, has termed the domain of the scopic.[8] De Bolla explores the visibility of visuality as a cultural construct, positing that vision is not entirely circumscribed by and through optics. His discussion of the environment of the pleasure gardens at Vauxhall, south of the River Thames in eighteenth-century London, reveals a whole range of viewing activities at work and play, demarking a 'metaphorics of the eye', which in his account begins to describe the anatomy and grammar of Enlightenment visuality. Using de Bolla's formulation, this chapter seeks to position George IV's 1822 visit to Edinburgh in the scopic domain. It offers a close reading of examples of visual culture in the form of paintings and engravings that were generated in response to the royal visit.[9]

---

[4] [Robert Mudie], *A Historical Account of His Majesty's Visit to Scotland* (Edinburgh, 1822), p. 113.

[5] [Mudie], *A Historical Account of His Majesty's Visit to Scotland*, p. 167, p. 214, p. 230.

[6] 13 September 1822. BL Add. MS. 29991 folio 34.   [7] NRAS, 1454/2/282.

[8] Peter de Bolla, 'The visibility of visuality: Vauxhall Gardens and the siting of the viewer', in Stephen Melville and Bill Readings (eds.), *Vision and Textuality* (Basingstoke: Macmillan, 1995), p. 283.

[9] The visual output of George IV's northern excursion has not been entirely overlooked to date: see James N. M. Maclean and Basil Skinner, *The Royal Visit of 1822* (Edinburgh: University of

Focussing on the hermeneutics of surface in the production of images – both official and unofficial – by various Scottish and English artists, including David Wilkie, William Home Lizars and John Wilson Eubank, it documents how the assembled Scots, a composite mosaic of cultures and classes, were imaged as a nation united internally and reconciled with the English. Effectively, this chapter considers those Scots who participated in the visit and the king himself as being both subjects and objects in an art historical narrative of nation-ness. The presentation and representation of Highland dress and textiles will be shown to function as a potent means for reifying Scottishness as a form of collective national identity.

The visual data will not be read in an art historical vacuum, however. It will be discussed in conjunction with the many textual descriptions of the visit that proliferated. These range from unpublished private correspondence, like Alexander Gordon's letter to Hugh Irvine, to daily newspaper reports, to *Historical Accounts* published contemporaneously. According to one such account, the Edinburgh newspapers greatly increased their print run during the duration of the royal visit, only to sell out a day or two after publication, with prices of as much as five guineas being demanded.[10] What is striking about the content of these eclectic textual sources is their shared subscription to what de Bolla has termed a 'metaphorics of the eye', from the profusion of figurative expressions that make visible the visual content of the royal visit.[11] This chapter argues that a multiplicity of visual experiences was proffered by the king's visit to Edinburgh. Not only in the production of traditional art historical media like paintings, engravings and sculpture, but also in the ways in which the city itself in terms of its architectural embellishments, its topographical landscape and its body politic were described as being revealed to the king in 'a sequence of theatrical and symbolically-loaded tableaux'.[12]

Edinburgh Department of Educational Studies, 1972); Gerald Finley, *Turner and George the Fourth in Edinburgh, 1822* (London: Tate Gallery, 1981); John Prebble's *The King's Jaunt: George IV in Scotland, August 1822* (London: Collins, 1988) incorporates a number of images; Mark Dorrian, 'The king and the city: On the iconology of George IV in Edinburgh', *Edinburgh Architecture Research* 30 (2006), pp. 32–36, reprinted in his *Writing on the Image: Architecture, the City and the Politics of Representation* (London: I.B. Tauris, 2015), pp. 13–21, focusses on the visit as an optical event but does not look at the visual output in terms of specific works.

10 *A Complete Historical Account of His Majesty King George the Fourth to the Kingdom of Scotland* (Edinburgh, 1822), Preface.

11 de Bolla, 'The visibility of visuality', p. 283.

12 Dorrian, 'The king and the city', p. 32. The conception of the body politic in this chapter derives from Anthony Smith's vertical axis for the ethnic community, see Anthony D. Smith, *National Identity* (London: Penguin, 1991), pp. 52–53. Smith concedes that 'the distinction between lateral and vertical ethnic communities is an ideal-typical one, and it conceals differences within each category while suggesting too sharp a division between the types'.

On more than one occasion there is an interface between the scopic and graphic regimes in the cultural productions that documented the visit. For instance, four outline engravings by William Home Lizars accompany Robert Mudie's *Historical Account of his Majesty's visit to Scotland*. They depict the landing at Leith (Figure 43), the procession towards the city (Figure 44), the procession to the castle and a view of the banquet in the Great Hall of Parliament House. *A Picturesque Sketch of the Landing of His Most Gracious Majesty King George IV* (Edinburgh, 1822) offers an eye-witness account of the king's entry that is conceptualised art historically – as a picturesque sketch. The pamphlet also provides a nomenclature for the twenty-five personnel mounted and on foot in an aquatint by William Turner (Figure 45), representing the king's arrival at Holyrood Palace. According to the accompanying text of *A Picturesque Sketch*, the 'sombre aspect and architectural gravity [of Holyrood Palace], served as a fine relievo to the brilliancy and sparkling animation of the sumptuous congregation'; with the cloud providing a backdrop for the king's carriage as it arrived at the entrance to the Palace.[13] Turner's image was exhibited at 63 Princes Street, Edinburgh and published by subscription as a copper plate print measuring twenty-four by eighteen inches. The exhibition of pictures has previously been identified by de Bolla as one the cultural environments in which the activity of looking takes place.[14] For Smith, the dissemination of paintings as prints and engravings to a wide audience is one of the means by which notions of the nation and national identity – which in his account are 'high level' abstractions – are articulated and communicated.[15] This chapter focusses on 'looking' as a means for registering a collective national identity that is reified through the dress of the participants in the spectacle; situating the spectacle as a series of tableaux of which individual scenes were represented in paintings, some of which were subsequently exhibited and engraved.

As John Prebble has surveyed the sequential events of the 'One and twenty daft days' that comprised the royal visit, this chapter will focus on the episodic rather than the entirety of the programmatic spectacle, although the proceedings of Thursday 15 August, the royal entry into the city, will be dwelt on in more detail.[16] The royal squadron arrived at the

---

[13] *A Picturesque Sketch of the Landing of His Most Gracious Majesty King George IV* (Edinburgh, 1822), 7.

[14] de Bolla, 'The visibility of visuality', p. 282.

[15] Anthony D. Smith, *The Nation Made Real: Art and National Identity in Western Europe, 1600–1850* (Oxford: Oxford University Press, 2013), p. 10 and p. 6.

[16] Prebble, *The King's Jaunt.*

THE LANDING of KING GEORGE THE IV AT LEITH: 15ᵀᴴ AUGUST 1822.

Edinburgh. Published by Oliver & Boyd.

Figure 43: W. H. Lizars, 'The Landing of King George the IV at Leith: 15th August 1822', from Robert Mudie's *Historical Account of his Majesty's visit to Scotland.* 55 × 21.3 cm. © University of Edinburgh.

Figure 44: W. H. Lizars, 'View of the royal procession advancing by Picardy Place, from the barrier where the keys of the city were delivered by the Lord Provost to His Majesty, 15th August 1822', from Robert Mudie's *Historical Account of his Majesty's visit to Scotland*. 55 × 21.3 cm. © The University of Edinburgh.

Figure 45: William Turner, *The arrival of His Most Gracious Majesty George IV at his ancient Palace of Holyrood on the 16th August, 1822,* 1822. 44.3 × 58.1 cm. City of Edinburgh Council – Edinburgh Libraries www.capitalcollections.org.uk.

port of Leith on Wednesday, 14 August, with the king disembarking at midday the following day. After the ship the *Royal George* had anchored, Sir Walter Scott went on board to present the king with the Silver Star, a gift from the Ladies of Edinburgh. Finley has read George IV's *adventus* by sea as providential, since it lacked the political overtones of an arrival by land, which would recall the advance of Government troops led by the Duke of Cumberland during the '45 uprising.[17] The term *adventus* is used here quite deliberately as one of the many historical referents invoked in descriptions of the royal visit is ancient Rome. For instance, one of the five *Letters to Sir Walter Scott, Bart. on the Moral and Political Character and Effects of the Visit to Scotland in August 1822, of his Majesty King George IV*, which were written by James Simpson two months after the visit and published anonymously in Edinburgh, recalls, 'No approach in dust-

---

[17] Finley, *Turner and George the Fourth in Edinburgh 1822*, p. 8.

covered carriages could impress the spectator in the same sort, with the scene of a gallant fleet walking the waters, with more than the common dignity of Britain's bulwarks because of its kingly charge – as if it said as it swept along "Caesarem veho!"[18] Simpson's narrative moves seamlessly between contemporary Britain and ancient Rome, maritime victory to imperial *adventus*, where the landing and disembarkation of the king at Leith harbour are described as being suitable to Britain's naval character. When the king steps on the pier, Simpson's narrative shifts backwards again, this time to a specific precedent in the annals of Scottish history, the arrival of Mary Queen of Scots from France. This kaleidoscopic rotation of historical chronology, where fragments of the past and present, are overlaid and of national identity, where Scotland is simultaneously an independent nation and a part of Britain, characterise many of the written accounts of the royal visit. For Samuel, such alleged continuities of nation are fictions – a device for connecting phenomena which are both analytically distinct and chronologically separated over time.[19] Much as in the scopic domain, where the eye was said to be 'no less gratified in the detail than with the general effect' of the spectacle, so Scottish history and identity are repeatedly being figured and reconfigured, viewed as an entirety and as details.[20]

David Wilkie and William Collins were two of the London-based artists who travelled from the capital city to Edinburgh 'for the purpose of being present at the Landing of the King'.[21] 'I have promised to give them a Letter to you', Lord Liverpool wrote to William Adam, on 6 August 1822. 'I shall be very much obliged to you if you would afford them all the assistance in your power in order that they may see the different ceremonies in the most advantageous manner as I am satisfied there are no spectators from whose Presence the Public & Posterity will derive so much benefit.' Thanks to the intervention of the first minister of the Tory administration in the form of a letter of introduction, Wilkie and Collins were afforded privileged views of the proceedings. Liverpool made the same request to Scott, as pageant-master of the visit, in an attempt to ensure that the spectacle would be represented pictorially for posterity by these favoured artists.[22] After the

---

18 [James Simpson], *Letters to Sir Walter Scott, Bart. on the Moral and Political Character and Effects of the Visit to Scotland in August 1822* (Edinburgh, 1822), pp. 43–44.

19 Raphael Samuel, 'Continuous national history', in Raphael Samuel (ed.), *Patriotism: The Making and Unmaking of British National Identity* (London: Routledge, 1989), volume 1, pp. 9–17 at p. 17.

20 *The Scotsman*, 24 August 1822, p. 267.   21 NRAS, 1454/2/281.

22 See Basil C. Skinner, 'Scott as pageant-master: The royal visit of 1822', in Alan S. Bell (ed.), *Scott Bicentenary Essays* (Edinburgh: Scottish Academic Press, 1973), pp. 228–237.

visit, Collins wrote to his mother that he was working on a large painting of the approach of the King to the pier at Leith, explaining 'I have seen so much of his [the king's] doings that I could paint a series of pictures, – but not one will I do (further than making sketches when I return) without commissions'.[23] The serial nature of the different ceremonies posed a significant obstacle for artists when trying to isolate a single event to capture on canvas. Hence J. M. W. Turner's 'King at Edinburgh' sketchbook in the Tate reveals a proposed *cycle* of paintings of the royal visit (Figure 46).[24] A double page contains eighteen small pencil sketches extending in two rows, with a nineteenth below. The upper row of images reads from right to left and snakes from left to right in the lower register. As far as it is possible to identify the compositional subjects, Turner's cycle documents the events in chronological order (with one exception which Finley thinks was omitted unintentionally), from Sir Walter Scott greeting the king on board the *Royal George* on 14 August, to the laying of the foundation stone for the National Monument on 27 August. Rather less ambitiously, William Collins envisaged a painting of the Embarkation of the King on 29 August as a companion piece to the Landing.[25] Collins seems not to have produced a completed canvas of the king's arrival at Leith (perhaps the hoped-for commissions were not forthcoming), but 'the Public & Posterity' continue to benefit from engravings and paintings by other artists who witnessed first-hand the event, including the Scottish artists William Home Lizars and Alexander Carse.

Lizars's engraving of the landing at Leith (Figure 43) is indebted to the panorama, an architectural apparatus built for displaying two enormous cylindrical paintings, whose name derives from the Greek for 'all' and 'view'.[26] Lizars divides the rectangular picture plane into two horizontal sections: with the royal squadron in the harbour below and the warehouses lining the shore above. The gangplank via which the king disembarks physically links the two realms of sea and land. On the far right, the drawbridge to the inner harbour is half raised. In keeping with Lizars's other engravings reproduced in Robert Mudie's *Historical Account*, the optical focus is less on the figure of the king as on the assembled citizen body. As Scott had explained in his anonymously published thirty-two-page directive for the royal visit, *Hints Addressed to the Inhabitants of*

---

[23] 28 August 1822. *Memoirs of the Life of William Collins* (London, 1848), I, pp. 205–206.

[24] Gerald Finley, 'J. M. W. Turner's proposal for a "Royal Progress"', *Burlington Magazine* 117 (1975), pp. 27–33, p. 35.

[25] 17 August 1822. *Memoirs of the Life of William Collins* (London, 1848), I, p. 206.

[26] Denise Blake Oleksijczuk, 'Gender in perspective: The King and Queen's visit to the Panorama in 1793', in Steven Adams and Anna Gruetzner Robins (eds.), *Gendering Landscape Art* (Manchester: Manchester University Press, 2000), p. 146.

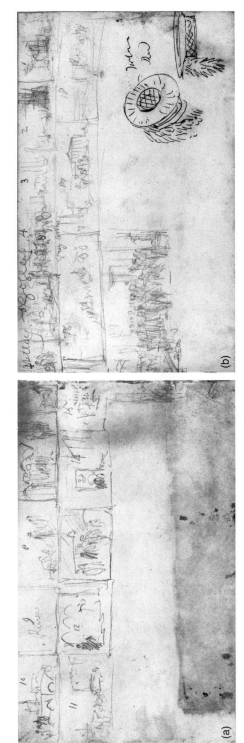

Figure 46: J. M. W. Turner. 'Designs for the "Royal Progress" series', 1822. Each page, 11.1 × 18.8 cm. © Tate, London 2019.

Edinburgh and Others, in Prospect of His Majesty's Visit by an Old Citizen
(Edinburgh, 1822): 'this is not an ordinary show – it is not all on one side. It
is not enough that we should see the King; but the King must also see US.'[27]
This statement makes explicit the visual reciprocity that was Scott's blue-
print for the royal visit.

Lizars's image of the landing at Leith (Figure 43) closely corresponds
with the text of one of James Simpson's *Letters* to Scott in which the king's
'countless subjects were marshalled in steadfast and deep alignment on
both sides of his route, compacted in gallery, balcony, and scaffold, without
end, stationed in every window, perched upon every height from which a
view could be caught of this most unusual of spectacles'.[28] From Lizars's
engraving, we might add ships' masts to Simpson's inventory of crammed
viewing spaces. Alexander Carse's large horizontal (160 × 362 cm) oil
painting depicts the king's embarkation from the opposite side of Leith
harbour to Lizars (Figure 47).[29] The overall view of the scene is simultaneously panoramic in its extent and telescopic in its rendering of detail.
Notice the monarch in the right foreground dressed in the uniform of an
Admiral of the Fleet and encircled by a group of dignitaries representing
the magistrates, deacons and trades of the town. Members of the Company
of Royal Archers line the king's route off to his right wearing their
distinctive dress 'with a Quiver full of arrows sticking at their Backs & a
white sattin scarf across their Bodies & green sattin Puffs on the sleeves & a
Feather in their Caps'.[30] Carse's painting contrasts the orderliness of the
ticketed (Figure 48) visitors with the more disordered elements of the
crowd, which includes a pickpocket making his way from the left to right
of the canvas. Furthermore, by representing the rear view of a shallow row
of spectators in the foreground, the external viewer seemingly joins those
in the painting to witness the king's historic arrival in Scotland.

From Leith harbour, the royal party joined a procession, which passed
along St Bernard Street, under a temporarily erected triumphal arch
inscribed 'Scotland hails With Joy The Presence Of Her King' and into
Constitution Street. The quotations from ancient Roman triumphs were
accentuated with a second arch inscribed in English *and Latin* 'O Happy
Day'. From here, the procession headed towards Edinburgh. 'No city in

---

[27] *Hints Addressed to the Inhabitants of Edinburgh and Others, in Prospect of His Majesty's Visit by an Old Citizen* (Edinburgh, 1822), p. 22.

[28] [Simpson], *Letters to Sir Walter Scott,* pp. 46–47.

[29] Carse's canvas still hangs in Leith Police Station, formerly Leith Council Chambers, built in 1827 prior to Leith becoming a parliamentary burgh in 1830.

[30] NAS, GD157/2548. Harriet Scott to her daughter, 16 August 1822.

Figure 47: Alexander Carse, *George IVth Landing at Leith*, 1822. 160.1 × 362 cm. City Art Centre, City of Edinburgh Museums & Galleries.

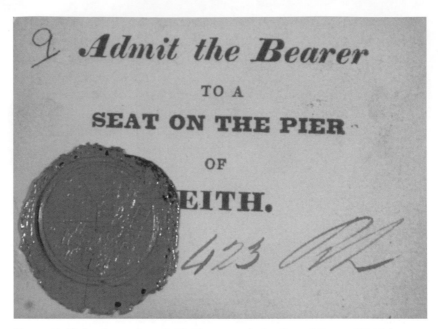

Figure 48: Ticket for a seat on Leith Pier to see the landing of George IV, 15 August 1822. 5.6 × 7.7 cm. Trinity House. © Crown Copyright HES.

Europe can boast a nobler avenue', proclaimed Scott of Leith Walk, into which it proceeded.[31] Another of Lizars's engravings (Figure 44) shows the king in the right foreground in his carriage – open to give a view of the king's person, according to *A Picturesque Sketch*.[32] The royal carriage has just passed under another arch where the Lord Provost presented the king with the keys of the city of Edinburgh. Lizars delineates a compact mass of the urban populace and also carefully demarcates the architecture of this part of the city. His extended view along Picardy Place towards York Place follows the forward movement of the royal cavalcade. One visitor saw the king enter the city by Leith walk, 'with all the pomp & parade on such a rare and magnificent occasion'.[33] Harriet Scott lived in the row of houses at 29 York Place and provided an eyewitness account of the procession in a contemporaneous letter to her daughter, 'nothing could go off better than the King's Entry, we began <u>looking</u> & <u>seeing</u> directly after breakfast for the Procession assembled in this street to go <u>to meet</u> the king'.[34] Mrs Scott's

---

[31] *Hints Addressed to the Inhabitants of Edinburgh and Others,* p. 11.

[32] *A Picturesque Sketch,* p. 4.

[33] D. G., 'Notes during a journey to Edinbro in July & August 1822', Beinecke Library, Osborn d283.

[34] Harriet Scott to her daughter, 16 August 1822. NRS, GD157/2548/2.

letter differentiates between different modes of viewing, looking and see-ing, so beginning to dissect the anatomy of the gaze.

From outside Harriet Scott's house at York Place, the procession made its way into St Andrew's Square and across towards Princes Street, effectively doing a short circuit around part of the grid of James Craig's New Town. 'Streets and squares of stately architecture, porticoes, columns, vistas, varied the effect at every turn', Simpson wrote in his *Letters*.[35] The literary accounts make clear that the left turn into Princes Street was the climax of the scopic spectacle for those *in* the procession, when the city of Edinburgh and its environs were revealed to the king's sight for the first time. As Scott reminded readers of his *Hints*, 'Scotland and Scotchmen are altogether a new subject for his [the king's] observation.'[36] Simpson proceeds to recount a visual rehabilitation of the view of the city through the king's unfamiliar gaze. 'The King's eye was on these [city, trophy and mountain], and, at the moment, they were new in their interest to the oldest inhabitant.'[37] Alongside the architecture of the New Town and the assembled body politic, the natural topographical landscape of Edinburgh was in the king's line of vision. For Simpson, the view of Calton Hill at the east end of Princes Street defied description; he does however explicitly describe it as a 'panorama'. According to an anecdote in the history of the panorama, it was the site of Calton Hill that inspired its invention as a large-scale, step-in spectacle, when an Irishman in his adopted city of Edinburgh in the 1780s sought to re-create the natural panorama that was the 360-degree view from the summit of the 350-foot hill showing the city, its surroundings and the distant Firth of Forth.[38] At least two visitors to Edinburgh, one before, the other after the royal visit, mention viewing Barker's panorama in London prior to their visits to Scotland: 'never was a copy more perfect [extolled Benjamin Silliman]. Indeed Edinburgh and its environs present a scene of unrivalled beauty and grandeur'.[39] One Charles Steade climbed the Calton Hill during a stay in Edinburgh in 1819, writing that the view from the summit of this 'rocky eminence' offered 'as great and admirable a variety of sea and land

---

[35] [Simpson], *Letters to Sir Walter Scott*, p. 57.

[36] *Hints Addressed to the Inhabitants of Edinburgh and Others*, p. 21.

[37] [Simpson], *Letters to Sir Walter Scott*, p. 59.

[38] Martin Kemp, *The Science of Art: Optical Themes in Western Art from Brunelleschi to Seurat* (New Haven, CT and London: Yale University Press, 1990), p. 213; Stephan Oettermann, *The Panorama: History of a Mass Medium* (New York: Zone Books, 1997), p. 100.

[39] Benjamin Silliman, *A Journal of Travels in England, Holland and Scotland and Two Passages over the Atlantic in the Years 1805 and 1806* (New Haven, 1820), III, p. 213. The other visitor was Revd John Skinner in 1825.

prospects, as can be formed in any part of Britain'.[40] 'Nature à Coup d'Oeil' – what these much-lauded prospects surveyed is represented in a series of four panoramic views taken from the top of Calton Hill beside the Nelson monument showing the east, north, west and south vistas (Figure 49a–d). This set of prints was published in 1823 after drawings made by Mary Stewart and dedicated to George IV. Stewart's earlier views of the city and its environs from Edinburgh's Blackford Hill were presented to the king during his 1822 visit. 'I really feel the highest gratification [she wrote to William Adam] in having been able to give so correct a representation of this country as that it should have been thought worthy of being presented to his Majesty.'[41] The later views coincided with the royal visit – the first plate looking east is entitled 'Artillery and tents on the Calton Hill during his Majesty George 4's visit to Scotland 1822' (Figure 49a) and others in the series will be referenced below.

One of Simpson's *Letters to Scott* continues by describing the view that greeted the king as the cavalcade headed towards the foot of Calton Hill: 'The first face of the eminence rose abrupt on the sight, a pyramid of human beings – bold, instant, imminent, – as if they had been formed in magic phalanx to bar the path. It was so near, that a vast pavement of human faces, in living mosaic, seemed to gaze with one steady eye, and hail with one heart and one tongue.'[42] Simpson's text describes a *trompe l'oeil*, where the mass of animated human spectators crammed onto Calton Hill coalesces into the inanimate features of the built environment, variously 'pyramid', 'pavement' and 'mosaic'. The passage demarcates a metaphorics of vision that is distinctly cyclopean – with one shared monocular view-point. The text of *A Picturesque Sketch* is more expansive, likening the Calton Hill to a section of a Roman amphitheatre

tessilated and studded with all the variety of life, beauty and elegance, rising in rows of thousand, and tens of thousands … Such was the beautiful aspect of the declivity, serpentening into perspective and aerial gradations, which lured the eye into the distance, where Arthur's Seat and Salisbury Craig raise their mountain monster heads, and by their bold imposing aspects arrest the powers of vision to view – to taste the magic change from shade to light, of lovely varying tints, and change of place, while the distant city world around its base, in hazy vapour curtain'd o'er, seem'd at first sight a distant sea.[43]

---

[40] [Charles Steade], *A Tour to the Highlands of Scotland and the Isle of Staffa with a Short Description of the Lakes of Windemere and Derwentwater*, 1819. YCBA, DA 865.S74
[41] NRAS1454/2/323, undated.   [42] [Simpson], *Letters to Sir Walter Scott*, p. 60.
[43] *A Picturesque Sketch of the Landing of His Most Gracious Majesty King George IV*, pp. 6–7.

Figure 49a–d: *Four panoramic views of the city of Edinburgh* (Edinburgh, 1823). (a) View from the door of Nelson's monument on the Calton Hill looking to the east; (b) View from the top of the Calton Hill, looking to the north; (c) View from the top of the Calton Hill by Nelson's monument looking to the west; (d) View from the walk on the top of Calton Hill, looking to the south. 1823. 22.1 × 60.2 cm. © The Trustees of the British Museum. All rights reserved.

The metaphorics of vision are repeatedly invoked in this evocative pictorial passage. The optical experience is represented as powerful and seductive; in motion, rather than fixed, where the eye is drawn from a more proximate aspect to the distant view of Arthur's Seat and Salisbury Craig (Figure 49d). Nor is vision the only sense invoked – a shift is affected from viewing to tasting as the scene itself transforms from shade to light. Becoming, as in Simpson's account, a kind of *trompe l'oeil* in which the far cityscape shrouded in mist 'seem'd at first sight a distant sea'; the reference to the sea recalling George IV's earlier nautical *adventus* at Leith harbour.

According to a report in *The Scotsman*, the promenade along Princes Street afforded 'one of the finest composition views of town and country, – mountain, hill, and precipice, – art and nature, – earth and sky, – that the world can furnish'.[44] John Wilson Eubank's 150.5 × 240 cm canvas (Plate XXV) represents this unrivalled composition, not from the worm's eye perspective of one of the procession, but the elevated vantage point of Calton Hill looking west (compare with Figure 49c). Much like *The Scotsman's* hyperbolic polarities, Eubank's canvas seems to defy classification according to art historical genres. It is a painting that is cityscape, landscape, portrait and history painting. The Calton Hill is tessellated with rows of spectators overlooking a panoramic view of the city and its environs. On the far right, a dropped handkerchief hovers bird-like, drawing our eye down on a vertical axis towards the procession making it way along Waterloo Place past the prison designed by Robert Adam and onto its destination, Holyrood Palace. *A Picturesque Sketch* noted the prison inmates 'in spite of their unhappy conditions, manifested their union of feeling ... by the display of banners of welcome'.[45] Eubank depicts the prison's façade punctuated by beams of light; its inmates viewing the royal procession in a temporary reversal of the prison's internal system of surveillance by which they were usually surveyed.

In the background of Eubank's canvas in the border between the earth and sky, are the mountainous forms of the natural landscape. These are testimony to the ancient, geological origins of the city, around which they form a natural border. Moving from extremity to centre, the painting continues to represent the historical strata of the built environment. By dividing the main body of the canvas vertically into two contrasting halves, Eubank maintains the division between the old and new towns of

---

[44] *The Scotsman*, 17 August 1822, p. 258.
[45] *A Picturesque Sketch of the Landing of His Most Gracious Majesty King George IV*, p. 6.

Edinburgh. The old town below on the left side of the image is represented as dark, dense and disordered: a ragged chaos of multi-storied tenements built upon steep slopes and winding streets. In J. G. Lockhart's *Peter's Letters to His Kinsfolk*, which he published under a pseudonym (Edinburgh, 1819), the builders of the old town are described as 'appear [ing] as if they had made nature the model of their architecture', where the crowded buildings 'are not easily to be distinguished from the larger and yet bolder forms of cliff and ravine, among which their foundations have been pitched'.[46] The old town appears an organic extension of the natural geological landscape. In contrast, Eubank's image of the new town built on a regular plan with its broad, straight streets, is bathed in a golden light. Its shining, rather than smoking, buildings are spacious and ordered. Register House is visible on the right. This public building designed by Robert and James Adam recorded the entire terrain of Scotland and its legal owner-ship. It was both record repository and working office, housing the govern-ment and legal offices concerned with the creation of the records.[47] The cosmic form of the seventy-six feet high dome with an external diameter of ninety-three feet has been read as part of the ideology of the New Town.[48] In Eubank's painting, the golden light permeating the New Town offers a visual metaphor for the Scottish Enlightenment whose urban birthplace was Edinburgh; the builders of this part of the city taking not nature as their model, but art, specifically ancient architecture. Descriptions of Edinburgh as the 'Athens of the North', the Athens to London's Rome, gained common currency from the early nineteenth century.[49] The dis-tinctive combination of its geological and topographical landscape, of mountains, plain, sea and acropolis, made Athens and Edinburgh natural equivalents; the parallels becoming more explicit when Edinburgh adopted Greek revival as its architectural vocabulary for the streets and squares, the educational, legal and civic buildings of the New Town. By the time of George IV's visit, a project to build a replica of the Parthenon as a National Monument to the Scottish servicemen killed in the Napoleonic Wars on the top of Calton Hill had been approved. Simpson wrote to Scott of the procession as it came up the east end of Princes Street, 'The panorama was

---

[46] [J. G. Lockhart], *Peter's Letters to His Kinsfolk* (Edinburgh, 1819), p. 3.

[47] Margaret H. B. Sanderson, *'A Proper Repository': The Building of the General Register House* (Edinburgh: Scottish Record Office, 1992), p. 10.

[48] See Thomas A. Markus (ed.), *Order in Space and Society: Architectural Form and Its Context in the Scottish Enlightenment* (Edinburgh: Mainstream, 1982), p. 9.

[49] John Lowrey, 'From Caesarea to Athens: Greek Revival Edinburgh and the question of Scottish identity within the Unionist State', *Journal of the Society of Architectural Historians* 60 (2001), pp. 136–157.

in front. One turn to the left, and the *Place des Victoires,* as the French would have termed it, came full in view! – the street of Waterloo [Waterloo Place], and the pillar of Trafalgar! – the cliffs of the *Acropolis,* whose summit was already prepared for the *Parthenon.*'[50] George IV's representatives attended the laying of the foundation stone for the National Monument during the royal visit on 27 August.[51] The 'pillar of Trafalgar' that Simpson refers to is a monument to Nelson in the form of an inverted telescope by Robert Burn erected on the Calton Hill. *A Picturesque Sketch* lauded the pillar as 'the proud national memento, to the memory of the hero whose nautical thunders restored the courses of the political world, of which it will stand, as the Herculean pillars, to the end of creation'.[52] Alongside the Trafalgar Pillar, the projected National Monument commemorated the 'firm bold and manly' Scots (as Scott put it) who served as active participants in the expansion and consolidation of Britain's global empire during the Napoleonic Wars.[53] 'the metropolis of Scotland is as healthy as any city or town in the British empire' pronounced Charles Steade in 1819 – an imperial view echoed by many visitors.[54]

Eubank's image (Plate XXV) is *more* than a portrait, or an urban landscape of the new and old towns, that Washington Irving during a visit to Edinburgh in 1817 conceptualised as the drawing room and the office to emphasise their distinctiveness.[55] It visually represents a historically significant event, the first royal visit to Scotland in a hundred and seventy years, since that of Charles II in 1650, *and* the first visit of a Hanoverian monarch since Scotland's political Union with England in 1707. Alexander Gordon bemoaned this point in his letter to Hugh Irvine quoted at the start of the chapter. The ant-like figures in the epoch-making procession form a dramatic, sweeping curve around the base of the Calton Hill; smoke emanating from the summit of the castle indicates the firing of the cannons; Eubank's historical canvas culminates in a contemporary vision of Edinburgh as a cultural metropolis that is modern and progressive in its

---

[50] [Simpson], *Letters to Sir Walter Scott,* p. 58.

[51] John Gifford, 'The National Monument of Scotland', *Architectural Heritage* 25 (2014), p. 54.

[52] *A Picturesque Sketch of the Landing of His Most Gracious Majesty King George IV,* p. 6.

[53] *Hints Addressed to the Inhabitants of Edinburgh and Others,* p. 21.

[54] [Charles Steade], *A Tour to the Highlands of Scotland and the Isle of Staffa with a Short Description of the Lakes of Windemere and Derwentwater,* 1819. YCBA, DA 865.S74. For Mrs Cox who made a thirty-one-day tour of Scotland from May to July 1822, Edinburgh was 'one of the noblest cities in the Empire'. NLS Acc. 12285 folios 28–29.

[55] S. T. Williams (ed.), *Tour in Scotland 1817 and Other Manuscript Notes by Washington Irving* (New Haven, 1927), p. 29.

urban improvements.[56] George IV's visit to Edinburgh in August 1822 was 'a remarkable event in our national annals' proclaims *A Historical Account of His Majesty's Visit to Scotland*, with the Scots themselves being figured as 'a highly improved and enlightened people' according to one of the *Letters to Sir Walter Scott*.[57]

The visit of George IV was designed to inculcate a rehabilitated view of Scots, that saw them as improved and enlightened, transformed from the domestic enemies of Jacobitism into compliant British subjects.[58] As master of ceremonies, Scott fabricated an erroneous pedigree for the monarch, in which 'King George IV. comes hither as the descendant of a long line of Scottish Kings. The blood of the heroic Robert the Bruce – the blood of the noble the enlightened, the generous James I. is in his veins . . . In short, we are THE CLAN, and our king is THE CHIEF.'[59] In what Simpson describes as 'a spirit of universal reconciliation', the bloody animosity between Jacobite Highlanders and previous Hanoverian monarchs was visually recast a spectacle of loyalty to George IV.[60] David Wilkie witnessed first-hand the 'the gathering of the Clans from the north', writing to Perry Nursey on 13 September that their 'alacrity and spirit [was] not unlike that their fathers showed in the 45 [they] have been with an equal disregard of consequences, been at the expense of fitting out a hundred men each that they might welcome in becoming form their great Chief of Chiefs. Those who appeared were the Macgrigors, the Drummons, the clanrannalds, the Sutherlands, and the Macdonals of Glengary.'[61] The precise number of clansmen varies according to different epistolary accounts. Sir Walter Scott wrote to MacLeod of MacLeod to bring half a dozen or half a score of Clansmen with him from the Isle of Skye 'so as to look like the Island Chief you are. Highlanders are what he [the king] will like best to see'.[62] Wilkie's letter suggests a hundred men per clan, while as many as a thousand is cited in a letter of Mrs. Louisa Forbes to Mrs MacLeod of MacLeod![63]

These Highland chiefs bought their clansmen to Lowland Edinburgh as loyal subjects to their newly designated clan chief, George IV. The

---

[56] My understanding of Edinburgh as a cultural metropolis, as opposed to a political or commercial one, is indebted to Ian Duncan, *Scott's Shadow: The Novel in Romantic Edinburgh* (Princeton, NJ: Princeton University Press, 2007), esp. pp. 8–20.

[57] [Mudie], *A Historical Account of His Majesty's Visit to Scotland*, p. 1; [Simpson], *Letters to Sir Walter Scott*, p. 35.

[58] As [Mudie] points out in *A Historical Account*, p. 3, the English saw all Scots as Jacobites.

[59] *Hints Addressed to the Inhabitants of Edinburgh and Others*, pp. 6–7.

[60] [Simpson], *Letters to Sir Walter Scott*, p. 72.   [61] BL, Add. MS. 29991 folio 34.

[62] 23 July 1822. NRAS, 2950/4/909.   [63] NRAS, 2950/4/1137/11.

Highlanders' congregated presence was visually stamped on the official proceedings by their distinctive tartan dress. Formerly part of the armoury of Jacobitism discussed in the previous chapter, the wearing of Highland dress in Scotland was outlawed in the wake of the '45 by an Act of Parliament. The Act was repealed in 1782 and by the royal visit of 1822 tartan was re-appropriated as a cloth of loyalty rather than sedition. Being attired in full Highland dress meant being swathed in layers of plaid, and appropriately armed. One of Simpson's letters to Scott observes how the Highlanders were drawing for George IV the same claymores, which their grandfathers had brandished seventy years before *against* George II.[64] Wilkie's letter wryly notes how at the Drawing Room held at Holyrood Palace on 20 August, the carriage of 'a Highland chieftain with the handsomest liverys accompanyd by 4 running footmen in the Highland dress armed with targets and Lochaber Axes as if in defence of the Ladies who lighted and entered the hall in elegant court dresses'. The former weapons of Highland martial culture mobilised during the '45 were re-cast as the prosaic trappings of polite Edinburgh society.[65] Wilkie's letter offers a further social critique of the event, where the equipages are judged in general to be inferior to those of a court in London. Yet the dialectic between England and Scotland, metropolitan centre and impoverished periphery, was no way as pronounced, or as controversial during the royal visit as that between the cultural identities of the Scottish Highlands and Lowlands. 'We are now all Jacobites, thorough-bred Jacobites, in acknowledging George IV', enthused the *Edinburgh Observer*, embracing Scott's contrived continuity between the Stuarts and Hanoverians.[66] The radical *Scotsman*, in contrast, insisted: 'too much has been done to give a Highland complexion to the whole of the exhibitions connected with the royal visit, as if nothing were Scottish but what is Highland'.[67] Scott's stage-managed pageantry perpetuated a homogenous vision of Scotland as a nation in which the exterior trappings of Highland culture formed a vital part of the scopic spectacle. In reality, Highland culture was facing social and economic crisis, rather than anything like the carnivalesque festivities perpetuated in Edinburgh in August 1822, that one newspaper report thought 'more grand..[than] the Fairy Tales of the East'.[68] The 'whole land was *tartanized*, in the royal eye [wrote Simpson

---

[64] [Simpson], *Letters to Sir Walter Scott,* p. 72.

[65] See David H. Caldwell, 'The re-arming of the clans, 1822', *Review of Scottish Culture* 21 (2009), pp. 67–86.

[66] Quoted in Prebble, *The King's Jaunt*, p. 206.   [67] *The Scotsman*, 17 August 1822, p. 258.

[68] *Glasgow Sentinel*, 21 August 1822. NRS, GD105/740/33.

in one of his *Letters*], from Pentland to Solway, much in the same manner as the Welsh might be made to overshadow the rest of the people of England'.[69] Franz Fanon's description of the decolonised culture that the intellectual leans towards as 'often no more than a stock of particularities. He wishes to attach himself to the people; but instead he only catches hold of their outer garments' seems an apt summary of Scott as pageant and wardrobe master for the 1822 royal visit.[70] He 'had to arrange everything [wrote Lockhart later in his *Life of Scott*] from the ordering of a procession to the cut of a button and the embroidering of a cross'.[71]

The Jacobite/Hanoverian impasse was the more chronologically distant uprising that the royal visit sought to retrospectively mend in a spectacle of loyalty. The other, more recent, was the so-called Radical War or Scottish Insurrection of 1820. When Lowland radicals in the counties of Ayr, Dumbarton, Glasgow and Renfrew announced on 1 April that a provisional government of Scotland was to be established, some 50–60,000 workers responded to a call for a national strike. According to Whatley what 'was virtually a state of open war existed between working class communities and the authorities'.[72] By 17 August 1822, the day of the Levee at Holyrood Place, a Miss Jane Fleming from Barochan in Renfrewshire would write from Edinburgh that 'no one could have guessed that Radicalism has ever been in fashion so completely is it now exploded'.[73] Even before the king disembarked from the royal yacht, on 14 August, Miss Fleming had noted 'Whig and Tory are equally loyal at present, and the wrongs of Queen Caroline forgotten in the expectation of the Monarch's condescending visit'. The radicals had flocked to support the estranged queen in part to mobilise the masses and as a means of conflating her oppression at the hands of George IV with their own. 'order & good behavior seem to govern all ranks', G. L. Meason wrote to the Revd Buchanan, 'The Country people throw down their sickles & run to the city, and the ripe corn stands. Numbers of them have paced on foot to town, saved their little pittance to get a peep of Royalty & turn back delighted at the little they see'.[74]

With George IV as the newly designated Chief of the Clan, it seems highly fitting for him to have dressed in the Stuart tartan (supposedly the

---

[69] [Simpson], *Letters to Sir Walter Scott*, p. 74.

[70] Franz Fanon, *The Wretched of the Earth* (London: Penguin, 2001), p. 180.

[71] J. G. Lockhart, *Life of Scott* (Edinburgh: T. C. & E. C. Jack, 1902), VII, p. 45.

[72] Christopher A. Whatley, *Scottish Society, 1707–1830: Beyond Jacobitism, Towards Industrialisation* (Manchester: Manchester University Press, 2000), p. 316.

[73] NRAS, 276/2/29.   [74] NRAS, 1948/4.

tartan of his ancestors!) on at least one occasion during the royal visit.[75] The single sartorial episode when the king wore Highland dress was to provide a lasting visual memory of the event and to perpetuate it as little more than a pantomimic charade. In contrast with the visual data discussed so far, the oil paintings and engravings by artists who witnessed first-hand the events in Leith and Edinburgh, graphic representations of the monarch's sartorial foray, or faux pas, into plaid provides a view of the proceedings that was in no way endorsed by members of the Edinburgh establishment, like William Adam, or the royal household. In a series of unofficial engravings published in London, the king is shown equip for a northern visit, to borrow the title of one of the satires. In this image by Charles Williams published prior to the king's embarkation (Figure 50), George IV is shown accompanied by his travelling companion, the former Lord Mayor of London, Sir William Curtis. Both men are wearing kilts, the king's cut dangerously high above the knee, and swathed in plaid. George wears the Orders of the Garter and Thistle; his uniform is embellished with voluminous epaulets and a bonnet of ostrich feathers. In the accompanying text, the king rebukes Curtis for wearing the Highland dress, saying the former Lord Mayor is too old for such 'freaks', unlike George himself who is 'every inch a Scot'. The irony is double-pronged, since George is represented as physically enormous, yet despite his many inches of flesh, he is genealogically, corporally, emphatically *not* Scottish.

Curtis to the right with his bottle-nose in profile, proclaims himself a loyal subject in adopting the tartan, but also cautions 'we must take care of the Lasses, for this dress is but little better than Achilles's fig leaf'. Curtis refers here to the impropriety of women viewing a naked bronze statue known as the Achilles monument to the Duke of Wellington (Figure 51) executed by the sculptor Richard Westmacott that was erected in London's Hyde Park a month before the royal visit in July 1822 (Figure 52).[76] The eighteen-foot high, thirty-two ton *Achilles* was a slightly modified bronze replica of one of the Quirinale horse tamers in Rome, also known as the Dioscuri, Castor and Pollux. Its identification as Achilles derived from a tradition that enjoyed currency in the early nineteenth century that the ancient sculptural pairing of Castor and Pollux was raised in honour of Achilles and was executed by the master-sculptor of fifth century BC Greece, Phidias. The bronze version of the Castor by Westmacott in

---

[75] A. V. B. Norman, 'George IV and Highland dress', *Review of Scottish Culture* 10 (1997), pp. 5–15, notes that 1822 was not the first time George IV wore Highland dress.

[76] My discussion is based on Marie Busco, *Sir Richard Westmacott, Sculptor* (Cambridge: Cambridge University Press, 1994), pp. 51–55.

Figure 50: Charles Williams, 'Equipt for a Northern Visit', c. 1822. 30.5 × 21.43 cm. City Art Centre, City of Edinburgh Museums & Galleries.

Figure 51: Richard Westmacott, *Achilles Monument*, 1822. Negative number: 832/8 (29 & 30). Conway Library, The Courtauld Institute of Art, London.

Hyde Park was cast from twelve, twenty-four pound French cannons captured during Wellington's victorious campaigns at Douro, Salamanca, Vittoria, Toulouse and Waterloo.[77] The refashioning of the *spolia* into sculpture cost £10,000 and funds were raised by a group of patriotic British women, hence its appellation in the popular press as the 'Ladies' man' or the 'Ladies' Trophy'. In a pre-emptive gesture insisted on by the

---

[77] Marie F. Busco, 'The "Achilles" in Hyde Park', *Burlington Magazine* 130 (1988), p. 921.

Figure 52: Alexander Nasmyth, *The Erection of Westmacott's Statue of Achilles*, 1822. 17 × 26.9 cm. National Galleries of Scotland.

gentlemen on the committee and designed to deflect moral objections, a fig leaf was attached to the genitalia of the colossal sculpture prior to its unveiling, but scandal still ensued among the public and in the press. Satirists had a visual riot representing the titillating aspects of gendered viewing, especially of polite, metropolitan British women getting an eye-full of Achilles. Curtis's topical comment about the kilt being little better than Achilles' fig leaf invokes a stereotypically negative view of Highland Scots as impoverished barbarians for their absence of underwear. Making the kilt equivalent to a fig leaf – at least in mixed company – for converging the eyes on the private parts that it is supposed to camouflage. By referring to the Achilles Monument, the unknown artist of this visual satire contextualises George IV and Curtis wearing of Highland dress in Edinburgh in terms of a topical public viewing scandal in the urban metropolis.

Both the king and Curtis wore Highland dress at the Levee at Holyrood Palace on 17 August. David Wilkie thought the former 'looked finer than I every saw him in any dress', while the latter bespoke 'a compliment which no alderman has ever paid that cloth before'.[78] Yet the satirical images deliberately contrived to conflate the wearing of tartan at the Levee at Holyrood Palace with the Drawing Room held three days later at the same location when the king wore Field Marshal's uniform. Harriet Scott described the king wearing tartan at the Levee in a letter to her daughter,

> with Buff colourd Trowsers like <u>flesh</u> to <u>imitate</u> his <u>Royal knees</u>, and little Tartan bits of stockings like other Highlanders half up his legs, & he looked very well only a little <u>huffle buffle</u> by all accounts, but I can tell you better how he looks when we see him . . . I am sorry to hear that everybody is presented to him [at the Drawing-Room on 20 August], so we Ladies are <u>all</u> to be <u>kissd</u> which is a great bore, & I think is very ridiculous, as if he was a new king <u>or</u> we were all new people.[79]

In contrast with the martial, masculine cast of much of the spectacle surrounding the royal visit, five hundred society women attended the Drawing Room, 'their trains sailing as they advanced to his Majesty', wrote Wilkie, who thought the scene 'very imposing'.[80] Predictably, the satires eliminated all traces of the august ceremony and reworked it, as, for instance, 'A Thousand warm receptions in the North' (Figure 53). In this image, the king lunges at one of the crowd of women brought forward to meet him, all richly attired in court dress and ornamented with jewellery and ostrich feathers. The right-hand side of the image and the speech bubbles above firmly locate the thousand warm receptions in the scopic

[78] BL, Add. MS. 29991 folio 34.   [79] 17 August 1822. NRS, GD157/2548/3.
[80] BL, Add. MS. 29991 folio 34.

Figure 53: 'A Thousand warm receptions in the North', 1822. 23.6 × 33.4 cm. © The City of Edinburgh Council. Licensor www.scran.ac.uk.

domain. 'My Eyes!' proclaims Curtis of the 'warm work' of escorting the ladies to meet their king. They in turn, adopt different optical accessories and modes of vision – one squints through an eye-glass in order to 'see all very plain', another obscures the view with her fan, while a third asks her to put the fan down to grant her a 'peep'. At least two of the women speak in thick Scottish accents, a ventriloquising echoed in a letter of 29 July from Mrs Louisa Forbes to Mrs Macleod of Macleod: 'All the Edin.ʳ dames are going to Court forsooth & truth to say there's none of us very bonnie but that we're to make up by being very <u>braw</u>.'[81] Forbes added that Mrs Macleod might 'get a new <u>train</u> at the Laird of Macleods expence – Gold & Silver & Tissue seems the dandy O'.

It is the king and Curtis who are cast as dandies in the engraved satires that constitute an enduring paper trail of the royal visit. In a third, even more explicit image by George Cruickshank, Geordie and Willie are said to be 'keeping it up' while 'Johnny Bull pays the piper!!' (Figure 54). This image forms the frontispiece to a play in verse entitled *Kilts and Philibegs!!!* in which Geordie, the Emperor of Gotham makes a northern excursion with Sir Willie Curt-his, the court fool. The title of the engraving makes a pointed economic projection – that it is the English who are bearing the financial burden of the royal visit to Scotland, while the subtitle of the piece pronounces itself as a 'serio-tragico-comico-ludrico-aquatico burlesque gallimaufry'. As in the previous example, the sartorial and social circumstances of the separate Levee and Drawing Room events are graphically conflated. Obese Geordie plants an imperial kiss onto the lips of one of the women who are assembled around him in an unappealing assortment of shapes and sizes. Renowned for his promiscuity, he misquotes Burns's 'Green Grow the Rashes O', 'The sweetest hours that ere I spent it was among the lasses O!'[82] His enormous sporran is represented as a fox's head with its hairy protuberance extending almost to the king's tiny feet. Next to him, the similarly rotund figure of Curtis – 'this voluptuous ignoramus' as he was dubbed in the memoirs of one onlooker – is doing a Scottish jig dressed in tartan with sausages around his neck and a carving knife and fork secured around his waist.[83] Wearing a turtle for a sporran, and clicking his fingers, Curtis extorts the emaciated, barefoot Scots piper to 'play up' on his bagpipes.

---

[81] NRAS, 2950/4/1137/11.

[82] John Morrison, *Painting the Nation: Identity and Nationalism in Scottish Painting, 1800–1920* (Edinburgh: Edinburgh University Press, 2003), p. 60.

[83] David Johnston. Quoted by Eric G. E. Zuelow, '"Kilts *versus* Breeches": The royal visit, tourism and Scottish national memory', *Journeys* 7.2 (2006), p. 46.

Figure 54: George Cruickshank, *Kilts and Philibegs!!!*, c. 1822. 13.3 × 20.8 cm. © The Trustees of the British Museum.

According to McMillen's research into matters chelonian, the turtle's existence in the eighteenth century was dual: being both comestible and material, food and object, making it 'a veritable walking banquet'.[84] During the royal visit to Edinburgh of August 1822, turtle soup was one of the dishes on the menu at the banquet at Parliament House, along with grouse soup, stewed carp and vension.[85] The soup was made from the head of the animal and was known for its aphrodisiac qualities and culinary rarity: it was a highly prestigious dish given the logistics of transporting West Indian marine turtles alive in freshwater tanks.[86] The woman conversing with Curtis in 'A Thousand warm receptions in the North' refers to the 'warm work' of eating this gastronomic delicacy in June (Figure 53). In contrast, a bowl inscribed royal porridge is situated between our protagonists (Figure 54). Even with the 'royal' appellation, Scotland's national dish made from oatmeal was one of culinary impoverishment. Either its contents are steaming, or the exuberant Geordie and Willie are farting profusely into it. The double row of sausages around the former Lord Mayor's neck illustrate the slang term 'alderman in chains', which is how a turkey garnished with sausages was dubbed, so making this derisive representation a graphic feast or veritable banquet for the senses – the eye, ear and mouth.

In our final satirical engraving again by George Cruickshank (Plate XXVI), Curtis is shown solo, full-length, filled-out and head-to-toe, or cockaded bonnet to cockaded and ribboned buskins, in tartan with a hirsute sporran and a basket-hilted sword and dirk. 'Bonnie Willie's' gaze is drawn in three-quarters view to the left and he is located in a stereotypically 'Scottish' Highland landscape, with the sea behind him to the left and mountains on the right, a thistle in the right foreground. This former Lord Mayor of London is depicted as having usurped the exclusive right of Highland clan members to wear their traditional dress. Coupled with this act of sartorial pilfering is further evidence of art historical plagiarism. Cruickshank's engraving deliberately evokes the series of large-scale oil on canvas portraits of Highland chiefs executed at full-length during the Regency by the so-called 'prince of Scottish portrait painters', the

---

[84] Krystal McMillen, 'Eating turtle, eating the world: Comestible *Things* in the eighteenth century', in Ileana Baird and Christina Ionescu (eds.), *Eighteenth-century Thing Theory in a Global Context: From Consumerism to Celebrity Culture* (Aldershot: Ashgate, 2013), p. 191 and p. 194.

[85] *Account of the Royal Visit of George IVth to Scotland* (Kilmarnock: H. Crawford, 1822), p. 19.

[86] Holgar Hoock, 'From beefsteak to turtle: Artists' dinner culture in eighteenth-century London', *Huntington Library Quarterly* 66 (2003), p. 42. See too Christopher Plumb, *The Georgian Menagerie: Exotic Animals in Eighteenth-Century London* (London: I.B. Tauris, 2015), 'Turtle travels far', pp. 61–74.

Edinburgh artist, Henry Raeburn.[87] Though Raeburn's first biographer, Allan Cunningham, described his subject as 'a favourite with all who wore tartan', his tartanised sitters actually constitute a tiny percentage of his portrait output.[88] Cruickshank's engraved portrait of Curtis is pictorially indebted to Raeburn's portrait of Colonel Alastair Ranaldson Macdonell of Glengarry (Plate XXVII), which was exhibited at the Royal Academy in London in 1812.[89] A review of the annual exhibition published in *The Examiner* described the portrait of Macdonell as follows: 'In his picturesque and rich Highland dress, his head turned in a reverse direction from his body, one arm akimbo, the other horizontally stretched out and his hand holding a musquet, he stands with an easy dignity characteristic of the head of a Clan.'[90] Cruickshank lampoons Curtis's adoption of the indigenous dress and triumphant pose of the military chief of a Highland clan by this obese English alderman. Glengarry's painted portrait is located in a vast interior space, where Highland weapons adorn the cavernous walls like trophies. Curtis's exterior topographical landscape finds parallels in other portraits in Raeburn's repertoire, including that of Francis MacNab.[91] 'The MacNab' as he was known is represented as autochthonous: his implacable facial features and indomitable pose echoing that of the mountainous landscape and the tumultuous skyscape. Raeburn's portraits of Highland chiefs have been read by Fintan Cullen as a form of nostalgic fiction. Despite their visual seduction as images of power, the clan system and traditional dress was 'more a fossil than a contemporary reality' of Highland life.[92] Cruickshank's engraving of Curtis extends the nostalgic fiction of Raeburn's portraits as a representation of the colonial appropriation of the dress of indigenous Highland culture.

Among surviving correspondence to the Lord Chief Commissioner, William Adam, is the following previously unpublished letter from Raeburn, dated 22 August 1822:

I have heard [he writes] that the King was so much pleased with the appearance and dress of a Gent.ⁿ in the highland garb that he had been requested by order of his majesty to sit for his picture to the king's Painter – now I believe I need not tell your Lordship, that the honour of being the King's Painter for Scotland and the salary

---

[87] Centre for Research Collections, The University of Edinburgh, La. IV. 20 R1 f3 (David Laing).

[88] Allan Cunningham, *The Lives of the Most Eminent British Painters, Sculptors and Architects* (New York: Harper & Bros., 1834), IV, p. 197.

[89] Duncan Thomson, *Raeburn: The Art of Sir Henry Raeburn, 1756–1823* (Edinburgh: Scottish National Portrait Gallery, 1997), no. 47.

[90] *The Examiner*, 5 July 1812, p. 428.   [91] Thomson, *Raeburn*, no. 46.

[92] Fintan Cullen, 'The art of assimilation: Scotland and its heroes', *Art History* 16 (1993), pp. 600–618.

attached to it has been enjoyed for forty years by a Mr Abercromby a rich man, bred a Clergyman and who never had a brush in his hand. How he is to acquit himself of this commission is not easy to say.[93]

The gentleman sitter of this projected portrait 'in the highland garb' remains unknown; as does whether the request was ever realised. Less elliptical is Raeburn's petitioning of Adam in an attempt to secure the royal commission for himself. Visual testimony of George IV's esteem for Highland garb is imaged in this official, whole-length portrait (279.4 × 179.1 cm) of the king by David Wilkie, dated 1829 (Plate XXVIII). Had Raeburn not died soon after being appointed King's Limner for Scotland in May 1823, it is reported that he would have executed the commission for the monarch's portrait in full Highland dress.[94] He was knighted by George IV at Hopetoun House outside Edinburgh on the final day of the royal visit on 29 August (a week after he wrote to Adam) and was one of seven artists examples of whose works were exhibited for the king in rooms adjacent to his closet at Holyrood. In a letter dated 19 August, William Adam explained how the works of the artists named by the king, Raeburn, Andrew Wilson, Hugh William Williams, Revd John Thomson, Alexander Nasmyth, Andrew Geddes and George Watson 'would enable His Majesty to judge of the state of the Art in this Country'.[95] The next and final chapter considers the conceptualisation of the 'Scottish School of painters' which first began to be documented in the Edinburgh press and periodical literature during the 1810s.

In rhetorical stature, Wilkie's official portrait (Plate XXVIII) is indebted to those of Raeburn already discussed, where the Hanoverian King George IV is cast in a visual realisation of Scott's directive 'we are THE CLAN, and our king is THE CHIEF'. The worm's eye view perspective places the viewer in an unequivocal position of subordination to the king whose Highland accoutrements were supplied by George Hunter & Co. of Edinburgh and London at a total cost of £1354.18.0.[96] Their account, dated 23 September 1822, confirms that the king's wardrobe on this occasion consisted of sixty-one yards of royal satin plaid, thirty-one yards of royal plaid velvet and seventeen and a half yards of royal plaid cashmere. The single most expensive item was the £375 badge for the king's bonnet, which was set with diamonds and other precious stones all held in

---

[93] NRAS, 1454/2/281.

[94] See Georgina Low's letter dated 3 September 1822 to her brother John in St Helena: 'The king, it is said, ordered him [Raeburn] to take a portrait of him in Highland garb, that he was dressed in at the levee.' Ursula Low, *Fifty Years with John Company* (London, 1936), p. 15.

[95] NLS, Acc. 12092/52.   [96] Royal Archives, GEO/MAIN/29600.

a wreath of golden thistles, surmounting a large emerald. For the king's Highland dirk (Plate XXIX), the dirk and knife blades were 'inlaid with gold' with a 'Crimson velvit scabbard, richly ornamented with chased gold mountings, with Royal Arm's of St Andrew, Thistle &c, top of the sea green Emerald, top of the knife Scotch Topase, top of the fork fine Amathyst' supplied for £262.10. Prebble has noted that in Wilkie's official portrait the colour and texture of the king's Highland clothes 'are discreetly muted' so that no badges or buckles of gold are visible, no jewelled weapons, goatskin or steel.[97] The same is true of the 'pair of fine gold shoe Rosets, with vibrating Center made of felegree gold, studied all over with variegated gems' supplied by Hunter & Co. for £94.10. Even so, the king is presented in his official portrait as a luxurious, almost exotic specimen of Highland prowess, at a time when, ironically, Highlanders were increasingly becoming an endangered species. This disparity between historical reality and scopic delusion was constantly at play during the royal visit to Edinburgh in August 1822.

David Wilkie's eyewitness account of the series of events that constituted the royal visit, in a letter to Perry Nursey dated 13 September 1822, has been quoted throughout this chapter. It describes the visual component of the proceedings as surveyed by his professional gaze: 'looking at it with the eye of a painter the variety and brilliancy of the costumes and buildings and scenery, seemed to recall those of the best times of the Art'.[98] Wilkie's juxtaposition of the visual culture of dress ('costumes'), with the built environment ('buildings') of Edinburgh and topographical landscape ('scenery') of its environs dominates many of the texts and images documenting the royal visit that we have looked at. His subsequent correspondence with Nursey records his perspicacious progress on a canvas devoted to some aspect of the visit. By November 1822, he has been 'considering and reconsidering [the visit] again, to work up some subjects from have made multitudes of sketches, with the King and without the King, but as yet without hitting upon anything to satisfy me. It presented in reality scenes of the greatest excitement, but to reduce these upon canvas seems the difficulty, and I have not yet been able to accomplish it.'[99] The difficulty of reducing spectacle onto canvas was given 'new force' in July 1823 when the Fife-born Wilkie was appointed Limner to the King for Scotland after Raeburn's death. He wrote to Nursey, 'it has converted me into a prisoner to a certain extent upon the public and being in regard to Scotland a non

---

[97] Prebble, *The King's Jaunt*, p. 76.　　[98] BL, Add. MS. 29991 folio 35.
[99] 26 November 1822. BL, Add. MS. 29991 folio 36.

resident, I feel desirous to make such application of my art that in spirit at least I may not be subject to the additional charge of being a Sinecurist . . . I am still engaged with the different sketches in hopes that something may grow out of it consistent with the ancient designation of my office.'[100] The completed canvas took another six to seven years to materialise, during which time Wilkie had a nervous breakdown and spent three years travelling abroad. Measuring 126 by 198.1 cm this was a large-scale visual representation of a state event (Plate XXX) whose crowded figural content make it appear to be a guest list of a court faction. The same is true of Rubens's *Coronation of Maria de' Medici*, which he saw in Paris in 1814 and which has been cited as a possible prototype for Wilkie's canvas.[101]

Rather than investigating its cosmopolitan, art historical genealogy, *The Entrance of George IV at Holyroodhouse* (Plate XXX) needs to be looked at as the culmination of the scopic spectacle on 15 August 1822; the official painterly production by Wilkie of an onerous royal appointment. Dressed in Field Marshal's uniform, the king arrives at the supposed ancient palace of his ancestors, the kings of Scotland, to be greeted by representatives of the Scottish nobles and peoples. The Scottish peoples consist entirely of women and children, so denoting George IV as *paterfamilias* and *pater patriae*. The keys to the Palace are presented to him by the kneeling figure of the 10th Duke of Hamilton, in full Highland dress. As hereditary keeper of the household, the Duke of Argyll stands at the entrance to the palace in his family tartan. Henry Lord Montagu made a pointed social comment in a letter to his mother, the Duchess of Buccleuch, in which Argyll appeared in Highland dress 'quite like a Highlander & a gentleman which few of our Highlanders look like. He seems as much at his ease as if he had always worn the dress.'[102] These aristocrats are represented by Wilkie as symbolically transferring the patrimony of Holyrood Palace to their king. On the left of the entrance, is the 4th Earl of Hopetoun in his uniform as Captain-General of the Royal Company of Archers and next to him, Sir Walter Scott. The Honours of Scotland consisting of the Crown of Robert I or Robert the Bruce is carried on horseback by Sir Alexander Keith, hereditary knight marshal. The sword of State presented to James IV by Pope Julius II in 1507 and the sceptre, fashioned during the reign of James V are

---

[100] 26 July 1823. BL, Add. MS. 29991 folio 40.

[101] H. A. D. Miles and David Blayney Brown, *Sir David Wilkie of Scotland (1785–1841)* (Raleigh: North Carolina Museum of Art, 1987), no. 32, p. 225. See Ronald Forsyth Millen and Ronald Erich Wolf, *Heroic Deeds and Mystic Figures: A New Reading of Rubens'* Life of Maria de' Medici (Princeton, NJ: Princeton University Press, 1989), p. 107.

[102] Montagu's letter of 18 August 1822 describes Argyll at the Levee, rather than the entrance to Holyrood. NRAS, 859/box 190/bundle 5.

presented by Keith's attendants representing the Countess of Sutherland and Earl of Morton. The ancient symbols of Scottish political power (Figure 55) had signified the king's presence at sittings of the Scottish Parliament following the coronations of Charles I and II in 1633 and 1651.[103] After the Union of the English and Scottish Parliaments in 1707, the symbols, divested of their political charge, were locked away in the Crown Room at Edinburgh Castle. They were rediscovered over a century later in 1818, when George IV as Prince Regent authorised at Scott's instigation, a royal warrant to search for the lost Honours. The Commissioners, including Scott, who were responsible for their unearth-ing in a sealed chest, compiled a detailed report of the proceedings accom-panied by a graphic inventory consisting of seven scale drawings executed in pencil, oil and ink by the Scottish artists William Home Lizars, John Thomson, William Allan and Andrew Geddes.[104]

The inclusion of the Honours in Wilkie's historical canvas (Plate XXX) and less noticeably, in the right background of his portrait of the king (Plate XXVIII), evokes their participation in one of the series of spectacles that constituted the royal visit to Edinburgh of August 1822. In a re-enactment of the pre-Union ceremony known as The Riding of the Parliaments, the Honours were escorted with the king in a procession on 22 August along the Royal Mile from Holyrood Palace to Edinburgh Castle. 'It seems a rather silly contrivance', wrote Lord Montagu, that the regalia should be carried from the Castle to the Palace so the king could carry it back to the Castle.[105] Whatever the behind-the-scenes preparative arrangements, it was the associa-tions of the fugitive spectacle that were designed to impress. 'This was a proud sight for Scotsmen to behold [proclaimed *A Narrative of the Visit of George IV to Scotland*]; and as it was in view, the days of Wallace and Bruce, and of those who ruled after them, – of the changes which time, and peace, and industry had effected, – could scarcely fail to actuate the thoughts and direct the reflections'.[106] Here again, a kaleidoscopic shift is effected in terms of the chronological sequence of Scottish history with a reference to the plebeian appeal of Wallace and Bruce. In much the same way, *A Historical Account of His Majesty's Visit to Scotland*, (Edinburgh, 1822) provides arguably the most prescient account of Wilkie's canvas (Plate XXX), in which the crowds 'seemed to consider the entrance of his Majesty within the Palace as completing the solemn inauguration of Him as King of Scotland, – as the actual revival, under

---

[103] Helen Smailes, *Andrew Geddes, 1783–1844: 'A Man of Pure Taste'* (Edinburgh: National Galleries of Scotland, 2001), pp. 51–52.
[104] NRS, SP12/2/15.   [105] NRAS, 859/box 190/bundle 5.
[106] *A Narrative of the Visit of George IV to Scotland* (Edinburgh, 1822), p. 51.

THE REGALIA OF SCOTLAND. *(From a Painting by Alex. Geddes.)*

Figure 55: 'Engraving of the Regalia of Scotland', from James Grant, *Old and New Edinburgh*, volume II. 10.2 × 14.4 cm. City of Edinburgh Council – Edinburgh Libraries www.capitalcollections.org.uk.

a modified form, of the Scottish monarchy'.[107] This is pure visual propaganda: a representation of the revival of the inauguration of a Hanoverian monarch as king of Scotland that was politically, if not ideologically, meaningless.

The cultural metropolis that was Edinburgh chose to commemorate the historic 1822 visit of their king with a colossal (335 cm high) portrait sculpture of George IV cast in bronze, for the sum of £3,000 (Figure 56).[108] The commission and erection of this statue will bring our account of the scopic spectacle in August 1822 to its conclusion. According to *A Narrative of the Visit of George IV to Scotland* (Edinburgh, 1822), the resolution was made at a general meeting of the Institution of the Fine Arts during the visit on 21 August for an equestrian statue of the king to be paid for by public subscription of three guineas for the gentlemen and one guinea for the ladies.[109] The choice of artist and preferred location would be determined by the king. We next hear about the proposed statue in an unsolicited overture to William Adam from the sculptor, Richard Westmacott, who was responsible for the controversial Achilles Monument to the Duke of Wellington in London's Hyde Park (Figure 51). In a letter dated the month after the royal visit, on 24 September, he

had hoped & I will not despair, that an occasion may still favour me in paying my respects to you & in distinguishing myself at Edinburgh. I hear that a compliment is intended to His Majesty for that place. My late success in Bronze & which in magnitude & difficulty of achievement is without a parallel for 1200 years might allow me some small hope of being thought of but I am a stranger in Edinburgh & yourself I believe my own friend if however you should hear that there is no immediate promise I should be highly flattered by being mentioned.[110]

Westmacott's technical prowess in reviving the ancient art of bronze casting could not begin to compete with the favoured reputation of Francis Chantrey among Edinburgh's civic and legal elite. Having already completed statues for the Faculty of Advocates at Parliament House of Henry Dundas, 1st Viscount Melville and Lord President Blair in 1818, with a third sculpture of Lord Chief Baron Dundas commissioned, Chantrey was the obvious candidate for the sculpture of the king.[111] Once the requirements shifted to a pedestrian statue rather than an equestrian one, the Edinburgh bronze was to be a

---

[107] [Mudie], *A Historical Account*, p. 109.

[108] Ilene Lieberman, Alex Potts and Alison Yarrington, 'An edition of the ledger of Sir Francis Chantrey, R. A., at the Royal Academy, 1809–1841', *The Walpole Society* 56 (1991/2), no. 196a.

[109] *A Narrative of the Visit of George IV to Scotland* (Edinburgh, 1822), 41. See NLS, AP.5.210.03.

[110] NRAS, 1454/2/282.

[111] Lieberman, Potts and Yarrington, 'An edition of the ledger of Sir Francis Chantrey', nos. 26, 28, 117a.

Figure 56: Francis Chantrey, *Pedestrian bronze statue of George IV on a granite plinth,* 1831. Photograph by John McKenzie.

variant of that by Chantrey already erected at Brighton. At committee meetings, the preferred location of the statue was debated at length, with the king said to be in favour of its erection at the Castle Battery.[112] This elevated viewpoint had featured in the official ceremonials of 22 August, when following a grand military procession to the castle, described by Simpson as being 'almost scenic', the king ascended the half-moon battery.[113] Simpson's letters recounts, 'While he [the king] looked round on the noble picture of city and country, land and sea, hill and valley, spread out before him and saw at one glance the assembled myriads of his subjects by whom he had just been hailed, he was himself visible to every eye'.[114]

Once again and for the final occasion, Simpson delineates the domain of the scopic, where the monarch's aerial view is described as a 'picture'. Like Eubank's painted canvas (Plate XXV), it is a picture that defies categorisation in Edinburgh's unusual topographical combination of cityscape, urban landscape, rural landscape and seascape. Simpson explicitly invokes the metaphorics of the eye in describing an optical exchange between the king and his subjects, in what may be viewed as the physical embodiment of Scott's directive: 'It is not enough that we should see the King; but the King must also see US.'[115] The glance that Simpson refers to is a specific viewing activity, which, in de Bolla's account, is ordered by and through the virtual spaces, in which it moves.[116] Norman Bryson's account of the glance seems opaque in this context as it is not furtive or concealing, but rather fleeting and all encompassing.[117] More relevant to our account is his differentiation of the glance from other viewing activities like the gaze. The gaze is prolonged and contemplative, regarding the visual field with an aloofness and disengagement, suggests Bryson. Simpson employed the term 'gaze' for the monocular viewpoint of the living mosaic of the Calton Hill. De Bolla proffers a third form of viewing activity: the look, a catoptric mode in which the eye requires self-reflection to register its own power to see and to recognise its instrumentality in visuality.[118] We might recall Mrs. Harriet Scott 'looking & seeing' as the procession passed in front of her house at York Place.

---

[112] W. E. K. Anderson (ed.), *The Journal of Sir Walter Scott* (London, 1972), p. 561 n. 5.

[113] [Simpson], *Letters to Sir Walter Scott*, p. 84.

[114] [Simpson], *Letters to Sir Walter Scott*, p. 85.

[115] *Hints Addressed to the Inhabitants of Edinburgh and Others*, p. 22.

[116] de Bolla, 'The visibility of visuality', pp. 284–285.

[117] Norman Bryson, *Vision and Painting: The Logic of the Gaze* (London: Macmillan, 1983), chapter 5, 'The gaze and the glance', p. 94.

[118] de Bolla, 'The visibility of visuality', p. 285.

When Chantrey supervised the erection of the statue of George IV in Edinburgh in 1831, its location had altered again and for the third time, from in front of Register House, to the aerial Castle Battery, to the heart of the New Town. Elevated on a pedestal of red Aberdeen granite eight feet high and positioned at the intersection of George Street (named after King George III) and Hanover Street (after the dynasty), George IV stands swathed in a robe with the sceptre in his right hand (Figure 56), forever gazing towards the Old Town with its castle on whose battery 'He was like Jove himself', enthused Jane Fleming.[119]

The visit of George IV to Edinburgh in August 1822 was a spectacle, or more properly a series of spectacles staged over successive days in the Debordian sense of operating 'as society itself, as a part of society and as a means of unification'.[120] It offered a fabricated view of Scots as a nation unified on several fronts: culturally, socially and politically. In the first instance, Scotland was afforded one collective cultural identity that was homogenous – propagated in a spectacle of sameness in which Highland and Lowland were concretised as coterminous. Residue of the hostility between the working classes and the establishment authorities in the Lowlands was nowhere visible. The plaided panorama that united Scots sartorially and socially at the same time reconciled them as a people willingly serving Britain's global empire, where the progeny of once rebellious Highland Jacobites participated in a spectacle of loyalty to their Hanoverian monarch, George IV. If the spectacle is ideology materialised, so derivative material forms perpetuate that ideology. The officially endorsed art historical output that the chapter has focussed on – the portrait and landscape paintings and the monochrome engravings – could not make the nation entirely real in the sense described by the title of Smith's 2013 monograph.[121] Not only as in Samuel's analysis, 'the idea of the nation, though a potent one, belongs to the realm of the imaginary rather than the real', but also because there was little room for realism in the ideologies that, like the participants themselves, jostled to be seen and to get a view of the proceedings.[122] According to Debord, the spectacle 'erases the dividing line between true and false, repressing all directly lived truth beneath the *real presence* of the falsehood maintained by the organisation of appearances'.[123] Only the satires reinstated the dividing line

[119] NRAS, 276/2/29.

[120] Guy Debord, *The Society of the Spectacle* (New York: Zone Books, 1994), p. 12.

[121] Smith, *The Nation Made Real.*   [122] Samuel, 'Continuous national identity', p. 16.

[123] Debord, *The Society of the Spectacle*, p. 153.

between true and false in graphically puncturing the carapace of the facade. For the most part, the visual culture produced about and around the royal visit passively reflected the falsehood of these choreographed appearances, offering a suitably panoramic view of Edinburgh as a cultural metropolis, with its breath-taking natural and man-made vistas and its ecstatic swarm of viewers, that included the king.

6 | Borders Bard

'The Exactness of the Resemblance': Sir Walter Scott and the Physiognomy of Romanticism[1]

The present century has no name in its annals of more enviable distinction than that of Sir Walter Scott; the victories of Napoleon were not so wide, nor his monuments so likely to endure.

North American Review 32 (1831)[2]

---

[1] The phrase 'physiognomy of Romanticism' is from Georg Lukács, *The Historical Novel* (London, Merlin: 1962), p. 34. He claims it is completely wrong to see Scott as a romantic writer, in terms of his subject matter and his manner of portrayal, so I am using his expression although not his application of it in this chapter. I am aware that my use of the term Romanticism requires some explanation of 'this often rather monstrous historical figment of retrospective definition', as Malcolm Chapman describes it in *The Gaelic Vision in Scottish Culture* (London: Croom Helm, 1978), p. 19. I have no desire to add to the dizzying, not to mention dazzling, definitions that proliferate. Not do I wish labour this point, which could easily become a chapter in itself. My own view echoes that of M. H. Abrams, *Doing Things with Texts: Essays in Criticism and Critical theory* (New York and London: Norton, 1989), p. 117, that the Romantic and Romanticism is 'one of those terms historians can neither do with nor make do without'. Like him, I am using the word as 'an expository convenience', while aware that Scott is normally excluded from the 'big six' – the English poets of what Miles calls Institutionalised Romanticism (Robert Miles, *Romantic Misfits* (Basingstoke: Palgrave Macmillan 2008), p. 7). I am consciously avoiding sub-categorisations such as more or less romantic, early/late, pre- or post, necromanticism or neo-, highly or anti-, located at its limits, its core or beyond. With the exception of William Blake, the study of British Romantic literature and the visual arts was described by Morris Eaves in 2006 as 'a vast underexplored critical wilderness': see 'The sister arts in British Romanticism', in Stuart Curran (ed.), *The Cambridge Companion to British Romanticism* (Cambridge: Cambridge University Press, 2006), p. 238 and p. 237. In addition to those texts cited in the footnotes, the following have informed my thinking about Romanticism as it was inflected in Scottish literature: Leith Davis, Ian Duncan and Janet Sorensen (eds.), *Scotland and the Borders of Romanticism* (Cambridge: Cambridge University Press, 2004); Andrea K. Henderson, *Romantic Identities: Varieties of Subjectivity, 1774–1830* (Cambridge: Cambridge University Press, 1996); Caroline McCracken-Flesher, 'Walter Scott's Romanticism: A theory of performance', in Murray Pittock (ed.), *The Edinburgh Companion to Scottish Romanticism* (Edinburgh: Edinburgh University Press, 2011), pp. 139–149; Fiona Robertson, 'Romancing and Romanticism', in Fiona Robertson (ed.), *The Edinburgh Companion to Sir Walter Scott* (Edinburgh: Edinburgh University Press, 2012), pp. 93–105; Fiona Stafford, 'Scottish Romanticism and Scotland in Romanticism', in Michael Ferber (ed.), *A Companion to European Romanticism* (Oxford: Blackwell, 2005), pp. 49–66. When revising the chapter, I repeatedly bore in mind Jerome Christensen's comment in *Romanticism at the End of History* (Baltimore, MD and London: Johns Hopkins University Press, 2000), p. 3: 'Historically constructed, Romanticism remains under construction in the history that we are making.'

[2] *North American Review* 32 (1831), p. 386.

In *Possible Scotlands: Walter Scott and the Story of Tomorrow* (2005), Caroline McCracken-Flesher characterises Scott as 'the architect of cultural Scottishness'.[3] Drawing on Homi Bhabha's seminal formulation of the nation as constructed through narrative, she positions Scott's writings as 'an act of national valuation situated between peoples and places, authors and audiences, past and future'.[4] Her own narrative, she explains, is 'concerned with the constant and mutual encroachments of life and literature, and see both as circulating uncertainty in a marketplace of ideas that is aesthetic and national'.[5] This chapter seeks to reposition the aesthetic by inserting art as the third leaf of a triptych, so to speak, with life and literature. The import of visual and material culture as part of the romantic endeavour becomes in this account an act of national valuation through the validation by Scott in his literary output of Scottish peoples and places, pasts in the plural as opposed to the singular and modernity, rather than McCracken-Flesher's 'future'. In its privileging of art, it expectedly focusses on artists and audiences; on the illustrations that accompanied Scott's published works and on Scott himself who was the sitter-subject in a veritable production line of painted portraits. Both illustrations and portraits are considered as symptomatic of the encroachment of art on life and vice versa. The strictures Scott imposed on the illustrations accompanying his texts will be seen to inform that of his own portrait representation as part of the sartorial realia of local Scottish identities rather than their pictorial speciousness. Audiences are invoked and evoked as the readers of Scott's poetic and literary productions; in the many reviews of the annual Royal Academy exhibitions published in the flourishing periodical press and in the tourists who visited Scott's house Abbotsford in the Scottish Borders near Melrose.

The prevailing view in the existing secondary literature concerning Scott's ambivalent attitude to the visual arts is here contested in the productive interplay between literature, art and life. The chapter considers Scott as a notably 'pictorial' writer – a claim that dates back to the earliest reviews of his poetry – including the ekphrastic portraits he creates through words in his novels and the fictional artist Dick Tinto, a character in the 1819 novel *The Bride of Lammermoor*. Material culture is represented through the history of collecting with the array of objects that Scott acquired, received and displayed at Abbotsford. Writing to Lady

---

[3] Caroline McCracken-Flesher, *Possible Scotlands: Walter Scott and the Story of Tomorrow* (Oxford: Oxford University Press 2005), p. 3.

[4] McCracken-Flesher, *Possible Scotlands*, p. 18.

[5] McCracken-Flesher, *Possible Scotlands*, p. 26.

Compton in 1818 that his house in the process of being remodelled was 'in the bravura style of building or if you will what a romance is in poetry or a melo-drama in modern theatricals ... a sort of pic-nic dwelling'.[6] In revisiting this vast and unwieldy subject the chapter will not attempt to disentangle the 'pic-nic' – the interwoven threads between life, literature and art. To do so would be anachronistic given that they constitute Scott's historical physiognomy, so much as to cast them as romantic objects or commodities. Because it was part of the wider cultural process of romantic commodification – the conversion of use value into exchange value – that saw Scotland the nation reinvented in its personification as Scott-land; a literary topos identified as part of the hyperbole of the obituaries discussed later in the conclusion.

The manifestly pictorial character of Scott's writing has often been noted by art historians, as it was by reviewers of his work writing in early nineteenth-century periodicals. Part of one such response to Scott's most celebrated poem, the *Lady of the Lake* was published in the London-based *Quarterly Review* for May 1810:

Never, we think, has the analogy between poetry and painting been more strikingly exemplified than in the writings of Mr. Scott. He sees every thing with a painter's eye ... It is because Mr. Scott usually delineates those objects with which he is perfectly familiar that his touch is so easy, correct and animated. The rocks, the ravines and the torrents which he exhibits, are not the imperfect sketches of a hurried traveller, but the finished studies of a resident artist, deliberately drawn from different points of view; each has its true shape and position; it is a portrait; it has its name by which the spectator is invited to examine the exactness of the resemblance. The figures which are combined with the landscape are painted with the same fidelity. Like those of Salvator Rosa, they are perfectly appropriate to the spot on which they stand.[7]

While much in this sensory passage seems self-explanatory regarding Scott's intuitive literary relationship with the visual arts, it is worth clarifying for the creative synergy as this reviewer saw it, between poetry and art. The piece refers to Scott's painterly eye and his virtuoso 'touch' in delineating the landscape through words. It particularly praises Scott's mastery for what we might designate an aesthetic of intimate knowledge, in which the distinctions between the visual and the haptic, the genres of poetry and painting, landscape painting and portrait painting and the formal

---

[6] *The Letters of Sir Walter Scott*, H. J. C. Grierson (ed.) (London: Constable, 1932–7), V, p. 91.

[7] *Quarterly Review* 3 (1810), pp. 512–513. Unless otherwise referenced, the press cuttings I have used are among those in the Corson Collection in the Centre for Research Collections, University of Edinburgh.

structures of words and images seem deliberately fluid. The review proceeds by invoking contemporary exhibition culture ('the spectator is
invited to examine') and the professional credentials of the author-artist,
where it characterises Scott's delineations as 'the finished studies of
a resident artist', rather than the 'imperfect sketches of a hurried traveller'.
Scott's figures, like those of the seventeenth-century Italian painter,
Salvator Rosa, are said to be recognisably autochthonous ('perfectly appropriate to the spot on which they stand'.). Scott's subsequent preference for
artists who were, to paraphrase the *Quarterly Review*, resident rather than
itinerant, in terms of their familiarity with his indigenous Scottish subject
matter, were, as we shall see, a considerable preoccupation in the commissions awarded to artists illustrating his poetic and literary corpuses.

Catherine Gordon quotes an edited version of the *Quarterly Review*
piece in a pioneering article published in 1971, on the bicentenary of
Scott's birth, when she presented the results of her systematic study of
the Royal Academy and British Institution exhibition catalogues issued
between 1805 and 1870.[8] During this sixty-five-year period, Gordon calculated that over 300 painters and sculptors exhibited more than 1,000
Scott-related works in portraiture, genre scenes, literary or historical subjects. Scott's literary corpus offered artists a surfeit of riches – publishing
twenty-six novels in eighteen years that furnished artists with an encyclo-
paedic thematic repertory, with subjects ranging chronologically from
ancient Byzantium to modern European history.[9] One review of *Ivanhoe*
(1819) in the Whig periodical the *Edinburgh Review* (1820) describes its
author like Shakespeare as a 'prodigy of fertility'; another, in the *London
Magazine* for 1826 is highly critical of *Woodstock, or The Cavalier* (1826),
characterising Scott as a dealer in old clothes who '*renovates* (we believe
that is the phrase) his old thread-bare stories'.[10] Whatever their critical
reception, by 1830, every one of the major novels written between 1814 and
1826 had become a source for popular narrative painting. Gordon identifies what she designates an oblique approach to Scott's works, where the
link between his writing and the productions by artists is tangential. By
inference, there was also a direct approach whereby artists faithfully translated his works into the visual domain, with a narrative fidelity rather than

[8] Catherine Gordon, 'The illustration of Sir Walter Scott: Nineteenth-century enthusiasm and
adaptation', *Journal of the Warburg and Courtauld Institutes* 34 (1971), p. 297, p. 316.

[9] B. S. Wright, '"Seeing with Painter's Eye: Sir Walter Scott's challenge to nineteenth-century art',
in Murray Pittock (ed.), *The Reception of Sir Walter Scott in Europe* (London: Continuum,
2006), p. 312.

[10] *London Magazine* 5 (1826), p. 173.

a visual potency in the transferral from page to painting.[11] According to this model, the visual arts are subordinate to the narrative compulsion of Scott's historical fiction.[12] Errington proposes a third model: a series of complex interactions between early nineteenth-century literature and painting that were not parasitic, or symbiotic but enjoyed a buoyant synergy.[13] Her all too brief discussion counteracts the still prevalent belief in the supremacy of text over image, that artists followed 'obediently behind him [Scott] like a troupe of dogs at heel'.[14] Errington's is an apposite simile given that Scott is frequently represented in painted portraiture accompanied by one or more of his domestic canine companions – another instance of the interplay between life and art.

One facet of Scott's extensive corpus of pictorial writing that has been hitherto untapped by art historians is that one of his minor fictional characters is himself an artist, albeit an obscure and professionally unsuccessful one.[15] Chapter 1 of *The Bride of Lammermoor* (1819), one of the two tales in the third *Tales of my Landlord* series, constitutes a metafictional frame for the entire novel which is set before or just after the union of the English and Scottish Parliaments in 1707.[16] It opens with a parodic biography of Dick Tinto, the artist friend and former schoolmate of the narrator of the incipient tale, the schoolteacher, Peter Pattieson. Tinto is introduced to the reader via his fabricated lineage. Said to be of the ancient family of Tinto from Lanarkshire, when in reality, Pattieson explains, Tinto's father was a tailor from the west of Scotland, from a fictitious

---

[11] B. S. Wright, 'Scott's historical novels and French historical painting, 1815–1855', *Art Bulletin* 63 (1981), pp. 274–275.

[12] Duncan Forbes, 'Scottish historical painting in the 1820s: Tory hegemony and the spectacle of literary celebrity', in Terry Brotherstone, Anna Clark and Kevin Whelan (eds.), *These Fissured Isles: Ireland, Scotland and British History, 1798–1848* (Edinburgh: John Donald, 2005), p. 155 (referring to William Allan's history paintings).

[13] Lindsay Errington, 'Sir Walter Scott and nineteenth-century painting in Scotland', in Wendy Kaplan (ed.), *Scotland Creates: 5000 Years of Art and Design* (London: Weidenfeld & Nicolson, 1990), p. 121.

[14] Jeanne Cannizzo, '"He was a gentleman even to his dogs": Portraits of Scott and his canine companions', in Iain Gordon Brown (ed.), *Abbotsford and Sir Walter Scott: The Image and the Influence* (Edinburgh: Society of Antiquaries of Scotland, 2003), pp. 115–135. See also J. P. Carson, 'Scott and the romantic dog', *Journal for Eighteenth-Century Studies* 33.4 (2010), pp. 647–661, which considers the centrality of dogs in Scott's life and novels.

[15] Richard J. Hill argues that the artist and illustrator of Scott's novels, William Allan, was the model for Dick Tinto: see his *Picturing Scotland through the Waverley Novels: Walter Scott and the Origins of the Victorian Illustrated Book* (Farnham: Ashgate, 2010), pp. 124–130.

[16] D. S. Butterworth, 'Tinto, Pattieson, and the theories of pictorial and dramatic representation in Scott's "The Bride of Lammermoor"', *South Atlantic Review* 56.1 (1991), p. 1. I accessed all Scott's written works as e-texts via the Corson Collection website at the University of Edinburgh: www.walterscott.lib.ed.ac.uk/etexts/externalindex.html

place called Langdirdum. Apprenticed to a sign painter, Tinto became adept at painting horses, which 'came to look less like crocodiles, and more like nags', until a moment of revelation, when 'The scales fell from his eyes on viewing the sketches of a contemporary, the Scottish Teniers, as Wilkie has been deservedly styled. He threw down the brush took up the crayons, and, amid hunger and toil, and suspense and uncertainty, pursued the path of his profession'. This is the second occasion on which Scott names David Wilkie in one of his novels. The first is in *The Antiquary* (1816), where the interior of a fisherman's house in which the body of Mucklebackit's son has been laid out for his funeral is described as being 'a scene which only Wilkie could have painted, with the exquisite feeling of nature than characterises his enchanting productions'. A review of the 1818 annual Royal Academy exhibition hoped that 'the challenge [in the *Antiquary*] should not be thrown out in vain, and that Mr. Wilkie would turn his attention to a subject to which he alone can do adequate justice'.[17] Thirteen years after *The Antiquary* was published, Scott wrote to Wilkie in a letter dated 23 January 1829: 'I am glad you are pleased with the tribute offered to you in The Antiquary, though it is a little selfish on my part; for, after all, how could I better convey an idea of any particular scene, as by requesting my reader to suppose that you had painted it.'[18] A third reference to Wilkie occurs in chapter 18 of the *Heart of Midlothian* (1818), where Jeanie Deans is reunited with her father and scrutinises him like a corporeal connoisseur 'at arm's length, to satisfy her mind that it was no illusion'.[19] Scott describes the details of his dress, from toe to tip, from the 'the very copper buckles' to 'the broad Lowland blue bonnet', lingering on David Deans's distinctive physiognomy. The pen portrait ends with the following self-referential remark: 'so happily did they [Deans's features] assort together, that, should I ever again see my friends Wilkie or [William] Allan, I will try to borrow or steal from them a sketch of this very scene'. On this and other occasions in his novels, Scott refers by name or cites the generic paintings of contemporary Scottish artists whose pictorial output, as we shall see imminently, included portraits of Scott himself.

Back in chapter 1 of the *Bride of Lammermoor*, Pattieson meets Tinto several years later in the village of Gandercleugh, where the artist is not longer painting signs, having graduated to painting faces for the fee of a guinea a head. In a passage that was to be repeatedly cited in other

---

[17] *Literary Gazette and Journal of the Belles Lettres* (1818), p. 123.   [18] NLS, MS. 1752 folio 7.

[19] The phrase 'corporeal connoisseur' is from Barbara Maria Stafford, *Body Criticism: Imaging the Unseen in Enlightenment Art and Medicine* (Cambridge, MA and London: MIT Press, 1991), p. 84.

contexts, including a scathing review of the annual Royal Academy exhibition in *The Athenaeum* for 1833, Pattieson explains how, 'Amid his wants and struggles, Dick Tinto had recourse, like his brethren [Joshua Reynolds], to levying that tax upon the vanity of mankind which he could not extract from their taste and liberality – on a word, he painted portraits.'[20] Living in a village with a limited clientele of sitters, economic necessity forced Tinto to revisit his earlier career as a sign painter, a profession which he euphemistically refers to as an 'out of doors' artist and for which he contrives an entire art historical genealogy in a single sentence: 'why should I shun the name of an out of doors artist? Hogarth introduces himself in that character in one of his best engravings; Dominichino, or somebody else, in ancient times, Morland in our own, have exercised their talents in this manner.' Moving first to Edinburgh, whose 'gentlemen dispensed their criticism more willingly than their cash, and Dick thought he needed cash more than criticism', Tinto the peripatetic painter continued south to London. Once based in the metropolis, he failed there too and died in obscurity. An obituary printed in the corner of the *Morning Post* referred to an advertisement announcing that a Mr. Varnish, printseller, had a very few drawings and paintings by Richard Tinto for sale – with which the nobility and gentry might wish to complete their collections of modern art. Pattieson describes London as 'the universal mart of talent, and where, as is usual in general marts of most descriptions, much more of each commodity is exposed to sale than can ever find purchasers'. In the importunate life story of this failed Scottish artist, Tinto's limited works only accrued a commodity value in the saturated metropolitan marketplace once he had died.

Having outlined this short biographical sketch of his former friend's unsuccessful artistic career and premature death, Pattieson recalls their previous conversations concerning the matter at hand – the narrating of the novel of the Bride of Lammermoor – to which Tinto had at some point envisaged an illustrated edition 'with heads, vignettes, and cul de lamps, all to be designed by his own patriotic and friendly pencil'. Among these conversations, Pattieson remembered that Tinto had complained that Pattieson's characters (in what is surely a pun on the latter's name) '*patter* too much', with 'nothing in whole pages . . . but mere chat and dialogue'. While Pattieson defends the dialogic narrative, Tinto advocates the

---

[20] *The Athenaeum*, (1833), p. 297. 'This tax has been levied with a merciless hand by artists of the year 1833 . . . Portrait . . . everywhere prevails', the review continued, stipulating that out of 1,107 paintings, around 600 were portraits and among 118 sculptures, eighty were portrait busts.

conjuring of images through words via a descriptive narrative, insisting that 'Description was to the author of romance exactly what drawing and tinting were to a painter; words were his colours, and, if properly employed, they could not fail to place the scene, which he wished to conjure up, as effectually before the mind's eye, as the tablet or canvass presents it to the bodily organ.'[21] The similarity between the arguments marshalled by Tinto and the early reviews of Scott's poems, that stress their pictorial quality, as in that devoted to the *Lady of the Lake* in the *Quarterly Review* for May 1810, is striking. Providing a visual demonstration for his argument, Pattieson recounts how Tinto produced a sketch from a portfolio from which he proposed to execute a preposterously colossal (fourteen foot by eight foot) canvas representing the interior of an Elizabethan hall, with a beautiful woman watching a debate between a young man who seemed to be urging a claim of right to the mother of the young woman. Though Pattieson recounts having admired the sketch, he was unclear as to its subject. Tinto proceeds to describe having visited the ruins of an ancient castle in the mountains of Lammermoor on the coast between East Lothian and Berwickshire. Staying for two or three days at a farmhouse in the neighbourhood, he had been told the history of the castle by his elderly landlady and had resolved to produce a history paint-ing – the most esteemed of the painterly genres – of the singular events that had taken place in it. '"Here are my notes of the tale," said poor Dick, handing a parcel of loose scraps, partly scratched over with his pencil, partly with his pen, where outlines of caricatures, sketches of turrets, mills, old gables, and dovecots, disputed the ground with his written memor-anda.' It was from this bricolage of preparatory images and fragments of text that Pattieson was to compose the story that follows concerning the *Bride of Lammermoor*; that climaxes in chapter 33, where the events imaged in Tinto's preparatory sketch, the confrontation between Edgar Ravenswood and Lady Ashton, observed by a silent Lucy Ashton, are narrated.

Prior to this narrative denouement, however, the memory of Tinto resurfaces in the novel, in chapter 26, in a description of a portrait in Ravenswood's apartment at the home of John the cooper:

A staring picture of John Girder himself ornamented this dormitory, painted by a starving Frenchman, who had, God knows how or why, strolled over from Flushing or Dunkirk to Wolf's Hope in a smuggling dogger. The features were,

---

[21] See Butterworth, 'Tinto, Pattieson, and the theories of pictorial and dramatic representation', p. 3.

indeed, those of the stubborn, opinionative, yet sensible artizan, but Monsieur had contrived to throw a French grace into the look and manner, so utterly inconsistent with the dogged gravity of the original, that it was impossible to look at it without laughing. John and his family, however, piqued themselves not a little upon this picture, and were proportionably censured by the neighbourhood, who pronounced that the cooper, in sitting for the same, and yet more in presuming to hang it up in his bedchamber, had exceeded his privilege as the richest man of the village; at once stept beyond the bounds of his own rank, and encroached upon those of the superior orders; and, in fine, had been guilty of a very overweening act of vanity and presumption. Respect for the memory of my deceased friend, Mr. Richard Tinto, has obliged me to treat this matter at some length; but I spare the reader his prolix though curious observations, as well upon the character of the French school as upon the state of painting in Scotland at the beginning of the 18th century.

This ekphrasis introduces a fictional portrait into the gallery of words that is the novel *The Bride of Lammermoor*.[22] The term ekphrasis is used in its mid nineteenth-century meaning, when it came to be reinterpreted as a special kind of description of art objects that was divorced from its rhetorical background in antiquity. If I am guilty of a 'cavalier treatment of an ancient term', it seems entirely in keeping with the humorous tone of the passage – Girder's portrait is no Homeric shield of Achilles or Keats's Grecian Urn.[23] Pattieson's description provides the reader with nuggets of information on the ekphrastic portrait as regards its anonymous émigré artist, the composition, with its gallic veneer, and its mode of display. The reported response of the viewer to this immaterial canvas conjured by prose – that it was 'impossible to look at it without laughing' – is less applicable to the genre of painted portraiture as to caricature, a particular mode of pictorial representation which Tinto had practised in his youth when apprenticed to his tailor father. Pattieson explains in chapter 1 how Tinto Senior's customers had begun 'loudly to murmur, that it was too hard to have their persons deformed by the vestments of the father, and to be at the same time turned into ridicule by the pencil of the son'. Both portraiture and caricature form part of the province of physiognomy, that in the so-called romantic period was a practice as well as a system, 'a subject area and a mode of inference' that involved the empirical study of the lineaments of a person's face to judge their nature.[24] Caricature is also

---

[22] John Hollander, 'The poetics of *ekphrasis*', *Word & Image* 4 (1988), pp. 209–218.

[23] Ruth Webb, '*Ekphrasis* ancient and modern: The invention of a genre', *Word & Image* 15.1 (1999), p. 8.

[24] Ludmilla Jordanova, 'The art and science of seeing in medicine: Physiognomy, 1780–1820', in W. F. Bynum and Roy Porter (eds.), *Medicine and the Five Senses* (Cambridge: Cambridge

a useful generic classification of Scott's pen portrait of Tinto. The sitter, John Girder, is said to have transgressed the stringent social codes within his village, in both the commissioning of his painted portrait and its display in his bedchamber. The satirical description of portraiture as 'a very over-weening act of vanity and presumption' recalls the earlier characterisation in chapter 1 of 'levying a tax upon the vanity of mankind'.

Pattieson's protracted musings on the preposterous portrait concerning its anonymous French artist, the sitter and his social pretensions, are contrasted with the potentially fascinating morsels of information that he chooses *not* to expand upon at the close of the passage, concerning Tinto's own thoughts on the character of the French school and the state of painting in Scotland at the beginning of the eighteenth century, when the novel is set. These were pressing cultural concerns by the early decades of the nineteenth century, as witnessed in an article entitled 'Remarks on the history of painting in Scotland' which was published two years before the *Bride of Lammermoor* in the *Edinburgh Magazine and Literary Miscellany* for 1817. It attempted to define the characteristics of a distinctly Scottish school of painters as follows:

> Many circumstances, it is true, contribute to produce and to modify the genius of a people; but there is a strong presumption, I apprehend, from the romantic character of the scenery of this country, the peculiar *naïveté* of our national character, and our decided tendency to catch what is striking and picturesque, either in the appearances of nature, or in the aspects of character – a tendency so unequivocally displayed in the idiom of our language that the genius of our artists would naturally display itself with the happiest effect, either in depicting the more romantic scenery of nature, or in expressing those peculiarities of our national manners which offer so many fine subjects for its exhibition.[25]

These 'Remarks' reveal how a national painterly tradition was codified in the early nineteenth-century periodical press. Its primary determinants are identified as the rendering of the inherent features of scenery and char-acter, where 'our decided tendency to catch what is striking and pictur-esque' in visual representation parallels a linguistic equivalence. Notice the repetition of 'romantic' in its contemporaneous description of the natural Scottish landscape. The idea of a homogenous school of artists, whose productions are essentially and profoundly 'Scottish' has enjoyed longevity

University Press, 1993), p. 122 and p. 124; Melissa Percival, *The Appearance of Character: Physiognomy and Facial Expression in Eighteenth-Century France* (Leeds: W. S. Maney for the NHRA, 1999), p. 44.

[25] *Edinburgh Magazine and Literary Miscellany* 80 (1818), p. 327.

in the historiography of Scottish art well beyond its preliminary articulations in print. It is this hoary canon, which is seemingly impenetrable, that the narrative of this book seeks to offer as an alternative account. It has effectively made a notion of 'Scottish' painting intractable – captive in an idealised concept of native genius forged two centuries ago, in the later 1810s and 20s.

One of the founder members of the Scottish School of portrait painters as it was classified in these early nineteenth-century Edinburgh periodicals was Henry Raeburn. If Wilkie was the Scottish Teniers, as Scott referred to him in the *Bride of Lammermoor*, then the elder statesman Raeburn was often dubbed the Scotch Reynolds. Scott refers to him by name in a passage in chapter 71 of *Waverley; or, 'Tis Sixty Years since* (1814), his novel dealing with the Jacobite uprising in 1745, in another ekphrasis, which describes a double portrait of the eponymous protagonist and the Highland chief, Fergus Mac-Ivor:

It was a large and spirited painting, representing Fergus Mac-Ivor and Waverley in their Highland dress, the scene a wild and rocky mountainous pass, down which the clan were descending in the background. It was taken from a spirited sketch, drawn while they were in Edinburgh by a young man of high genius, and had been painted on a full length scale by an eminent London artist. Raeburn himself, (whose Highland Chiefs do all but walk out of the canvas) could not have done more justice to the subject; and the ardent fiery, and impetuous character of the unfortunate chief of Glennaquoich was finely contrasted with the contemplative, fanciful, and enthusiastic expression of his happier friend.

Scott conveys an evocative impression of the fictional full-length double portrait through its studies of the contrasting characters of Mac-Ivor and his companion Waverley. He refers to the genealogical evolution of the portrait from sketch to oil, in its geographical passage from Edinburgh to London. The painting itself is said to be taken from a sketch drawn from life in Edinburgh and then painted from the sketch and enlarged to life-size by a London artist. Neither of the Edinburgh or London artists responsible for the portrait at its different evolutionary stages is referred to by name; only Raeburn, who is lauded for the extraordinary verisimilitude of his portraits of Highland chiefs (as in Plate XXVII), is afforded such an appellation.[26] Peacocke has pointed out that no illustrator ever rendered Scott's description

---

[26] Lynda Nead refers to the literary phenomenon of the walking portrait – as in Walpole's *The Castle of Otranto*. See her *The Haunted Gallery: Painting, Photography, Film c. 1900* (New Haven, CT and London: Yale University Press, 2007), p. 49. Thanks to Helen McCormack for this reference.

of the double portrait in graphic form – neither did they attempt a visual rendering of the John Girder portrait in the *Bride of Lammermoor*.[27] He also draws attention to the flagrant anachronism that is the mention of Raeburn in a novel dealing with the '45 rebellion, where the reference to the painter is 'the hook to pull the reader into Scott's own modernity'.

Of the co-authors of the *Bride of Lammermoor*, Frederick Burwick remarks: 'Dick Tinto, no less than Peter Pattieson, is Scott's narrative persona'.[28] In light of such identifications, it is tempting to map literature onto life, to read these ekphrastic passages from Scott's *Waverley* and the *Bride of Lammermoor* autobiographically, as the pointed musings of an author whose prodigious literary corpus was regularly issued and reissued in illustrated editions and who was himself repeatedly exposed as a sitter to the art and artifice of portrait painting including by 1819 two portraits by Henry Raeburn. McCracken-Flesher has characterised this as the 'constant and mutual encroachments of life and literature', to which we are inserting art as the third leaf in the romantic triptych.[29] Scott regularly blurred the distinctions between these categorisations, for instance in the idiosyncratic catalogue of his collection at Abbotsford, which remained unpublished during his lifetime. Its title *Reliquiae Trotcosienses, or the Gabions of the late Jonathan Oldbuck Esq. of Monkbarns*, linked the work to Scott's third novel, *The Antiquary* (1816) set during the British wars against Revolutionary and Napoleonic France, whose titular hero, Jonathan Oldbuck, has an estate at Monkbarns that had once formed part of the lands of the Abbey of Trotcosey. Scott defined a gabion within the manuscript as a curiosity of small intrinsic value, whether rare books or small articles of the fine or useful arts, a notably broad definition which tellingly encompasses the productions of literary, visual and material culture.[30] Yet once we try and extend the correspondences between Scott and Oldbuck more meaningfully, they seem to deliberately confound us. This is part of the dialogic push and pull or the simultaneous embrace and repudiation of the real that characterises Scott's Romanticism.[31] The redolent description

[27] E. R. Peacocke, 'Facing history: Galleries and portraits in *Waverley's* historiography', *European Romantic Review* 22.2 (2011), p. 187 and p. 203.

[28] Frederick Burwick, 'Competing histories in the Waverley novels', *European Romantic Review* 13 (2002), p. 265.

[29] McCracken-Flesher, *Possible Scotlands*, p. 26.

[30] Walter Scott, *Reliquiae Trotcosienses, or, the Gabions of the Late Jonathan Oldbuck Esq. of Monkbarns*, Gerald Carruthers and Alison Lumsden (eds.) (Edinburgh: Edinburgh University Press, 2004), p. 6.

[31] Ann Rigney, *The Afterlives of Walter Scott: Memory on the Move* (Oxford: Oxford University Press, 2012), sees push and pull as the key to understanding the afterlives of Scott's work; I would argue they are at work during his lifetime.

of Oldbuck's study published in the 1816 novel, bears little relation to Scott's counterpart at Abbotsford, whose interiors were being planned at the same date.[32] The reader first sees Oldbuck's sanctum through the unfamiliar eyes of his companion and first-time visitor to Monkbarns, Lovel. The view is initially distorted as the dust, disturbed by the uninvited cleaning of his niece and the chambermaid, settles. The eclectic mass of two- and three-dimensional objects in a variety of media (books, armour, bronzes, portraits) disarrayed on the floor, tables and chairs in a room furnished with oak panels and a tapestry, is reminiscent in its eclectic material content, if not the disordered display, of Scott's own collections. He writes:

numberless others [volumes] littered the floor and the tables, amid a chaos of maps, engraving, scraps of parchment, bundles of papers, pieces of old armour, swords, dirks, helmets, and Highland targets. Behind Mr. Oldbuck's seat (which was an ancient leathern-covered easy-chair, worn smooth by constant use) was a huge oaken cabinet, decorated at each corner with Dutch cherubs, having their little duck-wings displayed, and great jolter-headed visages placed between them. The top of this cabinet was covered with busts, and Roman lamps and paterae, intermingled with one or two bronze figures. The walls of the apartment were partly clothed with grim old tapestry ... The rest of the room was panelled, or wainscotted, with black oak, against which hung two or three portraits in armour, being characters in Scottish history, favourites of Mr. Oldbuck, and as many in tie-wigs and laced coats, staring representatives of his own ancestors. A large old-fashioned oaken table was covered with a profusion of papers, parchments, books, and nondescript trinkets and gewgaws, which seemed to have little to recommend them, besides rust and the antiquity which it indicates ... The floor, as well as the table and chairs, was overflowed by the same mare magnum of miscellaneous trumpery, where it would have been as impossible to find any individual article wanted, as to put it to any use when discovered.

Rather than its Abbotsford counterpart and the collections therein, the disarray of Oldbuck's study echoes Scott's account in *Paul's Letters to his Kinsfolk* (1816) of the detritus littering the field after the battle at Waterloo:

All ghastly remains of the carnage had been either burned or buried, and the relics of the fray which remained were not in themselves of a very imposing kind. Bones of horses, quantities of old hats, rags of clothes, scraps of leather, and fragments of books and papers strewed the ground in great profusion ... Letters, and other

---

[32] Clive Wainwright, *The Romantic Interior: The British Collector at Home, 1750–1850* (New Haven, CT and London: Yale University Press, 1989), p. 160.

papers, memorandums of business, or pledges of friendship and affection, lay scattered about on the field – few of them were now legible.[33]

The creation of domestic and foreign tourism in Scotland is often attributed to Scott, especially in the posthumous hyperbole of the obituaries, with Abbotsford as an unmissable destination on the Borders part of the tour. Yet more needs to be said about him as a consumer, as well as a contributor to mass tourism including his August visit to the site of Waterloo in Belgium just two months after the decisive defeat of Napoleon. Historians agree that Waterloo was a turning point in history for Britain and the participating nations, whether they were victorious or defeated.[34] For our purposes, it is strategic to position Waterloo and Scott's visit to the battlefield as a fulcrum in a narrative of modernity. From the 'field where legitimate government had trampled over the forces of anarchy and despotism' (writes Shaw, in a sentence that might have been written contemporaneously by the victors), Scott acquired objects of material culture for the collection at Abbotsford, including a cuirass and sword and a soldier's memorandum book.[35] Later conjuring a portrait of the 'magpie-like compositor' in *Paul's Letters to his Kinsfolk*, 'sifting through the ruins of Empire in search of the Romantic', as Shaw puts it.[36] According to this paratextual reading, Scott's literary persona is not so much Jonathan Oldbuck the antiquary as Dick Tinto, the artist, from whose 'parcel of loose scraps' Pattieson will compose the narrative of the *Bride of Lammermoor*.

Framed by the biographical portrait of the failed artist, Dick Tinto and including the ekphrastic portrait of John Girder, the *Bride of Lammermoor* parodies the art of portrait painting as an index of identity and a social institution of which by the time the novel was published in 1819, Scott was a veteran. Francis Russell's useful chronology of Scott portraits, published in his 1987 catalogue, has calculated that Scott sat for thirteen portraits by 1819, including two by Henry Raeburn and one, a family group at

---

[33] Yoon Sun Lee, 'A divided inheritance: Scott's antiquarian novel and the British nation', *English Literary History* 64.2 (1997), p. 554.

[34] Susan Colley, *Britons: Forging the Nation, 1707–1837* (New Haven, CT and London: Yale University Press, 1992), p. 323; Susan Pearce, 'The *matériel* of war: Waterloo and its culture', in John Bonehill and Geoff Quilley (eds.), *Conflicting Visions: War and Visual Culture in Britain and France, c. 1700–1830* (Aldershot: Ashgate, 2005), p. 209.

[35] Philip Shaw, *Waterloo and the Romantic Imagination* (Basingstoke: Palgrave Macmillan, 2002), p. 36. Pearce, 'The *matériel* of war: Waterloo and its culture', pp. 207–226, discusses material culture from the field of Waterloo but does not mention Scott's acquisitions.

[36] Shaw, *Waterloo and the Romantic Imagination*, p. 47. Shaw's chapter 1, 'Walter Scott: The discipline of history', pp. 35–66, discusses in detail Scott's poem *The Field of Waterloo* (published in 1816), where Scott 'first experienced the limits of poetic romance'. (38) His nine-volume biography of Napoleon was published in 1827.

Abbotsford, by David Wilkie. The inventory of his portraits on canvas and in sculpture – that vanity tax, as Scott put it in the *Bride* – would reach fifty-two by the time he died in 1832, making Scott one of the two most painted private figures of the late eighteenth and early nineteenth century; the other being the Duke of Wellington, the victorious commander of the British-led Allied army at Waterloo. This was quite an accolade for a man whose own physiognomy was judged to be unremarkable. 'Sir Walter's appearance certainly does not denote the extensive genius he has [a young Edinburgh woman recounted in her diary for January 1824] . . . His hair and eyes are light, and his lameness gives him an awkward appearance, but the charms of his conversation make his appearance forgotten'.[37] Because of his 'extensive genius', Scott was reported on at least one occasion as being 'absolutely besieged' by portrait painters; Washington Irving wrote to the artist C. R. Leslie from Paris in 1824: 'I am told the Great Unknown was absolutely besieged [at Abbotsford] by a legion of "panthers", that you really surrounded him – one taking a point blank elevation of him in full front – another in profile – another in rear – happy to sketch a likeness which ever side presented.'[38] Irving's second-hand account of Scott's multiple points of view for these parasitic artists echoes in reverse perspective a passage in the *Bride of Lammermoor*, where Tinto takes his sketch for the proposed colossal history painting and gazes at it 'as a fond parent looks upon a hopeful child . . . He held it at arm's length from me [Pattieson] – he held it closer – he placed it upon the top of a chest of drawers – closed the lower shutters of the casement, to adjust a downward and favourable light – fell back to the due distance, dragging me after him – shaded his face with his hand, as if to exclude all but the favourite object – and ended by spoiling a child's copy-book, which he rolled up so as to serve for the darkened tube of an amateur artist.' Tinto's chaotic exhibition of the sketch with its random placement and contrived lighting exposes him as one such amateur artist.

Francis Russell's catalogue contains some 233 inventoried items, consisting of sketches, paintings, portrait busts and full-length sculptures of Scott, arranged alphabetically by artist from William Allan to David Wilkie; a kaleidoscope of pictorial identities dating from when Scott was aged five or six years to various posthumous images, including a life-sized wax effigy by

---

[37] *Parties and Pleasures: The Diaries of Helen Graham, 1823 to 1826* (Edinburgh: Paterson, 1957), pp. 36–37.

[38] 8 December 1824. C. R. Leslie, *Autobiographical Recollections* (London, 1860), II, p. 160. Scott was not publicly acknowledged as the author of the *Waverley* novels until as late as 1827. His identity was, however, widely well known, as shown by Irving's letter.

Madame Tussaud's. The subtitle of Russell's work *A Study of Romantic Portraiture*, apparently refers to the chronological parameters of Scott's life, 1771–1832; it seems to adopt romantic as a period classification. Simultaneously, Russell's own take on portraiture is notably romantic in its idealisation of the genre. The assembled portraits of Scott offer a twofold commentary on their sitter, we are told, allowing us to follow his changing appearance and offer a series of separate, but related, impressions of his personality, where every likeness contributes 'to our experience of the man'.[39]

Russell's myopic view of painted portraiture as offering unmediated access to the 'real' Sir Walter Scott, might be contrasted with the observation of one of the panther-like artists, C. R. Leslie, who painted him in 1824 in a half-length portrait commissioned by George Ticknor (Figure 57).[40] Ticknor had visited Abbotsford in March 1819, writing that the house was 'a kind of collection of fragments of history . . . a kind of irregular, poetical habitation as ought to belong to him [Scott]'.[41] Prior to producing this portrait, which provides material testimony of Scott's burgeoning transatlantic reputation, Leslie wrote that 'All the portraits [of Scott] I have seen are somewhat like him, but none of them very strongly so'.[42] In a letter to his cousin in 1826, Scott judged his portrait by Thomas Lawrence (Figure 58) 'a very fair one and makes me think I may been a very illused gentleman on former occasions'.[43] Such was the widespread circulation of Scott's portrait in a variety of media that when Maria Edgeworth finally met him in Edinburgh in 1823 she recorded a disjuncture between the historical figure and his representation in literary, visual and material culture, where 'My first impression was that he was neither so large not so heavy in appearance as I had been led to expect by description, prints, bust & picture'.[44] One of the oil on canvas portraits of Scott included in Russell's catalogue actually capitalised on Scott's status as a seasoned portrait sitter when it was painted in 1828 (Plate XXXI).[45] Executed by James Northcote, a former pupil and biographer of Joshua Reynolds, from three recorded sittings, it is on a first glance a double portrait – a self-portrait of the artist shown armed with a palette and brush at work on

[39] Francis Russell, *Portraits of Sir Walter Scott: A Study of Romantic Portraiture* (London: F. Russell, 1987), p. 8.
[40] Russell, *Portraits of Sir Walter Scott*, no. 116.
[41] *Life, Letters and Journals of George Ticknor* (Boston, 1876), I, p. 283.
[42] C. R. Leslie, *Autobiographical Recollections* (London, 1860), II, p. 85.
[43] Russell, *Portraits of Sir Walter Scott*, p. 58.
[44] Quoted in Russell, *Portraits of Sir Walter Scott*, p. 2. Edgeworth is writing to her aunt in a letter dated 8 June 1823.
[45] Russell, *Portraits of Sir Walter Scott*, nos. 153 and 154.

Figure 57: C. R. Leslie, *Sir Walter Scott*, 1824. 91.5 × 71.1 cm. Photograph © 2019 Museum of Fine Arts, Boston.

a portrait of Scott for which he is sitting in Northcote's London studio. Installed on the bottom right of the canvas wearing a velvet Titian cap, Northcote represents himself standing before an enormous canvas of rectangular orientation.[46] The canvas is elevated on an easel that

---

[46] Ludmilla Jordanova, 'Picture-talking: Portraiture and conversation in Britain, 1800–1830', in Katie Halsey and Jane Slinn (eds.), *The Concept and Practice of Conversation in the Long Eighteenth Century, 1688–1848* (Newcastle: Cambridge Scholars Publishing, 2008), pp. 157–158.

Figure 58: Sir Thomas Lawrence, *Sir Walter Scott,* 1821–6. 161.7 × 132.9 cm. Royal Collection Trust/© Her Majesty Queen Elizabeth II, 2019.

corresponds with Scott's eye level and that is cropped by the right-hand vertical frame. Scott's portrait emerges in the bottom left of the canvas within a canvas. Scott the sitter is shown seated with his back to the shuttered studio window, in a three-quarter view to the external viewer. This in turn, is captured on canvas by the artist as a full-frontal view, with the fingers of his right hand resting on his chin. Portraits of female sitters hanging on the far wall of the studio gaze out and away from the more proximate encounter between portrait sitter and painter. On a table next to

Scott are some of the accoutrements with which he is regularly attired and cast as an author in the earlier painted portraits, including that by Lawrence (Figure 58) – a book, paper, and a quill in an inkwell. The original half-length canvas (96.5 × 124.5 cm) was commissioned from Northcote by Sir William Knighton, who is already familiar from the previous chapter as George IV's private secretary and physician. A member of the king's inner circle, Knighton's long-standing patronage of Northcote appears to derive from their shared descent in Devon, much like George Steuart and the Dukes of Atholl discussed in Chapter 2, which is further evidence of the long-standing patronage ties appended to local identities.[47]

Like Scott, citing the painterly productions of Wilkie or Raeburn in his novels, Northcote includes his own portrait in that of Scott (which is actually a double portrait) to bask in the reflected representational glory, or the cultural capital, of his celebrated sitter. In the artist's own words, 'I thought it a great honour to be on the same canvas with Sir Walter'.[48] At the Scott Centenary exhibition held in Edinburgh at the Royal Scottish Academy in July and August of 1871, 129 portraits of Scott were exhibited showing him from the ages of six to sixty (Figure 59). A review of the exhibition published in *Harper's New Monthly Magazine* the following year noted 'there were two Sir Walters, according to the eye that looked upon him. Some have painted the courtly baron in fine raiment, surrounded by luxury and grandeur; others have given us the rough Scotch countryman, with all his stumpiness of form and rude strength of feature.'[49] Northcote's 1828 portrait of Scott represents the identities of two interrelated Sir Walters on a single canvas – the experienced portrait sitter and renowned portrait subject.

If the portrait of Scott by Northcote is what we might designate intervisual – being a double portrait of Scott the literary celebrity with a self-portrait of the artist – an equally striking intertextual episode occurs with the reappearance of Dick Tinto in chapter 1 of Scott's *St. Ronan's Well* (1824). Here, the failed artist familiar from the earlier *Bride of Lammermoor* is, in the landlady Meg Dods's eyes, recast as 'the celebrated' Dick Tinto who, in what must have been during his sign-

[47] Mark Ledbury, *James Northcote, History Painting and the Fables* (New Haven, CT and London: Yale University Press, 2014), pp. 127–128. The original portrait is untraced; this reduced-size copy is now in the Royal Albert Memorial Gallery in Exeter. It has recently been reattributed to John Cawse after Northcote which merits further study.

[48] E. Fletcher (ed.), *Conversations with James Northcote, R.A.* (London, 1901), p. 130.

[49] *Harper's New Monthly Magazine* 44 (1872), pp. 324–325.

Figure 59: Frontispiece from the Scott exhibition catalogue, 1871. Showing portraits of Scott from age six to sixty arranged on an altar-like bookcase, from the top: a miniature painted in watercolour on ivory; marble bust by Francis Chantrey, 1820–1 (Figure 61); full-length oil on canvas by William Allan, 1831 and half-length oil on canvas by John Watson Gordon, 1830. © The City of Edinburgh Council.

painting phase, was responsible for repainting Dods's sign at Cleikum Inn, which the reader is told 'had become rather undecipherable; and Dick accordingly gilded the Bishop's crook, and augmented the horrors of the Devil's aspect, until it became a terror to all the younger fry of the school-house, and a sort of visible illustration of the terrors of the arch-enemy, with which the minister endeavoured to impress their infant minds.' Later in chapter 3, Meg admonishes one of her tenants, the artist Frances Tyrell, in her Scots dialect that he would 'never mak your bread' in the production of landscape sketches and associated views, but that 'Ye suld munt up a muckle square of canvass, like Dick Tinto, and paint folks ainsells . . . I warrant, ye might make a guinea a-head of them. Dick made twa, but he was an auld used hand, and folk maun creep before they gang.' In response, Tyrell was able to reassure his landlady that for the sketches he had shown her, he was often better paid than those artists who produced portraits or coloured drawings. 'He added, that they were often taken for the purpose of illustrating popular poems, and hinted as if he himself were engaged in some labour of that nature.' Once again, the temptation is to read Scott's text autobiographically, in which as an inferred illustrator of popular poems, the fictional Tyrell joins the cohort of early nineteenth-century English and Scottish artists who were commissioned to produce images to accompany his robust output of verse (his own popular poems) and later, his historical fiction. It is to these artists and their pictorialisation of Scott's Scottish subject matter that the chapter now turns as life continues to encroach on literature, to encroach on art in a centripetal direction.

In an often-quoted letter to Joanna Baillie, dated 30 March 1810, Scott discussed the illustrations executed by the English artist, Richard Westall to accompany his forthcoming poem, the *Lady of the Lake*:

You are quite right as to my private opinion of Westalls illustrations – they are barely [basely?] devised like almost every thing of the kind I ever saw – but what would have it availd to have said so to the artist or to poor Longman [the publisher] – the deed was done. By the way I understand there are two rival sets of illustrations in preparation for the Lady of the Lake, even before she makes her appearance. Both will probably be execrable for if Westall who is really a man of talent faild in figures of chivalry where he had so many painters to guide him, what in the Devils name will he make of Highland figures. I expect to see my chieftain Sir Rhoderick *Dhu* (for whom let me bespeak your favour) in the guize of a recruiting serjaint of the Black Watch and his Bard the very model of Auld Robin Grey upon a japand tea-tray.[50]

---

[50] *Letters of Sir Walter Scott*, II, p. 321.

In a brilliantly lucid exposition of the place of the real as well as the ideal in romanticism and visual culture for a middle class nineteenth-century audience, d'Arcy Wood cites this passage as proof of Scott's distaste for the commercial union of word and image; as epistolary evidence of what he identifies as echoes of the 'Romantic iconophobia' that pervaded Europe from the 1760s to the 1820s.[51] Taking J. M. W. Turner's illustrations to Scott's *Poetical Works*, published in twelve volumes from 1833 to 1834, d'Arcy Wood demonstrates how the images Turner produced during a tour with Scott and his publisher Robert Cadell of the Borders and Lowlands in the summer of 1831 are not illustrative in the strictest sense of directly imaging the content of Scott's poetry and prose. Rather, they document what he calls the Romantic tourist industry, where author, artist and publisher – 'the triumvirate of the illustrated book trade' – are shown as emblematic consumers of the Scottish landscapes delineated by Scott.[52] Hence in one vignette in volume 6, they are shown enjoying a picnic lunch overlooking a prospect of Melrose; in others Turner is shown sketching, alone at Loch Coriskin, or at Bemerside Tower, accompanied by Scott and Cadell who converse with a Miss Haig. Of the dozen engraved images, the final volume devoted to Scott's dramas (Figure 60) is a nocturnal scene illuminated by a crescent moon, in which the diminutive travellers make their way on horseback and in an open carriage across the River Tweed back towards Abbotsford. Appropriately enough their journey, and the last volume of the series, end back at the author's home in the Borders. This exterior view of Abbotsford executed as if on a large, turreted, vertical canvas is juxtaposed to either side with outline engravings of aspects of its interior spaces, furniture and objects. On the left, is a partial vista of the hall with two suits of full armour and a dog; on the right, Scott's sanctum sanctorum – his book-lined study with its writing chair, manuscript in progress and a portrait bust. For Stephen Bann in his discussion of the formation of historical consciousness, armour is 'the vehicle of a Romantic subterfuge in imagining what was empty to be full'.[53] Similarly, in

---

[51] Gillen d'Arcy Wood, *The Shock of the Real: Romanticism and Visual Culture, 1760–1860* (New York: Palgrave, 2001), pp. 174–175. See also Adele M. Holcomb, 'Scott and Turner', in Alan S. Bell (ed.), *Scott Bicentenary Essays* (Edinburgh and London: Scottish Academic Press, 1973), p. 199: 'Scott regarded the illustrations of his poems and novels as a concession to popular taste; the obligation was not one in which he took keen personal interest.'

[52] Wood, *The Shock of the Real*, p. 179.

[53] Stephen Bann, 'The sense of the past: Images, text and object in the formation of historical consciousness in nineteenth-century Britain', in H. Aram Veeser (ed.), *The New Historicism* (London: Routledge, 1989), p. 114.

Figure 60: After J. M. W. Turner, 'Abbotsford' vignette from the frontispiece of *The Poetical Works of Sir Walter Scott*, (Edinburgh, 1834), volume 12. © The University of Edinburgh.

Figure 60 the vacant writing chair and portrait bust opposite the suits of armour give the absent author/sitter/owner an adumbrated presence.

Since d'Arcy Wood has written so recently and so compellingly on Turner's published engravings, the remaining discussion will focus on artists other than Turner and their portraits of Scott's characters, rather than the pictorial landscapes onto which notions of Romanticism are so often mapped.[54] In other words, on the physiognomy of Romanticism rather than its topography.[55] D'Arcy Wood's rather hasty conclusions elsewhere in his chapter concerning Scott's 'indifferent' attitude to art need to be countered with a more nuanced reading of his epistolary correspondence.[56] In the first instance, because Scott's endlessly-cited letter to Baillie echoes her own damning but humorous critique of Richard Westall in a letter to Scott dated ten days earlier, in which she recounts having seen engravings taken from drawings by him for the *Lay* and *Marmion*.[57] Baillie attacks Westall's illustrations for their lack of fidelity to their literary source, hoping that in future Westall will have the goodness 'to represent your stories as you tell them. His death of Marmion might be the death of any man ... and for the broken sword he ought to brandish, if it were taken to give the artist a good rap upon the scull, it would be well employed'. Scott's reply certainly testifies to the popular commercial union between the pen and the pencil: two rival sets of illustrations were reported to be in the course of preparation for the *Lady of the Lake* even before the poem had been published. What Scott seems to particularly object to in Westall's illustrations is not the images *per se* as much as the English artist's lack of intimate knowledge of the Highland figures in his poem for which there were no existing pictorial precedents. Projecting that in the translation of the poem into a visual idiom, Westall would be guilty of a careless cultural stereotyping, whereby Scott's Highland chief Sir Rhoderick Dhu would be represented as an officer of the Black Watch Regiment and his Bard, as Auld Robin Grey upon a fashionable object of material culture: a lacquered tea tray. Too often, Scott's comments concerning the illustration of his works are taken out of context and at face value, which unhelpfully obfuscates the contours of his

---

[54] See too Sebastian Mitchell, *Visions of Britain, 1730–1830: Anglo-Scottish Writing and Representation* (New York: Palgrave Macmillan, 2013), chapter 6: 'Scott, Turner and the vision of North Britain', pp. 193–232.

[55] I am deliberately over-drawing the distinctions between portrait and landscape at this point.

[56] Wood, *The Shock of the Real*, p. 174.

[57] Baillie's letter is transcribed and reproduced in *Letters of Sir Walter Scott*, II, p. 321 n. 1.

reportedly contested relationship with the visual arts, a reading which this chapter seeks to challenge.

Scott articulated his visual preferences and prejudices in a well-known letter to George Ellis dated 21 August 1804. From a close reading, he emerges not so much as an iconophobe, indeed, he says that he should have 'liked very much to have appropriate embellishments' in *The Lay of the Last Minstrel*, as a disciplinarian in the appropriate visual codification of local traditions.

I should fear [John] Flaxman's genius is too classic to body forth my Gothic Borderers. Would there not be some risk of them resembling the antique of Homer's heroes rather than the iron race of Salvator [Rosa]? After all, perhaps nothing is more difficult than for a painter to adapt the author's ideas of an imaginary character, especially when it is founded on traditions to which the artist is a stranger.[58]

What plagued Scott, at least as far as we can ascertain from the content of his published letters, was less the embodying of his characters from Scottish history in visual form, as the veracity of their distinctive Highland/Lowland identities as manifest in their appropriate sartorial attire. In a letter to the artist B. R. Haydon, dated 7 January 1821, he explained, 'In general there is a great error in dressing ancient Scottish men like our Highlanders, who wore a dress, as they spoke a language, as foreign to the Lowland Scotch as to the English.'[59] Scott's letter ventriloquises, only without the barbed English xenophobia, one of his own literary creations, the militant Colonel Talbot, addressing Edward Waverley in chapter 27 of his novel of the same name:

Let them [Scottish Highlanders] stay in their barren mountains, and puff and swell, and hang their bonnets on the horns of the moon, if they have a mind: but what business have they to come where people wear breeches, and speak an intelligible language? I mean intelligible in comparison with their gibberish, for even the Lowlanders talk a kind of English little better than the negroes in Jamaica.

Here dress and dialect are the idiomatic sights and sounds of Scottish identity and for Talbot, not only part of a corpora of identity but links on an indexical chain that demarcates the register from civilisation to barbarism. Though the disparaging reference to the Lowlanders English as being little better than the negroes in Jamaica is little more than a rhetorical trope, it reinforces the wider imperial perspective adopted throughout this

---

[58] 21 August 1804, to George Ellis. *Letters of Sir Walter Scott*, I, pp. 226–227.
[59] *Letters of Sir Walter Scott*, VI, pp. 331–332.

narrative for renegotiating the borders between two distinct Scottish cultures that were demarcated as different by geography, language and dress: Highland Gaelic and Lowland Scots. To which this chapter is adding, via Scott's cultural patrimony, a third region of the Scottish Borders. John Gray has established the importance of distinguishing between border zones as peripheral spaces on the one hand and as frontier spaces on the other in terms of their implications for constructing local identities.[60] While his work focusses on the fourteenth to sixteenth centuries, his comments are readily applicable to Scott's 'policing' of the borders of the Scottish Borders in visual and material culture centuries later.

Scott's own portrait was subject to comparable strictures to the illustrations that accompanied his verse and prose in his insistence on propriety in its sartorial fashioning. The bulk of Scott's painted portraits dress the sitter-subject in contemporary clothing, which habitually consisted of a green coat, yellow waistcoat, light trousers and a black neckcloth.[61] In 1820, George IV commissioned a portrait of Scott from the king's Painter-in-Ordinary, Sir Thomas Lawrence (Figure 58), which was still unfinished four years later for the following reason, which Scott explained in a letter to Lady Abercorn:

the costume having never been settled. I don't like a real good picture to be quite in a modern dress ours being about the most unpicturesque possible. I might to be sure take the plaid about me as I sometimes do at public meetings of the Celtic Society. But I am no Highlander by birth or connection and to take their dress looks like assuming their own character which I would not do holding that of my own more highly.[62]

Despite the picturesque possibilities of rendering the warp and weft of Highland tartan in oil on canvas, Scott had no legitimate foundation on which to fashion himself such an identity – a social and sartorial privilege blithely overlooked by George IV and Sir William Curtis during their visit to Edinburgh in August 1822 as stage-managed by Scott and discussed in the previous chapter. What constituted Scott's 'own' dress was that of the Borders region where he lived at the extensively remodelled 'pic-nic dwelling' that was Abbotsford. This was the dress that he had repeatedly advocated to the artists directly and obliquely illustrating his works – for pictorial representations of his 'Gothic Borderers' and his spearmen of

---

[60] John Gray, 'Lawlessness on the frontier: The Anglo-Scottish borderlands in the fourteenth to sixteenth century', *History and Anthropology* 12.4 (2001), p. 381.

[61] *The Times* for 8 November 1824. Quoted in Russell, *Portraits of Sir Walter Scott*, p. 53.

[62] *Letters of Sir Walter Scott*, VIII, p. 201.

Tiviotdale from the ballad collection, Scott campaigned for the adoption of the Border tartan known as maud. Writing as early as 12 September 1803 to John James Masquerier, an artist commissioned to produce some drawings for the *Lay of the Last Minstrel* set in the Borders which were never published:

The Minstrel should wear over his dress what we call a *Maud* or Low Country plaid. It is a long piece of cloth about a yard wide wrapd loosely round the waist like a scarf & from thence brought across the breast & the end thrown over the left shoulder where it hangs loose something like a Spanish Cloak. It is not of Tartan but of the natural colour of the wool with a very small black check which gives it a greyish look.[63]

Scott is represented as a Borders bard enveloped in low country plaid in a monochrome marble portrait bust executed from life by Francis Chantrey in 1820 (Figure 61). Like Raeburn, who painted Scott on four occasions, resulting in portraits that proliferated in painted copies and engraved prints, Chantrey produced the definitive sculptural likeness that was mass-produced in casts, copies and relief medallions. He wrote to Sir Robert Peel, who had purchased a marble bust in 1838, that the bust of Scott was the only occasion on which he, the sculptor, had requested the sitter's presence, rather than being solicited by the sitter themselves or a third party.[64] This portrait produced without commission shows Scott 76 cm high turning to his left with the maud draped around him toga-like and fastened with a brooch. In a letter dated 18 December 1810, Scott had written to a Miss Smith of the 'great art [of putting on the plaid], and when done prettily is very becoming. I can only describe it by negatives. It is not like a Highland serjeant's, not is it *scarf-wise* like a shepherdess in an opera ... The plaid is fastened by a brooch, which should be large and showy ... All caps or bonnets, no hats'.[65] Chantrey sculpted Scott bareheaded, in what to his contemporaries appeared an animated, conversational mode. The year after the sittings, Scott's latest novel *Kenilworth* (1820) was published and in chapter 37, Chantrey is referred to in the same breath as Michael Angelo: 'The smile with which Leicester had been speaking, when the Queen interrupted him, remained arrested on his lips, as if it had been carved there by the chisel of Michael Angelo or of Chantrey; and he listened to the speech of the physician with the same immovable cast of countenance.' Scott cited Chantrey a second time in chapter 23 of *The Pirate* (1822), where the daughters of Magus Troil are described as

---

[63] *Letters of Sir Walter Scott*, XII, p. 379.   [64] NLS, MS. 3653 folio 209.
[65] *Letters of Sir Walter Scott*, II, p. 412.

Figure 61: Francis Chantrey, *Sir Walter Scott,* 1820. Height 76.2 cm. With the kind permission of the Abbotsford Trust.

continuing 'to sleep as softly and sweetly as if the hand of Chantrey had formed them out of statuary-marble'. In the juxtaposition of these two references to Chantrey, Scott shows an awareness of, on the one hand, the rigidity of sculpture and on the other, its sometime remarkable approximations of animation. And this from a writer who it is claimed based on readings of his epistolary correspondence was at best, indifferent to art and at worst, an iconophobe. Better to re-read the letters in question more carefully in order to comprehend the romantic synergy between art, literature and life that characterises Scott's historical physiognomy.

In 1828, Chantrey presented a marble bust to Scott 'as a token of esteem', so the accompanying dedicatory inscription chiselled on to it announced. Scott acknowledged its arrival a week later, in a letter to Allan Cunningham in which he mentions the 'great dispute' concerning its intended location in the interior at Abbotsford.[66] The 'only one capital' place was said to be a niche in the far end of the library, which had been occupied since 1825 by a plaster of Shakespeare's tomb and bust from Stratford-on-Avon. Scott had no desire to dethrone the bust of Shakespeare, cast by George Bullock at John Britton's instigation, although after his death in 1832, Scott's bust by Chantrey literally usurped the pedestal previously occupied by that of Shakespeare (Figure 62). At early as 1820, a review of *Ivanhoe* published in the *Edinburgh Review* quoted above, likened Scott's literary productivity to that of Shakespeare; the relationship between the two literary prodigies who shared the same initials becoming notably pronounced after Scott's death especially in the hyperbolic claims of the obituaries. *The Morning Chronicle* lauded Scott as a national Scottish hero: 'Cervantes has done much for Spain, and Shakespeare for England, but not a tithe of what Sir Walter Scott has accomplished for us.' The *Athenaeum*, meanwhile, situated him in a literary pantheon of British poetic worthies with Shakespeare, Milton, Burns and Byron, who 'have each, in their particular line, equalled or excelled him; but then he surpassed them all, save perhaps the first, in the combination of many various excellencies'. Scott's appellation as the Scottish Shakespeare (another evocative historical pairing like Wilkie as the Scottish Teniers; or Raeburn as the Scotch Reynolds), occurs again in a letter dated 21 February 1828 from Allan Cunningham to the artist William Allan. Allan was named by Scott with Wilkie in the episode in *Heart of Midlothian* where Jeanie Deans is reunited with her father, previously cited. In the letter in question, Cunningham requests 'a sketch or drawing from your hand of the study or library or armoury of our Scottish Shakespeare ... The study I hear is for work rather

---

[66] *Letters of Sir Walter Scott*, X, pp. 450–451.

BUST OF SIR WALTER SCOTT IN THE LIBRARY AT ABBOTSFORD

Figure 62: Bust of Sir Walter Scott in the library at Abbotsford. 1831. The Miriam and Ira D. Wallach Division of Art, Prints and Photographs: Print Collection, the New York Public Library, Image 3937729.

than show, but both library and armoury are picturesque, and what is far better are the habitation of the greatest genius our Island has had since the days of Milton'.[67]

The portrait Allan executed draws together the tripartite strands of this chapter – life, literature and art – by representing Scott in a space that is a concatenation, another form of pick-nickery, of interior fixtures, furniture and artefacts of material culture from Abbotsford (Plate XXXII). Allan incorporated objects that adorned the spaces stipulated by Cunningham in his letter, namely, the study, armoury, and library, alongside the contents of other rooms, including the chimneypiece in the hall. Scott sits full-length in the centre, reading a historical Scottish document – Mary Queen of Scots' proclamation for her marriage to Lord Darnley. The light from the window shines directly onto the document and is reflected back on Scott's face. 'To see S.ʳ W[alter] in perfection is to see him at Abbotsford when his anecdotes relative to his different curiosities are beyond measure amusing', wrote one Judith Beecroft in her journal of a tour in Scotland undertaken in the summer of 1824.[68] Fortunately for our purposes, Allan elucidated some of the other gabions in the commentary that accompanied the portrait when it was exhibited at the Royal Academy's 1832 exhibition, when a review in *Fraser's Magazine* trumpeted the equilibrium between art and literature, as follows: 'Allan's pencil is as forcible and graphic as the pen of Sir Walter himself, and like that, has conferred a certain indefinable charm upon the matter-of-fact things it touches'.[69] A line engraving by John Burnet (Figure 63) after Allan's portrait (Plate XXXII) further enables us to precisely identify the 'things' incorporated into it. They include the silver vase in front of the window on the table at the far left, which was gift from Lord Byron; the keys between the window and the bookcase from the old Tolbooth at Edinburgh; the sword suspended on the opposite side of the bookcase belonged to the Marquis of Montrose and was given to him by Charles I. Hanging on the right of the bookcase is an ancient border bugle, James VI's travelling flask and the sporran of Rob Roy M'Gregor. Claverhouse's pistol is displayed behind the bust of Shakespeare on the mantelpiece, with a brace below that belonged to Napoleon. The stag hound at Scott's feet is Maida. The left foreground and the top of the bookcase are littered with arms and armour including a targe, helmet and cuirass, with Scott the 'literary veteran' reading in what a review of the 1832 Royal Academy exhibition in the *Examiner* dubbed his 'warlike-looking study at Abbotsford'.[70]

---

[67] *Historical Manuscripts Commission. Laing Manuscripts* (London, 1925), II, p. 771.

[68] Judith Beecroft, Journal of a tour in Scotland, Summer 1824. NLS, MS. 29500 folio 47.

[69] *Fraser's Magazine* 5 (1832), p. 719.   [70] *Examiner*, 1 July 1832, p. 421.

Figure 63: John Burnet. *Sir Walter Scott, 1st bt.* Line engraving, printed by R. Lloyd, published by Hodgson, Boys & Graves, after Sir William Allan (Plate XXXII), published 25 March 1835. Plate size 56.2 × 40.9 cm; paper size 68.3 × 51 cm. © National Portrait Gallery, London. NPG D40595.

This chapter has endorsed Perry's contention that Romanticism is not 'a fixed historical object', as it has travelled across media, genres and disciplines in its pursuit of the productive interplay between life, literature and art.[71] The review of the 1832 annual Royal Academy exhibition published in *Fraser's*

---

[71] Seamus Perry, 'Romanticism: The brief history of a concept', in Duncan Wu (ed.), *A Companion to Romanticism* (Oxford: Blackwell, 1998), p. 9.

Magazine noted how the portrait of Scott by Allan impinged on the permeable boundaries of art historical genres in that it was a portrait and a history painting; a still life and an animal painting combined in one canvas. We might add an interior landscape, or objectscape to these classifications that simultaneously bordered and embroidered on life, art and literature: Rob Roy featured in Scott's 1817 novel of the same name; the keys from the Tolbooth were those in *The Heart of Midlothian* (1818) with the Highland campaign of Montrose providing the context for *A Legend of Montrose* (1819). In a letter of 1812 to Mrs Clephane, Scott described the broadsword of Marquis of Montrose and the gun of Rob Roy as 'my nick-nackatery'; elsewhere writing to Joanna Baillie that the former was 'a most beautiful blade. I think a dialogue between this same sword and Rob Roys gun might be composed with good effect.'[72] In Scott's *Bride of Lammermoor* the dialogic narrative was advocated by Pattieson; the descriptive narrative, by Tinto, both of whom have been identified as Scott's narrative personae.

If Romanticism is not a fixed historical object, then neither is physiognomy, whose definition as a subject area and a mode of inference has been applied throughout this chapter in its empirical trace of the form and character of Scott's romanticism. Physiognomy is a 'constantly shifting phenomenon' writes Percival in her study of the appearance of character in eighteenth-century France 'and ... the best way to understand it is in relation to a specific historical context'; or alternatively, as here, in relation to a specific historical individual who was one of the most painted figures of his generation.[73] In the last known portrait of Scott to be painted before his death (Plate XXXII), William Allan was to compose in visual form a dialogic narrative taking place about and around Scott the 'literary veteran' as a portrait sitter, subject and object; and as a collector and recipient of gabions both historical and contemporary. The threads between his life, literature and art, the dominant features of Scott's historical physiognomy, are knowingly entangled in a characteristically Romantic image that was subsequently exhibited and engraved.

---

[72] *Letters of Sir Walter Scott*, III, p. 69 and III, p. 100.
[73] Percival, *The Appearance of Character*, p. 83.

Conclusion: Scott-Land

> Scotland never owed so much to one man
>
> *Journal of Henry Cockburn*[1]

Post mortem, the custodians of Sir Walter Scott's memory were unable to agree on the preferred style of a monument to commemorate 'our departed friends Giant Genius'.[2] In 1832, the year that Scott died aged sixty-one, committees were appointed in London, Glasgow and Edinburgh with the purpose of erecting monuments to him in each of these urban centres. The London subcommittee for subscriptions was headed by the Duke of Portland, the Duke of Wellington, the Marquis of Stafford, the Earl of Aberdeen, Lord Montagu, Sir Robert Peel and the Lord Mayor. A second subscription committee for Glasgow included the Lord Provost and James Smith of Jordanhill. The secretary of the Edinburgh committee, James Skene, characterised the cultural metropolis that was Scott's native city as follows: 'this antient capital, the city of his birth, where his life was passed, where those imperishable works were produced which from his genius reflect so much glory on the literature of Scotland, and where after ages will naturally look for the chief monument to his fame'.[3] Like its London and Glasgow equivalents, membership consisted of 'the great and good', with representatives of the Scottish aristocracy and senior professional figures.[4] 'I hope the committee who are entreated with the decision may be men of real taste', one John S. Forbes wrote to Skene in May 1833.[5] The minutes of the Edinburgh committee record initiatives to raise monies beyond Scotland, in Germany and Paris; remittances were received from Russia, Spain, America and Calcutta, with solicitations to the Cape of Good Hope and New South Wales. Despite James Hogg's contention in a letter to the committee that '[Scott] has left a monument in every heart throughout the civilized world and every monument else will be degrading to him', they raised £6,000 by subscription and commissioned designs from the

---

[1] *Journal of Henry Cockburn; being a continuation of the Memorials of his time* (Edinburgh, 1874), I, p. 37.

[2] Francis, 14th Lord Grey. NRS, GD157/2027/12.   [3] NRS, GD157/2023/17.

[4] NRS, GD157/2027/1 (A. T. Gilbert).   [5] 18 May 1833. NLS, Acc. 12092/88.

Edinburgh-born artist, David Roberts.[6] Roberts provided two alternative options for the committee's perusal, the first of which was an Egyptian obelisk two hundred feet high; the second, a Gothic structure eighty-five or one hundred feet high.

After what the published minutes of the 1835 meeting describe as 'a long and deliberate discussion', the subcommittee of the general committee agreed on the proposed site of the monument – the east end of George Street in St Andrews Square – but there was no consensus among them as to the preferred design.[7] The pro-obelisk faction argued that a Gothic structure was more suited for a country town or village green; that it would appear out of place, being 'paltry and subdued' amidst the heavy masses of Edinburgh's built environment and that it would be perishable with no available funds for repair. The obelisk in contrast, would terminate a series of monuments that already punctuated the George Street vista that included, at the Hanover Street intersection, the bronze statue of George IV by Chantrey (Figure 56), which commemorated the king's historic visit to Edinburgh in August 1822. Its proponents contrasted the grand and severe style of an obelisk with the tracery and fretwork of the Gothic; offering an aesthetic endorsement of the former from the artist J. M. W. Turner.[8] The pro-Gothic faction retaliated with a series of counter arguments, of which the most striking was that an obelisk, in style, character, aspect and history, had no association with either Scotland or Scott. The Gothic style, in contrast, was said by its champions to be 'intimately associated with the events, eras, and characters, which occupied the genius of the man whose memory it is desired to honour'.[9] Invoking Scott's own predilection for Gothic structures, they insisted that this option would be *his* first choice. Here and on many other occasions, the iconising of Scott is based on publicly projected versions of his preferences in a continuous trafficking between the historical figure that was Scott and the posthumous icon.[10]

---

[6] NRS, GD157/2028/16.

[7] *Second report of the subcommittee for erecting a monument to Sir Walter Scott* (Edinburgh, 1835), p. 6.

[8] Scott had written to his publisher Robert Cadell in August 1831, that Turner was 'unquestionably [the] best judge of everything belonging to art'. Quoted by Adele M. Holcomb, 'Scott and Turner', in Alan S. Bell (ed.), *Scott Bicentenary Essays* (Edinburgh: Scottish Academic Press, 1973), p. 204.

[9] *Second report of the subcommittee for erecting a monument to Sir Walter Scott* (Edinburgh, 1835), p. 11.

[10] Nicholas Jagger, 'The iconising of Walter Scott', in Martin Hewitt (ed.), *Representing Victorian Lives* (Leeds: Leeds Centre for Victorian Studies, 1999), p. 108.

Having reached an impasse in divergent aesthetic styles in this commemorative tug of war, in the spring of 1836, the committee launched an open competition, offering prizes of fifty guineas each for the three best designs for a monument that incorporated both architecture and sculpture within a budget of £5000. Twenty-two Gothic structures, eleven statues, fourteen Grecian temples, five pillars, one obelisk and one fountain later, the subcommittee agreed on an architectural structure 135 feet high in the Gothic style designed by the Scottish architect George Meikle Kemp, whose details derived from Melrose Abbey (Figure 64).[11] Kemp submitted his design under the pseudonym John Morvo, the architect who was concerned with the rebuilding of Melrose Abbey in the Scottish Borders in the fifteenth century. His historicising architectural monument would incorporate a marble statue of Scott executed by the Edinburgh sculptor John Steell, whose equestrian statue of *Alexander and Bucephalus* and whose bust of Queen Victoria had reportedly attracted the attention of members of the sub-committee. A bronze statue was discouraged by J. S. Memes in a *Letter to John Steell* (Edinburgh, 1838) on the grounds that it 'never composes well as a portion of an architectural monument', as well as being aesthetically inappropriate ('cold, heavy, and dark') and historically vulnerable.[12] The intended location of the monument also shifted from the east end of George Street to, by December 1838, the foot of 'St David Street within the Gardens', where it was subsequently erected.

The foundation stone for the Scott monument was laid on 15 August 1840, the 69th anniversary of Scott's birth and the monument was inaugurated six years later (Figure 65). Among the many panegyrics reported verbatim in the Scottish press was the speech of the Lord Provost, the Right Honourable Adam Black, in which he extolled the monument's sequential efflorescence between the spheres of poetry, architecture and sculpture: 'even here we see how the glowing genius of the poet has stirred the soul of the architect, and awakened the talents of the sculptor, whose skilful chisel has moulded the rude block into the all but breathing form and features of Scotland's darling son [Figure 66]'.[13] At the inaugural dinner, the chairman envisaged the degree to which the nation of Scotland was indebted to Scott's literary endeavours as follows:

[11] *Third report of the sub-committee for erecting a monument to Sir Walter Scott* (Edinburgh, 1838).

[12] J. S. Memes, *Letter to John Steell, Esq. S.A. regarding the Scott monument* (Edinburgh, 1838), pp. 10–11.

[13] *Caledonian Mercury*, 17 August 1846. NLS, FB.m.55. [Four volumes of press-cuttings, photographs, engravings &c., relating to the work of Sir John Steell].

Figure 64: Design for Scott Monument. Lithograph presentation perspective issued to subscribers from a drawing by George Meikle Kemp. © HES and the Royal Incorporation of Architects in Scotland.

Figure 65: View of Scott Monument from the north. © HES.

Figure 66: John Steell, *Sir Walter Scott*, Scott Monument, Edinburgh. *c.* 1846. © HES.

The admiration won by his writings has been extended to his country; those who have been delighted with his delineations, have been attracted to the scenes which he has so beautifully described, and I may also say that even his own countrymen have viewed them with a deeper and increasing admiration, and as have been quaintly said, if his country had not received its name before, it might now have acquired the name of Scott-land.[14]

---

[14] NLS, FB.m.55

This affective patrimonial relationship – 'Scotland's darling son' – and the appellation, 'Scott-land', enjoyed widespread circulation by the Victorian 1840s, while the idea of Scott the individual author as delineating the nation of Scotland is a literary topos that occurs at least a decade earlier in his obituaries. For instance, in a passage endlessly cited in the secondary literature as from the *Morning Chronicle* for 26 September 1832, where Scott's genius is described as being 'eminently national. Our hills and vallies, our history, and our manners, are consecrated in his immortal pages. Thousands from foreign lands are yearly visiting our shores, to tread the localities which he has given to fame ... In the political scale of nations we may rise, or we may fall. In his pages we are a glorious people, and a favoured spot for ever!'[15] Actually, this obituary reproduces part of one that was first published in the *Edinburgh Evening Post* four days earlier on 22 September where it is described by its author as 'hurried paragraphs regarding the unrivalled genius' of Sir Walter Scott. 'His name was blazoned on the whole civilized world', exclaimed another obituary in the *Edinburgh Evening Courant*.[16]

After his death, his works were even seen as exerting a civilising influence in the British colonies, when in 1840, the Scottish governor of the penal colony of Norfolk Island purchased a set of the cultural phenomenon that was the Waverley novels for the edification of his Scottish inmates in an attempt to 'invest country and home with agreeable images and recollections [that] are too much wanting in the individual experience of our lower and criminal classes'.[17] The *Christian Observer* reviewed *The Pirate* (1822) in their March 1832 issue.[18] Though 'not very vehement admirers either of novels or novel reading', the latter a habit they considered to be 'to a very high degree inexpedient and injurious', the reviewer conceded the existence of Scott's 'innumerable readers in every corner of the empire' for whom the Waverley Novels in thirty-nine volumes had become an 'indispensible piece of furniture'. Scott the global publishing phenomenon had, it would seem, disseminated 'Scotland' in its literary manifestation and as requisite 'furniture' into every home across the British Empire and at least one far distant penitentiary.

[15] Unless referenced otherwise, the press cuttings I have used are among those in the Corson Collection in the Centre for Research Collections at the University of Edinburgh.

[16] *Edinburgh Evening Courant*, 24 September 1832, n.p.

[17] Katie Trumpener, *Bardic Nationalism: The Romantic Novel and the British Empire* (Princeton, NJ: Princeton University Press, 1997), pp. 256–257.

[18] *Christian Observer*, 22 March 1832, p. 157, p. 167.

The commission and inauguration of the Scott monument in 1830s and 40s Edinburgh draws our narrative concerning the cultural contours and detours of identity to its chronological and methodological conclusion. For in the obituaries and reviews that proliferated in print across the British Empire and which coincidentally often echo Scott's own literary descriptions that they eulogise, Scotland as a nation had finally found a son to embody her cultural significance. 'if it be a Monument I hope no English architect may have anything to do with it', E. L. Bulwer had written to the fledgling committee in October 1832.[19] The memorial as erected was both a tribute to Scott – executed in a style he would have chosen himself according to the arguments marshalled by the pro-Gothic faction – and a celebratory bastion of cultural Scottishness in its union of the singular achievements of native Scots in the fields of literature, architecture and sculpture. The Scott Monument became an axiom of Scottishness – an emanation of Scottish cultural identity focussed on the cultural significance of one man and located on his monument situated between the Old and New Towns in the nation's capital city.[20]

In seeking to invest the elastic concept of identity with a renewed analytic purchase, each of the preceding chapters has sought to demonstrate how it was variously represented, manifested and iterated in visual and material culture. Part I focussed on the corpora of Scottish identity as being framed by geography, although not in the traditional sense of a geography of art survey text, by looking first at a phalanx of Scots travelling on their grand tours in Europe, and then proceeding onto the epistolary identities of George Steuart and Claud Alexander, working respectively as an architect in London and for the East India Company in Bengal. Using a focussed chronological sample, from the 1760s to the 1780s, Part I enabled us to see a variety of identity categories wax and wane in equivalent cosmopolitan, metropolitan and colonial contexts. Part II focussed on the tripartite territories of Scotland, the Highlands, Lowlands and Borders across a more expansive timeframe, from around the last of the Jacobite uprisings, the '45, to the death of Sir Walter Scott in 1832. This part of the book leant towards collective identities and their enduring reification in dress and textiles as part of the armoury of

---

[19] NRS, GD157/2022/21.

[20] Tom Mole argues the Scott Monument not only contributed to a pantheon in Edinburgh – forming part of what he calls a pantheonic axis with the Nelson monument and National monument on Calton Hill – but was a micropantheon in its own right. See his *What the Victorians Made of Romanticism: Material Artifacts, Cultural Practices and Reception History* (Princeton, NJ: Princeton University Press, 2017), p. 151.

Jacobitism, as a plaided panorama or spectacle of loyalty to George IV and – focussing on Sir Walter Scott – in pursuit of the integrity of Borders Scottish identity rather than its pictorial speciousness.

One of the persistent limitations of identity as an object of study lies in its apposite conceptualisation. As the historian Stephen Conway has written, 'We can [. . .] conceive of identities in layers, but the problem with this approach us that it implies inner and outer, or fundamental and superficial, or some other form of ranking. Better perhaps to visualize the different identities as related to each other, like the sides of a multi-faceted precious stone. Which identity caught the sun and shone the most brightly depended upon time, place and circumstance.'[21] Here, identities are conceptualised as the sides of a precious stone, reminding us of the Earl of Buchan's characterisation of Scotland as a medallion of ancient sculpture in his 1784 anniversary speech to the Society of Antiquaries, quoted and discussed in the introduction. For the historian of visual and material culture there is no need for such similes as identity is already reified in the richly populated objectscape that constitutes her primary data; that this narrative proposes as manifestations embodied or emblematic of a messy, undulating constellation of identity categories – personal, political, occupational and national – rather than fixed concentric rings.

'National character is not a procrustean bed', proclaims Pevsner, in the *Englishness of English Art*.[22] Discussing the style of Robert Adam in chapter 5 on 'Blake and the Flaming Line', Pevsner is forced to confront his Scottishness, choosing to allude to it, rather than to enunciate it. He writes, 'no distinction can be made between Scottish and English qualities. This does not mean that there are no specifically Scottish qualities' – only that Pevsner fails to articulate what these might be.[23] These opaque qualities can, he argues 'be detected in the peculiar freshness of [Henry] Raeburn', in the so-called Ossianic work of the Runciman brothers and John Brown. We looked at Robert Adam and Alexander Runciman's Ossianic painted scheme at Penicuik House in Chapter 2 (Figure 22); at portraits by Raeburn in Chapters 5 (Plate XXVII) and 6. This narrative eschews Scottishness as an ahistorical style, discernible or otherwise, although it has focussed on the preliminary articulations of a national painterly tradition in early nineteenth-century press and periodical culture in Chapter 6.

---

[21] Stephen Conway, 'Scots, Britons and Europeans: Scottish military service, *c.* 1739–1783', *Historical Research* 82 (2009), p. 114.

[22] Nikolaus Pevsner, *The Englishness of English Art* (London: British Broadcasting Corporation, 1956), p. 194.

[23] Pevsner, *The Englishness of English Art*, p. 144.

Across the chapters of this book as a whole, Scottishness has been revealed as a national identity which was superseded and enhanced in alternative geographical contexts; offering a sense of cohesion, transformation and regulation as an instrument of both insurrection and loyalty to the state at distinct historical periods.

'[F]or the Face of Things so often alters, and the Situation of Affairs in this *Great British* Empire gives such new Turns ... that there is Matter of new Observation every Day', remarked Daniel Defoe in the preface to the first edition of his *A Tour thro' the whole Island of Great Britain, divided into circuits or journies*.[24] The *Tour* was on its ninth edition by 1779. According to Turner, it became a 'national institution' during the eighteenth century, 'the common property of the ever-improving nation it describes', with from 1742, an entire volume devoted to Scotland. '*Scotland* is here describ'd with Brevity, but with Justice', explained Defoe, taking pains to insist on his own authorial objectivity: 'as I shall not make a Paradise of *Scotland*, so I assure you I shall not make a Wilderness of it. I shall endeavour to shew you what it really is'. Despite Defoe's laudable intentions, he can never represent Scotland 'as it really is' – only as it is perceived to be by him.[25] This book has celebrated the multiple, processual identities for Scots and Scotland that proliferated within representation between 1745 and 1832, that in the case of the Highlands shifted between these dates from a previously uncharted wilderness to a 'fairyland' delineated by Sir Walter Scott.[26] It has sought to place them, as all discourse is placed, somewhere between these polarities, even as and when they were at stake.[27]

---

[24] Katherine Turner, 'Defoe's *Tour*: The changing "Face of Things"', *British Journal for Eighteenth-Century Studies* 24 (2001), pp. 189–206.

[25] Tom Keymer, 'Smollett's Scotlands: Culture, politics and nationhood in "Humphry Clinker" and Defoe's "Tour"', *History Workshop Journal* 40.1 (1995), p. 125.

[26] Thermuthis Collinson describes Loch Achray in Perthshire a 'fairyland' in his A Tour through some of the southern and western counties of Scotland, BL, Add. MS. 36454 folio 56.

[27] Stuart Hall, 'Cultural identity and diaspora', in Nicholas Mirzoeff (ed.), Diaspora and Visual Culture: Representing Africans and Jews (London: Routledge, 2000), p. 21.

Bibliography

Archives & Manuscripts

Bedfordshire Archives and Record Services

L30/9/17   Lucas of Wrest collection

Beinecke Library

Osborn c569   Thomas Watkins, Travels in a series of letters from a gentleman
                to his father, in the years 1787, 88 & 89

Osborn d283   'Notes during a journey to Edinbro in July & August 1822'

British Library (BL)

Add. MS. 29991   David Wilkie letters to Perry Nursey

Add. MS. 33685   Revd John Skinner, Account of a tour through the Kingdom
                   of Scotland with views (1825)

Add. MS. 36454   Thermuthis Collinson, A Tour through some of the southern
                   and western counties of Scotland (1812)

Add. MS. 45421   David Anderson Papers

Add. MS. 57321   Sir John Moore Papers

Cambridge University Library, Department of Manuscripts and University Archives

The Buxton Papers

Centre for Research Collections, The University of Edinburgh

Corson Collection
Laing Manuscripts

Clackmannanshire Archives

PD239   Johnstone of Alva papers

Glasgow City Archives

TD 1681   Bogle Papers collection

Highland Archive Centre (HAC)

D766   Fraser Tytler of Aldourie

Lewis Walpole Library

Miscellaneous Manuscripts

National Library of Scotland (NLS)

Acc. 8278	Anon, Tour in Scotland, 1794
Acc. 9260	Papers of Michael Moncrieff Stuart
Acc. 12017	Photocopy of a journal, A tour through part of England and Scotland by Eliza Dawson in the year 1786
Acc. 12092	Papers of the family of Skene of Rubislaw, related Scottish families and the family of Sir Walter Scott
Acc. 12285	A Tour in Scotland by Mrs Cox with Mr and Mrs Favell, 24 May to 6 July 1822
Adv. MS. 29.3.14	Letters and papers, 1777–1809, of David Steuart Erskine, Earl of Buchan
Adv. MS. 32.6.16–25	Robert Forbes, Bishop of Ross and Caithness, manuscript of 'The Lyon in Mourning'
Dep. 175	Gordon Cumming of Altyre and Gordonstoun Papers
FB.m.55	Four volumes of press-cuttings, photographs, engravings &c., relating to the work of Sir John Steell
MS. 1003	Miscellaneous Letters
MS. 1539–45	Journal kept by Sir William Forbes, 6th Bart., of Pitsligo, of a tour taken on the Continent with his wife and daughter, 1792–3
MS. 1750–3	Copies, mostly typewritten, of letters of Sir Walter Scott, collected by Herbert Grierson, when he was preparing the centenary edition of Scott's letters but rejected from printing
MS. 3653	Sir Walter Scott

MS. 6322	A Tour through parts of the Highlands of Scotland in 1780. By Jacob Pattison (junior) of the University of Edinburgh.
MS. 16004 Lynedoch Papers:	Letters, 1775–90, of Jane, Duchess of Atholl, to her sister, Hon. Mary Graham.
MS. 19200	Autograph journal of a tour in the Highlands undertaken by Warren Hastings in 1787
MS. 29500	Judith Beecroft, Journal of a tour in Scotland, Summer 1824, by Mrs and Miss Beecroft

National Records of Scotland (NRS)

SP12	Regalia papers
GD18	Papers of the Clerk family of Penicuik, Midlothian
GD24	Papers of the family of Stirling Home Drummond Moray of Abercairny
GD25	Papers of the Kennedy family Earls of Cassillis
GD105	Papers of the Duff family of Fetteresso
GD110	Papers of the Hamilton-Dalrymple family of North Berwick
GD112	Papers of the Campbell family Earls of Breadalbane
GD113	Papers of the Innes family of Stow, Peeblesshire
GD121	Papers of the Steuart Fotheringham Family of Pourie, Fotheringham, Murthly and Strathbraan
GD155	Papers of the Maxtone Graham family of Cultoquhey, Perthshire
GD157	Papers of the Scott family of Harden, Lords Polwarth, Berwickshire
GD206	Papers of the Hall family of Dunglass, East Lothian
GD248	Papers of the Ogilvy family Earls of Seafield
GD267	Papers of the Home-Robertson family of Paxton, Berwickshire (Home of Wedderburn)
GD345	Papers of the Grant family of Monymusk Aberdeenshire
GD393	Boyd Alexander

National Register of Archives for Scotland (NRAS)

105	Haig family of Bemersyde, Roxburghshire
180	Royal Company of Archers
234	Atholl Estates
276	Fleming family of Barochan, Renfrewshire
783	Scrymgeour-Wedderburn family, Earls of Dundee
859	Douglas-Home family, Earls of Home
905	Fairlie family, Ayrshire & India

1454   Adam family of Blair Adam, Fife
1500   Forbes-Irvine family of Drum, Aberdeenshire
1948   Macbeth and Maclagan, Solicitors, Rothesay
2171   Earl of Annandale and Hartfell
2177   Douglas-Hamilton Family, Dukes of Hamilton and Brandon
2614   Macpherson family of Blairgowrie, Perthshire
2950   Macleod family of Macleod, Dunvegan, Isle of Skye

Royal Archives

GEO/MAIN/29600

Royal Institute of British Architects

DaFam/1–2   Archive of the Dance Family

Yale Center for British Art

DA 865.S74   [Charles Steade], *A Tour to the Highlands of Scotland and the isle of Staffa with a short description of the lakes of Windemere and Derwentwater*, 1819

Primary Printed Sources

A complete historical account of His Majesty King George the fourth to the kingdom of Scotland (Edinburgh, 1822).

A description of the paintings in the Hall of Ossian at Pennycuik, near Edinburgh (Edinburgh: A. Kincaid and W. Creech, 1773).

A narrative of the visit of George IV to Scotland (Edinburgh, 1822).

A picturesque sketch of the landing of his most gracious majesty King George IV (Edinburgh, 1822).

Account of the royal visit of George IVth to Scotland (Kilmarnock: H. Crawford, 1822).

Argyll, Duke of, *Intimate Society Letters of the Eighteenth Century* (London: S. Paul & Co., 1910), 2 volumes.

Brady, Frank and Pottle, F. A. (eds.), *Boswell on the Grand Tour: Italy, Corsica and France, 1765–1766* (London: Heinemann, 1955).

Bristed, John, *Antroplanomenos; or a pedestrian tour through parts of the Highlands of Scotland in 1801* (London, 1803).

Cunningham, Allan, *The lives of the most eminent British painters, sculptors and architects* (New York: Harper & Bros., 1834), 5 volumes.

Fergusson, James (ed.), *Letters of George Dempster to Sir Adam Fergusson, 1756–1813* (London: Macmillan, 1934).

Fletcher, E. (ed.), *Conversations with James Northcote, R.A.* (London, 1901).

Forbes, Robert, *The Lyon in Mourning*, Henry Paton (ed.) (Edinburgh, 1895–96), 3 volumes.

Gardenstone, Francis Garden, *Travelling Memorandums made in a tour upon the continent of Europe in the years 1786, 1787 and 1788* (Edinburgh, 1795), 3 volumes.

Garnett, Thomas, *Observations on a tour through the Highlands and Western Isles of Scotland* (London: T. Cadell and W. Davies, 1800), 2 volumes.

Hurd, Richard, *Dialogues on the uses of foreign travel; considered as part of an English gentleman's education* (London, 1764).

Johnson, Samuel, *A Journey to the Western Islands of Scotland*, Ian McGowan (ed.), (Edinburgh: Canongate, 1996).

Journal of Henry Cockburn; being a continuation of the Memorials of his time (Edinburgh: Edmonston & Douglas, 1874), 2 volumes.

Lockhart, J. G., *Life of Scott* (Edinburgh: T. C. & E. C. Jack, 1902), 10 volumes.

Leslie, Charles Robert, *Autobiographical Recollections* (London, 1860).

[Lockhart, John Gibson], *Peter's Letters to his Kinsfolk* (Edinburgh: W. Blackwood, 1819).

Low, Ursula, *Fifty years with John Company* (London, 1936).

McNayr, James, *A Guide from Glasgow, to some of the most remarkable scenes in the Highlands of Scotland* (Glasgow: Courier Office, 1797).

Memes, J. S., *Letter to John Steell, Esq. S.A. regarding the Scott monument* (Edinburgh, 1838).

Memoirs of the Life of William Collins (London, 1848), 2 volumes.

Moore, John, *A View of Society and Manners in Italy* (London: W. Strahan & T. Cadell, 1781), 2 volumes.

A View of Society and Manners in France, Switzerland, and Germany (London: W. Strahan & T. Cadell, 1779), 2 volumes.

[Mudie, Robert], *A Historical Account of His Majesty's Visit to Scotland* (Edinburgh, 1822).

Otter, William, *The Life and Remains of the Rev. Edward Daniel Clarke* (London, 1824).

Pennant, Thomas, *A Tour in Scotland* (Chester: John Monk, 1771).

A Tour in Scotland and Voyage to the Hebrides (Dublin: A. Leathley, 1775), 2 volumes.

Poole, Herbert Edmund (ed.), *Music, Men and Manners in France and Italy, 1770, being the journal written by Charles Burney* (London: Folio Society, 1969).

Second report of the subcommittee for erecting a monument to Sir Walter Scott (Edinburgh, 1835).

Scott, Walter, *Reliquiae Trotcosienses, or, the gabions of the late Jonathan Oldbuck Esq. of Monkbarns*, Gerald Carruthers and Alison Lumsden (eds.) (Edinburgh: Edinburgh University Press, 2004).

The Letters of Sir Walter Scott, H. J. C. Grierson (ed.) (London: Constable, 1932–7), 12 volumes.

[Scott, Walter], *Hints addressed to the inhabitants of Edinburgh and others, in prospect of his Majesty's visit by an old citizen* (Edinburgh, 1822).

Silliman, Benjamin, *A journal of travels in England, Holland and Scotland and two passages over the Atlantic in the years 1805 and 1806*, 3rd edition (New Haven: S. Converse, 1820), 3 volumes.

[Simpson, James], *Letters to Sir Walter Scott, Bart. on the moral and political character and effects of the visit to Scotland in August 1822* (Edinburgh: Waugh & Innes, 1822).

Spence, Elizabeth Isabella, *Letters from the North Highlands during the summer 1816* (London, 1817).

Sketches of the present manners, customs and scenery of Scotland (London, 1811).

Third report of the sub-committee for erecting a monument to Sir Walter Scott (Edinburgh, 1838).

Walker, Ralph S. (ed.), *The Correspondence of James Boswell and John Johnstone of Grange* (London: Heinemann, 1966).

Wendeborn, Gebhard Friedrich August, *A view of England towards the close of the eighteenth century* (London, 1791), 2 volumes.

Williams, S. T. (ed.), *Tour in Scotland 1817 and other manuscript notes by Washington Irving* (New Haven, CT, 1927).

Secondary Sources

Abrams, M. H., *Doing Things with Texts: Essays in Criticism and Critical Theory* (New York and London: Norton, 1989).

Adam Smith, Janet, 'Some eighteenth-century ideas of Scotland,' in N. T. Phillipson and Rosalind Mitchison (eds.) *Scotland in the Age of Improvement* (Edinburgh: Edinburgh University Press, 1970), pp. 107–124.

Alexander, David, *Richard Newton and English Caricature in the 1790s* (Manchester: Whitworth Art Gallery, 1998).

Anderson, Benedict, *Imagined Communities: Reflections on the Origin and Spread of Nationalism* (London: Verso, 1983).

Appadurai, Arjun, *The Social Life of Things: Commodities in Cultural Perspective* (Cambridge: Cambridge University Press, 1986).

Archer, Mildred, *India and British Portraiture, 1770–1825* (London: Philip Wilson, 1979).

Arnold, Dana, *Cultural Identities and the Aesthetics of Britishness* (Manchester: Manchester University Press, 2004).

Auerbach, Jeffrey, 'Imperial Boredom', *Common Knowledge* 11.2 (2005), pp. 283–305.

Bailey, Richard W., 'Scots and Scotticisms: Language and ideology', *Studies in Scottish Literature* 26 (1991), pp. 65–77.

Baines, Paul, 'Ossianic geographies: Fingalian figures on the Scottish tour, 1760–1830', *Scotlands* 4.1 (1997), pp. 44–61.

Bann, Stephen, 'Historicizing Horace', in Michael Snodin (ed.), *Horace Walpole's Strawberry Hill* (New Haven, CT, and London: Yale University Press, 2009), pp. 117–133.

'The sense of the past: images, text and object in the formation of historical consciousness in nineteenth-century Britain', in H. Aram Veeser (ed.), *The New Historicism* (London: Routledge, 1989), pp. 102–115.

Under the Sign: John Bargrave as Collector, Traveler and Witness (Ann Arbor: University of Michigan Press, 1994).

Bannet, Eve Tavor, *Empire of Letters: Letters, Manuals and Transatlantic Correspondence, 1688–1820* (Cambridge: Cambridge University Press, 2005).

Barnard, Toby and Clark, Jane (eds.), *Lord Burlington: Architecture, Art and Life* (London: Hambleton, 1995).

Barrell, John, 'Sir Joshua Reynolds and the Englishness of English art', in Homi K. Bhabha (ed.), *Nation and Narration* (London: Routledge, 1999), pp. 154–176.

Basker, James G., 'Scotticisms and the problem of cultural identity in eighteenth-century Britain', *Eighteenth-Century Life* 15.1 & 2 (1991), pp. 81–95.

Baucom, Ian, *Out of Place: Englishness, Empire and the Locations of Identity* (Princeton, NJ: Princeton University Press, 1999).

Bennett, A. G., *Fans in Fashion: Selections from the Fine Arts Museums of San Francisco* (Rutland: Fine Arts Museum of San Francisco, 1981).

Bhabha, Homi K. (ed.), *Nation and Narration* (London: Routledge, 1990).

Bickham, Troy, 'Eating the Empire: intersections of food, cookery and imperialism in eighteenth-century Britain', *Past & Present* 198 (2008), pp. 71–109.

Black, Jeremy, *The British and the Grand Tour* (London: Croom Helm, 1985).

Blench, B. J. R., 'Symbols and sentiment: Jacobite glass', in Robert C. Woosnam-Savage, *1745: Charles Edward Stuart and the Jacobites* (Edinburgh: HMSO, 1995), pp. 87–102.

Bolla, Peter de, 'The visibility of visuality: Vauxhall Gardens and the siting of the viewer', in Stephen Melville and Bill Readings (eds.), *Vision and Textuality* (Basingstoke: Macmillan, 1995), pp. 282–295.

Bonehill, John and Daniels, Stephen, 'Designs on the landscape: Paul and Thomas Sandby in North Britain', *Oxford Art Journal* 40.2 (2017), pp. 223–238.

Bourdieu, Pierre, *Outline of a Theory of Practice* (Cambridge: Cambridge University Press, 1977).

Bowen, H. V., *The Business of Empire: The East India Company and Imperial Britain, 1756–1833* (Cambridge: Cambridge University Press, 2006).

Bowers, Terence, 'Reconstituting the national body in Smollett's *Travels through France and Italy*', *Eighteenth-Century Life* 21.1 (1997), pp. 1–25.

Bowron, Edgar Peters, *Pompeo Batoni: A Complete Catalogue of His Paintings* (New Haven, CT: Yale University Press, 2016), 2 volumes.

and Kerber, Peter Björn *Pompeo Batoni: Prince of Painters in Eighteenth-Century Rome* (New Haven, CT and London: Yale University Press, 2008).

and Rishel, Joseph J. (eds.), *Art in Rome in the Eighteenth Century* (Philadelphia, PA: Philadelphia Museum of Art, 2000).

Brady, Frank, 'So fast to ruin: The personal element in the collapse of Douglas, Heron and Company', *Ayrshire Archaeological and Natural History Society* 11.2 (1973), pp. 27–44.

Brant, Clare, *Eighteenth-Century Letters and British Culture* (Basingstoke: Palgrave Macmillan, 2006).

Brewer, John, 'Between distance and sympathy: Dr John Moore's philosophical travel writing', *Modern Intellectual History* 11.3 (2014), pp. 655–675.

Brooks, George R., 'A portrait by Anton von Maron in the Busch-Reisinger Museum', *Gazette des Beaux Arts* 67 (1966), pp. 115–118.

Brown, Bill, 'Thing theory', *Critical Enquiry* 28.1 (2001), pp. 1–22.

Brown, Iain Gordon (ed.), *Abbotsford and Sir Walter Scott: The Image and the Influence* (Edinburgh: Society of Antiquaries of Scotland, 2003).

Brown, Peter, *The Cult of the Saints: Its Rise and Function in Latin Christianity* (London: SCM Press, 1981).

Brubaker, Rogers and Cooper, Frederick, 'Beyond "identity"' *Theory and Society* 29 (2000), pp. 1–47.

Bryant, G. J., 'The Scots in India in the eighteenth century', *Scottish Historical Review* 64 (1985), pp. 22–41.

Brydall, Robert, *Art in Scotland: Its Origin and Progress* (Edinburgh: W. Blackwood & Sons, 1889).

Bryson, Norman, *Vision and Painting: The Logic of the Gaze* (London: Macmillan, 1983).

Burton, Antoinette, 'Introduction: on the Inadequacy and the Indispensability of the Nation,' in Antoinette Burton (ed.) *After the Imperial Turn: Thinking with and through Nation* (London and Durham, NC: Duke University Press, 2003), pp. 1–23.

Burwick, Frederick, 'Competing Histories in the Waverley Novels', *European Romantic Review* 13 (2002), pp. 261–271.

Busco, Marie, *Sir Richard Westmacott, Sculptor* (Cambridge: Cambridge University Press, 1994).

Busco, Marie F., 'The "Achilles" in Hyde Park', *Burlington Magazine* 130 (1988), pp. 920–924.

Butler, Richard W., 'Tartan mythology: the traditional tourist image of Scotland', in Greg Ringer (ed.), *Destinations: Cultural Landscapes of Tourism* (London: Routledge 1998), pp. 121–39.

Butt, John, *The Industrial Archaeology of Scotland* (Newton Abbot: David & Charles, 1967).

'The Scottish cotton industry during the industrial revolution, 1780–1840', in L. M. Cullen and T. C. Smout (eds.), *Comparative Aspects of Scottish and Irish Economic and Social History, 1600–1900* (Edinburgh: Donald, 1977), pp. 116–128.

Butterworth, D. S., 'Tinto, Pattieson, and the theories of pictorial and dramatic representation in Scott's "The Bride of Lammermoor"', *South Atlantic Review* 56.1 (1991), pp. 1–15.

Bynum, Caroline Walker, *Metamorphosis and Identity* (New York: Zone Books, 2005).

'Why all the fuss about the body? A medievalist's perspective', *Critical Inquiry* 22.1 (1995), pp. 1–33.

Cage, R. A. (ed.), *The Scots Abroad: Labour, Capital, Enterprise, 1750–1914* (London: Croom Helm, 1985).

Caldwell, David H., 'The re-arming of the Clans, 1822', *Review of Scottish Culture* 21 (2009), pp. 67–86.

Cannizzo, Jeanne, '"He was a gentleman even to his dogs": Portraits of Scott and his canine companions', in Iain Gordon Brown (ed.), *Abbotsford and Sir Walter Scott: The Image and the Influence* (Edinburgh: Society of Antiquaries of Scotland, 2003), pp. 115–135.

Cant, R. G., 'David Steuart Erskine, 11th Earl of Buchan: Founder of the Society of Antiquaries of Scotland', in Alan S. Bell (ed.), *The Scottish Antiquarian Tradition: Essays to Mark the Bicentenary of the Society of Antiquaries and its Museum, 1780–1980* (Edinburgh: Donald, 1981), pp. 1–30.

Carson, J. P., 'Scott and the romantic dog', *Journal for Eighteenth-Century Studies* 33.4 (2010), pp. 647–661.

Castle, Terry, *Masquerade and Civilisation: The Carnivalesque in Eighteenth-Century English Culture and Fiction* (London: Methuen, 1986).

Causey, Andrew, 'Pevsner and Englishness', in Peter Draper (ed.), *Reassessing Nikolaus Pevsner* (Aldershot: Ashgate, 2004), pp. 123–144.

Caw, James L., *Scottish Painting Past and Present, 1620–1908* (Edinburgh: T. C. & E. C. Jack, 1908).

Chalmers, Alan, 'Scottish prospects: Thomas Pennant, Samuel Johnson and the possibilities of travel narrative', in Lorna Clymer and Robert Mayer (eds.), *Historical Boundaries, Narrative Forms: Essays on British Literature in the Long Eighteenth Century in Honor of Everett Zimmerman* (Newark: University of Delaware Press, 2007), pp. 199–214.

Chalus, Elaine, 'Fanning the flames: women, fashion and politics', in Tiffany Potter (ed.), *Women, Popular Culture and the Eighteenth Century* (Toronto and London: University of Toronto Press, 2012), pp. 92–112.

Chapman, Malcolm, *The Gaelic Vision in Scottish Culture* (London: Croom Helm, 1978).

Charlesworth, Michael, 'Thomas Sandby climbs the Hoober Stand: The politics of panoramic drawing in eighteenth-century Britain', *Art History* 19 (1996), pp. 247–266.

Chartier, Roger, 'Culture as appropriation: Popular cultural uses in early modern France', in Steven Laurence Kaplan (ed.), *Understanding Popular Culture: Europe from the Middle Ages to the Nineteenth Century* (Berlin and New York: Moulton, 1984), pp. 229–254.

Chatterjee, Partha, *The Nation and its Fragments: Colonial and Postcolonial Histories* (Princeton, NJ: Princeton University Press, 1993).

Chaudhuri, K. N., *The Trading World of Asia and the English East India Company, 1660–1760* (Cambridge: Cambridge University Press, 1978).

Cheape, Hugh, 'The culture and material culture of Jacobitism', in Michael Lynch (ed.), *Jacobitism and the '45* (London: Historical Association Committee for Scotland and the Historical Association, 1995), pp. 32–48.

Cherry, Deborah and Harris, Jennifer, 'Eighteenth-century portraiture and the seventeenth-century past: Gainsborough and Van Dyck', *Art History* 5.3 (1982), pp. 287–309.

Christensen, Jerome, *Romanticism at the End of History* (Baltimore, MD and London: Johns Hopkins University Press, 2000).

Christian, Jessica, 'Paul Sandby and the military survey of Scotland', in Nicholas Alfrey and Stephen Daniels (eds.), *Mapping the Landscape: Essays on Art and Cartography* (Nottingham: University Art Gallery, 1990), pp. 18–22.

Clark, Anthony M., *Pompeo Batoni: A Complete Catalogue of his Works* (Oxford: Phaidon, 1985).

Clark, Jane, 'Lord Burlington is here', in Toby Barnard and Jane Clark (eds.), *Lord Burlington: Architecture, Art and Life* (London: Hambledon, 1995), pp. 251–310.

Clive, John and Bailyn, Bernard, 'England's cultural provinces: Scotland and America', *William and Mary Quarterly* 11.2 (1954), pp. 200–213.

Cohen, Michèle, *Fashioning Masculinity: National Identity and Language in the Eighteenth Century* (London: Routledge, 1996).

'The Grand Tour: constructing the English gentleman in eighteenth-century France', *History of Education* 21.3 (1992), pp. 241–257.

'The Grand Tour: national identity and masculinity', *Changing English: Studies in Culture and Education* 8.2 (2001), pp. 129–141.

'Manliness, effeminacy and the French: Gender and the construction of national character in eighteenth-century England', in Tim Hitchcock and

Michèle Cohen (eds.), *English Masculinities, 1660–1800* (London: Longman, 1999), pp. 44–62.

Cohn, Bernard S., *Colonialism and Its Forms of Knowledge: The British in India* (Princeton, NJ: Princeton University Press, 1996).

Coleridge, Anthony, 'The 3rd & 4th Dukes of Atholl and the firm of Chipchase, cabinet-makers', *Connoisseur* 161 (1966), pp. 96–101.

Colley, Linda, 'Britishness and otherness: An argument', *Journal of British Studies* 31.4 (1992), pp. 309–329.

   Britons: Forging the Nation, 1707–1837 (New Haven, CT and London: Yale University Press, 1992).

Coltman, Viccy, 'The aesthetics of colonialism: George Chinnery's portrait of *Gilbert Elliot, 1st Earl of Minto*, 1812', *Visual Culture in Britain* 17.2 (2016), pp. 1–26.

   'Material culture and the history of art(efacts)', in Anne Gerritsen and Giorgio Riello (eds.), *Writing Material Culture History* (London: Bloomsbury, 2015), pp. 17–31.

   'Party-coloured plaid? Portraits of eighteenth-century Scots in tartan', *Textile History* 41.2 (2010), pp. 182–216.

   'Scottish architects in eighteenth-century London: George Steuart, the competition for patronage and the representation of Scotland', in Stana Nenadic (ed.), *Scots in London in the Eighteenth Century* (Lewisburg, PA: Bucknell University Press, 2010), pp. 91–108.

   'Sojourning Scots and the portrait miniature in colonial India, 1770–1780', *Journal for Eighteenth-Century Studies* 40.3 (2017), pp. 421–441.

Constantine, Mary-Ann and Leask, Nigel (eds.), *Enlightenment Travel and British Identities: Thomas Pennant's Tours in Scotland and Wales* (London: Anthem Press, 2017).

Conway, Stephen, 'Scots, Britons and Europeans: Scottish military service, *c.* 1739–1783', *Historical Research* 82 (2009), pp. 114–130.

   'War and national identity in the mid-eighteenth-century British Isles', *English Historical Review* 116 (2001), pp. 863–893.

Cooke, Anthony, *The Rise and Fall of the Scottish Cotton Industry, 1778–1914* (Manchester: Manchester University Press, 2010).

Corp, Edward, T. (ed.), *Lord Burlington, the Man and His Politics: Questions of Loyalty* (Lewiston, NY: Edwin Mellen Press, 1998).

   'Maurice Quentin de la Tour's portrait of Prince Charles Edward Stuart', *Burlington Magazine* 139 (1997), pp. 322–325.

Craig, Maggie, 'The fair sex turns ugly: Female involvement in the Jacobite rising of 1745', in Yvonne Galloway Brown and Rona Ferguson (eds.), *Twisted Sisters: Women, Crime and Deviance in Scotland since 1400* (East Linton: Tuckwell Press, 2002), pp. 84–100.

Cross, Anthony, 'Cultural relations between Britain and Russia in the eighteenth century', in Brian Allen and Larissa Dukelskaya (eds.), *British Art Treasures from Russian Imperial Collections in the Hermitage* (New Haven, CT and London: Yale University Press, 1996), pp. 16–35.

Cullen, Fintan, 'The art of assimilation: Scotland and Its heroes', *Art History* 16 (1993), pp. 600–618.

and Morrison, John (eds.), *A Shared Legacy: Essays on Irish and Scottish Visual Art and Culture* (Aldershot: Ashgate, 2005).

Curtin, Philip D., *Death by Migration: Europe's Encounter with the Tropical World in the Nineteenth Century* (Cambridge: Cambridge University Press, 1989).

Dalgleish, George, 'Objects as icons: Myths and realities of Jacobite relics', in J. M. Fladmark (ed.), *Heritage and Museums: Shaping National Identity* (Shaftesbury: Donhead, 2000), pp. 91–102.

Darby, Michael, 'Jacobite Garters', *Victoria and Albert Museum Bulletin* 2.4 (1966), pp. 157–163.

Daston, Lorraine, *Biographies of Scientific Objects* (Chicago and London: Chicago University Press, 2000).

(ed.), *Things that Talk: Object Lessons from Art and Science* (New York: Zone, 2004).

Daunton, Martin and Halpern, Rick (eds.), *Empire and Others: British Encounters with Indigenous Peoples, 1600–1850* (London: UCL Press, 1999).

Davis, Leith, Duncan, Ian and Sorensen, Janet (eds.), *Scotland and the Borders of Romanticism* (Cambridge: Cambridge University Press, 2004).

Debord, Guy, *The Society of the Spectacle* (New York: Zone Books, 1994).

Devine, T. M., *Scotland's Empire, 1600–1815* (London: Allen Lane, 2003).

The Tobacco Lords: A Study of the Tobacco Merchants of Glasgow and their Trading Activities, c. 1740–90 (Edinburgh: Donald, 1975).

and McCarthy, Angela (eds.), *The Scottish Experience in Asia c. 1700 to the Present: Settlers and Sojourners* (Cham, Switzerland: Palgrave Macmillan, 2017).

Dingwall, Christopher, 'Gardens in the wild', *Garden History* 22 (1994), pp. 133–156.

'The Hercules Garden at Blair Castle, Perthshire', *Garden History* 20 (1992), pp. 153–172.

'Ossian and Dunkeld: A hall of mirrors', *Scotlands* 4.1 (1997), pp. 62–70.

Donnachie, Ian and Hewitt, George, *Historic New Lanark: The Dale and Owen Industrial Community since 1785* (Edinburgh: Edinburgh University Press, 1993).

Dormont, Richard, *British Painting in the Philadelphia Museum of Art from the Seventeenth through the Nineteenth Century* (London: Philadelphia Museum of Art in association with Weidenfeld & Nicolson, 1986).

Dorrian, Mark, 'The king and the city: On the iconology of George IV in Edinburgh', *Edinburgh Architecture Research* 30 (2006), pp. 32–36, reprinted in his *Writing on the Image: Architecture, the City and the Politics of Representation* (London: I.B. Tauris, 2015), pp. 13–21.

Duffy, Michael, *The Englishman and the Foreigner* (Cambridge: Chadwyck-Healey, 1986).

Duncan, Ian, *Scott's Shadow: The Novel in Romantic Edinburgh* (Princeton, NJ: Princeton University Press, 2007).

Durie, Alastair, '"Scotland is Scott-Land": Scott and the development of tourism', in Murray Pittock (ed.), *The Reception of Sir Walter Scott in Europe* (London: Continuum, 2006), pp. 313–322.

'Tourism in Victorian Scotland: The case of Abbotsford', *Scottish Economic and Social History* 12 (1992), pp. 42–54.

Eaves, Morris, 'The sister arts in British Romanticism', in Stuart Curran (ed.), *The Cambridge Companion to British Romanticism* (Cambridge: Cambridge University Press, 2006), pp. 236–270.

Entwistle, Joanne, 'Fashion and the fleshy body: Dress as embodied practice', *Fashion Theory* 4.3 (2000), pp. 323–347.

The Fashioned Body: Fashion, Dress and Modern Social Theory (Cambridge: Polity, 2000).

Epstein, James, 'Radical dining, toasting and symbolic expression in early nineteenth-century Lancashire', *Albion* 20.2 (1988), pp. 271–291.

Errington, Lindsay, 'Sir Walter Scott and nineteenth-century painting in Scotland', in Wendy Kaplan (ed.), *Scotland Creates: 5000 Years of Art and Design* (London: Weidenfeld & Nicolson, 1990), pp. 121–135.

Fanon, Franz, *The Wretched of the Earth* (London: Penguin, 2001).

Farquhar, Helen, 'Some portrait-medals struck between 1745 and 1752 for Prince Charles Edward Stuart', *British Numismatics Journal* 17.7 (1923–4), pp. 170–225.

Fielding, Penny, 'Writing at the North: Rhetoric and dialect in eighteenth-century Scotland' *The Eighteenth Century* 39.1 (1998), pp. 25–43.

Finlay, Richard J., 'Caledonia or North Britain', in Dauvit Broun, Richard J. Finlay and Michael Lynch (eds.), *Image and Identity: The Making and Re-making of Scotland through the Ages* (Edinburgh: John Donald, 1998), pp. 143–156.

Finley, Gerald, 'J. M. W. Turner's proposal for a "Royal Progress"', *Burlington Magazine* 117 (1975), pp. 27–33+35.

Turner and George the Fourth in Edinburgh, 1822 (London: Tate Gallery, 1981).

Finn, Margot C., 'Colonial gifts: Family politics and the exchange of goods in British India, *c.* 1780–1820', *Modern Asian Studies* 40.1 (2006), pp. 203–231.

Forbes, Duncan, 'Scottish historical painting in the 1820s: Tory hegemony and the spectacle of literary celebrity', in Terry Brotherstone, Anna Clark and Kevin Whelan (eds.), *These Fissured Isles: Ireland, Scotland and British History, 1798–1848* (Edinburgh: John Donald 2005), pp. 141–162.

Ford, Brinsley, *Dictionary of British and Irish Travellers in Italy, 1701–1800* (New Haven, CT and London: Yale University Press, 1997).

'A portrait group by Gavin Hamilton: with some notes on portraits of Englishmen in Rome', *Burlington Magazine* 97 (1955), pp. 372–378.

Forsyth, David (ed.), *Bonnie Prince Charlie and the Jacobites* (Edinburgh: National Museums Scotland, 2017).

Forth, Christopher E. and Crozier, Ivan (eds.), *Body Parts: Critical Explorations in Corporeality* (Oxford: Lexington Books, 2005).

Francis, Grant R., 'Disguised Jacobite glasses', *Burlington Magazine* 69 (1936), pp. 174–176.

Fraser, William, *The Chiefs of Grant* (Edinburgh, 1883), 3 volumes.

French, Henry and Rothery, Mark, '"Upon your entry into the world": Masculine values and the threshold of adulthood among landed elites in England, 1680–1800' *Social History* 33.4 (2008), pp. 402–422.

Fulford, Tim and Kitson, Peter J. (eds.), *Romanticism and Colonialism: Writing and Empire, 1780–1830* (Cambridge: Cambridge University Press, 1998).

Garside, Peter, 'Picturesque figure and landscape: Meg Merrilies and the gypsies', in Stephen Copley and Peter Garside (eds.), *The Politics of the Picturesque: Literature, Landscape and Aesthetics since 1770* (Cambridge: Cambridge University Press, 1994), pp. 145–174.

Geary, Patrick J., *Furta Sacra: Thefts of Relics in the Central Middle Ages* (Princeton, NJ: Princeton University Press, 1978).

   Living with the Dead in the Middle Ages (Ithaca, NY and London: Cornell University Press, 1994).

Gifford, John, 'The National Monument of Scotland', *Architectural Heritage* 25 (2014), pp. 43–83.

Gikandi, Simon, *Maps of Englishness: Writing Identity in the Culture of Colonialism* (New York: Columbia University Press, 1996).

Gillis, John R. (ed.), *Commemorations: The Politics of National Identity* (Princeton, NJ: Princeton University Press, 1994).

Gilroy, Amanda and Verhoven, W. M., *Epistolary Histories: Letters, Fiction, Culture* (Charlottesville and London: University Press of Virginia, 2000).

Gleason, Philip, 'Identifying identity: A semantic history', *Journal of American History* 69.4 (1983), pp. 910–931.

Gold, John R., and Gold, Margaret M., *Imagining Scotland: Tradition, Representation and Promotion in Scottish Tourism since 1750* (Aldershot: Scolar Press, 1995).

Goodsir, Sally, 'George Steuart and Robert Adam: A professional relationship revealed', *Georgian Group Journal* 18 (2010), pp. 91–104.

Gordon, Catherine, 'The illustration of Sir Walter Scott: Nineteenth-century enthusiasm and adaptation', *Journal of the Warburg and Courtauld Institutes* 34 (1971), pp. 297–317.

Graham, Ian Charles Cargill, *Colonists from Scotland: Emigration to North America, 1707–1783* (Ithaca, NY: Cornell University Press, 1956).

Gray, John, 'Lawlessness on the frontier: The Anglo-Scottish borderlands in the fourteenth to sixteenth century', *History and Anthropology* 12.4 (2001), pp. 381–408.

Greene, Jack P., 'Empire and identity from the Glorious Revolution to the American Revolution', in P. J. Marshall (ed.), *The Oxford History of the British Empire: Volume II, the Eighteenth Century* (Oxford: Oxford University Press, 1998), pp. 208–230.

Gregg, Stephen H., 'Representing the nabob: India, stereotypes and eighteenth-century theatre', in Tasleem Shakur and Karen D'Souza (eds.), *Picturing South Asian Culture in English: Textual and Visual Representations* (Liverpool: Open House, 2003), pp. 19–31.

Grosvenor, Bendor, 'Bonnie Prince Charlie returns to Edinburgh', *Country Life* 11 May 2016, pp. 122–125.

Guha, Ranafit, 'Not at home in Empire', *Critical Inquiry* 23.3 (1997), pp. 482–493.

Gust, Onni, 'Remembering and forgetting the Scottish Highlands: Sir James Mackintosh and the forging of a British Imperial identity', *Journal of British Studies* 52 (2013), pp. 615–637.

Guthrie, Neil, *The Material Culture of the Jacobites* (Cambridge: Cambridge University Press, 2013).

Gutiérrez, Natividad, 'The study of national identity', in Alain Dieckhoff and Natividad Gutiérrez (eds.), *Modern Roots: Studies of National Identity* (Aldershot: Ashgate, 2001), pp. 3–17.

Hall, Catherine, 'William Knibb and the constitution of the new Black subject', in Martin Daunton and Rick Halpern (eds.), *Empire and Others: British Encounters with Indigenous Peoples, 1600–1850* (London: UCL Press, 1999), pp. 303–324.

and Rose, Sonya O., *At Home with the Empire: Metropolitan Culture and the Imperial World* (Cambridge: Cambridge University Press, 2006).

Hall, Stuart, 'Cultural identity and diaspora', in Nicholas Mirzoeff (ed.), *Diaspora and Visual Culture: Representing Africans and Jews* (London: Routledge, 2000), pp. 21–33.

Hamilton, Douglas J., *Scotland, the Caribbean and the Atlantic World, 1750–1820* (Manchester: Manchester University Press, 2005).

Hamilton, Henry, 'The failure of the Ayr Bank, 1772', *Economic History Review* 8.3 (1956), pp. 405–417.

Hancock, David, *Citizens of the World: London Merchants and the Integration of the British Atlantic community, 1735–1785* (Cambridge: Cambridge University Press, 1995).

Handler, Richard, 'Is "identity" a useful cross-cultural concept?' in John R. Gillis (ed.), *Commemorations: The Politics of National Identity* (Princeton, NJ: Princeton University Press, 1994), pp. 27–40.

Harrison, Mark, '"The Tender Frame of Man": Disease, climate and racial difference in India and the West Indies, 1760–1860', *Bulletin of the History of Medicine* 70.1 (1996), pp. 68–93.

Harvey, Karen, 'Barbarity in a teacup? Punch, domesticity and gender in the eighteenth century', *Journal of Design History* 21.3 (2008), pp. 205–221.

'Ritual encounters: Punch parties and masculinity in the eighteenth century', *Past & Present* 214 (2012), pp. 165–203.

Hart, Avril and Taylor, E., *Fans* (London: Victoria & Albert Museum, 1998).

Hazard, Erin, 'The Author's House: Abbotsford and Wayside', in Nicola J. Watson (ed.), *Literary Tourism and Nineteenth-Century Culture* (Basingstoke: Palgrave Macmillan, 2009), pp. 63–72.

Henderson, Andrea K., *Romantic Identities: Varieties of Subjectivity, 1774–1830* (Cambridge: Cambridge University Press, 1996).

Hill, R. J., *Picturing Scotland through the Waverley Novels: Walter Scott and the Origins of the Victorian Illustrated Book* (Farnham: Ashgate, 2010).

Holcomb, Adele M., 'Scott and Turner', in Alan S. Bell (ed.), *Scott Bicentenary Essays* (Edinburgh: Scottish Academic Press, 1973), pp. 199–212.

Hollander, John, 'The poetics of *ekphrasis*', *Word & Image* 4 (1988), pp. 209–218.

Holloway, James and Errington, Lindsay, *The Discovery of Scotland: The Appreciation of Scottish Scenery through Two Centuries of Painting* (Edinburgh: National Gallery of Scotland, 1978).

Holm, Christiane, 'Sentimental cuts: Eighteenth-century mourning jewelry with hair', *Eighteenth-Century Studies* 38.1 (2004), pp. 139–143.

Hoock, Holgar, 'From beefsteak to turtle: Artists' dinner culture in eighteenth-century London', *Huntington Library Quarterly* 66 (2003), pp. 27–54.

Hoppit, Julian, 'Financial crises in eighteenth-century England', *Economic History Review* 2nd series, 39.1 (1986), pp. 39–58.

   Risk and Failure in English Business, 1700–1800 (Cambridge: Cambridge University Press, 1987).

   (ed.), *Parliaments, Nations and Identities in Britain and Ireland, 1660–1850* (Manchester: Manchester University Press, 2003).

Hughes, G. Bernard, *English Snuff-Boxes* (London: MacGibbon and Kee, 1971).

Hunter, Margaret, 'Mourning jewellery: A collector's account', *Costume* 27.1 (1993), pp. 9–22.

Irvine, James (ed.), *Parties and Pleasures: The Diaries of Helen Graham, 1823 to 1826* (Edinburgh: Paterson, 1957).

Irwin, David, 'A 'picturesque' experience: The Hermitage at Dunkeld', *The Connoisseur* 187 (1974), pp. 196–199.

   and Irwin, Francina, *Scottish Painters at Home and Abroad, 1700–1900* (London: Faber, 1975).

Jagger, Nicholas, 'The iconising of Walter Scott', in Martin Hewitt (ed.), *Representing Victorian Lives* (Leeds: Leeds Centre for Victorian Studies, 1999), pp. 101–112.

Jenkins, Ralph E., '"And I travelled after him": Johnson and Pennant in Scotland', *Texas Studies in Literature and Language* 14.3 (1972), pp. 445–462.

Johns, Christopher, M. S., 'Portraiture and the making of cultural identity: Pompeo Batoni's *The Honourable Colonel William Gordon* (1765–66) in Italy and North Britain', *Art History* 27 (2004), pp. 382–411.

Jones, Ann R., and Stallybrass, Peter, *Renaissance Clothing and the Materials of Memory* (Cambridge: Cambridge University Press, 2000).

Jones, Lindsay (ed.), *Encyclopedia of Religion* (Detroit and London: Thomson/Gale, 2005).

Jordanova, Ludmilla, 'The art and science of seeing in medicine: Physiognomy, 1780–1820', in W. F. Bynum and Roy Porter (eds.), *Medicine and the Five Senses* (Cambridge: Cambridge University Press, 1993), pp. 122–133.

'Picture-talking: Portraiture and conversation in Britain, 1800–1830', in Katie Halsey and Jane Slinn (eds.), *The Concept and Practice of Conversation in the Long Eighteenth Century, 1688–1848* (Newcastle: Cambridge Scholars Publishing, 2008), pp. 151–169.

Joseph, Betty, *Reading the East India Company, 1720–1840: Colonial Currencies of Gender* (Chicago and London: Chicago University Press, 2003).

Juneja, Renu, 'The Native and the Nabob: Representations of Indian experience in eighteenth-century English literature', *Journal of Commonwealth History* 27.1 (1992), pp. 183–198.

Kaiser, Thomas E., 'The drama of Charles Edward Stuart: Jacobite propaganda and French political protest, 1745–1750', *Eighteenth-Century Studies* 30.4 (1997), pp. 365–381.

Karras, A. L., *Sojourners in the Sun: Scottish Migrants in Jamaica and the Chesapeake, 1740–1800* (Ithaca, NY and London: Cornell University Press, 1992).

Kemp, Martin, *The Science of Art: Optical Themes in Western Art from Brunelleschi to Seurat* (New Haven, CT and London: Yale University Press, 1990).

Keymer, Tom, 'Smollett's Scotlands: Culture, politics and nationhood in "Humphry Clinker" and Defoe's "Tour"', *History Workshop Journal* 40.1 (1995), pp. 118–132.

Kidd, Colin, *British Identities before Nationalism: Ethnicity and Nationhood in the Atlantic World, 1600–1800* (Cambridge: Cambridge University Press, 1999).

'North Britishness and the nature of eighteenth-century British patriotisms', *Historical Journal* 39.2 (1996), pp. 361–382.

Kiernan, Victor, 'Scottish soldiers and the conquest of India', in Grant G. Simpson (ed.), *The Scottish Soldier Abroad, 1247–1967* (Edinburgh: John Donald, 1992), pp. 97–110.

Koditschek, Theodore, 'The making of British nationality', *Victorian Studies* 44.3 (2002), pp. 389–398.

Kumar, Krishnan, *The Making of English National Identity* (Cambridge: Cambridge University Press, 2003).

'Nation and Empire: English and British national identity in comparative perspective', *Theory and Society* 29.5 (2000), pp. 576–608.

Kupperman, Karen Ordahl, *Indians & English: Facing Off in Early America* (Ithaca, NY: Cornell University Press, 2000).

Langford, Paul, *A Polite and Commercial People: England, 1727–1783* (Oxford: Oxford University Press, 1989).

'South Britons' reception of North Britons, 1707–1820', in T. C. Smout (ed.), *Anglo-Scottish Relations from 1603–1900* (Oxford: Oxford University Press, 2005), pp. 143–169.

'Tories and Jacobites 1714–51', in L. S. Sutherland and L. G. Mitchell (eds.), *The History of the University of Oxford: Volume V, the Eighteenth Century* (Oxford: Clarendon, 1986), pp. 99–127.

Lawson, Philip and Phillips, Jim, '"Our Execrable Banditti": Perceptions of nabobs in mid-eighteenth century Britain', *Albion* 16.3 (1984), pp. 225–241.

Leask, Nigel, 'Fingalian topographies: Ossian and the Highland tour, 1760–1805', *Journal for Eighteenth-Century Studies* 39.2 (2011), pp. 183–196.

Ledbury, Mark, *James Northcote, History Painting and the Fables* (New Haven, CT and London: Yale University Press, 2014).

Lee, Yoon Sun, 'A divided inheritance: Scott's antiquarian novel and the British nation', *English Literary History* 64.2 (1997), pp. 537–567.

Lelièvre, F. J., 'Jacobite glasses and their inscriptions', *The Glass Circle* 5 (1986), pp. 62–74.

Leneman, Leah, *Promises, Promises: Marriage Litigation in Scotland, 1698–1830* (Edinburgh: NMS Enterprises Ltd, 2003).

Lenman, Bruce, 'The Scottish Episcopal clergy and the ideology of Jacobitism', in Eveline Cruickshanks (ed.), *Ideology and Conspiracy: Aspects of Jacobitism, 1689–1759* (Edinburgh: Donald, 1982), pp. 36–48.

Lester, Alan, 'Constructing colonial discourse: Britain, South Africa and the Empire in the nineteenth century', in Alison Blunt and Cheryl McEwan (eds.), *Postcolonial Geographies* (New York and London: Continuum, 2002), pp. 29–45.

Lieberman, Ilene D., Potts, Alex, and Yarrington, Alison, 'An edition of the ledger of Sir Francis Chantrey, R. A., at the Royal Academy, 1809–1841', *The Walpole Society* 56 (1991/2), pp. 1–343.

López, Rosa, 'The garter: Function and seduction', *Datatèxtil* 13 (2005), pp. 4–19.

Lowenthal, Cynthia, *Lady Mary Wortley Montagu and the Eighteenth-Century Familiar Letter* (Athens and London: University of Georgia Press, 1994).

Lowrey, John, 'From Caesarea to Athens: Greek Revival Edinburgh and the question of Scottish identity within the Unionist State', *Journal of the Society of Architectural Historians* 60 (2001), pp. 136–157.

Löwy, Michael and Sayre, Robert, *Romanticism against the Tide of Modernity* (Durham, NC and London: Duke University Press, 2002).

Lukács, Georg, *The Historical Novel* (London: Merlin, 1962).

Lutz, Deborah, 'The dead still among us: Victorian secular relics, hair jewelry and death culture', *Victorian Literature and Culture* 39 (2011), pp. 127–142.

Macdonald, Murdo, 'Finding Scottish art', in Glenda Norquay and Gerry Smyth (eds.), *Across the Margins: Cultural Identity and Change in the Atlantic Archipelago* (Manchester: Manchester University Press, 2002), pp. 171–184.

Macinnes, Allan I., 'Scottish Jacobitism: In search of a movement', in T. M. Devine and J. R. Young (eds.), *Eighteenth-Century Scotland: New Perspectives* (East Linton: Tuckwell Press, 1999), pp. 70–89.

MacInnes, Ian, 'Mastiffs and spaniels: Gender and nation in the English dog', *Textual Practice* 17.1 (2003), pp. 21–40.

Mackenzie, John M., 'Empire and national identities: The case of Scotland', *Transactions of the Royal Historical Society* 8 (1998), pp. 215–231.

and Devine, T. M. (eds.), *Scotland and the British Empire* (Oxford: Oxford University Press, 2011).

Mackillop, Andrew, 'Europeans, Britons and Scots: Scottish sojourning networks and identities in Asia, *c*. 1700–1815', in Angela McCarthy, *A Global Clan: Scottish Migrant Networks and Identities since the Eighteenth Century* (London: Tauris Academic Studies, 2006), pp. 19–47.

'The Highlands and the returning nabob: Sir Hector Munro of Novar, 1760–1807', in Marjory Harper (ed.), *Emigrant Homecomings: The Return Movement of Emigrants, 1600–2000* (Manchester: Manchester University Press, 2005), pp. 233–261.

'Locality, nation and empire: Scots and the Empire in Asia, *c*. 1695–*c*. 1813', in J. M. Mackenzie and T. M. Devine (eds.), *Scotland and the British Empire* (Oxford: Oxford University Press, 2011), pp. 4–83.

Maclean, James N. M., and Skinner, Basil, *The Royal Visit of 1822* (Edinburgh: University of Edinburgh Department of Educational Studies, 1972).

Macmillan, Duncan, 'The canon in Scottish art: Scottish art in the canon', *Scotlands* 1.1(1994), pp. 87–103.

Scottish Art, 1460–2000 (Edinburgh: Mainstream, 2000).

Macmillan, J. Duncan, '"Truly national designs": Runciman's Scottish themes at Penicuik', *Art History* 1 (1978), pp. 90–98.

Malley, Shawn, 'Walter Scott's Romantic Archaeology: New/Old Abbotsford and *The Antiquary*', *Studies in Romanticism* 40.2 (2001), pp. 233–251.

Mandler, Peter, 'What is "national identity"? Definitions and applications in modern British historiography', *Modern Intellectual History* 3.2 (2006), pp. 271–297.

Manners, Victoria, and Williamson, G. C., *John Zoffany, R.A.* (London: John Lane, 1920).

Mannings, David, 'Notes on some eighteenth-century portrait prices in Britain', *Journal for Eighteenth-Century Studies* 6.2 (1983), pp. 185–196.

Mari, Francesca, 'The microhistorian', *Dissent* 60 (2013), pp. 81–86.

Markus, Thomas A. (ed.), *Order in Space and Society: Architectural Form and Its Context in the Scottish Enlightenment* (Edinburgh: Mainstream, 1982).

Marshall, P. J., 'British society in India under the East India Company', *Modern Asian Studies* 31 (1997), pp. 89–108.

   East Indian Fortunes: The British in Bengal in the Eighteenth Century (Oxford: Clarendon Press, 1976).

   'Private British investment in eighteenth-century Bengal', *Bengal Past and Present* 86 (1967), pp. 52–67.

   'The white town of Calcutta under the rule of the East India Company', *Modern Asian Studies* 43 (2000), pp. 307–331.

McCausland, Hugh, *Snuff and Snuff-Boxes* (London: Batchworth, 1951).

McCracken-Flesher, Caroline, *Possible Scotlands: Walter Scott and the Story of Tomorrow* (Oxford: Oxford University Press, 2005).

   'Walter Scott's Romanticism: A theory of performance', in Murray Pittock (ed.), *The Edinburgh Companion to Scottish Romanticism* (Edinburgh: Edinburgh University Press, 2011), pp. 139–149.

McCullen, J. T., 'Tobacco: A recurrent theme in eighteenth-century literature', *The Bulletin of the Rocky Mountain Modern Language Association* 22.2 (1968), pp. 30–39.

McGilvary, George K., *East India Patronage and the British State: The Scottish Elite and Politics in the Eighteenth Century* (London: Tauris Academic Studies, 2008).

McMillen, Krystal, 'Eating turtle, eating the world: comestible *things* in the eighteenth century', Ileana Baird and Christina Ionescu (eds.), *Eighteenth-Century Thing Theory in a Global Context: From Consumerism to Celebrity Culture* (Aldershot: Ashgate, 2013), pp. 191–207.

McNairn, Alan, *Behold the Hero: General Wolfe and the Arts in the Eighteenth Century* (Liverpool: Liverpool University Press, 1997).

Meyer, Arline, 'Re-dressing classical statuary: The eighteenth-century "hand in waistcoat" portrait', *Art Bulletin* 77.1 (1995), pp. 45–63.

Miles, H. A. D., and Brown, David Blayney, *Sir David Wilkie of Scotland (1785–1841)* (Raleigh: North Carolina Museum of Art, 1987).

Miles, Robert, *Romantic Misfits* (Basingstoke: Palgrave Macmillan, 2008).

Millen, Ronald Forsyth, and Wolf, Ronald Erich, *Heroic Deeds and Mystic Figures: A New Reading of Rubens' Life of Maria de' Medici* (Princeton, NJ: Princeton University Press, 1989).

Miller, Daniel, *Stuff* (Cambridge: Polity Press, 2010).

Mirzoeff, Nicholas, *Bodyscapes: Art, Modernity and the Ideal Figure* (London and New York: Routledge, 1995).

Mitchell, Sebastian, *Visions of Britain, 1730–1830: Anglo-Scottish Writing and Representation* (New York: Palgrave Macmillan, 2013).

Mitchison, Rosalind, 'Patriotism and national identity in eighteenth-century Scotland', in T. W. Moody (ed.), *Nationality and the Pursuit of National Independence* (Belfast: The Appletree Press, 1978), pp. 73–95.

Mole, Tom, *What the Victorians Made of Romanticism: Material Artifacts, Cultural Practices, and Reception History* (Princeton, NJ: Princeton University Press, 2017).

Monod, Paul Kleber, *Jacobitism and the English People, 1688–1788* (Cambridge: Cambridge University Press, 1989).

'A Restoration? 25 years of Jacobite studies', *Literature Compass* 10.4 (2013), pp. 311–330.

Pittock, Murray and Szechi, Daniel (eds.), *Loyalty and Identity: Jacobites at Home and Abroad* (Basingstoke: Palgrave Macmillan, 2010).

Moore, John, *A View of Society and Manners in Italy* (London, 1781), 2 volumes.

Morrison, John, *Painting the Nation: Identity and Nationalism in Scottish Painting, 1800–1920* (Edinburgh: Edinburgh University Press, 2003).

Murdoch, Alexander, 'Scotland and the idea of Britain in the eighteenth century', in T. M. Devine and J. R. Young (eds.), *Eighteenth-Century Scotland: New Perspectives* (East Linton:Tuckwell Press, 1999), pp. 106–121.

Murray, Arthur C., *The Five Sons of 'Bare Belly'* (London: John Murray, 1936).

Myrone, Martin, *Bodybuilding: Reforming Masculinities in British Art, 1750–1810* (New Haven, CT and London: Yale University Press, 1995).

Navickas, Katrina, '"That sash will hang you": Political clothing and adornment in England, 1780–1840', *Journal of British Studies* 49.3 (2010), pp. 540–565.

Nead, Lynda, *The Haunted Gallery: Painting, Photography, Film, c. 1900* (New Haven, CT and London: Yale University Press, 2007).

Nechtman, Tillman, W., 'A Jewel in the Crown? Indian wealth in domestic Britain in the late eighteenth century', *Eighteenth-Century Studies* 41.1 (2007), pp. 71–86.

Nabobs: Empire and Identity in Eighteenth-Century Britain (Cambridge: Cambridge University Press, 2010).

'Nabobs Revisited: A cultural history of British Imperialism and the India Question in late eighteenth-century Britain', *History Compass* 4.4 (2006), pp. 645–667.

Nevinson, J. L., 'Vandyke dress', *Connoisseur* 157 (1964), pp. 166–171.

'Vogue of the Vandyke dress', *Country Life Annual* 1959, pp. 25–27.

Newman, Gerald, *The Rise of English Nationalism: A Cultural History, 1740–1830* (London: Weidenfeld & Nicolson, 1987).

Nicholson, Eirwen E. C., 'Evidence for the authenticity of portrait-engraved Jacobite drinking-glasses', *Burlington Magazine* 138 (1996), pp. 396–397.

'The oak v. the orange tree: Emblematizing dynastic union and conflict, 1600–1796', in Bart Westerwell (ed.), *Anglo-Dutch Relations in the Field of the Emblem* (Leiden: Brill, 1997), pp. 227–251.

'"Revirescit": The exilic origins of the Stuart oak motif', in Edward T. Corp (ed.), *The Stuart Court in Rome: The Legacy of Exile* (Aldershot: Ashgate, 2003), pp. 25–48.

Nicholson, Robin, *Bonnie Prince Charlie and the Making of a Myth: A Study in Portraiture, 1720–1892* (Lewisburg, PA: Bucknell University Press, 2002).

Norman, A. V. B., 'Arms and Armour at Abbotsford', *Apollo* 76 (1962), pp. 525–529.

'George IV and Highland dress', *Review of Scottish Culture* 10 (1997), pp. 5–15.

Normand, Tom, '55° North 3° West: A panorama from Scotland', in Dana Arnold and David Peters Corbett (eds.), *A Companion to British Art: 1600 to the Present* (Chichester: Wiley-Blackwell, 2013), pp. 265–288.

Novotny, Jennifer, 'Polite war: Material culture of the Jacobite era', in Allan I. Macinnes, Kieran German and Lesley Graham (eds.), *Living with Jacobitism: The Three Kingdoms and Beyond, 1690–1788* (London: Pickering & Chatto, 2014), pp. 153–172.

Oettermann, Stephan, *The Panorama: History of a Mass Medium* (New York: Zone Books, 1997).

Oleksijczuk, Denise Blake, 'Gender in perspective: The King and Queen's visit to the Panorama in 1793', in Steven Adams and Anna Gruetzner Robins (eds.), *Gendering Landscape Art* (Manchester: Manchester University Press, 2000), pp. 146–161.

Palmeri, Frank (ed.), *Humans and Other Animals in Eighteenth-Century British Culture: Representation, Hybridity, Ethics* (Aldershot: Ashgate, 2006).

Park, Katharine, 'Was there a Renaissance body?', in Walter Kaiser and Michael Rocke (eds.), *The Italian Renaissance in the Twentieth Century* (Florence: Olschki, 2002), pp. 321–335.

Parker, J. G. 'Scottish enterprise in India, 1750–1914', in R. A. Cage (ed.), *The Scots Abroad: Labour, Capital, Enterprise, 1750–1914* (London: Croom Helm, 1985), pp. 191–219.

Peacocke, E. R., 'Facing history: galleries and portraits in *Waverley's* historiography', *European Romantic Review* 22.2 (2011), pp. 57–86.

Pearce, Susan, 'The *matériel* of war: Waterloo and its culture', in John Bonehill and Geoff Quilley (eds.), *Conflicting Visions: War and Visual Culture in Britain and France, c. 1700–1830* (Aldershot: Ashgate, 2005), pp. 207–226.

Pearsall, Sarah M. S., *Atlantic Families: Lives and Letters in the Later Eighteenth Century* (Oxford: Oxford University Press, 2008).

Pentland, Gordon, '"We speak for the Ready": Images of Scots in political prints, 1707–1832', *Scottish Historical Review* 90.1 (2011), pp. 64–95.

Percival, Melissa, *The Appearance of Character: Physiognomy and Facial Expression in Eighteenth-Century France* (Leeds: W. S. Maney for the NHRA, 1999).

Perry, Seamus, 'Romanticism: The brief history of a concept', in Duncan Wu (ed.), *A Companion to Romanticism* (Oxford: Blackwell, 1998), pp. 3–11.

Pevsner, Nikolaus, *The Englishness of English Art* (London: British Broadcasting Corporation, 1956).

Pinnington, Edward, *Sir David Wilkie and the Scottish School* (Edinburgh, 1900).

Pittock, Murray, 'The Aeneid in the Age of Burlington: A Jacobite text?', in Toby Barnard and Jane Clark, *Lord Burlington: Architecture, Art and Life* (London: Hambleton, 1995), pp. 231–249.

Material Culture and Sedition, 1688–1760: Treacherous Objects, Secret Places (Basingstoke: Palgrave Macmillan, 2013).

The Myth of the Jacobite Clans (Edinburgh: Edinburgh University Press, 1995).

'Treacherous Objects: Towards a theory of Jacobite material culture', *Journal for Eighteenth-Century Studies* 34.1 (2011), pp. 39–63.

Plumb, Christopher, *The Georgian Menagerie: Exotic Animals in Eighteenth-Century London* (London: I.B. Tauris, 2015).

Pointon, Marcia, *Brilliant Effects: A Cultural History of Gem Stones & Jewellery* (New Haven, CT and London: Yale University Press, 2009).

Portrayal and the Search for Identity (London: Reaktion, 2013).

'"Surrounded with brilliants": Miniature portraits in eighteenth-century England', *Art Bulletin* 133 (2001), pp. 48–71.

'Wearing memory: Mourning, jewellery and the body', in Gisela Ecker (ed.), *Trauer tragen – Trauer zeigen: Inszenierungen der Geschlechter* (Munich: Fink, 1999), pp. 65–81.

Port, M. H., 'Town house and country house: Their interaction', in Dana Arnold (ed.), *The Georgian Country House: Architecture, Landscape and Society* (Stroud: Sutton, 1998), pp. 117–38.

'West End palaces: The aristocratic town house in London, 1730–1830', *The London Journal* 20 (1995), pp. 17–46.

Porter, Roy, *Bodies Politic: Disease, Death and Doctors in Britain, 1650–1900* (London: Reaktion, 2001).

'History of the body', in Peter Burke (ed.), *New Perspectives on Historical Writing* (Cambridge: Polity, 1991), pp. 206–232.

Pottle, Frederick A., *James Boswell: The Earlier Years, 1740–1769* (New York: McGraw-Hill, 1966).

Prebble, John, *The King's Jaunt: George IV in Scotland, August 1822* (London: Collins, 1988).

Prown, Jules D., 'Mind in matter: An introduction to material culture theory and method', *Winterthur Portfolio* 17.1 (1982), pp. 1–19.

Raeburn, Michael, Voronikhina, Ludmila and Nurnberg, Andrew (eds.), *The Green Frog Service* (London: Cacklegoose Press, 1995).

Ragussis, Michael, 'Jews and other "Outlandish Englishmen": Ethnic performance and the invention of British identity under the Georges', *Critical Inquiry* 26.4 (2000), pp. 773–797.

Raleigh, John Henry, 'What Scott meant to the Victorians', *Victorian Studies* 7 (1963), pp. 7–34.

Rappaport, Erika, '"The Bombay Debt": Letter writing, domestic economies and family conflict in colonial India', *Gender & History* 16.2 (2004), pp. 233–260.

Raven, James, *Judging New Wealth: Popular Publishing and Responses to Commerce in England, 1750–1800* (Oxford: Clarendon Press, 1992).

Redford, Bruce, *Venice and the Grand Tour* (New Haven, CT and London: Yale University Press, 1996).

Ribeiro, Aileen, *The Art of Dress: Fashion in England and France, 1750 to 1820* (New Haven, CT and London: Yale University Press, 1995).

 The Dress Worn at Masquerades in England, 1730 to 1790, and its Relation to Fancy Dress in Portraiture (New York and London: Garland, 1984)

Richards, Eric, 'Scotland and the uses of the Atlantic Empire', in Bernard Bailyn and Philip D. Morgan (eds.), *Strangers within the Realm: Cultural Margins of the First British Empire* (Chapel Hill and London: University of North Carolina Press, 1991), pp. 67–114.

Richardson, H. E., 'George Bogle and his children', *Scottish Genealogist* 29 (1982), pp. 73–83.

Riddy, John, 'Warren Hastings: Scotland's benefactor', in Geoffrey Carnall and Colin Nicholson (eds.), *The Impeachment of Warren Hastings: Papers from a Bicentenary Commemoration* (Edinburgh: Edinburgh University Press, 1989), pp. 30–57.

Rigney, Ann, 'Abbotsford: Dislocation and cultural remembrance', in Harald Hendrix (ed.), *Writers' Houses and the Making of Memory* (New York and London: Routledge, 2008), pp. 75–91.

 The Afterlives of Walter Scott: Memory on the Move (Oxford: Oxford University Press, 2012).

Rix, M. M., and Serjeant, W. R., 'George Steuart, Architect, in the Isle of Man', *The Journal of the Manx Museum* 6 (1962–3), pp. 177–179.

Robertson, Fiona, 'Romancing and Romanticism', in Fiona Robertson (ed.), *The Edinburgh Companion to Sir Walter Scott* (Edinburgh: Edinburgh University Press, 2012), pp. 93–105.

Rosenthal, Angela, 'Unfolding gender: Women and the "secret" sign language of fans in Hogarth's work', in Bernadette Fort and Angela Rosenthal (eds.), *The Other Hogarth: Aesthetics of Difference* (Princeton, NJ and Oxford: Princeton University Press, 2001), pp. 120–141.

Ross, Ian, 'A bluestocking over the border: Mrs Elizabeth Montagu's aesthetic adventures in Scotland, 1766', *Huntington Library Quarterly* 28.3 (1965), pp. 213–233.

Rothschild, Emma, *The Inner Life of Empires: An Eighteenth-Century History* (Princeton, NJ: Princeton University Press, 2011).

Rothstein, Eric, 'Scotophilia and *Humphry Clinker*: The politics of beggary, bugs and buttocks', *University of Toronto Quarterly* 52 (1982–3), pp. 63–78.

Rowan, Alistair J., 'After the Adelphi: Forgotten years in the Adam brothers' practice', *Journal of the Royal Society of Arts* 122 (1974), pp. 659–710.

Russell, Francis, 'Notes on Luti, Batoni and Nathaniel Dance', *Burlington Magazine* 130 (1988), pp. 853–855.

 Portraits of Sir Walter Scott: A Study of Romantic Portraiture (London: F. Russell, 1987).

Sahlins, Peter, *Boundaries: The Making of France and Spain in the Pyrenees, 1659–1868* (Berkeley: University of California Press, 1989).

Samuel, Raphael (ed.), *Patriotism: The Making and Unmaking of British National Identity* (London: Routledge, 1989).

Sanderson, Margaret H. B., *'A Proper Repository': The Building of the General Register House* (Edinburgh: Scottish Record Office, 1992).

Robert Adam and Scotland: Portrait of an Architect (Edinburgh: HMSO, 1992).

Sanger, Alice E., 'Sensuality, sacred remains and devotion in Baroque Rome', in Alice E. Sanger and Siv Tove Kulbrandstad Walker (eds.), *Sense and the Senses in Early Modern Art and Cultural Practice* (Farnham: Ashgate, 2012), pp. 199–215.

Sankey, Margaret and Szechi, Daniel, 'Elite culture and the decline of Scottish Jacobitism, 1716–1745', *Past & Present* 173 (2001), pp. 90–128.

Schlarman, Julie, 'The social geography of Grosvenor Square: Mapping gender and politics, 1720–1760', *The London Journal* 28 (2003), pp. 8–28.

Schwarzer, Mitchell, 'Origins of the art history survey text', *Art Journal* 53.4 (1995), pp. 24–29.

Seddon, Geoffrey B., *The Jacobites and Their Drinking Glasses* (Woodbridge: Antique Collectors' Club, 1995).

de Seta, Cesare, 'Grand Tour: the lure of Italy in the eighteenth century' in Andrew Wilton and Ilaria Bignamini (eds.), *Grand Tour: The Lure of Italy in the Eighteenth Century* (London: Tate Gallery, 1996), pp. 13–19.

Sharp, Richard, *The Engraved Record of the Jacobite Movement* (Aldershot: Scolar Press, 1996).

Shaw, Philip, *Waterloo and the Romantic Imagination* (Basingstoke: Palgrave Macmillan 2002).

Sheumaker, Helen, '"This Lock You See": Nineteenth-century hair work as the commodified self', *Fashion Theory* 1.4 (1997), pp. 421–445.

Shields, Juliet, *Sentimental Literature and Anglo-Scottish Identity, 1745–1820* (Cambridge: Cambridge University Press, 2010).

Siegfried, Susan L., 'Picturing the battlefield of victory: Document, drama, image', in Satish Padiyar, Philip Shaw and Philippa Simpson (eds.), *Visual Culture and the Revolutionary and Napoleonic Wars* (Routledge: London and New York, 2017), pp. 213–245.

Simpson, Kenneth, *Protean Scot: The Crisis of Identity in Eighteenth-Century Scottish Literature* (Aberdeen: Aberdeen University Press, 1988).

Skinner, Basil, 'A note on four British artists in Rome', *Burlington Magazine* 99 (1957), pp. 237–239.

Scots in Italy in the Eighteenth Century (Edinburgh: Scottish National Portrait Gallery, 1966).

'Scott as pageant-master: The royal visit of 1822', in Alan S. Bell (ed.), *Scott Bicentenary Essays* (Edinburgh: Scottish Academic Press, 1973), pp. 228–237.

'Some aspects of the work of Nathaniel Dance in Rome', *Burlington Magazine* 101 (1959), pp. 346–349.

Slater, John, 'The Strand and the Adelphi', *Journal of the Royal Society of Arts* 71 (1922), pp. 19–32.

Smailes, Helen, *Andrew Geddes, 1783–1844: 'A Man of Pure Taste'* (Edinburgh: National Galleries of Scotland, 2001).

Smethurst, Paul, 'Peripheral vision, landscape and nation-building in Thomas Pennant's tours of Scotland, 1769–72', in Benjamin Colbert (ed.), *Travel Writing and Tourism in Britain and Ireland* (Basingstoke and New York: Palgrave Macmillan, 2012), pp. 13–30.

Smith, Anthony D., *The Nation made Real: Art and National Identity in Western Europe, 1600–1850* (Oxford: Oxford University Press, 2013).

     National Identity (London: Penguin, 1991).

Smout, Christopher, 'Tours in the Scottish Highlands from the eighteenth to the twentieth centuries', *Northern Scotland* 5.1 (1982–3), pp. 99–121.

Smout, Thomas Christopher, 'Perspectives on the Scottish identity,' *Scottish Affairs* 6 (1994), pp. 101–113.

     'Problems of nationalism, identity and improvement in later eighteenth-century Scotland', in T. M. Devine (ed.), *Improvement and Enlightenment* (Edinburgh: John Donald, 1989), pp. 1–21.

Smylitopoulos, Christina, 'Portrait of a nabob: Graphic satire, portraiture and the Anglo-Indian in the late eighteenth century', *Revue d'art canadienne* 37 (2012), pp. 10–25.

     'Rewritten and reused: Imaging the Nabob through "Upstart iconography"', *Eighteenth-Century Life* 32 (2008), pp. 39–59.

Spivak, Gayatri Chakravorty, *Outside in the Teaching Machine* (New York and London: Routledge, 1993).

Stafford, Barbara Maria, *Body Criticism: Imaging the Unseen in Enlightenment Art and Medicine* (Cambridge, MA and London: MIT Press, 1991).

Stafford, Fiona, 'Scottish Romanticism and Scotland in Romanticism', in Michael Ferber (ed.), *A Companion to European Romanticism* (Oxford: Blackwell, 2005), pp. 49–66.

Standen, Edith A., 'Instruments for agitating the air', *Metropolitan Museum of Art Bulletin* 23.1 (1965), pp. 243–258.

Steegman, John, 'Some English portraits by Pompeo Batoni', *Burlington Magazine* 88 (1946), pp. 56–63.

Stewart, Keith, 'Towards defining an aesthetic for the familiar letter in eighteenth-century England', *Prose Studies* 5 (1982), pp. 179–192.

Stewart, Rachel, *The Town House in Georgian London* (New Haven, CT and London: Yale University Press, 2009).

Strawhorn, John, 'The background to Burns. Part II: Industry and commerce in eighteenth-century Ayrshire', *Ayrshire Collections* 4 (1958), pp. 182–215.

Synnott, Anthony, 'Shame and glory: A sociology of hair', *British Journal of Sociology* 38.3 (1987), pp. 381–413.

Szechi, Daniel, *The Jacobites: Britain and Europe, 1688–1788* (Manchester: Manchester University Press, 1994).

Tague, Ingrid H., *Animal Companions: Pets and Social change in Eighteenth-Century Britain* (University Park: Pennsylvania State University Press, 2015).

Taylor, Charles, 'Modernity and identity', in Joan W. Scott and Debra Keates (eds.), *Schools of Thought: Twenty-Five Years of Interpretative Social Science* (Princeton, NJ and Oxford: Princeton University Press, 2001), pp. 139–153.

Taylor, Miles, 'John Bull and the iconography of public opinion in England, *c.* 1712–1929', *Past and Present* 134 (1992), pp. 93–128.

Teltscher, Kate, 'Writing home and crossing cultures: George Bogle in Bengal and Tibet, 1770–1775', in Kathleen Wilson (ed.), *A New Imperial History: Culture, Identity and Modernity in Britain and the Empire, 1660–1840* (Cambridge: Cambridge University Press, 2004), pp. 281–296.

Thom, Danielle, '"William, the Princely Youth": The Duke of Cumberland and anti-Jacobite visual strategy, 1745–46', *Visual Culture in Britain* 16 (2015), pp. 269–286.

Thomson, Duncan, *Raeburn: The Art of Sir Henry Raeburn, 1756–1823* (Edinburgh: Scottish National Portrait Gallery, 1997).

Tobin, Beth Fowkes, *Picturing Imperial Britain: Colonial Subjects in Eighteenth-Century British Painting* (Durham, NC and London: Duke University Press, 1999).

Travers, Robert, 'Death and the nabob: Imperialism and commemoration in eighteenth-century India', *Past and Present* 196 (2007), pp. 83–124.

Trevor-Roper, Hugh, 'The invention of tradition: The Highland tradition of Scotland', in Eric Hobsbawm and Terence Ranger (eds.), *The Invention of Tradition* (Cambridge: Cambridge University Press, 1983), pp. 15–41.

Tromans, Nicholas, *David Wilkie: The People's Painter* (Edinburgh: Edinburgh University Press, 2007).

Trumpener, Katie, *Bardic Nationalism: The Romantic Novel and the British Empire* (Princeton, NJ: Princeton University Press, 1997).

Turner, Katherine, 'Defoe's *Tour*: The changing "Face of Things"', *British Journal for Eighteenth-Century Studies* 24 (2001), pp. 189–206.

Tytler, Graeme, '"Faith in the Hand of Nature": Physiognomy in Sir Walter Scott's fiction', *Studies in Scottish Literature* 33.1 (2004), pp. 223–246.

Vaughan, William, 'The Englishness of British Art', *Oxford Art Journal* 13.2 (1990), pp. 11–23.

Vincent, Susan, *Dressing the Elite: Clothes in Early Modern England* (Oxford: Berg, 2003).

Wahrman, Dror, 'Change and the corporeal in seventeenth- and eighteenth-century gender history: or can cultural history be rigorous?', *Gender & History* 20.3 (2008), pp. 584–602.

'The English problem of identity in the American Revolution', *American Historical Review* 106.4 (2001), pp. 1236–1262.

The Making of the Modern Self: Identity and Culture in Eighteenth-Century England (New Haven, CT and London: Yale University Press, 2004).

'National society, communal culture: An argument about the recent historiography of eighteenth-century Britain', *Social History* 17.1 (1992), pp. 43–72.

Wainwright, Clive, *The Romantic Interior: The British Collector at Home, 1750–1850* (New Haven, CT and London: Yale University Press, 1989).

Walsham, Alexandra (ed.), *Relics and Remains* (Oxford: Oxford University Press, 2010).

Watson, Nicola J., 'Readers of Romantic locality: Tourists, Loch Katrine and *The Lady of the Lake*', in Christoph Bode and Jacqueline Labbe (eds.), *Romantic Localities: Europe Writes Place* (London: Pickering & Chatto, 2010), pp. 67–79.

Webb, Ruth, '*Ekphrasis* ancient and modern: The invention of a genre', *Word & Image* 15.1 (1999), pp. 7–18.

Webster, Mary, *Johan Zoffany, 1733–1810* (New Haven, CT and London: Yale University Press, 2011).

Weschenfelder, Klaus, 'Belisar und sein Begleiter: Die Karriere eines Blinden in der Kunst vom 17. bis zum 19. Jahrhundert', *Marburger Jahrbuch für Kunstwissenschaft* 30 (2003), pp. 245–268.

Westover, Paul, *Necromanticism: Traveling to Meet the Dead, 1750–1860* (Basingstoke: Palgrave Macmillan, 2012).

Whatley, Christopher A., *Scottish Society, 1707–1830: Beyond Jacobitism, Towards Industrialisation* (Manchester: Manchester University Press, 2000).

White, Jerry, *London in the Eighteenth Century: A Great and Monstrous Thing* (London: Bodley Head, 2012).

Whyman, Susan E., *The Pen and the People: English Letter Writers, 1660–1800* (Oxford: Oxford University Press, 2009).

Wilson, Kathleen, 'Citizenship, empire and modernity in the English provinces, c. 1720–1790', *Eighteenth-Century Studies* 29.1 (1995), pp. 69–96.

(ed.), *A New Imperial History: Culture, Identity and Modernity in Britain and the Empire, 1660–1840* (Cambridge: Cambridge University Press, 2004).

Wilton-Ely, John, 'Lord Burlington and the virtuoso portrait', *Architectural History* 27 (1984), pp. 376–381.

Withers, Charles, 'The historical creation of the Scottish Highlands', in Ian Donnachie and Christopher Whatley (eds.), *The Manufacture of Scottish History* (Edinburgh: Polygon, 1992), pp. 143–156.

Wood, Gillen d'Arcy, *The Shock of the Real: Romanticism and Visual Culture, 1760–1860* (New York: Palgrave, 2001).

Woolf, Noel, *The Medallic Record of the Jacobite Movement* (London: Spink & Son Ltd, 1988).

Wright, B. S., 'Scott's historical novels and French historical painting, 1815–1855', *Art Bulletin* 63 (1981), pp. 268–287.

'"Seeing with the Painter's Eye: Sir Walter Scott's challenge to nineteenth-century art', in Murray Pittock (ed.), *The Reception of Sir Walter Scott in Europe* (London: Continuum, 2006), pp. 293–312.

Wrigley, Richard, *The Politics of Appearance: Representations of Dress in Revolutionary France* (Oxford: Berg, 2002).

Wu, Duncan (ed.), *A Companion to Romanticism* (Oxford: Blackwell, 1998).

Young, Hilary (ed.), *The Genius of Wedgwood* (London: V&A, 1995).

Zuelow, Eric G. E.,'"Kilts *versus* Breeches": The royal visit, tourism and Scottish national memory', *Journeys* 7.2 (2006), pp. 33–53.

Index

Page numbers in *italics* indicate a figure. References to plates are given in the form *Pl.V*